THE RUSSIAN COUNTESS

Escaping Revolutionary Russia

Edith Sollohub

IMPRESS BOOKS

First Published 2009
by Impress Books Ltd
Innovation Centre, Rennes Drive,
University of Exeter Campus, Exeter EX4 4RN

Reprinted 2010
Reprinted with amendments 2010
Paperback edition 2011, reprinted 2012, 2013, 2017
Second edition with Foreword published 2017 (HB), 2018 (PB)

Typeset in Garamond by Swales & Willis Ltd, Exeter, Devon
Printed and bound in the UK by Short Run Press Ltd, Exeter, Devon

British Library Cataloguing in Publication Data
A catalogue record for this book is available from the British Library

ISBN 13: 978–1–911293–07–1 (hardback)
ISBN 13: 978–1–911293–06–4 (paperback)
ISBN 13: 978–1–911293–20–0 (ebook)

Dedicated to the memory of Nicolas Sollohub, who admired, cherished and supported his mother in her lifetime, and who was determined to preserve her writings so that her story would be known.

CONTENTS

CONTENTS

BORDER CROSSINGS
A Foreword to the Second Edition
Robert Chandler, April 2017

Edith Sollohub was intelligent, perceptive and endowed with the gift of trust. She trusted her intuition, and her intuition did not let her down. Time and again during her two years in Soviet Russia, in situations where the wrong choice would have meant death, she trusted the right person. It is the same with her writing, which is clear and straightforward. She had an important story to tell and she trusted its power; she saw no need for artifice.

As a young girl, Edith was independent and determined. As a young wife and mother, however, she seems to have been somewhat lost. It was after the Revolution, when she was in her early thirties and with sole responsibility for her three sons, that she fully came into her own, developing new strengths and gifts and showing ever more resourcefulness.

She earned money by pulling heavy loads on sledges. Devoted servants brought her food from her confiscated estate. She shot ducks on Lake Ladoga. She became adept at helping starved, frozen horses that have slipped on icy streets back onto their feet – a common sight during the bitterly cold winters of those years, and the subject of a warm, generous poem by Mayakovsky. Edith survived thanks to luck, generosity of spirit and an intuitive understanding of people from all walks of life.

There are moments when her unpretentious narrative attains true spiritual depth. In the winter of 1919–20 she attempted suicide. Her sons are safe in Estonia by then, but she herself is trapped in Moscow. Despairing, unable to obtain a permit to leave the country, she decides to walk out into the midwinter forest until she dies of exposure. Unexpectedly, she meets a German (probably a former prisoner-of-war) coming towards her. He asks where he can find food and shelter. 'He had fled the forests in search of a warm fire, and a piece of bread. He wanted to live – why? He had the courage to want to live, even here where everything was strange to him, where he was not wanted [. . .] "Come, I'll show you the way," I replied, and we walked up the long deserted street, back into the heart of the town. I did lead him to shelter – and did he not lead me back to life?'

This real-life parable is remarkable in many ways. For all her despair, Edith is guided by love; she chooses this particular way of committing suicide because of her love for the Russian forest. Setting off to die in a place she loves, she encounters the man who will save her. Most remarkable of all, she allows herself to *learn* from this strange figure – himself perhaps close to death – who makes what must have seemed exasperating demands and so frustrates her plans. Edith never again attempted suicide.

* * *

I never knew Edith Sollohub but, three years after her death, when I was fifteen, a boarder at Winchester College, I began studying Russian. My teacher was her son, Nicolas. The course was intensive; we were a small class and we had six lessons a week. The Count (as I still think of him) was a gifted and imaginative teacher, actively involved in developing new teaching methods with an emphasis on the spoken language. It was, of course, difficult for us to spend much time in Russia, but this probably only increased his determination to make Russian a living language for us.

After leaving Winchester, I stayed in touch with the Count and saw him and his family a number of times over the years.

After attending his funeral in 1990, however, I lost touch with his widow Valerie and it was only twenty years later, after the first publication of *The Russian Countess*, that we met again. As Valerie was leaving, I gave her copies of two of the books my wife and I have translated from Russian. Valerie asked me to sign them. In the second book I wrote: ". . . with deep gratitude for the Count's kindness and patience towards me."

Noticing a flicker of a smile on Valerie's face, I explained that I was thinking of the seemingly endless patience with which the Count, day after day, had corrected my pronunciation. I had had speech difficulties as a child. Not only had my French pronunciation always been atrocious, but I had also been slower than other children to manage such common English sounds as 'sh' and 'th'. I had been a troubled child, and these difficulties had been one of my symptoms.

Valerie then explained that she had smiled because she remembered her husband once saying of me, 'I don't know what the trouble is, but I can see he's really trying.' This moved me; I felt moved that the Count had understood how hard I was trying, moved that he had cared enough to mention this to his wife, and moved, above all, by his modesty. He could see that I was troubled; he understood that he would be unable to help with regard to my deeper problems; at the same time, he trusted that, through patience and kindness, he could at least help with the more surface difficulties. And he succeeded; though far from perfect, my Russian pronunciation is acceptable. And I would like to think that, as the years pass, he may, however slowly, be passing on to me a little of his patience – a patience clearly learned, at least in part, from his mother. He certainly succeeded in passing on to me his love for the Russian language, and his love for a country he never himself felt able to visit.

* * *

Edith Sollohub finally escaped from Soviet Russia by enrolling as a Red Army nurse during the Polish-Soviet war of 1919–21.

Her descriptions of the tired, demoralized Red Army are memorable and can usefully be read alongside the more romantic picture painted by Isaac Babel in his *Red Cavalry* stories. Most remarkable of all, however, is Edith's account of how she managed to cross the front line.

Edith crossed the front line by not crossing it. Instead, she allowed *it* to cross *her*. At a time when the Poles are advancing and her unit has been ordered to retreat, she packs up her medical equipment in good time, asks for permission to go and say goodbye to her landlady and then hides in an out-of-the-way hut she has earmarked for precisely this purpose. Thirty-six hours later, when the fighting appears to have died down, Edith emerges into what is by then Polish territory. Soon afterwards she manages to rejoin her sons.

This too is close to being a parable. There are times in all our lives when the best thing to do is – in an intelligent way – nothing. And Edith's story may even have a particular relevance to the work of a translator. Sometimes it may seem impossible to translate some particular perception or understanding across a linguistic frontier. All one can do is to put oneself in the right place and wait: an answer may come in an unexpected manner.

FOREWORD

My Russian mother-in-law, Countess Edith Sollohub, born Edith Natalie de Martens, was well known in pre-revolutionary St Petersburg for accompanying her husband Alexander on shooting trips and for being outstandingly accurate with her gun. She was also the daughter of a high-ranking Russian diplomat, and was the mother of three young sons who would have been destined in due course to join the social and intellectual elite of imperial Russia. The Revolution of 1917 put an end to all that. By December 1918 her husband was dead, her children separated from her by the closing of the frontiers, and her own life in danger. These memoirs are her account of how she faced these disastrous events. They reveal how the courage and determination she had shown in earlier times now helped her to endure hunger, imprisonment, and loneliness. Her reunion with her sons in 1921 made the months of danger and deprivation finally worthwhile.

By the time I knew her, Countess Edith Sollohub was an old lady, fluent in four or five languages, glad to have helped her sons survive and become established in Western Europe. Her youngest son, a grown man in his 50s but still "little Nic" to her, was a teacher of modern languages in England, making use of the skills she had passed on to him. While struggling to cook and keep house for him, she liked to tell stories about her escape from Russia, and I had the privilege of hearing some of these in her own voice, with its distinctive accent and intonation. (One could still hear traces of the Scottish governess.) I learned that, quite soon after she reached the safety of France in the 1920s, she taught herself to type and began to record the story of her escape. She took a job as a typist in order to support herself and her sons in a one-room apartment in Paris. Only later, when her sons had grown up, did she have time to write the anecdotes about her childhood, her marriage and – above all – the influence of her father.

The memoirs were written entirely in English which – even more than French – became her preferred method of communication. No translation has been required. Such editing as was necessary lay in the chronological ordering of the typescripts and manuscripts that she had accumulated over the years. Most of the material was typed, with many deletions, overtyping and handwritten corrections. Her sons were able to use their knowledge of her handwriting to decipher any handwritten pages. On the advice of friends, and to avoid repetition, some childhood reminiscences have been omitted, and some shooting stories have been streamlined. But from the time of the outbreak of the Revolution onwards, the narrative is given in its entirety.

It was always her hope that her memoirs would find their way into print. When she died in 1965 she left the manuscripts to her youngest son. He, in turn, died in 1990 and as his widow I have been proud to prepare these memoirs for publication.

Valerie Sollohub, widow of Count Nicolas Sollohub,
June 2009

Note

In order to preserve the authenticity of the author's own voice, transliterations from the Russian have been given mostly in the form she used, even if not necessarily conforming to a standard system. Baltic place-names have been left in the German forms which were current in Edith's own circles (e.g. Dorpat for Tartu, Reval for Tallinn). Polish place-names in the text were subject to spelling irregularities, which have now been re-shaped into some sort of consistency. Finally, where the names of certain key figures in the escape story had been replaced by initials in the original manuscript (because those people were still alive at the time of writing and should not have been identified), it has not been possible to discover or reinstate those names.

ACKNOWLEDGEMENTS

The work of editing this book has been made easier by the help of many good friends and family members – in England, France, Germany, Italy and Switzerland. In particular I wish to thank Edith's cousin in Basel, Johanna Müller-Vonder Mühll, who has been constant in her support over the years and who provided a number of family photographs. Thanks also to Angela Pullen for typing the first draft, working tirelessly to decipher Edith's original manuscript, to historian friends Mark Stephenson and Peter Gwyn for their encouragement, and to Catherine Hobey and Elizabeth Gordon for help with editing. Finally I am indebted to the younger, computer-literate generation – my daughters Maria, Alexandra, Katherine and Natalia Sollohub – for essential help in preparing the final typescript and placing it with the publisher.

PREFACE

I was born in Pavlovsk, near St Petersburg, on August 3rd, 1886. Both my parents were Russian though of Baltic origin, and were Lutheran Protestants which meant that they did not belong to the established "state-church". My father was Professor of International Law at the University of St Petersburg, at the Lyceum and the Law School, as well as being a member of the Ministry of Foreign Affairs. His name, Friedrich von Martens (or Frédéric de Martens in French), had to be russianised and changed to Fyodor Fyodorovich Martens when he was acting for the Ministry. His work at the Ministry and the frequent special diplomatic missions abroad as well as a wide circle of friends brought us children in contact with international life from our earliest days. Foreigners were not strangers for us and we were taught to understand their points of view and to respect the habits and customs of various nations. Our first dancing lessons, when we were small girls of five or six, were with children from various embassies, and the daily papers lying on Father's desk were newspapers not only in Russian but also in French, English, German, Dutch and Italian.

My brother Nicholas was six years older than I, and we had two younger sisters, Catherine and Mary. Our first languages were Russian, which we spoke in the nursery with our nurse, and French which was spoken at table with our parents. In winter, when we were at home in Petersburg, at Panteleimonskaya 12, on the corner of Mokhavaya Street, the "Ptichia Komnata"

(Birds' Room) was our realm. This was a large playroom in which there were two big cages full of canaries. Old Niania, who had started as my brother's nurse and who remained in our household for thirty-six years (until she died in the spring of 1918), looked after the canaries as well as the children, for she was extremely fond of all animals and birds. The Ptichia Komnata was a kingdom of its own where, under Niania's benevolent eye, we were free to do all we wanted, and we fully enjoyed our rights and privileges.

My mother Catherine was the daughter of Russian senator Nicholas von Tuhr. As her health suffered in the cold climate of northern Russia, she preferred to spend the early weeks of spring abroad, in Germany, Italy or Switzerland, and we often accompanied her on her travels. Travelling for us meant good hotels, special menus for us children, and the chance to study the table manners, tones of voice and styles of speech in the different countries we visited. Then in the summer months we went to Waldensee, the property which my father bought near Wolmar, in Livonia, and which played an important part in our lives as children and through the years of war and revolution. In those childhood years the memories are of long walks, the rides in the "lineika" to distant forests along the River Aa, the great mushroom hunts, the games of tennis and the grand birthday parties of both parents. Of the Russian provinces far away from Petersburg we knew little. I remember listening spellbound when the author Sir Donald Mackenzie Wallace came to lunch with Father and told us stories about the Russian provinces – a sort of mysterious, veiled country to which one did not travel, for there were no hotels, no "waters" to be drunk for the good of one's health, and no ancient ruins to be visited and admired. After my marriage I came to know and love the Russian countryside, and this knowledge was useful to me when the bad times came.

All this stands for an introduction to the life story of an old woman. A long life is behind me, so long that it looks like a book full of pictures, some clear, some vague, full of light and bright moments and full of blanks – where I failed to see or understand what I should have seen or understood at the right moment. What I have lived through is not yet really history, it is still personal experience. But the further time takes me from past events connected with my life in Russia the more this first part of my life appears as a series of pictures passing before my eyes. Perhaps this is the moment to look back, to recapitulate things seen and lived, in a more objective light. The pictures are not less vivid; on the contrary they have acquired a clearness which they did not have when the personal reaction was still acute, and when events could not be recalled without bringing with them a pang of sharp pain.

And now I am at the point where a huge question mark bars my way: where to start, and what to say? I must dive back into the past which looks at me through the eyes of so many familiar and dear faces, like those of Father and Mother and Niania and our first dear governess Mimi, old cooks, old coachmen, the gardeners and gamekeepers and animals that played so great a part in life at our country place. They all smile at me and try to give me confidence. But I feel hand- and tongue-tied and must turn first, as in childhood, to my father for the strength and support that he always gave me.

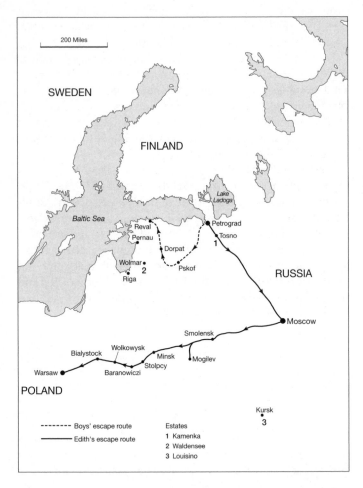

Map showing position of the family estates and direction of escape routes

1

FATHER

The word "Father" conjures up a range of images in my mind. He was the centre of my world, a reliable friend and the source of always new and thrilling interests. One of my first recollections of him is closely connected with Mereküll, a seaside place on the southern shores of the Finnish Gulf. I must have been three years old at most. I was playing on a sandheap in front of the house when Father came up, riding on a huge brown horse. He called someone who lifted me on to the saddle and I had thus my first ride, which seemed quite wonderful. From that day on Father must have taken me on his horse more or less every day as I recall the different views I had from this terribly high seat. I still remember the smell of the saddle and of the hot horse, and being a little afraid of the big panting nostrils when Father tried to make me give the horse a piece of sugar on the flat palm of my hand.

Father was a friendly, happy figure appearing on my Petersburg horizon either in the doorway of the dining room or in that of our playroom, a figure I always felt so full of sympathy that I could turn to him with all my little interests and could be sure of his cheering words when I showed him something new. It was with Father that I first got the trick of reading. It was in his study, on a sunny winter morning, just before lunch. My father was writing at his desk and I was playing with a small Russian reader and bricks on the carpet. My brother had already taught me the printed letters and I could read – or guess – the words on the front of shops. In fact these small shops, such as greengrocers, butchers, and hairdressers, used to have a brightly coloured picture advertisement of their trade, obviously in view of the number of illiterate people, especially country folk. How much I read and how much I guessed from these advertisements I cannot say, but here the little reader lay open in front of me; I found some of the letters I already knew from my daily walks with my brother and his governess, and as I saw these letters grouped into small words it suddenly dawned upon me that I could say them quickly in the same sequence, link them into one sound and this sound popped up as a word, a word which made sense. I was delighted at my discovery and, rushing up to Father with my book, read off word after word from a paragraph on the right page of the book. Father approved of my performance and I can still hear myself saying proudly to him "Look, now I can read!" and he laughed heartily and sent me to go on reading on the carpet without disturbing him.

What puzzled me for quite a time, and where I had to ask Father for an explanation, was why the servants spoke of Father as "the General" and addressed him as "Your Excellency", and why Father did not wear military uniform if he really was a general? I still remember his amused smile and then his very serious explanation about civil service titles in Russia corresponding to military ones. But I was a bit disappointed for I had hoped to hear that he might be a regular military general and wear a general's uniform always! As it was, he wore his Ministry of Foreign Affairs uniform only on solemn occasions, and it was not really satisfactory in my eyes as it had no shoulder pieces and the sword was a meagre affair discreetly slipped into a side slit in the longish uniform coat. But the redeeming point was that Father's chest on these big, official occasions was covered with all sorts of fascinating stars and medals and he had a number of wide bright silk ribbons which crossed his chest, ran over the shoulder and across the back to meet both ends in a large flat bow on the hip. It was fun to see all these stars, to have an explanation of their reasons, to visualise as I did later the whole world map on Father's chest, and to learn the names of so many outlandish countries. Invariably when he had to go out in uniform I repeated proudly the names of those orders he had on at the given time and Father was amused at my memorising names which obviously meant nothing to me. When I admired some showy star, Father always told me that of all the fancy orders the one he cherished most was the small silver grey Maltese Cross which he always wore on a black ribbon round the neck – whatever the occasion to wear the uniform might be. "This is the order given me by the Queen of England and only a few people in Russia have it," he told me when I was still very small. But I remembered his words and looked at the modest looking cross with respect. It is also the only one that I succeeded in getting out of Russia, and I gave it to my eldest son who had it as the only souvenir of his grandfather.

It is about that time that the Oxford – or Cambridge – gown rose up on my nursery horizon. Father had just returned from England where he had been officially received at either Oxford or Cambridge and was showing Mother his gown and mortar-board. Of course we children were thrilled at the sight and I was laughing heartily over them as they were a totally unknown sight and made me think that Father had them to "dress up" as we children did when playing. But Father stopped me laughing by saying that the dress received was a great honour that the old high universities conferred on outsiders from time to time and that such insignia were to be respected. Then my attitude changed completely and I felt proud of Father having been given this honour in such a far-away place as England. Many years later, during the Russian Revolution, when a Communist house-searching party opened old trunks and boxes which were stored away in an unused room, I saw again the gown and trembled lest it tempted the searchers by its good cloth and be misused by them – the childish feelings of deep respect

3

for this gown came back so vividly. But fortunately there were other things which attracted the greedy "proletarian" eyes and the old gown remained to finish its days – how? I do not know, since I had to leave my house to escape from Russia.

Through the Oxford gown, England had acquired a shape – a meaning for me – and when Father took me out for a ride on his horse or allowed me to spend a few minutes in his study after lunch, I always listened with interest to all he told me about that mysterious country. Willingly I picked up my first notions of English from the governess or tutor who taught my brother, and the first sentence I picked up at an extremely early age was "Please, not in front of the children!" or something of the kind.

As I grew bigger, the walks with Father, the long talks with him – or rather listening to his stories about history or the country – all these filled my spare time, when I was temporarily free from the rule and guidance of the governesses. I remember the Sunday rides on a cold winter's day when Father suddenly appeared in the playroom and told me to dress quickly to go out with him in the one-horse sleigh – these were the rides I loved best. Our governess, Mimi, hurried to see me dressed in the thick coat, the knee-high felt boots, the woollen scarf round the neck and the muff for my hands – and off I went with Father.

The horse always seemed to run particularly well on these occasions – it always was the best horse on these days – and the coachman sat so proudly on his seat right in front of me, with the small leather-covered clock pinned to his coloured belt just at the level of my eyes. The wind cut my face, Father held me fast and I hid behind the sheltering back of the coachman when the frost bit my cheeks. We went out of town, on to the Islands with their parks and closed villas, with the white palaces of Yelagin and Kammenyi Ostrov showing faint lights in the distance, the latter the palace of Princess Helen, a princess I imagined to be beautiful and who was rather a disappointment to me when a little later, as a girl of twelve or so, I saw her

4

in the house of friends and discovered that she was a very strict and serious-looking old lady (as I thought then) but with a kind expression in her eyes when she smiled at us children.

Yes, these drives with Father were lovely and towards the end I always hoped that he would give the coachman the order to come back along the Nevsky and stop at Conradi's. I felt quite guilty in cherishing this hope when the drive had been so lovely, but there it is, "la gourmandise" does play a part in the life of a child of seven, eight, nine, and Conradi was the big "confiseur", the brightly lit, warm, brilliant shop where hundreds of varieties of sweets were displayed in the most alluring boxes. I do not remember many occasions when Father forgot to give the expected order and I can feel even now the whiff of warm air full of the most alluring smells meeting us as we entered this shop. Father made his choice: sweets for Mother, for the coming dinner party, and then: "What would you like to have for yourself and Katya?" I already knew – there they were, the old favourites – the round, transparent, many-coloured caramels in round glass boxes. And Father would buy these boxes for each of us – and one extra, for Mimi – and we waited until the parcel was brought to us well packed in white paper and tied with a coloured ribbon.

We then went home, but often stopped on the way to buy Mother some flowers. My Father's favourite place was the shop called "Fleurs de Nice", a semi- basement place in the Mokhavaya where two brothers, Frenchmen, showed their selection of cut flowers which were sent in bamboo baskets direct from Nice. The choice was remarkably varied when I think of the difficulties one had at the time with the despatching of fresh flowers, which left the blessed climate of Nice to arrive forty-eight hours later in the bitter frost of St Petersburg. There were bowls and bowls of anemones, marguerites, renoncules, mimosas, carnations, roses, and many more, and they all seemed to be none the worse for their long journey. A large bunch was soon made up, well packed in layers of soft cotton wool and then in thick white paper, and we walked back up the steps, with Father carrying the bunch of flowers as if it were a baby, and got into the sleigh before getting out of it again only a few paces further on in front of our door. These drives were a joy and even the cup of tea I was given on my return tasted good – although I generally did not care for tea at all.

The great days for us were when Father and Mother went to a Court function. They looked beautiful, I thought, Father in uniform with lots of decorations on his chest, and Mother lovely in the Court dress or long evening dress with a train and with a fur coat over it. And on the next day Father used to give us some specially wrapped sweets from the palace, from the Emperor's supper we were told. I expected these sweets to be particularly good and tasty but I invariably found them much less tasty than the ones we got on Sundays from Conradi; so I praised the palace sweets ostentatiously, and then felt guilty because I was not keeping entirely to the truth.

Another recollection is connected with Christmas and with Father's and Mother's anniversary of their wedding-day. Before these "great days" Father sometimes took me to choose a present for Mother and it was with the greatest pride that I went out with him, promising not to tell anyone about the things we were going to see. Father had generally already chosen the present but just wanted to have another look and ask my opinion, as he so nicely put it. Off we went in the sleigh, crossed the Nevsky along the Sadovaya to a large market building, all arcades and endless shops, in through a low gate into the inner precincts of this market, through quiet, snow-covered passages until the coachman stopped at a cross-roads where we stepped out and entered a small shop poorly lit by a hanging petrol lamp. I always wondered how Father could have thought of finding a nice present for Mother in this dingy place but soon realised that, dingy or not, the place hid lovely things and the man there was both pleasant and apparently a wise and well-informed specialist. He was called Saveliev, was tall and thin, wore a high fur cap over his longish grey hair and very thick spectacles. He had few things on show in the glass boxes of his counter but he generally produced some sort of iron or wooden box out of which came really lovely things: necklaces, brooches, bracelets, chains, pins, and so on. It was a fascinating array of jewels and I only regret that I was too small then either to appreciate them properly or to follow the stories connected with them and which Saveliev seemed always ready to tell. Father and Saveliev discussed at length the merits of this or that piece which came into consideration for Mother and finally Father would turn to me, saying: "What would give really a lot of pleasure to Mother, do you think?" I knew immediately which piece I would have chosen. What a joy then for me when on the great day this very piece appeared on the table as the present for Mother and I could proudly tell her: "I have already seen it, and I helped Father choose it."

The mornings at home I always think of are those very dark sort of smoky wintry mornings in our town house. Old Niania was finishing her coffee behind the door of our nursery and my sisters were still sleeping fast in their cots with the white lace hangings. I slipped out on the quiet and washed and dressed – probably scanty washing – in a hurry, anxious to slip out of the room without being heard by our governess whose bedroom was next door. Niania offered me a bun and on tip-toes I made my way downstairs in that funny grey and smoky light. The Ptichia Komnata looked ghostly with the large rocking horse, the rocking boat, the ladder and ropes and rings and trapeze, all motionless, all asleep. I hurriedly took my books – always several as I never knew which would be my favourite at the given moment, and ran into my father's study where the footman would be sure to have already lit a fire. There, in front of the cheerfully gleaming fire I lay down on the white bear skin, flat on my tummy, and started my reading. The footman quietly moved round the place dusting and putting things in order by the light of one lamp burning in the middle of the room, and I read by the light of the fire.

It was a lovely time. All so quiet in the house; no traffic in the street, and only the nine clocks in the study ticking busily as if anxious to keep up one with the other. And when one of them began to strike eight all the others hurried to strike too, and I closed my books and went into the drawing room to start my violin practice. The standing lamp near the piano had to be lit, my skeleton-looking music stand pushed near it, and with my violin under my chin I started producing the wailing sounds of exercises, scales, arpeggios. Little by little daylight penetrated through the curtained windows and by half past eight the house was awake and alive again. Morning coffee was served in the dining room, my father was there, always brisk and bright, the sisters were down too and the governess all ready to start on her daily task of improving our minds and behaviour. Only my brother was late – but then it was to be expected for he was never on time and was always being reprimanded by my parents, his governesses and tutors. The coffee was so good, the buns so crisp, the butter so fresh and I felt so happy to have had that bit of a morning all to myself, all my own, on the bear skin rug (with Father's special permission), that to start the daily drudgery of boring lessons at nine o'clock did not seem so hard to face.

Most of these memories date from the happy times when Mimi was our governess. Yes, here is the word that echoes through my childhood: the governess! My brother, six years older than myself, had a French governess, Mlle Gousset, who also kept an eye on me during meals. (I do not remember when I was promoted to lunching with the grown-ups – it must have been very early.) It was from her that I learned French before realising it was a foreign language, and I have spoken French ever since with my parents and with my sisters. Mlle Gousset was round all over, a round head with beady but kind eyes, the round top part of her body encased in a tight bodice fastened down the front with many beady black buttons, and the round-looking lower part of her body supported, as I thought, on rounded bow legs underneath her long skirts.

When the time came for Katya and me to have a governess of our own, it was Mlle Schmiderlet, from Lausanne – our

8

good "Mimi", the very kind and devoted but strict govern-ess who taught us to make endless additions of tremendously long figures, who insisted on our knowing by heart the names of all the Cantons of Switzerland and all the Departments of France, who tried to instill in us a dutiful love for all our sour maiden aunts, who made us dust our playroom (or rather the nick-nacks we had there) every Saturday morning, and who implanted in us a great respect for the French language and an unerring knowledge of French grammar.

Learning was not a bothersome task nor did it imply any scenes or dramatic punishments. It all worked smoothly and at the end of the week I got my silver coin of 20 kopeks from Father – unless I had had more than fifteen mistakes in a dicta-tion during that week.

There was peace in our nursery during the Mimi era, an undis-turbed peace reigned throughout it as Mimi and old Niania understood each other – in some mysterious Russo-French language, and Mimi respected Niania, which seemed to me the essential and unquestionable element ruling our life. For Niania knew everything (except reading): she knew what was right or wrong in the nursery, she ordered about and taught the various Dunias and Mashas, our nursery maids, put an imme-diate stop by means of a strict glance to any unnecessary talk on their part, and reprimanded them with a quiet "This is not to be said in front of His Excellency's children!" That Niania could neither read nor write did not worry me: why should she? She knew things anyhow and could tell us such long and interesting stories about her own home in Archangel, about her Zyrianin uncle who lived by hunting sables and foxes in the northern forests and who turned up only twice a year in Archangel to sell the pelts and to buy powder and ammunition. Perhaps my love of shooting can be partly traced back to these stories? I don't know.

Yes, Niania knew all we needed or did not need. Once, when the doctor prescribed some bitter-tasting syrup against a cold and we made a fuss about taking it, Niania quietly poured it out into the pail saying to Mother: "This medicine cannot be good for the children if they object to it so violently." And Mother did not protest but meekly said: "All right, Niania, I'll ask the doctor to prescribe something else when he comes." I remember so well this episode as I lay cuddled up under my blanket watching Niania pour the dark brown liquid away, Mother looking on rather shocked – and I was holding my breath and waiting for what would come next. Would we be scolded? Or was Niania right after all? And she was right, just as she was right when she opened the small window pane, the "fortochka", in the coldest part of the winter, having ordered us to take cover, head and all under the blankets, adding: "His Excellency insists on the nursery window being opened before the night – clean air will never harm anyone." Running our life on this principle she took us out every day, in all weathers, reminding us to rub our cheeks and noses so as not to get them frozen. "Even crows fall smitten with frost," she added, and never tired of repeating how she had taken me out to the Summer Garden on so cold a day that we could count the dead crows lying on the snow. On such occasions the walks were short and we had thick knitted white veils, something like Scottish shawls, tied over our faces.

Yes, Niania, I see her as the kind yet strict spirit ruling over our childhood and I cannot separate any event of it from the picture or memory of her reactions or remarks. It was a blissful era – the co-rule of Mimi and Niania. But it had to end one day, a dark winter day when Mimi, in tears, left us and we wondered where she had gone. And shortly after this break a new governess turned up. It was my first experience of "trouble in the air", an experience which was to grow into a haunting danger for four long years, under the rule of Aline Kegeler, or Kegeler the Terrible.

Fräulein Kegeler did not contribute to simplifying life; she was from the start of the day offended. Whether she found a good reason for an offence or not did not matter as she was on the defensive in any case and ready to attack any possible

10

or impossible or improbable offender. As I was the eldest of her pupils it was my fate to get the first – and hardest – blow of her bad temper. And certainly there were many and frequent outbursts of this temper.

For the first two years of her stay with us, that is from the time I was twelve, she really made me cry many, many times, for she always accused me of not telling the truth – a thing that had never happened to me before. It took me a long time to become philosophical about these accusations, which ended finally when, during our morning walk one day in the snow-covered Summer Garden, I took out of my pocket a note book and pencil and kept on writing down numbers as Frl. Kegeler was scolding me vehemently. "What are you writing?" she finally asked me angrily. "Just how many times you accuse me of telling lies – I have counted seventeen so far," I replied. One can imagine her reaction. But it did not worry me in the least by then – and inwardly I was thrilled at the success of my plan.

Frl. Kegeler was very energetic – and she did look funny when excited. I always enjoyed it even though her shouts infuriated me, and roused in me indignation and a spirit of contradiction. One thing I did learn during these stormy morning lessons: I saw how ridiculous and undignified it looks to get excited, to vociferate, to gesticulate – and I learned to control myself and be reserved and quiet to a degree which only redoubled the anger of Frl. Kegeler. Only sister Katya seemed to have the knack of getting along more or less peacefully with this governess. Sister Katya seldom did anything wrong, always knew her lessons perfectly, used her excellent memory for her work – and without becoming distracted as I was inclined to do. And Katya, with her golden heart, loved Frl. Kegeler and tried not to anger her.

I wanted so much to tell Father about my difficulties under the rule of Frl. Kegeler. I felt somehow guilty not to tell him all that came to my mind or all that weighed on my heart; I felt that he expected me to say it all, but I just had not got the courage to do so. It was a complex feeling: was it fear of being scolded? Not so much that as the fear of creating difficulties or disturbances at home. I knew that Mother had many worries of which we did not speak, which we did not even know about for years but which we felt existed and made Mother sad and worried – and therefore unapproachable for us. It was a family drama with our grandfather, a drama that lasted for several years until he died when I was fifteen. Mother was entirely lost in these worries; Father took her abroad two or three times a year when he had to go on various missions and obviously this was in order to give her a rest. Meanwhile we believed we had been put in the hands of the given governess and had to put up with it and face life as best we could.

In spite of his very frequent absences abroad, Father's wishes were law in the house at all times. In the nurseries we always heard that this or that was to be done "because His Excellency wanted it that way". Old Niania referred to such wishes whenever nursery maids or servants were given instructions, and even governesses were politely reminded by Niania in this same way. There was an unwritten law in our lives, as natural as a law of nature which is not contested or discussed but simply accepted. Father never became agitated or impatient; I rarely heard him raise his voice – only once or twice against a coachman who had been drunk when driving the carriage. Otherwise Father's earnest face did not change; he seemed to be always absolutely certain of doing the right thing – at least of being absolutely sure of not committing an injustice. I think his quiet manner and his straight approach to a question influenced the others and made them accept Father's orders unquestioningly and with ease. As he himself had had a very difficult time in his early life he probably understood the feelings of people working for their living and must have been just in demanding from others what could be demanded and not more. When I think back I never heard from any of the servants (and children so often got to overhear comments from the servants) any word of bitterness, or complaint, or anger. Father had, it seemed, an inborn feeling of justice and an unquestioned conviction that through justice alone human beings could exist and progress. I am glad for his sake that his death in 1909, at the age of 62, spared him the heartbreak of seeing his convictions and his life's work trampled underfoot. When my mother died four years later in 1913 it was another sad blow, soon to be overshadowed by the outbreak of war. I came to realise that it was better that they had gone, that they did not have to witness the destruction and ruin of all they loved and cherished.

2

TRAVELS

So much of one's childhood is linked to the schoolroom – in my case our playroom in Petersburg, with our canaries, our toys, my brother's gymnastic apparatus and the reliable and hard-wearing furniture such as the old red plush sofa with the carved back, along which I used to walk in stockinged feet until I fell, and which let me bounce so nicely and never broke its springs. But there was another important side to our life when the winter routine was set aside and when, after much excited preparation and packing, we set off on our spring and summer travels.

In spring my mother generally tried to avoid staying in Petersburg during the cold rough winds of March, and left for Baden-Baden where her father and her uncle had a large property.

How thrilled we were, Katya and I, when we were considered old enough to travel with her. The long train journey was an experience in itself, and we loved the wagons-lits with two-tiered bunks and wide corridors where we could run around during the day. It was a journey of two nights and two days, with only one longer stop – at Berlin. There were no restaurant cars, and so provisions were taken in a large basket. Cold boiled chicken was the main standby, and to our great joy we were allowed to eat it without fork or knife – just gnaw the bones to our hearts' delight. When, a couple of years later, restaurant cars were introduced we were highly opposed to this innovation because it meant giving up the cold-chicken-gnawing delight. Everything in the provision basket tasted particularly good and even cold rissoles, which I would have objected to in everyday life, had their charm and were welcome.

Then there was the excitement of the Russian border at Verzhbolovo, and a few minutes later the small German town of Eydkuhnen. We all marched out of our carriage, passed all sorts of barriers with passports and papers and finished in the large well-lit restaurant of Verzhbolovo where we found excellent food – a hot beetroot soup was my favourite, followed by stewed fruit. The restaurant at Eydkuhnen has left no impression on me, perhaps because we never ate there, having had a meal on the Russian side. We had to change trains, of course, because of the difference of gauge: the Russian was a few inches wider than the general European gauge and I was persuaded from my earliest days that this was a measure to prevent the Germans invading Russia – a thought that always puzzled me: why should they want to invade us? Once in the German train, I remained glued to the window in order to see how the Germans lived and what struck me most were the tidy rows of village houses, tidy roads and tidy looking fields. We passed the station of Trakehnen where I knew there were good horses and I always hoped to see some at the station. Later we approached Koenigsberg and just before reaching it there was a spot from where one could see the sea – just a line on the horizon, but it always thrilled me and I waited anxiously for that moment.

The night was spent on the train, with an early arrival at Friedrichstrasse Bahnhof, Berlin. It was a grey murky day as a rule when we stepped down from the train, past lots of porters, down the steps to street level and across the open space to the Hotel Continental where we were met with bows and greetings and "Excellenz" and escorted to our rooms. As it was very early, about 6 a.m., Mother went to bed and we were expected to do the same. But Niania and our governess never managed to get us into bed and we played in our dressing gowns on the large double beds, building houses with endless pillows and quilts until breakfast was brought in. A breakfast of croissants and butter and jam with coffee and milk. It all tasted extremely good. Generally we stayed a day or two in Berlin but the stay never left any special impression on me except that the Unter den Linden looked wide and airy and that the toy shops in a side street were extremely interesting.

In the evening of the second day we left for Baden, where we arrived next morning. Arriving first at Baden-Oos we had to get into a small train which took us very soon into the real Baden-Baden. Here, at the station, everything seemed friendly, as even from the train we could see Uncle's landau with two brown horses and Anton on the box. After my first visit this was like coming home to good old friends. A long drive through the Lichtenthaler Allee, then up on the right, past the Menshikov villa, we reached our private drive which branched right to Uncle Charles' villa and left to Grandfather's house. Everything was unchanged: the same trees, bushes, flowers, the same gravel on the back yard, the same old cook Lisa running out to meet us. "My Lisa" I called her, as she had once been my own nurse for a couple of months when Niania had been ill. It was through "my Lisa", there in Grandfather's house, that I saw a kitchen for the first time. Lisa invited us children to have a cup of coffee one afternoon when all the grown-ups had gone out somewhere. What struck me was the cleanliness and brightness of that kitchen and the nice white table at which we sat eating lovely home-made biscuits. I had not imagined that a kitchen could be a friendly looking spot; we were strictly forbidden to go to the kitchen at home. I suppose this measure was due to the large number of servants we had there, and large number of tradesmen, delivery boys, and so on, who came and went.

Life in Grandfather's villa in Baden-Baden was smooth, ordered and happy for us children as we had the very large grounds to play in all day, a pond to sail toy boats on, plenty of walks in the extensive orchards and a spacious sandpit to dig in and build sandcastles. This sandpit had a great attraction: sometimes, towards the end of the afternoon, deer would appear on its edge in search of fresh grass which was plentiful in the orchard. Sometimes hares ran through the grass and along the edge of the pit – all coming from the mountainside above. The grass grew taller there, the wild flowers were many and varied and it was a great joy when old coachman Anton came to mow it and to make lovely high haystacks in which we could hide.

Coachman Anton was my great and special friend. As sister Katya had to be pampered after her bad winter cold and bronchitis I was left a little on my own, and the first thing I did was to run to the stables and spend all the time that I could there. The smell of the horses attracted me: Hector and Achilles were two lovely big brown horses. Anton looked after them with love. The carriages were shining and clean, the harnesses were polished and Anton seemed always to have something to do either in the stables or in the carriage house.

Anton always spoke to me explaining all he did and telling me stories about horses and their tastes and desires, so that I learned German and could chatter fluently with him. One day, as we drove out in the landau for an afternoon "coffee-expedition" to a place where there was a cafe with a lovely view, Mother heard me speaking with Anton as I sat next to him on the box where I was allowed to drive the horses. To Mother's horror she noticed that the German I spoke was Badisch dialect and she decided that as I knew so much it would be right to teach me proper German, and I was given regular German lessons as soon as we returned home.

Father used to play tennis on the Lichtenthaler Allee courts, right in front of our Quettighof where a special terrace had been made which allowed us all to look at the courts without having to go down. Often tea or coffee would be served on this terrace when there was to be an interesting game to watch. Next to this terrace was the wall of Prince Menshikov's stables; his property ran alongside ours up the hill. He was a famous figure in Baden-Baden: an old man with a white pointed beard who drove every afternoon in an open carriage drawn by a troika of light grey or white horses, a Russian coachman on the box. It was a lovely sight and I was proud of it. My uncle, named Kolya, mother's youngest brother, was extremely fond of horses and used to spend hours in Menshikov's stables, practising his Russian on the coachman perhaps. And one great day Uncle Kolya fetched me as we were playing in the garden and took me to the big stone wall which separated the two properties. There he showed me a breach in the wall through which he could crawl into the stable yard, and we crept through to have a look at the horses. He knew all their names and ages and it was clear that the coachmen and stable boys knew and trusted him. I was thrilled and proud to have an uncle who was a welcome guest in the stables of Menshikov.

Our first visit to Baden-Baden was followed in the autumn by a short stay at The Hague where Father had to attend an international conference. (This was the autumn of 1893.) We were parked in the Grand Hotel de Scheveningen which was half empty then, so late in the season. But my recollections are very vivid and very bright. The sea had a great attraction for me and I was happy that our window looked on to the long, sandy beach. The weather was often unfriendly and we could not play near the sea, so we repaired to the sand-dunes and had lovely digging parties there, well sheltered from the wind. On the beach we built enormous sandcastles which were flooded little by little by the incoming tide and it was really thrilling to stand behind our fortifications waiting for the first wave to swamp them. In the morning the beach was strewn with dead fish, large shells and sea stars which we carefully collected and which my brother Kolya hung up in his room to dry. I still remember the awful smell of his room with all these beasts hanging about at the window, drying.

Niania did not like the hotel – she found it was not clean enough. Besides, she always asked for the good Dutch herring which at home was the best sort of herring one could get.

She was sure that she would find it better still here, but was completely disappointed and never got tired of saying: "I've been in Holland and there they did not have any good Dutch herring – none."

There were some summers when we went to Switzerland. The snow-covered mountains impressed me enormously and I was never tired of admiring them and of wondering how the snow stayed there throughout the summer while we ran about at the foot of the same mountains in thin muslin dresses, sleeveless and open-necked.

One day we went out for a drive up the mountain side and as we were driving up a valley we all got out of the landau and walked along the road. On our left was a narrow stream, the water bubbling over the rocks, and Father told us that this was the Rhine, the very beginning of it. I had seen the Rhine as a huge river further down, in Germany, and it took me some time to realise that any large river is bound to start as a small brook – and when I did I was really proud of having seen the Rhine in its infancy. It was along that same road that I gathered a bunch of small flowers which caught my fancy because of their sweet scent and their silvery-white velvety stems and leaves. Father told us then about all the lovely flowers growing in the Alps and described the edelweiss and the blue gentian as the best and the rarest of them all. It was a lovely drive – Mother falling gently asleep as soon as she got into the carriage. We always teased Mother for not being able to keep awake when in a carriage.

It was a great joy to come back to Petersburg in the autumn and to see all the familiar old toys and the bird cages in the Ptichia Komnata. I had few dolls and none of them were dear to me: they were just there because aunts and uncles gave them to me but they did not attract me in the least. I much preferred the papier-mâché grey rocking horse, who – like all horses of his breed – lost his tail immediately and remained with a hole instead – a deep hole into which my chalks and pencils disappeared never to see daylight again.

We did not go abroad every year. In 1892 we spent part of the summer in Peterhof, in a dacha taken by my parents as my mother could not travel at the time. I disliked the house and the garden – it all looked gloomy and I think it must have been a very cold and unfriendly summer. I well remember the palaces at Peterhof, the fountains and lakes which I admired but which offered no free spot for proper games. One had to walk led by one's nurse and keeping to the sand-covered paths. How tempting the sea looked when glimpses of it appeared between the trees to the north. I always asked Father to be taken there but he answered that there were no nice beaches and no place for us to play.

In October, on the 15th, my sister Mary was born. It was a great surprise when Father announced to us at breakfast that we had another little sister. Kolya was furious: "I have enough with two sisters – I don't want a third one! Please, Father, send her away somewhere!" I felt very thrilled and was delighted when Father took us into the room to see the new baby, but was rather disappointed as the baby looked very small and very shrivelled and uninteresting. Soon I got used to her and a couple of months later I was very pleased to push her pram about from room to room; and when one day the baby went off to sleep as I was wheeling the pram through the Ptichia Komnata, I was really proud of my achievement.

In the spring of 1894 Father fell ill and was apparently very ill with rheumatic fever and heart weakness. There were nurses in the house and we children had to keep very quiet in our nurseries. Mother looked worried – I don't actually remember her face but I do remember the atmosphere of worry and anxiety. And then, a little later, Mother called me one day to come and see Father. On tip-toes I followed her into the bedroom and – I got a shock: Father was lying in bed and had a regular poivre-et-sel beard! I had never seen him in bed before, and I had never imagined that he could have a beard. He looked very pleased to see me and told me to sit down on the chair near his bed and as I was evidently short of conversation (still terrified by the beard) he told me to tell him a story. The only thing I could think of was Little Red Riding Hood and I started conscientiously from the beginning and worked myself into the story. But then, oh dear, it seemed a dreadful thing to tell someone lying in bed that the wolf ate up the grandmother – who was also lying in bed. I faltered and stopped and could think of nothing more to say; fortunately at that moment Mother came in and said that Father must be tired and that I had better come with her back to the nursery.

A few weeks later we were sent to the country, to a place where Mother had to go because of her weak lungs. It was called Pogulianka, and was on the river Dvina in the Vitebsk province. Mother had taken a dacha there and we were sent in advance as my father could not travel yet.

The dacha turned out to be very pleasant: a wooden house with a veranda, large rooms, a kitchen outside the house and linked with it by a covered gallery, thus eliminating all kitchen smells from the house; a large garden which was actually the pine forest, untouched and unspoiled, surrounded by a wooden fence; a few flower beds at the foot of the terrace; high bushes separating the place from the neighbours; nice sandy soil and a sandy road leading to the river.

The great attraction of Pogulianka was – the horses. There was a settlement of Tartars there with hundreds of mares and their foals. The Tartars milked the mares, made the milk ferment and sold it then to people who had come to the place to take a special cure in mares' milk, called Kumiss. This was the cure my mother had to take and, combined with the good dry air full of the scent of pine trees, it was supposed to do a great deal of good to anybody suffering from weak lungs. These Tartars willingly sold the foals for the ridiculous price of one rouble per head, and I begged Mother and Father when they joined us later on to buy me one of these foals. But I could not keep it in our Ptichia Komnata in winter, it was clear – so I had to give up the idea.

I think the cure must have done my mother a lot of good, for we returned to Pogulianka the next year, and as Father was in good health then there was much more gaiety and move-ment in the house. First of all, Father decided to play tennis, a game totally unknown in the Russian provinces. He found some English people who were in Pogulianka too and with their help arranged a grass court at the back of our dacha, at the foot of a green grassy slope. He played there daily and taught my brother too, while I ran round and picked up the balls with delight. It was a good, smooth lawn and my father was quite pleased with it. When he and his friends rested I looked for mushrooms, maslenniki, on the grassy slopes or played imagi-nary shooting games with my popgun. How I wanted to try William Tell's apple trick using Katya's head for the apple! But I was told once and for all that the gun would be taken from me if I ever tried to point it at someone.

My brother, then thirteen or fourteen, had become an enthu-siastic fisherman and hunter. Stanislav, the footman, was very keen on both these sports and after years in our service had become the trusted man in the house and the one who accom-panied us on our travels. He took the boy out in the early hours of the morning either to fish in the Dvina or to shoot wild duck on one of the numerous lakes around Pogulianka. By lunch-time they came home, muddy and exhausted, bringing fish or duck or partridges, happy and pleased with their long morning. I envied my brother and was never tired of hearing his stories about the exploits of the day. These stories were certainly suf-ficient to awaken in me the latent interest and love I had for this kind of sport. Once or twice we went in a large "lineika" to some of the places Kolya had been to when shooting and he explained to me on the spot all the advantages of this or that position for finding duck, or the different ways of finding cover when waiting for the birds to rise at dawn. It was not wasted on me and I well remember his lessons.

Using my beloved popgun, I was shooting one day at sparrows on the stable roof, when the spring gave way too quickly (I had not withdrawn my finger in time) and the iron rod caught my finger, cutting off a piece of flesh. It hurt and bled, but what frightened me more was that my gun might be taken from me. So I sucked the poor finger, hid in the stables and waited there until the lunch gong rang when I reluctantly had to appear in the dining room, the finger wrapped in my now rather dirty handkerchief. Fortunately for me someone had turned up unexpectedly for lunch and the attention of the grown-ups was diverted from us children. Later someone did notice but I made fun of it all and having asked Niania for a bit of clean linen I tied it up and it healed without any explanation being required.

The following year, in January 1895, a very new and unpleasant situation arose. The manservant Stanislav, who had been many years with us and who had been a devoted help to Father in his serious illness, turned out to be a thief. We children were all devoted to Stanislav: he had been my brother's mentor throughout the summer, taking him out shooting and fishing; my father had always entrusted him with all necessary purchases for the house and his work as butler and footman had been impeccable: he was quick, quiet, never forgot a thing, served well and was always on time. One could not have expected more from any man. And then – suddenly – the news broke that he had been stealing! Apparently he was a gambler – Niania had warned Mother about it as she knew that Poles were rather inclined that way. And indeed Stanislav had lost money playing cards. Twice my father had given him fairly large sums of money to pay some bills and – according to Stanislav – the money had been lost. But still no one really suspected him. Then, one day after a big dinner party, my mother decided (urged on by Niania) to look over the silver, and here she discovered that the boxes were empty and that Stanislav had been juggling with it all the time, taking some silver to the pawn shop in order to get out something which he had pawned earlier but was now needed for a certain occasion, and even pawning my father's summer clothes to get other things out. I remember my mother's disturbed face as she passed the door of the Ptichia Komnata after having discovered that the silver boxes were empty. Suddenly there was no Stanislav to be seen, the maids did the serving; there was a dead silence about him. And one evening strange men walked through the butler's office and down the passage to the servants' quarters and I heard they were the police – to have a look at Stanislav's room. I was awe-struck as I had never thought of the police except as the men standing at cross-roads, saluting my father when we passed in the sleigh or helping us across the street when we went with Niania to the Summer Garden. And here they were in our house . . . it felt queer and strange. And after this I never heard any more about Stanislav – only a rumour that he had had to go to prison for theft. The thought of his disgrace, and the visit from the police, cast a shadow over the whole household which did not lift for many weeks.

3

PETERSBURG

In Petersburg, social events for us children centred round our dancing lessons. I mention dancing lessons and my thoughts go back to the very beginning, to those lessons which we started at the early age of three or four – all in the houses of friends – and which we and our little friends of the same age continued until we were about eleven. They took place every Saturday and were always happy occasions in spite of the humour of our different governesses.

At three o'clock the closed carriage, a landau, waited for us at the door while upstairs we put on our thick coats, caps close over our ears, thick felt boots, and dangled from our hands the little bags containing our dancing shoes. Naturally, all these lessons belonged to the winter seasons, as in summer everybody left town and we were seldom there from the beginning of May until the end of September or even into October. At last we were ready and trotted down the stone staircase with its dark red carpet to the hall where dear Platon, the old red-haired porter, greeted us with smiles and bows and rushed in his long, dark blue livery coat with big brass buttons to open the double doors leading into the street. He lived under the staircase in a mysteriously dark narrow passage room which had a small door at the end opening on to the courtyard. For years I looked with awe at this black hole from which Platon emerged in all his six-foot height as if he were a jack-in-the-box popping out and stretching to its normal size with a jerk. His parted curly red beard enhanced his beaming smile and his small blue eyes disappeared in a mass of wrinkles. At the entrance to his den stood his writing desk on which people left letters, visiting cards, notes, and so forth. With what pride Platon drew my attention one day to the nice carved oak table and matching looking-glass that appeared instead of the plain white set that I had always seen there: "Come, baryshnia, and admire my presents. All her Excellency's doing . . . may God bless her!" and he reverently lifted his cap, while I frankly admired the great improvement and enjoyed the sight of Platon's delighted face. For days he would stop me to have another appreciative look at his "truly ministerial" desk. When a few days later my mother gave him also a carved chair to match, his joy seemed boundless.

When I think back it must have been amusing to see the little girls huddled in warm and clumsy clothes emerge out of them in airy, light frocks and dancing shoes. This metamorphosis took place in the nursery or in some secluded part of the hall in the house where the dancing lessons were to be. It involved slipping off thick stockings and felt boots, thick knitted pants or trousers, all discreetly discarded behind the protecting skirts of the governess. Then, hair brushed and dancing shoes on our feet, we walked into the salon to join the other children.

Here, besides our two little hosts and their small brother (who spoke Russian with a decided English accent as the nurse he had had from the cradle was English), about a dozen other children were assembled. I remember among them the two children of the Dutch Minister, the daughter of the Belgian Minister, the mischievous son of the Counsellor at the Danish Legation and the three children of a diplomat from Sweden. Punctually at 3.30 the "Balletmeister" – our dancing master – appeared on the threshold of the salon: in tails, impeccably correct, slim and slightly perfumed, he stopped on entering, rounded very slightly his arms, gave a general bow and, if the hostess was present, walked straight up to her to bow most respectfully in front of her. If she was absent, he would walk up to the piano, closely followed by his accompanist the piano player, also in tails, a small bearded little man with black-rimmed eyes.

A slight clap of hands by our dancing master and we all stood in a row facing him, with all our governesses sitting along the wall behind us. With a few chords on the piano, a well-known minuet by Mozart played slowly and the lesson started with the Court etiquette: the low sweeping curtsey demanded of the girls, while the boys had to click their heels to the music, slowly, noiselessly and to bow as we plunged down on bent knees. If the hostess was present, this part of the lesson finished by each of us having to walk up, to music, to the hostess and to perform our curtsey before her, with a word of approval from the dancing master or a gentle remark on the mistake committed (but we were never made to repeat it so as not to hurt our feelings). The boys had to come forward and kiss the hand of the hostess. When the hostess was absent, the girls did not have to perform, but the boys had to walk up to the dancing master and bow to him, while he made a few remarks on their general "tenue".

After this rather boring part of the lesson, the music changed to some gay tune and we started various exercises in "positions" or steps of dances such as the valse, polka and mazurka. The latter was my favourite dance at the time: it meant moving, running to music, with the whole lot of us in movement, girls doing their easy, light step, the boys clicking heels desperately, hopping about clumsily, each of them to be later taken separately for special training by the master. We had to go in pairs and when there were too few boys I always volunteered to dance the boys' part and learned assiduously their special steps, which were quite different from ours, the girls'.

The few minutes rest between the dances were generally disturbed by over-zealous governesses who whispered some remarks to their pupils or pulled about at our dresses. The lessons ended with a "polonaise" when we had to walk to music, in pairs, past the hostess or the place where she should have been, bowing as we passed. I still remember some of the tiny little girls' deep curtseys which landed them on the floor, or the boys' clumsy low bows. Then, with a general graceful bow to the audience and a small bow to us children accompanied by a gentle smile, our dancing master vanished with his faithful small shadow of an accompanist behind him.

After the lesson came our really enjoyable time. We all trooped into the dining room where a big table was laid with cakes and sweets and fruit and where we could have tea or chocolate – with our governesses shadowing our movements. Fortunately, neither my sister nor I were particularly keen on rich cakes and thus never ran the risk of overeating ourselves, whereas many of our little friends unavoidably had more than they should, and governesses' tales of woe reached our ears later. The hustle and bustle at the tea table started when the children tried to sit next to their friends or to avoid their "antipathies". I was at the time very fond of two brothers, one my age, the other a little younger, who were the same height as I was and who shared my interest in dogs and horses – or at least I thought they did. We had a lot to talk about together, but one day, as we gathered in the big salon after tea to start some sort of noisy game, the older boy roused my temper and before I knew what I was doing I found myself beating him, shaking him hard and even today I can feel the frail thin shoulder bones in my hand. Governesses pounced on us, separated us, indignant at such a lack of manners. My poor governess especially was in sheer distress for it was unpardonable for a big girl of eleven to fight a boy. What was it? Why this extraordinary lack of discipline and manners? Red in the face, hot, furious, I only remember myself saying: "I had to beat him: he told me I was lying!" In fact, I still recall this deep feeling of disgust that any-one could disbelieve my words; I had never experienced it and it brought my feelings to the boil. And what had the poor boy doubted? I remember it exactly: he did not believe that I had hit a target of a certain size at a distance of twenty strides with

28

my brother's little Montecristo rifle. He did not believe that I could shoot – and that was too much for me. This incident was the first one when I realised how much shooting meant to me.

Another incident connected with these dancing classes was my first acquaintance with real English girls. I spoke English, I had met grown-up English friends of my parents, but I had never seen English children. And one day there appeared two new little girls at our class; they had long wavy hair, the eldest was very tall and lanky and had brown hair, the other one was much shorter, fairer and very slight too. And both had long brown stockings! This was something quite novel for us as we all had long black stockings and small blackbronze shoes. And I thought these brown stockings very pretty and really smart. The little girls did not dance particularly well, nor did we talk much together as the big one seemed too old for me to talk to (she was about thirteen) and the little one too young. We looked at each other during the lesson but as they did not remain for the games and left immediately after tea, our acquaintance remained at this point, for they only came two or three times. Strangely enough, nearly sixty years later I met the "big" girl in England, in Winchester – and we did speak then, a lot even, sharing our reminiscences of Russia, and her presence in Winchester was a real blessing for me when I came there as a newcomer in my old age.

There came a time when we outgrew the young children's dancing class. After a winter's dancing lessons with "grown-ups" – that is, with girls and boys of 16 and 17 – where we two little ones were rather bored though much spoilt by the older ones, Katya and I joined a class at the house of some American friends of my parents. The father of Ben and Horatio was, as far as I can remember, Counsellor at the American Embassy and they had a charming flat overlooking the Neva, right opposite the St Peter and St Paul Fortress. I loved these lessons and enjoyed them immensely as there were many more boys than girls and we had a lot of fun and good games after the usual tea. The drive to the house at the hour of dusk on a cold wintry day was a source of ever renewed joy: the stretch of the ice-covered river, the lights shining silvery in the blue twilight, the creaking of the carriage wheels on the hard frozen snow, the large and solemn looking palaces bordering the quays – all this enhanced the charm of the outing as we scarcely ever got out of the house after dark. The lessons were run on the same lines, but the master here was an older man and the pianist was a woman – not as impressive. The three Tower boys, sons of the American Ambassador, were my great friends and together with the hosts and Sié, the son of the Chinese Ambassador, we made a cheerful band – if not exactly a good dancing class.

One day, at the dancing class, my Chinese friend Sié told me mysteriously "My father is going to call on yours tomorrow and Mr Lou is to go with him as his interpreter. Some big political question to be discussed – you know?" Of course I did not know but would not show it and tried to make a knowing face. The next day after lunch I asked my father casually whether he was expecting Mr Tang You and Mr Lou. "You seem well au courant of affairs" said my father, laughing. "In fact I am expecting them today at three, so don't practise your music then." (The piano was in the drawing room next to Father's study.) Fortunately I had no lesson at three, and decided then and there to have a good look at the two Chinamen when they walked through the drawing room. It was easy to hide lying flat under the big sofa and the only difficulty was to reach this observation post unnoticed. All went well, and I was ready and all eyes when the two Chinamen in lovely coloured dress, black caps and pigtails were ushered in. My father met them and, speaking French, invited them into his study. The Ambassador smiled and grunted something unintelligible whereas Mr Lou, the young and slim secretary, answered in fluent French. I wondered whether Father suspected my presence somewhere for he seemed to look round casually, but I was perfectly sure that he could not see me under the sofa. As soon as the place was clear I crept out, listened for any sounds and swiftly skipped into the schoolroom where I was supposed to be doing my prep. No one there: everything had worked out well, and I was very pleased to have seen the father of Sié in all his glory, for Sié had told me about the big pink stone (I hope I still remember this right) which his father had the right to wear on his black silk cap as a Mandarin of a certain rank.

More recollections crowd my memory and one of them is the visit of the Japanese great man, Marquis Ito. I had heard of him through conversations at lunch and heard also that he was to call on Father some time during the afternoon. Luckily it was just after tea when we were back from our second walk, and I succeeded in catching sight of the small Japanese in a top hat being ushered into the study. My father was hurrying forward to meet him and I heard the start of their conversation. To be truthful, I thought the footman from the Japanese Embassy looked more impressive, with his plumed hat and gold-braided coat. Still, the importance of the visitor was quite clear to me after all the conversations I had heard at table about him and his great work in modernising his country; he was a hero, I thought, and felt proud of having seen one.

Another call of interest was that of M. Delcassé, whom I caught sight of from our balcony as his open carriage with two horses, the plumed footman and gold-braided coachman, stopped at our door. A very small man in a high top hat (it looked particularly high because of the smallness of the man) stepped alertly down and walked briskly up the steps. There was no chance of seeing him closer, as I had to stay on the balcony until he had disappeared into Father's study, but I heard a great deal about him later and often remembered this visit when he played such an important part in Franco-Russian relations.

All these diplomatic connections and foreign policy conversations fascinated me from a very early age, and Father did not mind my putting questions and asking him for explanations. I think he was glad that I showed a keen interest whereas my brother Kolya, my elder by six years, seemed rather indifferent or at least very slow. Some years later, when I was nearly grown up, I read a great deal of diplomatic correspondence and history, specialising in foreign relations and international policy in general. It was easier then than it would be now, for the field was relatively restricted and one did not have to take into account all the countries of Asia and Africa and South America – without mentioning the North Pole, South Pole and the space between the earth and the moon . . . Individuals then really meant something in diplomacy and it was always interesting to meet, even just to see, these people on whom so much depended.

As winter closed in we used to look forward to more parties and, of course, the excitement of Christmas. But first there was St Catherine's day, which of all the saints' days was the most popular and best known by both young and old. There were many Catherines in Russia, it was a very favourite name, and the 24th of November was the only day connected with that Saint. Sweet shops and flower shops prepared their best displays for this date and by the evening all of them looked well plundered – in fact, quite sold out.

The morning post brought letters and cards of congratulations and flowers were delivered to the house throughout the day. Naturally I am speaking of a house where there was a Catherine. At home we had my mother and my sister who were Catherines and next door to us were friends with a similar arrangement. The mothers generally received friends for tea in their sitting rooms whereas the daughters had their friends in the dining room with chocolate and cakes. From 3.30 onwards people seemed to drop in incessantly, until well after seven. Men generally brought flowers or boxes of sweets which were intended for the younger Catherines. With the winter cold and frost, which had often set in by that date, the flowers were wrapped up in layers of paper and sometimes even of light cotton wool and I still see the young footman, a clumsy village boy called Fedka, struggling with the wraps, strings and papers, before handing them back to the impatient owner waiting to deliver his offering to the Catherine of the place. The chocolate or tea party for the younger set was just the usual performance, with the difference that the boys had to go away after a short stay as they had to squeeze in a few more "Catherine calls" before dinner. In our case things were easier, as the two Catherines in the apartment above ours had many friends in common with us and the boys just ran up or down stairs – trying not to mix up the flowers they had brought.

Then came Christmas. We had been dressing the large tree which stood as usual in the dining room against the window and reached right up to the high ceiling. Father and my brother were doing the top decoration, we girls were doing the bottom branches and we tried to keep our governess away as she was sure to want to introduce some novelty in the decoration – and we were terribly conservative about it. The old favourite toys had their duly fixed places: the black monkey with a flag in his hand was always in the middle, near the trunk; the little golden coach – to the left; the sledge with brown horses – to the right; and so on. On the very top was fixed the golden angel with a silver star and from under his feet cascades of different chains linked together the tips of the widening branches. The finishing touch – the silver rain – was always dealt with by Father, and in later years by my brother, whose own speciality was the distribution of the candles.

It was December 24th, we had no more lessons and were full of the holiday spirit with two long weeks of free time before us. Mother was busy at the other end of the dining room arranging on a large table trays and dishes with all the most attractive sweets and fruit one could have. On a separate table were lined up ten soup plates in which Mother distributed the sweets for the servants. From time to time we ran across the room to have a closer look – and taste – at the nuts, raisins, pâtes de fruits, and endless varieties of delicious things looking particularly tempting when piled in great quantities on trays and in flat crystal dishes.

Then came the evening – at last. The dinner was too long, the service so slow – although we were generally alone but for some old friend, such as Mother's old Russian governess or our own dear Mimi. After dinner we children were parked in the playroom and waited there until called in at eight. Only my brother had the right to help Father and the footman to light the candles on the tree while Mother was arranging the presents on the long dining room table pushed along the wall. I knew what the tree would look like, I knew the effect of the many candles against the very dark red of the window curtain – and yet it was always a new and breathtaking sight when the door opened and we walked in from the big drawing room, all the children together, and we formed quite a little crowd as my three cousins arrived punctually at ten minutes to eight. A squint at the table, at the end where the grown-ups' presents lay, and in that particular, special year I remember seeing the dark red leather case which contained the surprise for Mother.

Two Christmas days remain as particularly happy ones for me as far as presents go. Once, when I was eleven, I found waiting for me an entire outfit of a Russian naval officer – and it simply took my breath away. With what pride I told my violin teacher that this outfit was mine when he had just been asking which of the boys, my cousins, had received it. I can still see his raised eyebrows and amused face and remember my feeling of indignation that he did not seem to admire this present as much as I did. The other time was when at seventeen I found waiting for me my first real shotgun, a 20-calibre, and two boxes of cartridges. This was an even greater joy, for I had been asking Father to allow me to buy this gun with my own money, which I had been saving year after year. Finally, shortly before Christmas, when Father was at some conference abroad, I had written again and again asking him for his permission, begging him to say "yes" – such an easy word. And actually a few days before he came home, Father had sent me a telegram with the one word "Oui" – and I had been overwhelmed with joy. A little intrigue had been played behind my back, with Father delaying his permission so as to prevent my getting the gun myself, as he and Mother had made up their minds to give it me as a Christmas present.

For weeks before Christmas one of our favourite occupations was to plan the Christmas tree for the orphanage of the Orthodox Church of St Panteleimon – Niania's church, as we called it. There were about thirty children there, boys and girls, aged from four to twelve. All wore cotton overalls, generally of small red and white checks; they all had their hair cut very short and looked like boys, but some of the children had fancy earrings and, as a child, I thought that this was done in order to make it easier for the teachers to distinguish the girls from the boys.

I liked preparing the presents, arranging separate parcels of material for dresses, gloves, socks and handkerchiefs; it was fun buying all the different sweets and nuts and fruit and then filling the little gaily-coloured cotton bags which we had been sewing during our reading-aloud hour. Although I hated sewing, I never objected much to this work as it was easy, did not require attention and was bright in colours. Then there was the fun of packing all these things into individual parcels, tying them up with pink ribbons for girls and blue ribbons for boys, and the joy of seeing the stack of parcels grow more and more impressive.

When finally the great day arrived, there was the bustle of the departure of linen baskets filled with parcels carried by two maids, who took them in advance to the orphanage. How well I remember the drive there in the closed carriage, the turning left into the "crooked" street, as we called it, dark and dull with its low houses and modest little shops with painted shutters. The house of the orphanage was a two-storied building painted yellow, with a narrow staircase and small low rooms. I always thought it all looked small and smelt stuffy; the teachers had dresses or silk blouses which seemed too tight for them; the children stood crowded together, closely pressed against each other, among the narrow benches and the slanting desks. Somehow, everything looked as if it could not spread out comfortably. Only the priest with his full red beard, with his broad smile and ample robes, seemed to have plenty of space everywhere to spread at his ease.

A Christmas tree stood in the right hand corner, with its white candles, silver stars and a few sweets hanging on red, pink and blue ribbons. It was pretty as a Christmas tree is always pretty, but again there was too little room for it with all our parcels piled on two tables right and left of it.

Then the distribution began – my sister Katya at one table, myself at the other, helped by a tightly-bloused and much curled teacher who was always redolent of some sweet sickly perfume. Niania and sister Mary sat with the other teacher and the priest watching the distribution. The children looked clean, scrubbed and certainly happy; they thanked awkwardly but I felt that they were pleased and were anxious to have a peep into their parcels. The teacher whispered from time to time pointing out a particularly good pupil who had deserved a better present.

After the distribution came the speech of thanks, a few words by the priest as a rule, and once by some municipal councillor who had come for the occasion. He was also a Senator and apparently he knew my father. He had a double beard parted on both sides of a red and round chin, and he was extremely amiable and talkative.

After the speech the children sang for us and this part of the festivity was really the nicest – at least I always enjoyed it and waited for it with impatience. The tree was still lit, the children in their pink-tinted pinafores stood in three groups (according to voices) near the tree, the priest sat at the harmonium, conducting the choir and playing a few chords of accompaniment. Old Niania, whom we considered something like a "dame-patronesse" of this orphanage, sat upright on a chair, her white lace bonnet and kerchief framing so well the fine face with the clever black eyes, the firm mouth and well-cut nose, and the snow-white hair parted over the high forehead. Our maid Emma stood behind her also in her Sunday-best clothes, a big coral brooch pinned under her chin on the white silk front of her blue dress. My sisters and I sat right and left of Niania and the double-bearded Senator was next to me – as I was the eldest.

The children sang – and they sang remarkably well. The little choir was so well drilled, so rhythmic, and the three voice-parts blended so well together that it always impressed me greatly. Church songs and prayers opened and ended the little concert and, in between, the children sang folk songs and children's songs, sometimes duets, trios and quartets. It was amazing to see these children – often with blank and uninteresting faces – sing with ease and true understanding and pleasure, I always thought. This was real Christmas for them, and it was sad when the final National Anthem was sung; I regretted that the music had come to an end and that I would not hear it again until the following year.

I was anxious to go now, but, conscious of my duty and responsibility, I tried to talk to the teachers, to ask about the lessons and about the school Christmas party, while waiting impatiently for Niania to give the signal for departure. The children all came to see us off and I remember them standing in the doorway of the tiny hall, gaping at us as we got into our warm clothes – the high felt boots, the fur-trimmed coats, fur caps and the thick white "bashlyk" headscarf over the shoulders. They looked attentively at each garment as we put them on and seemed to find it all very fascinating for their eyes got rounder and rounder. Then Niania got into her fur coat, put the thick plaided shawl over her shoulders, hung the muff on the black silk cord, and with a last hand-shake to the priest and the teachers we filed down the narrow staircase, Emma following us with the empty linen baskets. As we came out into the street the air seemed to be so brisk and clear, the evening so dark, with the dim light of the paraffin street-lanterns, and the snow reflecting this light in a narrow circle. The carriage was waiting for us; we all scrambled in and drove home noiselessly in the deep snow through silent streets.

In the long weeks of winter one of our most enjoyable pastimes was to go skating in the Tauride Gardens. The Tauride Palace, which became so well known after the Duma occupied it in 1905, was familiar to us in our childhood as a place of retirement for the old ladies who had held Court appointments in their younger days – and as a place where we could change into skating clothes or get warm after skating. The Palace was spacious and light with large windows, enormous halls, lofty ceilings and lovely parquet floors. The old ladies occupied some of the apartments in the wings of the Palace, the rest was closed except in winter when one part, to the right of the central hall, was left open for us skaters. A number of footmen attached to the Court service looked after us: they took care of our coats and strapped on our skates, for at that time not all skates were fixed to the boots. We had skates of various types which had to be screwed or clamped to the boots – and screwed tight, as otherwise the foot had no proper hold over them. Once the skates were fixed we walked on them through several reception rooms – with only a few sofas or chairs in them – until we reached the glass door leading straight out on to an ice track which finished with a steep dip onto the frozen surface of the large pond.

Close by the pond were, to my joy, some "Russian mountains", tall wooden erections with steps one side and an ice-covered slope the other. On the top was a little platform surrounded with benches and from that platform you slid down the iced hill on a small steel sledge covered with a thick upholstered cloth or velvet covered cushion. These sledges were lifted to the platform on a chain supplied with hooks and wound up by hand by one of the palace gardeners. It was such fun to sit on the sledge, keeping one's feet with the skates well together in front of it and to fly down the very steep slope at a pace that cut one's breath, especially on very cold days when eyelashes and loose ends of hair coming out from under caps were covered with hoar frost.

Later, when the Duma had moved into the Palace, the skating was taken over by the Officers of the Chevaliers Garde.

A pavilion built on the edge of the pond served as a dressing place, and there were no Court footmen any more to buckle our skates. But we had the Regiment's band playing on Sunday afternoons and we naturally enjoyed it all very much – having grown up by then and enjoying the sport as well as being with our friends. One of the young men was Alexander Sollohub, later to become my husband. He was an excellent skater and was very fond of dancing on the ice, but I never managed to be a good partner for him and he had difficulty in finding suitable partners of his standard. But there was one place where we could skate together, and that was down the "Russian moun-tains" whereby he skated backwards and I held his hands com-ing down facing him. The strain on the feet was very great as we had to keep steady without giving way to the bumps or cuts in the ice which occurred after a milder day. I was really terrified and yet thrilled at the same time, and only too happy when he called me to skate down with him. Skating down the mountains alone was something I could already do quite eas-ily, and I practised it eagerly in the mornings when there were only children and their governesses using the rink. How well I remember the sight of all those governesses and nurses wad-dling along behind the wooden pushchairs used by learners! The long skirts which were the fashion then did not make the thing easy, I must say, and I admire now the courage and endurance of those English and French women in facing up to the intense cold of our northern winter.

Finally, it was spring again. No skating any more: snow melting everywhere. In the streets it looked like dirty choco-late ice cream; in the squares and gardens it was dirty grey and transparent on the top; on the roofs it melted rapidly during the day, thundering down in great clumps, and freezing into lovely long icicles overnight. The sparrows sat on the edge of the roof and twittered; the pigeons talked and preened them-selves; the crows and rooks sat on the gaunt branches of the black and lifeless trees and looked around for suitable nesting places. As to the river Neva – it showed something new every day: the traffic across on the ice was closed, the little electric tram across had been stopped and the rails hurriedly removed; the ice was still solid, but the large openings made in it to cut ice blocks for private cellars gave it an abandoned look and the water in them was black and sinister; once or twice I could still catch a glimpse of a seal coming to rest in the sunshine at the edge of one of these holes but when it slid back into the water a lot of broken ice fell in after it. A few more days and the ice might "move" as we used to say, and we would hear the grinding of the ice blocks pressing on each other, squeezing the lighter ones up on top, and breaking with a dull roaring noise. It was impressive and beautiful, fascinating to watch. The sun shone warmly but the air was still cold and hard frost could be expected at night.

It was a time of hard learning for all of us, whether we were at school or at home. It was the time for the last drill before examinations. We two sisters did not go to school until we were sixteen but we had to pass "control" examinations every year at some school chosen by our parents and teachers. The idea was to see whether we really had followed the programme of the general studies and were on a level with girls of our age. How I hated these exams. Besides the terror and fear they provoked, there was the horror of the masses of schoolgirls I was suddenly required to meet. Really I only had to see them run in and out of the classrooms, but that was enough; I was terrified of girls and had no girlfriends outside the family at all. They all looked to me sophisticated and nearly grown up, whereas I dreamed of remaining a child as long as possible. Perhaps it was the sign that my childhood was really a very happy and sheltered one for I never longed for any independence, knowing probably by instinct that independence also meant new responsibilities and I dreaded them as I dreaded the whole idea of growing up.

However, all went well as a rule, but I think the success was partly due to my looking years younger than I was and the teachers never believed that I intended to sit for an exam which they thought much beyond my years. Frankly, I guessed this at the time, and enjoyed the fact that with my long hair loose and my sailor dress my success in the oral exams was pretty nearly assured – except perhaps in mathematics where I was really very weak. Unfortunately it was a subject which was taken very seriously for girls as well as for boys, and the amount of mathematics we were taking terrifies me when I think back. Only the exams in French and German were easy. There were no exams in English as it was not an obligatory subject.

Oh, the joy when this trial was over! By then spring had really arrived and our special treat was to be taken after dinner to the Islands – a set of islands in the mouth of the Neva where parks with shady avenues and groups of lovely trees led to the point, from which one had a wide open view over the estuary and the Finnish Gulf. We drove there in the open landau, along the quay, across the Neva and through unknown parts of the town until, after more bridges across arms of the river, we came to the Yelagin Island, the best of all, where we could pick the first wild white anemones and hear the first nightingales. It was a festive night for we had evening tea with the grown-ups and went late to bed. It was cold and damp coming home but we did not mind for it was spring after all and soon, very soon we would go to the country, to our beloved country house where such a different carefree life awaited us.

The best spring in town that I can remember is the one when I stayed alone with Father as my mother and the sisters were in Italy and I had to do my finishing exams. I had been at school – a day school a few steps from our house – and I had to sit for these exams rather late in May, taking them with the rest of the class. It was tiring but at times quite interesting. I could ask my father lots of questions on history and could consult the books in his library undisturbed by my new governess Miss Cummins, who did not interfere in my work. Books lay round me on the carpet, open here, with bookmarks there, and I would plunge into one for one question, follow it up in another and another – with the result that I never got through one half of the questions that had to be prepared or revised for. There was always so much new to read about, so many new views opening, so many details giving a better, clearer idea of the subject. When the sun shone brightly Father would come into the study with the words: "What about a tour on the Islands?" to which I agreed with delight, of course.

And sometimes there were good games of tennis in the mornings, when my friends and cousins were free between their exams. We used to play then in the front garden of the State Bank building, as my uncle Timashev was Head of the Bank and two of his sons, who were our age, were quite keen on tennis – though they did not play well. My future husband and a friend of his often managed to get some time off too (they were also in the midst of their exams) and we had very happy games of doubles with my governess sitting and yawning on a garden seat and aunt Timashev bringing us some biscuits or sweets.

Better still were the mornings when I could have a ride either in the riding school or in the Summer Gardens, but I never enjoyed those rides in the side saddle as much as I did later when riding astride.

Time flew and the house began to give signs of closing up for the summer: upholsterers appeared carrying furniture to be repaired, dust-covers were slipped over the rest and the rooms looked strange and clumsy, though cool and clean. The carpets were rolled into enormous sausages, with naphthaline and turpentine and other smells hanging in the air and making you cough. Summer was really on the threshold and when the huge suitcases and travelling baskets appeared in our nurseries and playroom – then no learning could penetrate my head any more. The maid was packing, I was pushing my own treasures in between the layers of clothing and only concerned myself with the packing of my violin, my gun, my tennis racquet and riding kit. Books went in large wooden boxes, so many books for all of us to read and to prepare for next winter's work, looking so harmless now packed side by side between thick layers of newspapers. Men tramped up one morning and grunting and sweating carried down all this luggage which had to be sent partly in advance. And two, three days later we were going at last, Father seeing us off – he preferred not to travel with the family though. The long drive to the railway station, the Varshavsky Voksal, for the eight o'clock train, the smoky station, the long express train – all this was like a dream, for I was already there, in Waldensee, with all my thoughts and feelings.

4

WALDENSEE

I loved this house, Waldensee, which my father had bought so as to give us a country home. It was near Wolmar in Livonia, one of the Baltic provinces, and Father could make frequent visits there on his way to and from international conferences at The Hague which took up much of his time in the years leading up to The Hague Peace Conference of 1899. The conversation at table turned more and more to international events. The Spanish–American war broke out in 1898; we heard it discussed at table during lunch and the impression was stunning for sister Katya and me. We realised suddenly that history was not a thing of the past as we had thought, but that it was going on in our own time – though at a distance. I don't think I had any premonition of possible dangers, but my faith in history being just history and nothing more was gone. A feeling grew in me quite soon that things were changing, developing and that they might touch us too, however well we were sheltered in our parents' home. Reading some story which dealt with the great French Revolution I suddenly became terrified by the thought that things of that kind could also happen to us – and this thought never quite left me. Later, the revolutionary movement of 1904–5 in Russia brought back to my mind this fear of my childhood – an apprehension confirmed by the events of 1917. However, these dark thoughts did not spread any lasting shadows over me as a child and I think I enjoyed my childhood as fully as little girls of our circles could. And for me the summers in Waldensee were the best times of all.

The early mornings in our country home were so varied that I cannot select the best – they were all "best" in their own way. Our bedroom had closed wooden shutters but through the chinks I could see the sun, and then punctually at half past six my dog Kars managed to open the door (I suspect good old Niania helped him, as she could not resist the pleading eyes of a dog or a child). He was supposed to be a Siberian laika, the dog that was used throughout Northern Siberia for tracking elk, lynx, ermine and squirrel. But poor Kars had a blemish in his pedigree: his ears did not stand up as they should, his tail curled up triumphantly and his paws were too small – to mention only a few of his faults. But I did not care, he was my devoted friend and the keenest dog I ever had. He would wake me by putting his front paws on my shoulders and poking his nose into my neck – I knew it meant "get up" and no call could have been more welcome. Dressing, washing, brushing my hair took little time, I fear, and Kars and I were soon out of the room leaving sister Katya still asleep. We ran (for we both always ran) to the stables to be on time for the grooming of the horses – blissful hours when I stood there under the heavy stone arches of the stables watching Ivan cleaning, brushing, trimming the horses, and the long friendly conversations we had then, all about horses and their tastes, nature and whims. As I loved horses I took it all in very keenly, and certainly learned a lot during these hours, even though our conversation ran in infinitives as Ivan only spoke Latvian, which I did not know, and a sort of "short-hand" German. Sometimes the old father-in-law turned up and sat on an oak chest smoking his pipe and grunting some remarks which I could never understand, but he amused me because of his fear of horses: the moment one of them became restless, tickled by a brush or annoyed by a fly, the old man would quickly slip to the back of the chest which served him as a protective bastion.

By eight o'clock the horses were ready and happily munching their breakfast. Ivan had gone home for his coffee and I ran to the veranda where our breakfast was waiting. But on my way I stopped at the carnation beds to pick the prettiest one – a brilliant red or else a red and white striped one – to put on my father's plate for his button-hole.

After breakfast Father and I went round the "domain" as we called it: he wanted to have a look at the flower gardens, the hot-house, the stables and the fruit garden. I had so much to tell him then about the horses and the dogs, the fruit and the vegetables and I wonder how he had the patience to listen to it all, or if he did not listen to let me chatter so. But as I think back now it must have been quite a help for him to learn about the wishes of Ivan and the thoughts of Ernest the gardener through me and not through them directly, as they both had great difficulty in expressing themselves in either Russian or German. As we passed through the kitchen garden and orchard I had to taste the new radishes, pulling them out of the ground and washing them in the dewy grass, or sample the gooseberries and currants. When the apple crop was ripe it meant tasting the apples and with Father following my example we managed to eat quite a few fallen apples before we had done the rounds of the orchard. It was a lovely moment of the day with the long shadows of the trees falling on the grass-covered paths, with the dew still glistening on the longer blades, with the bees humming in the trees and the flower-beds of "flowers for cutting" looking a blaze of colour – the rows of asparagus plants framing them in light, feathery green.

It was also a blissful time because we had no regular lessons. The governess had no right to pin us down to books – and how I enjoyed this feeling of freedom. One of them had tried to limit my freedom at Waldensee by insisting on my telling her where I was going to be during the morning. But I soon found a way out of this trouble by reciting to her the names of all the places I possibly could be – with the result that she never could know where I actually was, and she soon gave up asking me.

But there were also very different mornings in the country when I reached fourteen and was allowed to go alone to our small woods across the fields. They too ended at eight o'clock when Father wanted me to be there for breakfast with him. But they started at dawn, and Kars was my companion, along with the Montecristo, my brother's little rifle. Those were perfect mornings with the sun just rising, with the mists lingering over the low, wet meadows, with the stubble fields grey with cobwebs. The run across the fields was short, the path straight and Kars kept to "heel" as long as there was no temptation. The moment we approached the little forest which stretched in a narrow band along the river, Kars was off like a dart and I saw no sign of him until I heard him barking up a tree after a squirrel. The excitement began then: Kars jumped up at the trunk of a tree, panting and following with his sharp eyes any movement in the branches. The squirrel, tired or frightened by the barking, jumped from tree to tree and Kars, following it, barked in a high distressed voice all along the course while I tried to shoot the squirrel, firing bullet after bullet until I finally brought it down. Then, we both dashed for it. If Kars was first I was really in a plight for he would not let me touch the prey, but I insisted on having it in order to cut off the tail for which I would get a premium of 20 kopeks, the usual reward given to the gamekeepers. How many times Kars bit me – involuntarily, I am sure – as we struggled for possession of the poor dead squirrel! How many times I came home dangling the squirrel tails tied with dry blades of grass and hiding the handkerchief tied round a bleeding hand or arm, in fear of the governess making a scene over it and stressing the importance of disinfection, the danger of dogs' bites, and so on. But never mind – Kars and I had had our sport and we came home hot and tired, creeping round the back of the stables to my room for a quick tidy-up before breakfast. Unforgettable mornings which gave me so much joy, which taught me to shoot accurately, to share the keen sporting spirit of my dogs, and to rely upon myself.

On warm summer days it was not easy to make up one's mind about the next morning: would it be the forest and shooting or would it be the river and fishing? Of course my fishing was the most primitive affair: I knew few fish, I knew very little about their tastes and habits and just as little about the baits and the hooks. But I loved fishing in the primitive way that I used to do it, either with Father fishing before sunset from the little bridge or my fishing alone on the lake which fascinated me. At sunrise again, Kars and I would leave the house cautiously; I took the heavy oars, my fishing tackle and a bucket for bailing the water out of the boat and off we went to the forest, then through it to the river where the boat was chained. On the bank, in the soft murky earth there were enough worms to fill my little box in a few minutes; a large stone which served as an anchor was hidden in the nearby bushes, and we could set out undisturbed, rowing down stream in the shade of the huge dark spruce growing on our bank of the river.

After a mile and a half the river widened, becoming a sort of lake with wide belts of rushes reaching far into the distance. This is where I dropped anchor and settled down to fish, with Kars curled up for a snooze in the bottom of the boat if it was dry enough or on the wider seat in the bows. And I fished, fished patiently for hours and very rarely caught anything. But it was so beautiful on the glassy surface of the lake, it was so fascinating watching the wild duck families starting their day's hunt for food among the reeds, it was so quiet and so far from anybody that I enjoyed every minute and rowed home reluctantly, annoyed to have to return to the hustle and bustle of everyday life. Only Kars was disappointed on those mornings for he saw that I carried no gun, and crossing through the forest he looked longingly at the trees hoping to spy a squirrel.

There were some special dates during the summer months in Waldensee that provided us children with a lot of excitement, fun and interest. In fact, these dates had more meaning for the grown-ups as they were those of traditional festivities in the various estates of the neighbourhood and we children generally participated only in those which took place in our own house. But even when our parents and their friends staying at our house were going to one of these big parties (generally dinners at 7.30, sometimes tea at 4.30 followed by the dinner party) we had a lot of fun. I spent hours before the departure watching the coachman Ivan polishing, dusting, inspecting all the harnesses and carriages, giving a last brushing to the seats, a last stroke of a brush with some mysterious tar-smelling stuff on some parts of the wheels. It was fascinating to watch him and when Lisa, his wife, joined him and brushed his livery and the funny coachman's cap and stretched on her hands the gloves she had just washed for him, – then I knew that it was time to watch for the most interesting part of the show, the harnessing of the four-in-hand. I was terribly proud of this four-in-hand and had no eyes any more for the usual caleche which followed the big landau and which had only two horses – one of them even being the farmer's horse. On these days Ivan did not allow us to climb into the carriage and drive round to the front door – our shoes would soil the carpet. So I ran behind the carriage and enjoyed this run just as much as I did the usual ride. It was grand to see the four horses pull on, the gardener's boy holding the front pair who never could start without prancing about. Ivan had his most serious face; his beard lay well brushed like a red fan on his chest, his long whip, the new one, stood up like a mast in front of him and all the metal parts of the harness were so glittering, so bright that the sun played on them and they sent sparks on the steps of the terrace.

Father stood ready – always the first and always on time – with his light summer suit and brown soft hat and my carnation in his buttonhole. Mother came out looking so elegant and pretty in her light foulard dress, with her white shoes and large white hat with masses of ostrich feathers on it. I admired her and thought that fortunately there were many years still to pass before I would have to get into such clothes and hats and gloves. I patted my scruffy sailor shirt and felt the supply of apples in its deep recesses and was thoroughly happy.

My mother's birthday on the 27th July was the occasion for us to return hospitality to our Baltic friends. Long skirts, large-brimmed hats with scores of hat pins fixing them to buns, curls and rolls of hair, a little powder and no rouge – this is what I see when I think of my mother's birthday party at Waldensee.

Fortunately the long skirts did not concern me at the time, nor did the hats, and my mane of thick brown hair was held together by a ribbon – white for the festivity. Brilliant sunshine in the early morning when, after my daily visit to the stables where Ivan was grooming the horses, I had to be in good time for breakfast. Mother in her white silk dressing gown sat in the chair highly decorated with branches of lime trees and many flowers. She looked like some Eastern deity amongst these wild shades of green and bright colours. The table was covered with flowers and there was the big birthday cake in the shape of a "Bretzel" surrounded by red and white carnations. How promising the almonds half baked into its surface looked now, and how impatiently I waited for the opportune moment to slip my knife into the chink of the fattest almond, to snap off the top half of it, if my governess did not catch me in this manoeuvre. But fortunately she was too long admiring Mother's presents – all put around Mother's place – the jewels from Father, some paintings from sister Katya, some jig-saw work of my production, books, vases from other members of the household. The almonds off the cake were awfully good, my brother competed with me, and Father gave us a warning glance – better stop for the time being. We heard murmuring and shuffling of feet on the gravel outside and then the high-pitched voices of the women on the farm singing song after song, with words unknown to us, but all in praise of Mother. Their white kerchiefs gleamed in the sunshine, they were half hidden by the herbaceous border in full bloom, their voices were so shrill but never a wrong note even in the audacious chords and variations to which two or three men's voices gave a droning background. Mother thanked them from the steps of the terrace, and patted the heads of the blue-eyed fair-haired children clinging to the embroidered aprons of the younger women. The shrivelled yellow-faced babka (old woman), Ivan's mother, laughed and cracked a joke apparently; we missed it, but all laughed heartily.

It was a lovely day; we were enjoying everything. Brother Kolya was finishing the most complicated arrangements for the evening's illuminations: fireworks and paper lanterns were fixed in intricate designs all along wires drawn across the lawn between the rows of lime trees and all along the drive. Katya and I helped him eagerly and ran up and down stairs with loads of lanterns, candles, sticks and hooks. Kolya wanted more sticks, his fireworks were to be grander than ever – and I ran off to the little wood to cut young elders in the thicket. Kars was at my heel but he did not bark joyously for he saw that I had no gun – not much fun, he thought. And how lovely the wood was, teeming with life – insects, flies and birds filling it with their sounds. Kars was off – he barked furiously and jumped up along the trunk of a pine tree. I tried to see where the squirrel went – for it was always a squirrel when Kars behaved like that – the elder sticks could wait; and we followed, Kars and I, the squirrel in its flight from tree to tree. I craned my neck to see it in the top branches of a transparent luminous birch; I screwed up my face and looked through my fists when it disappeared in a dark spruce. Kars was exhausted, panting like an engine, drops fell from his flapping pink tongue and his golden-brown eyes looked at me pathetically: "Why don't you get it?" they seemed to ask.

We must go – get the sticks – I patted Kars, talked to him and showed my empty hands. "No gun – nothing . . ." and we went back on the soft carpet of thick dark green moss, back into the thicket where my sticks lay on a bed of twigs and leaves that I had already stripped off. How strong the smell of freshly cut wood was in the morning, how it mixed with the heavy scent coming from the peat-bog close by.

The weather was too lovely. We could not miss our swim in the river and, leaving all further preparations for the afternoon, we went off to the river. The men were there already – we had to wait for them to come up the path through the wood where Mother had had a bench put, "belle vue" as we called it. It really was a pretty view, over the tops of trees from a sand cliff, along the shaded brook and towards soft slopes of fields with a few farm buildings hidden among apple trees. We thoroughly enjoyed the brisk swim in a cold stream. From the steps of the bathing hut our governess corrected the swimming and counted the seconds we took to swim to the old spruce which had slid down the sand cliff the previous spring and now hung low over the surface of the water. The brook was dark green there and shoals of little fish swam in and out of the hollows under the tree's arched roots. The sun made bright round spots and the red sand of the cliff was reflected in ever-moving ripples at the bend of the brook. There were crawfish there, but as I could not dive I couldn't lift the stones under which they hid.

Luncheon that day was particularly good – fortunately the special delicacies, ordered from Petersburg, arrived in time; the chef had produced marvellous "pirog" cake, and the well-cooled hock was much appreciated by us all, with the exception of sister Mary. She sat next to Mother, her plate surrounded by pet toys – all animals – who came in turn to attend at meals; not more than three at a time was the law put down by Mother.

By three o'clock all arrangements for the illuminations and fireworks were ready and we looked anxiously at the sky where a few long puffy clouds had appeared. Our governess – after her nap – came out to see that we got ready in good time, for although the neighbours were invited to dinner some of them had already arrived. These were generally the very distant neighbours who were a good two or three hours' distance from us and whose horses would need a long rest before they started on the homeward trip. The nearest neighbours were some two miles off and they too frequently came early, to have a game of tennis or because the old gentleman was particularly anxious to chat with Father and Mother and could not do so to his heart's content when all the other guests were assembled.

Niania was waiting in our bedroom to do our hair. She brushed it down energetically, especially mine which always seemed terribly tangled and full of moss, twigs and leaves. The white frocks lay on the beds, the coloured belts hung on the back of the chair, the shoes were so distressingly white – useless for the dewy evening grass when the fireworks started. Kars pricked up his ears as he lay near my bed, and I heard the distant rumbling of wheels over the wooden bridge down the drive. Katya and I hurriedly buckled the belts, pinned the brooches and made a little bet between ourselves as to who the first guests would be. From our narrow window on the west side we could see the avenue down to the first hill. There was movement there: a carriage – whose horses? Knieriem? No, Kokenhof! No, Rantzen! . . . we called out in turn trying to guess the owners by the colour of the horses. Well, it was Rantzen: the four heavy black horses, the spacious landau and the coachman we disliked as he always looked grumpy and hit his horses.

On the terrace Father and Mother greeted the guests. Father was so smart in his light grey suit with the light tie and the pearl pin in it. In his buttonhole he wore the deep red carnation I gave him that morning. Mother was lovely as usual in her blue pastel foulard dress with a long gold and sapphire chain round her neck. Of course Kolya was not ready – I saw him peeping over the edge of the window upstairs, pulling his tie straight and still in shirt sleeves. Even on Mother's birthday he couldn't be ready on time.

As a rule the first guests were older people who were quickly left to the care of the parents. Little by little all of the expected visitors turned up and often enough they brought with them their friends who might be staying with them at the moment, so that one never quite knew how many people would actually be seated at table. When there were young people we took them round the garden, the stables, for a sail on the pond in a very shaky little boat, and even for a quick walk in my beloved little forest.

Well, the dinner went along its usual lines: Mother's health was drunk with champagne after the first speech made by one of her two neighbours, the two who always sat on her right and on her left and who always competed with each other as to who was to snatch the right moment for that speech. Mother looked very pretty, the flowers on both tables were lovely, many more flowers filled the vases as each guest had brought a huge bunch; the speeches flowed easily and we, the young ones, went round the table touching our glasses of champagne with the older people or stood up singing "Hoch soll sie leben". As soon as it got dark Kolya started the fireworks while we lit the paper lanterns all round the house and in the garden. The men sat on the terrace sipping their drinks and smoking; the women – well I don't know where they were; and the young people ran round the garden seeing to the lanterns which caught fire with a gust of wind, or just walked and chatted. Then came the horrid moment when Father called me and told me to "play something". I dutifully took out my violin, Mother sat down at the piano, the guests crowded into the sitting room, the study and the small salon. Only a few of the older men were independent enough to stay where they were over their drink. And then I started; how I hated it, and how I must laugh at it all now, half a century later. But then it was the thing to do, I could not protest, but I felt that Mother quite shared my feelings. However, Father was pleased and so proud of my playing that the performance had to be gone through – finishing with Grieg's "An den Frühling", which was a piece I really loved and which made me forget the unpleasantness of the moment.

As well as being beautiful, my mother was also very talented, with an interest in music, literature and painting. I could catch glimpses of Mother's world through the person of Akavavna, my mother's Russian governess. Her name was in fact Alexandra Nikolayevna Velsovskaya, but this was too long for us children and we contracted it into "Akavavna". She was a dumpy, lively little woman with black eyes, no figure and a strong limp. I loved her for her endless stories and fairy-tales which she could tell or read in the same even, clear voice without ever getting tired. She often read aloud to my mother while Mother was painting; she read fast and equally well in Russian and French, and they generally stopped at the end to discuss the chapters just read. Her tone was clear and keen and I am sure that her judgements must have been worth noting: there was nothing futile, superficial or haphazard in her tone. Both Father and Mother had the greatest respect for her and often discussed the latest trend of literature with her. I know that it is from these discussions that I got my first ideas about Turgenev, Tolstoy and the later modern writers.

The servants at Waldensee, were they loyal Russian sub-jects even though Russian was a language they scarcely spoke? Their world was so close to ours, but for us it was a world that remained largely unexplored. I feel very fortunate that in thinking of all these people there is not the faintest taint of bitterness in my recollections and certainly a great deal of gratitude towards many among them. The regret arises that I may not always have appreciated the kindness, devotion and patience of many old servants, probably because it was all taken for granted. But looking back now after many years and from entirely different surroundings, I see more clearly the human element in our relations with our servants, both in the Baltics and in Russia, and realise that we, too, were taken for granted in a way and the servants would not have had us different from what we were. Of course, there were a few among our servants who changed their attitude towards us – who withdrew from our horizon and were swallowed up in the rising tide of "conscious citizens" as they thought they had become, thanks to the revolution. But these were only few, and came from among those who had not been personally well known to us – they were not old servants. And, after all, would one blame them? They had to face their families, their

surroundings with the new ideas; and with curses being showered upon us, they were looked at askance for having been in
our service, for having protected our property against the new
upcoming class. Some vanished discreetly, afraid of coming
across us but never seeming to have been active against us. A
few became openly hostile.

But all these things were far in the future and unimaginable
in those sheltered childhood years. Year after year we returned
to our dear Waldensee. By the time I was seventeen, I was
the proud possessor of a delightful 20-calibre shotgun – the
Christmas present from Mother and Father when they finally
and reluctantly gave in to my request. Of course there was no
shooting for me in winter while we were still in Petersburg. I
waited more impatiently than ever for the spring, to go to the
country, to try my new gun. And finally we were there and
finally too the shooting season opened. After June 29th the
ducks on the lake had no peace – I was down hiding in rushes
whenever I could escape Kars' watchful eye. He was excellent
with squirrels but he still had no idea about water fowl and
rushed right down into the water with much splashing and
noise whenever he spied duck anywhere.

Then came the real shooting season – my first with a proper
gun – after September 1st, when I was invited to the real shoots
together with my brother, and when he and I wandered off
every morning at 6 a.m. for a private shoot with our large, inefficient and disobedient golden pointer, Nimrod. We trudged
through forests and woods, moors and swamps, rarely bringing home anything but a stray moor-hen or a hare at the best,
but the satisfaction was great and I learned a lot, training my
eye to follow the birds I had not paid much attention to before
– my game having been squirrels until then.

One day we were invited to a regular shooting party, starting early in the morning. By 6 a.m. my brother and I were on
the road. I was driving my favourite horse, Miru, in the small,
light four-wheeler and we arrived on time to join the rest of the
party. To our annoyance we could only stay for the morning,

since we were required to return home soon after midday. Still, we enjoyed the shooting; the hares were scarce as they usually were on this estate, but I was alone on the stand and this meant a lot of exciting moments anyhow. By noon we were ready to go home and left with our guns well packed in their cases. I was driving again, as Kolya highly disliked horses and anything connected with them. The distance was not great – some five miles – along the high road first and then along a small forest road for a short cut.

We were rolling briskly along the last bit of the high road, which dipped here into a small valley through which ran a brook with wooded banks – hazelnut bushes in fact – when I noticed three men with double-barrelled guns crossing the road from the field above and disappearing into the brushwood. They were not known to me, and this struck me as strange for the shooting rights were very strictly upheld in these parts of the country and I knew the few people who had the right to go shooting here. I told Kolya to look at them carefully so that we could report these men to the gamekeeper of the place; and at that very moment three shots resounded one after the other in quick succession. Our brown mare bolted forward as the shots came from close by, from the bushes to the left. I held the reins tighter to straighten her but let her go as fast as she could. My brother looked round rather puzzled: "Do you think that was meant for us?" he asked slowly. "I don't see for whom else, after all," was my reply, "there's not much game in these bushes right beside the road." We drove up the hill, turned to the right and from the ridge there I could see the three men standing at the edge of the brushwood, their guns on their backs.

Our coachman Ivan, when told about the occurrence, shook his head and said, "Times are getting bad, you must not drive alone, Miss Edy, as you generally do – one never knows." I did not like the idea of having my beloved drives or rides curtailed.

The same evening a friend of ours drove his carriage drawn by two horses along the same high road some five or six miles further up. As the road led through a dense pine forest, five shots fell, all from shotguns, and riddled the hood of the carriage, stuck in the coachman's thick coat and grazed the man's hand. We concluded that this was the work of the same three men who had first tried their luck on us.

All too soon we were near the end of this, my first shooting season as a fully fledged "gun". One day, which had been very unsatisfactory with little game and few shots as the dogs seemed to be bent on chasing the hares round and round outside the area where the guns were posted, I found myself sharing a stand with our neighbour Konrad Knieriem. It was a quiet and colourful October day, the forests looked friendly and still smelled of mushrooms (or, rather, toadstools as the season of edible mushrooms was over). Kolya and I had been invited to go shooting with Konrad and I was enjoying every minute of it – the only sad note being the thought that in two days' time we were to leave Waldensee and go to Petersburg for the winter as usual. I tried not to think of it and to enjoy these last moments as one can enjoy things so intensely when one is eighteen.

Konrad, our host, was sharing the stand with me as the line had to be shortened in this last beat – and there was not much game to be expected by then. I quite liked Konrad after all: he was six years my senior, the age of my brother. He liked shooting and riding and was probably very kind. He was now in charge of running his father's estate and was keen on improving it. His looks . . . well he certainly was not attractive with his rather stuffed figure, arms sewn on to a body that looked as though it had just come from the upholsterer. Black hair and a small dark moustache, above which hung such a long, sad nose! He had a fascinating way of twiddling his moustache right and left when he felt self-conscious – and this happened very often. He was shy and quiet, he had never anything much to say and fully realised that this was a drawback when at a party. However, when he and I were together he always managed to chat quite happily, telling me all about his horses and dogs, his farm plans and his shooting. There were also other topics of conversation with him and my father always teased me for managing to draw something out of Konrad the silent.

There we were, waiting for a stray hare to slip away from the hounds barking somewhere in the distance. And we chatted in subdued tones keeping a sharp eye on the glade in front of us. But conversation did not flow easily today. Poor Konrad had even less to say than usual and I tried to find the dog–gun–horse topic which would wake him up. Giving up my attempts as of no avail, I mentioned again, probably for the tenth time, how sad I was to go away to Petersburg. This time Konrad suddenly became quite voluble trying to make me a glowing picture of the lovely life I should have now, just grown up and in the capital (where he himself had never been). I was not so sure that I liked the idea of grand balls and big parties, having always feared the moment when that life would have to be faced. And I went on repeating how much I preferred my country home and country life which seemed so much simpler and clearer to me.

"You really prefer the country?" said Konrad after a moment's silence, his whiskers twiddling frantically under his long nose. "Yes, I do, even though there is so much that I love also in town – music for instance." The whiskers stopped twiddling; Konrad was obviously thinking and then said, "You know, you need not leave the country – you could stay . . ." I laughed. "Alone? I don't think it would do, even though I would not mind it." Konrad's whiskers became frantically agitated. "No – not alone – the decision is with you . . . you could stay!" I looked away a bit worried. This sounded strange, too incoherent for Konrad's normal way of expressing himself, and the little blue eyes peered intensely at me.

Poor Konrad, he did not know what to say next. We were silent; from the corner of my eye I could see the agitation of his whiskers – too funny and pathetic – and what did he mean, really? I felt too shy to ask him to explain.

59

The dogs came to our rescue. The favourite, Turco, managed to chase a hare towards us. "Shoot!" I called. "There on the right!" Konrad obediently levelled his gun, shot – and missed. "How stupid – I think it was an easy shot?" said Konrad, disconcerted. "I don't know, perhaps you could not see it well," I put in, still in a daze after our strange conversation. "Of course, I should have let you shoot, you must have more practice, you must stay here! Won't you? . . ." and the whiskers started anew and the little blue eyes looked kind. "Yes, I do need practice – I'll try . . ." and I saw to my relief the gamekeeper and my brother coming up the ride.

Was it an offer of marriage? Looking back I think I see now that that was what he meant – and I do not regret that the question remained unanswered.

5

MARRIAGE

My childhood was coming to an end, and I could no longer keep this unwelcome thought out of my mind. What next? Marriage? Yes, that is what would be expected of me. Or more studies? No – boys could become students, but this was not yet a suitable career for well-brought-up young girls.

Father often spoke of students, those of the St Petersburg University, and I used to picture in my mind the young men in their drab black uniform with blue collar – an ugly uniform, I thought. At that time talk about students often got very lively, the subject seemed always to be an acute one and the students appeared to be very little concerned with studies (schoolboys had had that job). The students were always involved in rioting, proclaiming something, or generally protesting about all sorts of things. I was too young to understand the political situation, but old enough to realise that something was going seriously wrong with the students as a whole. Those I saw seemed harmless enough, though they looked terribly unwashed with their untidy hair and sallow faces; they used to call at our house to ask Father for his advice on their further studies and future careers, but I only caught a swift glimpse of them if I happened to be in the hall when they were shown into my father's reception study. And yet these same students must be extremely restless creatures as they were always involved in street riots, protest meetings and noisy gatherings. There were tales of Cossacks having scattered the meetings near the Kazan Cathedral and I never passed there without a shudder, visualising the mounted police and Cossacks charging the students and brandishing their whips, looking so fierce when represented on the cheap popular propaganda sheets.

I was terrified when during such rows my father insisted on going to the University. I well remember one special occasion in the winter of 1903 – or perhaps 1902 – when students' rows were very numerous. Father had to give a lecture at the University. The students had been restless for several days, and tales of Cossacks having had to charge them were circulating throughout the town. I felt sorry for the students but thought it wrong to go in for rioting instead of working. I remember my father coming out of the study with my mother accompanying him and insistently repeating: "Please, be careful, it would be better if you did not go . . . it is dangerous . . ." and Father, as he kissed her goodbye, saying simply: "Don't worry, dearest, I know them – they are not bad boys." And with this he left.

Lunch was a little delayed that day. We were waiting for Father, and Mother looked very worried and walked in and out of her boudoir into the drawing room and back again. At last the bell rang and Father came in. He and Mother exchanged a few words, and then we sat down to lunch. Only afterwards, when the grown-ups had their coffee in the drawing room, did Father start telling us about his experiences of the morning. He told us how he had walked into the lecture room and found only a couple of students there; how others soon came streaming in, whereupon he talked to them about the nobility of the students' vocation. He told us how well they understood and agreed with what he was saying, and that after his lecture they carried him in triumph in their arms through the whole building as far as his carriage – to the great alarm and consternation of the coachman.

My governess at that time, Miss Cummins, was more of a companion than a teacher, now that my own studies were almost finished. We had one wonderful interest in common – a love of listening to good music. I remember especially the visits of the great conductor Nikisch to Petersburg. Whenever Nikisch came it meant many more evenings at the symphony concerts in the Nobility Hall – and it also meant those early morning drives to the large hall where the public was admitted to the general rehearsals of these concerts. There was something novel, nearly mysterious in these rehearsals: the dimly lit hall, the dark corridors leading to it, the absence of liveried attendants, strange looking "civilians" opening the doors and merely indicating to you from a distance the seats you could take, instead of leading you up to them. The large white columned hall of the Dvorianskoe Sobranie was barely lit except above the orchestra, it was a little cold, everyone sat in their overcoats and furs, everyone seemed absorbed in the music and there was none of the gazing around and the calculating looks that one had in plenty in the evenings.

The public was quite a puzzle to me: lots of bearded men with spectacles, lots of young women in very plain winter clothes, lots of young men looking like students, I thought, partly because of the rather untrimmed hair and doubtful collar arrangements; some of the girls I knew – or knew only by sight if they belonged to the older set. I loved this atmosphere for I felt that everyone had come here for this one and only purpose: to hear the lovely music, to hear it undisturbed and hear it actually being "made" or worked at.

Nikisch appeared there, not as the great musician who – in evening dress and baton in hand – would stand in front of the orchestra for the evening performance, but as a man whose will imposed itself upon the other men in the orchestra – a man who was truly their leader. He stopped them short if something did not quite please him; he made brief, quick remarks, gave signs of impatience or of appreciation, repeated two or three times a certain passage – humming a measure or two to show the accentuation – and frequently put in a joke which was not for the public but cheered the musicians. To hear them again the same night, to hear the music I had followed so closely and attentively in the morning, gave me the greatest satisfaction. I would now enjoy it altogether – the lovely setting, the brilliant light in the white hall, the evening dresses, gay colours and this same music which seemed to flow so easily now following the leadership of Nikisch – playing so entirely to the setting, forming part of it.

Beethoven, Liszt, Wagner – all were given with such artistic finish that each one appeared at the moment as the best – at least to us young and enthusiastic people. Beethoven was my favourite although some Liszt thrilled me even more with its brilliancy and undaunted flow – but I did not dare admit it. The classical drill from early childhood still played a great part in my judgements, expressions and opinions; I was closely controlled by this strict education, by the "right and wrong" as settled and fixed by the other generations. However, new trends did carry us away and in music too the admiration for Wagner was fairly unanimous among the young and little understood by the older people, who shook their heads in dismay at the loud outbursts of trumpets and frenzied crescendos of violins leading up to an exalted summit chord and dissolving then in a cascade of mellowed gurgling rippling notes. "Mad," said some, "a genius but abnormal," said others, whilst we young ones sat listening intently, overwhelmed by this new wealth of sounds and impetuous expression of feelings. For us, Wagner was but a new era in music – we were not aware of his importance as a leader of German national sentiment nor his influence on future political development. Few people realised at the time the spirit of his great operas – *The Ring* in particular – or followed his philosophical ideas. It was the impression of the music and the novelty of its expression that struck the young generation, and Nikisch knew Wagner and made his orchestra understand him too. No wonder that we felt tired after the concert, tired from the strain of listening, of living these dramas in symphonies, of visualising a world so very different from the one surrounding us and into which we now reluctantly returned.

Lost in sounds and impressions, in feelings of light and shade, I walked slowly behind my mother and my father in the silent crowd, in which the usual society chatter seemed for once to be suppressed and slow in surging up. And then the funny faces of the sleepy footmen waiting with our fur coats in the wide passages, the burst of cold air through the swinging door, the quaint calls for various coachmen and the screech of wheels on the hard frozen glittering snow brought me back to actual life and invariably the first feeling was a real and healthy hunger. The drive home was quick and how pleasant a sight was the dining room table with the steaming samovar, the plates of various sandwiches, biscuits, cakes and the boat-shaped silver bowl of fruit.

It was through our conversations at the dining-table that I was gradually made aware of events in the rest of the world, and also of the increasingly difficult political situation inside Russia in 1904 and 1905. I remember particularly the year 1905 when Russia experienced revolutionary upheavals after the end of the unsuccessful war against Japan. As far as I know there were strikes all over the country but mainly in Petersburg and in Moscow. In the autumn of 1905 we had innumerable processions in Petersburg, demanding this or that; we witnessed mass meetings on the Champ de Mars, and we heard of the encounters of the strikers with the police – somewhere, generally, on the outskirts of the town. And one day a strike by the postmen and of all post office employees was declared. My father was indignant and full of blame for the postal workers. Then and there he sent letters to the editors of two of our largest daily newspapers in St Petersburg. The contents of these were unknown to me, but the very next day it was clear that things had been stirred up: in the school where I attended a few courses every girl assailed me with expressions of admiration for Father, telling me that their parents had followed his initiative and were offering their services. I felt terribly ashamed not to be "in the know" at all. What had Father written, in fact?

What was his very brilliant suggestion? Fortunately Father was at home when I came back and over luncheon I could ask for the explanations I wanted. Apparently Father had written that if the strikers wanted to stop work and leave the whole town without postal services, we – the inhabitants – should give them a proof of our independence and take up the services voluntarily, dividing the tasks among us according to our possibilities. The idea was picked up without hesitation: people got together according to districts and the very next day we got our letters and papers and even telegrams delivered once a day. Father and many older gentlemen undertook the distribution of the post along certain streets in the course of the morning; ladies and young girls drove to the various postal offices and sorted the incoming and outgoing post, and young men who were acquainted with the working of the telegraph volunteered to remain on duty at the centres after school ready to deliver these telegrams to their destinations. This organisation worked so well that in a couple of days the strike finished in a flop and the strikers came back to work.

But the leftish press had been really roused and was spitting fire and flame at my father. Articles with endless accusations were written in the daily papers and posters abusing Father appeared on the walls. But what struck me most were the caricatures of Father; I felt terribly hurt that anyone dared make fun of him, and at the same time I could not help laughing at some of the drawings which were really quite amusing. The first one I saw made me feel unhappy and disgusted; it was on the front page of the paper which I was just taking upstairs from the hall table, so I could not help seeing it and felt very awkward giving it to Father. But as soon as he saw it, he burst out laughing and said to me: "This is an amusing one; give it to me and I'll put it into the general file where I want to keep them for posterity!" And opening his filing desk he took out quite a fat blue file and spread before me numbers of newspapers – Russian and even foreign ones – all dealing with the postal strike and many of them illustrated with either portraits of Father or caricatures of him. I felt quite reassured in my feelings, had a good laugh at some of the pictures and only regretted that some of the newspapers were in languages I could not read.

The following spring of 1906 brought the historic moment of the opening of the Duma, our first parliament. It was an April day, the sun shone brightly, the air was light and clear and blue and everything looked festive – at least so I thought.

My father had not been very well recently and had decided not to go to the tiring ceremony. But my mother was keen not to miss the occasion and gladly accepted the offer of her brother-in-law, my uncle Timashev, who suggested taking her to the Palace. I don't remember now whether it was before lunch or immediately after that they were to leave, but it must have been about that time for I succeeded in taking an excellent snapshot of my mother in her Court dress on the steps of the balcony door of the drawing room. It was a very good photograph, one of those I regret most not having any more. The Court dress was the Russian prescribed dress; colours were according to taste (except for ladies in waiting and demoiselles d'honneur) but the cut was, as far as I remember, definitely fixed for all alike: very low cut décolleté, straight silk dress buttoned all down the front with large buttons – often jewelled ones – the back worked into a wide long train; and the sleeves cut from the shoulders into two long hanging sleeves, the bare arms free from the top. On the head the usual Kokoshnik, the diadem-like head-dress of velvet or silk on a semi-circle of harder material, decorated with jewels, often a row of pearls running all round the edge, pearl loops hanging down along the lower edge to fall on the forehead. It was a most effective dress and Mother looked so well in it.

Uncle Timashev, who was a Minister at the time, had special entrance permits and Mother was sure to have a good place. They returned after several hours; no one knew when to expect them as the ceremony would take time and the crowds were sure to make the traffic slow. Anyhow, Mother came home very happy (much to Father's relief, I remember) and told us during dinner all about the proceedings. The Emperor's speech from the throne had not been very impressive, apparently, and much concern was being expressed about it. All other speeches came off according to plan, but there had been no real enthusiasm – at least this is what I remember and what we seemed to regret. At first, with the lovely spring day, the bright sunny morning, it had seemed to me that great new expectations were in the air – and in the hearts of the people. But by the evening these hopes seemed to have dwindled; at least, this was my own very youthful impression.

These were the main events that I remember during those few years that led from my childhood to my marriage. By the summer of 1906 I was engaged to be married to Count Alexander Sollohub, my friend Sasha from those happy times on the skating rink and tennis court. My parents were to let us have an apartment in town, and for our country house there was Kamenka, a property that Sasha had bought some 80 versts (50 miles) to the south of Petersburg.

Sasha's childhood had been very different from my own. He was born on his family's estate, Louisino, near Kursk on May 1st, 1884. When he was four years old his father fell ill, was taken to Moscow and died there. His mother took him to Moscow with her at that time, but afterwards they returned to Louisino where his mother stayed all year round, working hard and managing the estate.

When Sasha was about twelve years old, he was taken to Voronezh to school, and he lived there every winter with his mother until he was seventeen. At seventeen he came to Petersburg, passed his exams and entered the 4th Class of the Lyceum – the last "silver collar" class. He worked well and loved his time at the Lyceum, living partly at home and partly at school – as the boys were expected to live there. He was "General ot Fronta" when he came into the 1st Class (the highest one), with a golden collar and sword. His duty was to see to the discipline, to take parades of all boys when any ceremony took place, to review them all every day as they filed into the dining hall for meals, and to see – as far as possible – that all boys behaved properly when out of the school and kept strictly to regulations in clothes and manners. When meeting in the street, the boys gave the military salute; they were never allowed to wear civilian clothes, could not go to restaurants (at any rate, not into the large public rooms), had to wear white gloves, button up all the buttons on their uniform coats, and were only allowed to wear their small winter caps if the thermometer went below −15°C. Sasha loved all these traditions and took them all very seriously.

In 1903, or about that time, Sasha bought Kamenka from a big industrialist named Franz Franzevitch Utemann. As his mother could not manage both places, and as she was very attached to Louisino where she had worked all these years, an uncle was entrusted with the superintendence of Kamenka. A permanent manager was placed there, with the uncle being supposed only to give general directions. The uncle held this post for three years and was well paid for it, but managed to get to Kamenka only twice – once to shoot elk, and another time for the capercailzie shooting in spring. He did not take the work seriously and allowed such misusage that the whole place was on the verge of ruin when Sasha took it over himself in 1906.

In the spring of that year Sasha finished at the Lyceum with the 2nd Gold Medal. And in June we became engaged and Sasha decided that he would now take over Kamenka, leaving Louisino to his mother. He would also enter state service – as the boys from the Lyceum were expected to do – and join the Imperial Chancellery, where they had plenty of leisure and were not obliged to be present. His service there never lasted more than a few weeks each year, and dwindled down to casual visits from time to time. Eventually Sasha decided not go on with the work there, for Kamenka needed all his attention.

Sasha's mother insisted on my going to see my future home, and Sasha was keen on my coming there in October for a two-day shoot. So we were packed off, sister Katya and I, and joined my future mother-in-law at the Nikolayevsky station. The old lady was certainly very impressive, with her stern expression on a decidedly ugly face – with large features and a mass of grey hair. She walked slowly, held herself very straight and had very little to say at any time.

We took the train to Tosno, and after that there was a three hours' drive from the station – sitting in silence and feeling weighed down by the grey, damp autumnal weather. The forests bordering the road never seemed to end and when we at last reached open fields I had a sense of relief: more space, more free breathing, I thought. And there stood Kamenka: no impressive castle (I had not expected it to be), but a cosy looking wooden two-storied shooting lodge sheltered from the north by huge fir trees and overlooking a sort of lawn, in the centre of which stood an enormous lime tree. Very soon this would be my home. I wondered . . . and preferred not to think in advance. In a haze of impressions I walked round the place, visited the stables, the manège which impressed me a lot, the huge cow-house looking like a Chinese pagoda, the abandoned uncared-for garden which seemed to have great possibilities, and in the same haze I duly talked at dinner and spent the evening in the red salon, until finally it was bedtime.

What a relief to go to sleep and to forget the problems which I felt now beginning to surge up around me. How should I behave, now that I was engaged? Was this the right thing to say? Was that the right thing to do? Should I smile all the time? Should I ask endless questions on running a house, on caring for cows and pigs? Was I still myself, or did I have to creep head and all into the mould prepared for me, duly bearing the label "Girl happy – getting married next month"? This label crushed me, crippled me, for how would I be able to live up to the expectations of all the people surrounding me? Enough to make anyone downcast, when I think of it now. Still – I knew I had to bravely face my new life and the duties looming on the horizon, and try to ignore those worrying thoughts that kept reappearing at odd moments when I was alone.

There I was, a complete stranger and complete novice in everything concerned with running a house, facing my future mother-in-law and the household of servants at Kamenka. Everyone looked at me inquiringly as if sizing me up and drawing their own conclusions. Fortunately at the time I was not in the least conscious of evil-minded and suspicious natures or of gossip-loving tongues, and only thought of the tasks facing me and of the proper way of facing them. Obviously a sense of duty had been well drilled into us as children. Perhaps the austere looks of my future mother-in-law accentuated all these apprehensions and robbed me of the modest ration of self-assurance that I may have had. Anyhow, the hours in the house dragged slowly on, the conversation seemed to be stretched out over topics of dogs and horses, but even there I felt a novice and all I said seemed limp and pretty helpless.

The early morning departure for a day's shoot with beaters was a huge relief. The old lady presided over the breakfast and saw us off: Sasha, the estate manager Baron Fersen and myself – we were only three guns. Sister Katya, who did not care for shooting, remained at home and I knew she would find plenty of things to do or to interest her in and out of the house.

The day's shoot was thrilling and exciting. The enormous stretches of forests were new to me; the vast moors over thousands of acres impressed me; and the variety of game was fascinating. Of course I shot badly: waiting for a hare I was suddenly called upon to shoot at a hazel hen and hesitated which barrel to use in accordance with the number of the cartridge in them; or then a neat swish of wings would resound immediately after the first call of the beaters and I was too late to aim at the lovely huge capercailzie passing over my head. On taking our places at another stand Sasha would tell me: "Mind, keep a good look out for there might be elk in this drive, but don't shoot them as you may make a mistake and shoot at an elk cow. Besides, your 20 calibre gun with shot is not really suitable for big game," and I would be left there trembling with terror and wondering what to do if an elk really came out near me! To shoot a cow would have been a never-forgotten shame, and to miss any game would mean bringing shame on Sasha that he had chosen such a clumsy girl for his wife. But to let it pass – as if unnoticed – would be just as bad with all these beaters and gamekeepers looking on. I must admit that I was glad when the last beat was over . . . and my little achievements did not look bad. It had been a very tiring day, but I did not dare admit it either to Katya or to myself.

The next day was perhaps less worrying but no less tiring as it rained steadily and the wet clothes weighed such a lot towards evening. By that time Katya had had a good look at the library and after dinner she eagerly pointed out to me many interesting publications which in later years became great friends of mine.

Summing up these two days in my mind I felt grateful that things had gone smoothly, that I had not shot an elk cow nor missed too good a shot at capercailzies; also, I had not shown signs of my tiredness and my future mother-in-law had been as gracious – and, at the same time, as distant – as she could be. But I had the feeling that Katya did not have great illusions about the "pleasant character" of the old lady. Baron Constantin Fersen and his wife had been quite cheerful and supplied a "third element" in an atmosphere which without them might have been a little strained. They had been married only two years. The Baron was a gentle, hesitant but friendly man, and his wife was a girl whom I had met before her marriage at the house of our nearest neighbours at Waldensee. Although we had not really been friends we had many topics of conversation in common, and this had helped during the dinners and evenings at Kamenka.

Early on the third day we duly left, Katya and I in the first carriage and Sasha with his mother in the second. Three good hours of steady trot brought us to Tosno station, and after an hour and twenty minutes in the train we were in Petersburg. Our old coachman was waiting for us at the station – and I felt really relieved and happy to get home.

In my heart I felt somehow guilty and ungrateful. Surely I should have had an effervescent feeling of happiness? I should have been elated at having seen my future home. And yet I just could not rouse these feelings in my heart. The most pleasant impressions for me had been the shooting trips into the endless silent forests and – as far as home was concerned – the large stables, the riding school, the smell of horses and harness. The people had been pleasant to me but at the same time all so distant and so scrutinising – at least so it had seemed on this first visit.

We were married on Sunday, November 12th, 1906, at the Lyceum Church and travelled at once to Kamenka for our honeymoon. Rather the wrong setting for a honeymoon, with the absence of sun, with the cold and damp, and the grey short hours of daylight. But we had both been abroad with our families that summer, and at Kamenka we could make the most of enjoying the shooting season.

We were married on Sunday, and today it was Tuesday. It was all very new to me – so unfamiliar in its quietness, in the absence of music and of the various interests which had, until now, filled my days in Petersburg. To my relief, the household seemed to run by itself. The house was warm and spacious, there were plenty of interesting books, and we both sat reading – reading and waiting. We were waiting, I was told, for the gamekeepers to come to report at about noon. What they were to report about I did not exactly know, and I dared not ask. So we just waited and read – not very attentively on my part. I was tired of sitting, and had been waiting ever since breakfast. But I had not had the courage to go out for a stroll, as Sasha had decided: "We must stay here and wait." Fortunately, there was a delightful dog, the white Samoyed Belka, who had immediately adopted me, and who now wagged her tail when I smiled at her as she lay curled on the brightly coloured oriental carpet. What a beauty she was, with her large, brown, expressive eyes. And the eyes said now: "Come out for a walk, won't you?" And the tail wagged quicker and the black nose seemed to move, sniffing for fresh air.

"I think Belka would like to go out for a stroll, don't you? Might we not take her out a little?" Sasha looked up from his book. "By all means, take her out in the garden. You'll find your way?" He smiled. "I'll stay here and wait."

Yes, I had forgotten this "wait". But Belka had understood about the walk and was up and alert. I must go; she was too delightfully confident, and I could not let her down. A few minutes later we were out in the garden and at the foot of the hillock in the meadow where no one could see us, and I ran with Belka as I always used to with my own Kars in Waldensee. I came back along the foot of the hillock, and then walked demurely up to the top with Belka still jumping round me asking for more fir cones and sticks to be thrown for her. Dear Belka! How many times she cheered me.

In the warm and cosy red drawing room Sasha was still reading, with piles of books at his side. He looked up as I came in, and smiled. "You liked your walk? None of the men has come yet, and it's nearly noon. We'll have to wait." And he was back in his book. I also picked up a book, and Belka licked herself clean with discreet noises.

A tap at the door. "Come in!" said Sasha, putting aside his book and looking eagerly at the door. Our estate manager Baron Fersen sidled in, pushing his pince-nez into place.

"Sidor has just come, and he reports that some five or six elk – two of them males, he thinks – are in the Kudrovskaya Dacha, district no. 27, I think . . ." said the Baron in hesitating tones.

"Good. Thank you, Baron. Perhaps you would kindly send Sidor here – I want to give him his orders. You'll come with us, won't you?"

"With the greatest pleasure. Thank you. You see, when I last saw elk, three weeks ago, I think . . . or was it a month . . ."

"Did you? Oh, I see. But would you kindly send Sidor? I must give him orders at once, as it is already late." Sasha seemed quite used to dealing with the Baron's slow and never-ending sentences.

"Of course, of course, no time to be lost – with elk in particular. Yes, we'll be ready . . ." and, sidling somewhat more quickly, he disappeared through the doorway.

Sasha turned to me apologetically. "You'll see, he is a good fellow, but not very quick. I sometimes wonder how he will run the place here."

A knock at the door and Sidor came in with his straggly yellow hair brushed well back behind his ears, his moustache drooping. His report was apparently quite satisfactory, although I couldn't quite make it all out. Anyhow, no more waiting. Luncheon was to be served immediately, and we were to start at one o'clock.

Everything worked to perfection. The luncheon was not underdone, my clothes were right and ready, the boots well oiled. Sidor had laid out the cartridge belts in the hall and seen to the guns, and at one o'clock exactly we got into a light sledge, Sasha driving. There was really too little snow for a sledge, but the deep, hard-frozen ruts would have been too much for the wheels and springs of a light dogcart. So we were jerked and shaken and thrown right and left, with the sledge creaking and groaning, and the horse sliding and stumbling, and Sasha using language which sounded pretty bad to me.

The beaters and the gamekeepers were waiting at the spot where the sledges were to be left. All eyes were turned on me, and all mouths gaped open wide, for here was the new mistress, who went shooting with her husband – a thing almost unheard of – and who even used a gun. This was something really new.

In the meantime, instructions were given in muffled voices; the Baron fussed about with the reels of red flags; Sasha adjusted his thick-rimmed shooting glasses – and we set off in single file along the narrow ride. There were to be two stands only, for, being totally inexperienced with elk, I was to remain with Sasha. The Baron drew the first number, and I noticed that Sidor smiled under his moustache. I guessed that the second stand must be the better one, and the Baron did not seem to be a great favourite with the people.

We had not waited very long before the beaters started. Their shouts seemed to advance like a wall, slowly, steadily, straight towards us. I stood a stride or two behind Sasha, not daring to move and feeling certain that I could never hear the elk amidst all the noise made by the beaters.

All of a sudden I saw Sasha stretch out his neck and peer intently into the undergrowth in front of us. A distressing sort of undergrowth, looking light and sparse, but so muzzy and confusing in the variety of grey and green patches that I could not distinguish anything. Suddenly, Sasha levelled his gun and shot. At last I saw large, dark shapes moving swiftly between the young aspen and willow bushes – three, four shapes. They made no noise, they seemed to glide. One of them floundered. I wanted to call out something, but a second shot rang out as Sasha swiftly turned, and another elk – this time I saw him well in the clearing – crashed heavily, head forward.

"What? Two?" I muttered, unable to believe my eyes. "Yes – and a right and left too!" exclaimed Sasha, hugging me round the shoulders. I rarely saw him as happy as he was then.

The beaters came out hurriedly, Sidor trotted up the line towards us, and the Baron sidled up quite fast, calling out: "Did you get him? They passed me in the thicket. Perhaps if I . . ."

"I got two – right and left!" said Sasha. "The big one first, as he passed following closely behind two cows. The younger one must have been hidden by the old one to begin with. I saw him only as he darted forward after the shot, the cows remaining just a couple of yards behind him."

"Ninety-eight strides to the first," announced Sidor, approaching us and counting loudly. "And some 120 strides to the second, I should think," said Sasha as we walked towards the first elk. What a lovely big animal, antlers spread wide apart, some twelve points on the mighty head.

A photograph was taken by the Baron as the elk were brought home and the *Illustrated London News* published it in 1912. Like all my photographs, it was lost in the Russian Revolution, but 25 years later my youngest son secured a back number of the magazine and I was able to look at it again and to visualise so vividly the past, and the impressions of this first elk shoot.

After our honeymoon in Kamenka we spent the Christmas holidays in town as our flat there was ready by then. I cannot really recall any special events connected with that period. Life went on its usual way with friends coming and going, parties and charity bazaars, ballet and dull visits to old dowagers. It was all quite familiar and yet new at the same time, and I still felt extremely shy and lost when people came to call officially or when we had to ask to a meal people we did not really know: people who came from the Kursk province for instance – a world totally unknown to me. But in January I was to see it for the first time when Sasha and his mother were called to Kursk on urgent business, and I went with them to their family estate, Louisino.

6

LOUISINO

The park at Louisino was old and had been laid out on broad lines. Lime trees formed broad avenues, lilac hedges had been planted to hide the view of the village, acacias edged the paths in the park. A row of tall pyramid-poplars grew along the fence beyond which a deep ditch separated the park from the high-road. Stables, a coach house and a small house for visitors were within easy reach of the big old house. A small Roman Catholic chapel was hidden in the park, where Mass used to be cel-ebrated from time to time when Sasha's grandmother, Sophie Wielhorsky, lived there. I think Sasha spent the first two years of his life in the old house, which must have been very cosy with its terrace, columns and queer sash windows which were a very unusual sight in Russia. But his mother wanted to move nearer to the farm so as to keep an eye on the work, and so Sasha's father then built a new house close to the farm build-ings and at the very edge of the estate, near where the church, the priest's house and garden touched the boundary. The big house and all surrounding buildings were deserted and locked, part of the furniture having been removed to the new house. This furniture was big and old, mostly made in the very begin-ning of the nineteenth century by the home carpenters. Large mahogany and birchwood tables and sofas, tall bookshelves and looking-glasses all gave an idea of the size of the rooms they had been made for. The books in the bookshelves were part of the Freemason library of the great grandfather Wielhorsky. This library seems to have been known for its value and for the number of important books on this special subject. There were volumes dating back to 1570 and some were written in Latin, some in old German, French and English. Together with the library, Sasha's father had inherited the collection of insignia or decorations which had belonged to the same Wielhorsky, who had been the Grand Master of the Freemason Order in Russia. All these things had been safely transferred to the new house before the old house and all the buildings surrounding it had burnt down, when Sasha was three years old. A man from the village had set fire to it – out of vengeance, some said, because his cattle had been driven out of our forest; others said he was just a revolutionary peasant. Anyhow, nothing remained but a mass of ruins, large vaulted basements, and the little chapel which stood a short distance away.

These ruins were a solemn sight, but I loved to ride in the park along the avenues of tall trees and through the apple orchards, which were surrounded by a double row of huge lime trees planted very close together and a high wickerwork fence to protect the fruit trees from the steppe winds. And I loved to ride, too, outside the park where the fields stretched smooth, without fences, without ditches, far into the distance. The roads were mere tracks, ploughed over when the peasant was too lazy to lift his plough. The earth was light, black, rich; not a stone to be found anywhere.

The revolutionary wave which had swept over all of European Russia in 1905–1906 had had strong repercussions in that part of the Kursk province. Fourteen farm buildings at Louisino, as well as the stables, had been burnt down by the villagers; the cattle had been scattered among different villages and the horses from the stud, which had acquired quite a name in the region, were sold at sales organised by the socialist estate manager and the village school-mistress (a socialist too) behind the back of the owners. Now that the uprising had been quenched, there remained the accounts to be settled, and they were very muddled accounts – if, indeed, one could apply that name at all to the total disorder that reigned.

It was a very cold January when we made the journey, with masses of snow, and we cuddled deep into our fur coats, our high felt boots reaching far over our knees, and good fur caps and bashlyks over head and shoulders. We were two nights and half a day on the way – half a day being spent in Moscow, which was looking its best in the glorious wintry sunshine, with its innumerable church towers and the white Kremlin walls. The train reached Dmitriev, our small district town, early in the morning and we took a cab to the local hotel. That was a new experience for me! I had travelled a lot abroad and had rather definite ideas about hotels although I had not seen any outside the usual "best" class. My mother-in-law had ordered two rooms and we were taken up straight away. Ours was large and bright with its light wallpapers; there were a table and two chairs, one dim electric light bulb hanging sadly on the wire in the middle of the room and there were no washing arrangements to be seen. When Sasha asked the boy about it he got the pleasant answer: "Here, at the end of the passage, is the washing arrangement for the rooms on this floor." We looked along the passage and saw at the end of it, near the window, a small water-tank fixed to the wall – obviously the water supply – and a china basin on an iron three-legged stand with a bucket nearby. "Is that all?" we asked, and the boy readily explained: "You can go and wash any time – not so many people use the washstand." This was consoling but not exactly encouraging. So for the next five days I had to watch when there was no one in the passage and then rush to the washstand, press up the nail fixed in the bottom of the water-tank, and catch the gentle dribble of water into one cupped hand to wash my face. It was a most unsatisfactory system.

I don't think we ever ate at the hotel, preferring to call on various landowners, some of them living in the little towns as their places had also suffered during the riots. But most of the day was taken up by endless interviews with the former manager, Fashchuk, a most unprepossessing small man with a quick elusive glance and a rapid flow of words. My mother-in-law did not mince her words with him. In fact, he had behaved abominably: when she left her estate in the autumn of 1905 to get back to Petersburg where Sasha was finishing his studies, Fashchuk had been left in charge of the whole place, stud, cattle – a big herd of selected Simenthaler cows numbering 125 as far as I remember, and the gardens and orchards. The school-mistress occupied part of the house and was to keep my mother-in-law informed of all happenings. Some time in late autumn the riots began and Fashchuk, together with the school-mistress, organised a sale of 140 horses and the cattle on the premises and distributed part of the livestock free of charge to the poorer villagers. Soon after the sale someone set fire to the stables, the cowhouses, sheds and barns – fourteen buildings altogether – and finally to the house itself, although some kind hands were found to rescue part of the furniture from the fire. The manager's own dwelling remained unharmed as well as the vine house and other glasshouses and a few smaller outbuildings.

And now my mother-in-law was trying to pin Fashchuk down to give a coherent account of all these happenings. As the revolutionary socialist attempt had failed, soldiers had been sent to keep down any further outbreaks. Fashchuk was at a loss to find any explanations. He threw a lot of the responsibility on the back of the school-mistress, who had in the meantime improved her position by marrying Prince P, a socialist member of the First Duma, and she was therefore – as times ran – pretty well out of reach of any prosecution. A few weeks later I saw her in a restaurant in Kursk – a very good looking woman who carefully avoided recognising Sasha and his mother as we passed the table where she and her husband were sitting. It gave me a strange feeling to see how political conditions could affect and restrict the proper working of the law.

The conversations with Fashchuk dragged on and on, and I don't remember what the results finally were. Anyhow, between then and our next visit to Kursk the Louisino estate was restored to some kind of order, and continued to be run by my mother- in-law and her secretary Savatyevna – a rather unpleasant small and sour-looking person. I am afraid they ran the show not very successfully as there were always complaints on the part of the servants and endless arguments and very bitter admonition from the two ladies. There was a definite feeling of distrust, dislike and antagonism in the place and I did not wonder that Sasha never wanted to run that estate, even though it was the family place and he had been born there. The difficulties seemed to crop up at every step: servants ran away without warning and they were sent away more or less in the same manner; things disappeared in stables and sheds; cows were not milked at the proper time; the butter was not properly washed, nor delivered in time to the station from where it was sent to Kiev. Everywhere there was something going wrong and angry words flew readily through the air. Savatyevna did not raise her voice when angry but I soon noticed that she said things in such a sour biting way that it was worse and hurt people more. A day spent at home was really a painful day for me, and once even Sasha admitted that he could not stick it and offered to go for a long ride until the evening "so as not to hear all these rows!" He had never before commented on the atmosphere so it must really have got him down that day.

How willingly I followed him for a ride. It was the country there that was really our joy: endless spaces to ride over, no proper roads – just tracks, perhaps a wood on the horizon. These were the last woods before the pure steppes, the last shallow valleys with slopes covered in brushwood, an occasional green patch of meadow looking like an oasis in the dry, black earth fields, valleys where the horses stepped slowly as if enjoying the soft green grass under their hooves. We went to our distant oak forest where I saw for the first time in my life new log cabins standing in rows, ready and waiting to be taken away with the onset of winter and the establishment of the sledge roads. These izbas had been sold en bloc to some new settlement in the next province; they looked like toys and smelt so good – fresh wood and no paint. As we rode slowly home I thought how different this landscape was from our northern forests, but – yes – I was beginning to feel that I could learn to love and understand this part of Russia too.

In the August of 1907 we did not go to Louisino but remained in Petersburg where, on Saturday, August 6th, our son Vladimir was born. I had gone out that morning to see the annual Apple and Honey fair, which was held only a few hundred yards away in the large open square near the blue-topped church of Spasso-Preobrazhenie. I had never seen it before, as we never stayed in town in summer, and I knew about the fair only from Old Niania. She always told us that, from that day on, apples could safely be eaten, whereas before that date, ripe or not ripe, apples were better left alone. Even for Niania's sake I had never been able to keep to this rule.

The fair was certainly worth seeing: boxes, baskets, wheelbarrows and carts all full of apples of every possible shape, kind and colour. And barrels and jars of honey of all shades of amber, gold and brown. There were masses of flowers, too, and I was happy to get a big bunch for the house as there were no flower shops open anywhere in Petersburg in August. These turned out to be birthday flowers for Vladimir, for that very evening at 11.20 he greeted this world with a loud and cheerful howl. He weighed 10 Russian pounds which was apparently quite a good weight – but I had never seen a new-born baby and it was a shock to look upon the quaint, ugly little creature. The newly promoted grandparents assured me that he was a normal and fine baby, and so did the nurses and the doctor; but I fear that Sasha and I both had our doubts – which, however, we kept discreetly to ourselves.

After four weeks I took my baby son to Waldensee as my mother wanted me to have a little country air – and we had a most delightful autumn with good weather right into October. All winter was spent in Petersburg in our flat on the Mokhavaya: the niania was most efficient and handled the

baby well. I never dared touch him and was terrified when
I was obliged to watch over him for a few hours when the
niania had to go out. It was so frightening to have to lift him
or change his clothes – everything seemed so loosely knit and
soft. Anyhow, he seemed to grow satisfactorily and, although
a bit pale, he was always in good health.

In spring I took the baby again to Waldensee, where we
spent two delightful months. My father was delighted with
his grandson – and so was my mother. By then Vladimir was
already quite independent in his tastes: he spent the day on a
rug in the garden, surrounded by toys, and generally standing
on his head, hands and feet – and greeting newcomers by looking through the gate of his legs. His two faithful friends were
the St Bernard, Beno, and my faithful old Kars. They lay close
to the rug – but not too close, as Vladimir always tried to play
with them, and they both preferred to lie in peace. There was a
charming photo of Vladimir sitting on the rug with my shooting hat on his head, and Beno – three times his height – sitting
beside and looking down at him.

After August 15th, my father's birthday, we went to Louisino
to show Vladimir to his other grandmother. The train journey,
via Riga, Dvinsk and Briansk, was terribly long and very tiring. Niania and I pinned thin bed covers to the seats of the
First Class carriage – where we were sure to be alone – so that
Vladimir could roll in peace and cleanliness on that seat to his
heart's content. We did have a few scenes with him when he
insisted on walking or crawling on the floor, but on the whole
it was not too bad and we arrived in the morning early at the
station – Dmitriev. I must mention that the journey had been
complicated by the presence of our two gun dogs, the faithful Sport and the slow and good-natured Fingo, as well as my
violin and the four shotguns which we also preferred to carry
ourselves.

The stay in Louisino was very pleasant. The nursery was
a nice sunny room, and the niania was reliable in everything.
Vladimir was starting to speak then, and he started walking

alone in September, I think. An amusing incident happened soon after we arrived at Louisino. On Sunday, after Mass, the priest used to come to my mother-in-law's house for lunch. I had not met him yet and Sasha introduced him. The priest, a funny, haggard little man who was known for drinking too much, looked at me with astonished eyes and, stroking his beard pensively, said: "*This* is the young Countess! And I thought there'd be something to look at! I thought I'd have time to eat a bun before I walked round her!" Sasha burst out laughing, I laughed politely too – not understanding the sense of this apparent joke. Sasha told me later that the priest, like all country people, valued a woman according to her weight, and the fact that one could eat a bun before having had time to walk around a woman was regarded as a high compliment to her. I am glad I could never give this satisfaction to the local people. Many times after that, when I met the priest on the road, he asked me confidentially whether I did not feel a pain in my chest – suspecting me obviously of having tuberculosis as a reason for my being slender. When I assured him that I felt perfectly well he always said, shrugging his shoulders: "I can't understand it then – you have plenty of cream and flour, cakes and bread – why on earth are you so thin?" Once we came across him as we were going out shooting (a bad omen to meet a priest before shooting, but we had to forget it!); he stopped us and, leaning on the mudguard of the high brake said to me: "Now I understand! If you go shooting – and riding as I saw you the other day – well then, you can't expect the cream and cakes to keep you up!" We had a good laugh over this final conclusion and he never bothered me any more.

Sasha and I spent our days shooting and riding – a real joy for me to be away from the ties of household and nursery. I was not so nervous about shooting with Sasha as I had been at first and I was full of interest in the various kinds of game to be found on the Louisino estate.

An interesting sport which I saw now for the first time was the bustard shooting of early autumn, when the birds came to

Edith's father, Friedrich von Martens (1845–1909), Professor of International Law at the University of St Petersburg, is pictured here in civilian dress. When this photograph was taken Edith would have been about 10 years old.

Fyodor Fyodorovich Martens (the Russianised version of Friedrich von Martens' name) is seen here wearing the imperial uniform of the Ministry of Foreign Affairs, together with various medals and accolades from foreign governments.

A corner of the study in the St Petersburg apartment, Panteleimons-kaya 12, where her father first helped Edith learn to read.

The salon in the St Petersburg apartment, furnished in the fashion-able French style, with a grand piano for musical evenings.

Waldensee, in Livonia, bought in the 1890s as a country residence conveniently placed for Professor Martens' travels to The Hague and other west European cities. On the right of the picture, his three young daughters are seated in a donkey-cart.

Coachman Ivan at Waldensee, with carriage and newly planted avenue of trees. 1898.

A formal portrait of the three Martens sisters in 1898. On the right, Edith (aged 12), on the left, Katya (10), and between them Mary (6) refusing to face the photographer.

Another formal portrait in 1903: Mary (11), Katya (15) and Edith (17) with their mother Catherine von Martens.

feed in the stubble. The great bustard looks rather like a goose on unusually long legs, but it has a dignified and sometimes extremely swift walk. They look really magnificent walking on the green autumn-sown wheat or the freshly ploughed black earth. Their plumage looks nearly white in spite of being well shaded with light grey and brown, and the movement of their long necks keeps in time with their demure strides. They bend to peck to right and left in a somewhat nonchalant manner, but they show great alertness, suddenly stretching out their necks at a hint of danger. They are very difficult to approach, the more so as they usually keep to open spaces.

The first time I saw a group of some twelve or fifteen bustards was from a hiding place lying flat on the ground amidst some high stubble. Sasha was also hidden, about 80 yards to my left. Gradually the birds approached, a little towards the left and so heading straight for Sasha. I could visualise him lying in the stubble like myself, his gun ready, his finger on the trigger, and perhaps pushing impatiently into place his dark-rimmed shooting spectacles.

Suddenly there came a distant neighing. One of our horses was getting impatient – if only the groom could keep them quiet. The light four-seater brake had brought us to our positions about an hour ago, after we had sighted the birds from a considerable distance. We had decided to try our luck and had left the road to drive slowly across the stubble several hundred yards from the birds. Then, one at a time we had dropped – or, rather, rolled – off the brake on the side away from the birds. It was a kind of dive one had to take, hugging the gun with one arm and stretching out the other to soften the fall.

First Sasha had rolled out – it had been more complicated for him as he had with him his shotgun and also a Winchester rifle – and then came my turn, and I had plunged head first into the stubble, keeping the muzzle of my gun high so as not to get it full of earth. The order then had been to lie motionless and wait. So far everything had worked well – if only the horses would keep quiet. But no! They neighed again, and the birds stopped abruptly to look round. What bad luck! A few more yards and Sasha could have had a shot, relying on the excellent range of his 12-bore.

I held my breath and waited. And then, suddenly, there was another noise – the high-pitched screeching of wheels in need of greasing. I peeped cautiously over my shoulder, and there on the high-road a long trail of dust was rising and my ear caught the wild strains of the Kamarinskaya, the well-known dancing song of the steppes. Loud and slow at first, it grew faster and faster and louder and louder, shouted lustily – and huskily – by a strong young voice, evidently someone returning from town after a successful visit and a few strong drinks.

"The fool! The idiot!" I thought, scarcely daring to look at our birds. But how lovely they looked now as they stretched their long necks, spread their wings, took a few running steps and rose into the air. Then came the short, dry crack of a rifle. One of the birds swayed, seemed to leap in the air and fell clumsily to the ground. The others were in full flight; it was a lovely sight. I could not look at the white bundle now lying motionless in the stubble.

Sasha got up and hurried towards the bird, calling out, "That idiot would have spoilt the day if I had not had my rifle!"

Spoilt? True, there would have been no bag, but for me it certainly would not have meant a spoilt day; the excitement, the suspense and the sight of the big birds in flight would, I knew, always remain a vivid picture – and even the husky song had its charm.

Besides our gun dogs we also kept a pack of borzoi hounds at Louisino. We had twelve of them; they had been given us by the Grand Duke Nicholas from his famous kennels. They were used for hunting wolves in the autumn, when the presence of wolves began to make itself felt. The wolves became more audacious at this time of year, and rumours would reach us from the villages that calves and foals had disappeared while grazing in the harvested fields or in the wooded valleys.

Pictures and descriptions generally connect wolves with a wintry landscape, with deep snow and vast forests. It is true that the wolf looks his best in winter when his coat is thick and fluffy, when his colours are vivid and well marked, when walking through deep snow makes him carry his head high and forces him to adopt a light gait. However, when hunted in autumn by borzois the wolf also makes a magnificent picture of strength and swiftness.

It is difficult to see a wolf against the brown and yellow colours of autumn, but borzois – unlike other dogs – have very little sense of smell and when they hunt they rely exclusively on their eyesight, which is remarkably sharp. They are so eager in the chase that, with eyes only for their quarry, they are apt to run head foremost into a hedge or a tree or any similar obstacle and are not infrequently injured or killed in that way. This is why hunting with borzois can be done only in flat and obstacle-free country.

I remember in particular one day which turned out to be eventful in the series of hunts of that year. Actually the events were not important, but they marked the day as one of interest and amusement. Firstly, our estate manager lost his golosh; secondly, our best rider was pulled clean off his horse by his own borzois; and, thirdly, we took a big, old wolf which had been the terror of the villages for miles around.

We set out rather late that morning on a dull and damp autumn day. It had been raining hard throughout the night, and we wondered whether it would be worth while hunting at all, as the wolves would probably keep close to the thicket. However, it cleared up a little and by nine o'clock we were on our horses, four riders and two or three borzois each. The borzois, tall and slender with their long silken coats, fawn, black and white, or black and fawn, looked around eagerly with their small ears slightly cocked, their heads raised, their eyes attentive and keen. Large iron rings in their collars allowed for easy movement of the long leash which passed through the rings of two or even three dogs at a time. Single borzois were rarely

used. Both ends of the leash were held by the rider. One end
could be tied to his arm, but the other had to lie loosely in his
hand, for at a given moment he needed to let it go instanta-
neously, or run the risk of being swept off his mount by the
forward dash of his borzois – should they spy the game before
he did.

We set out in good order with two gamekeepers holding
a couple of hounds which were to help us detect the wolves
in the small thickets of brushwood scattered here and there
among the fields. The soil was still wet and sticky. We came
near a small island of brushwood where wolves and foxes
often took cover, and as we were taking our stands round it I
noticed the absence of our estate manager, who was an excellent shot and a good huntsman in general but a very poor rider.
There he was, some way behind us, turning his horse right and
left, backwards and forwards, making his dogs obviously nervous as he pulled their leash in all directions.

"Pavel Ivanovich, what are you doing there? Have you lost
something?" I asked him as I rode up in haste and noticed that
he was bending low over the saddle, apparently searching for
something on the ground. He looked up and reddened, his
short-sighted eyes blinking through his very thick glasses.

"So sorry to delay you, but I have lost one of my
goloshes."

"One of your goloshes? You ride in goloshes?" and I noticed
a shiny rubber golosh on his left riding boot.

"Yes – no – you see, I come off my horse so often without
intending to, and as it has been raining all night I thought it
would be reasonable . . ." and he did not finish his sentence.

"Come along, come along, we can look for it later," I said,
turning away so as to conceal a smile that I could not suppress,
and Pavel Ivanovich followed me back to our stands.

The hounds went through the brushwood copse – no trace
of game apparently – and so we left our stands and talked
quietly together, the men smoking cigarettes while the gamekeepers led the hounds along the stretch of unmown grass

and thistles adjoining the copse. Our friend, a cavalry officer and an excellent rider, had twisted the loose end of his leash round his wrist. I warned him timidly, for he was a good huntsman and I did not feel entitled to give him advice. He laughed good-naturedly: "I'll have time to let go if necessary. See – the hounds are bored, evidently there is no game here."

He bent down over his closely clasped hands, trying to light a cigarette in the strong wind, but a second later he was down flat on his stomach, his borzois wresting themselves free from his hold, just as I, more or less instinctively, had let go the loose end of my leash to release my three borzois.

The gamekeepers were shouting, their hounds were giving tongue now, and in a flash I saw the shape of a large wolf emerge from the far end of a row of high thistles; behind him were my three borzois followed by two of our friend's. This was annoying, for my three worked well together, and I wondered if the others might interfere with them. The wolf was gaining ground and making straight for the forest on the horizon. We followed at full gallop, the distance between us and the wolf seeming to shorten gradually. My three borzois were leading now, and I could already make out their tactics: the two on the flanks were speeding up, bending like tightened bows and straightening out like arrows a second later – a lovely sight, perfect lines. The centre one continued at the same even and steady pace, sure, methodical, undisturbed. There! The borzois on the flank had now caught up with the wolf – they even seemed to overtake him – when, as if on some unseen signal, they suddenly turned sharply towards the wolf and pounced on him simultaneously from right and left. The centre one, dashing forward with sudden fury, leapt up and buried his teeth in the back of the wolf's neck, the other two holding the prey on both sides. The animals toppled over in a bundle, rolled over several times and stopped.

It had been a lovely sight and an exhilarating gallop, but I hated to think of the end of the wolf. Panting and wagging their feathery tails, my three borzois came up to me for praise

– which they well deserved after such magnificent work. The side glance they threw to their two rivals made me think of rather poor sportsmen glad to show off.

The wolf was a big animal – probably the one which had been terrorising the villages – and we were glad to have caught him. I was proud of the excellent work of my hounds but sorry for our friend, the cavalry officer, whose borzois had valiantly done their best but, not having been released in time, had wasted the first precious seconds of the race. Besides, he himself did not see anything to laugh about in his fall, and had so many excuses and explanations to offer that we never dared tease him about it.

As to Pavel Ivanovich, he managed to stay on his horse throughout the day, and only on the way home suddenly fell off when his horse, recognising its stable companions in an adjacent field, made a rather unexpected dash to the left. The lonely golosh came in useful at the end.

If wolves had to be hunted in winter, one could either hunt them in the "classical" way, that is, with beaters and red flags and a line of guns, or in a less elegant but sometimes more effective manner with the aid of a peasant sledge and a suckling pig. In December the wolves used to gather in packs and, real-ising that "l'union fait la force", would begin to attack people on the roads – single peasant sledges or even sledges travelling together when the peasants, well curled up in their sheepskin coats, had fallen asleep with their horses following the lead of the first sledge. They were, in fact, easy targets as I myself found out later when my Caucasian wolfhound, Topka, developed a liking for pulling sleeping peasants off their sledges on to the road where they would wake up very startled at feeling the large black nose of Topka smelling them with uncertain intentions. As a result poor Topka had to be put on the chain, as this joke of his did not quite fit with the rules of safety on the high-road.

In December, then, the wolf question became more press-ing, a solution more urgent. It was at this time of year that we had our best fun with the wolves. If there was a full moon during the Christmas holidays, things could work really well. Several friends would assemble at our house and after a good dinner and lots of black coffee – to keep us awake – we would start out at about ten in the evening, taking one or two peasant sledges, which were low and flat with no seats but filled with lots of fresh straw and covered with a thick rug. Dressed in our warmest fur-lined coats, with thigh-high felt boots and fur caps with ear-flaps, and fur-lined or knitted gloves, we would settle on these sledges, half lying, half sitting. The leading sledge would take on board a suckling piglet kept snugly warm in a woollen blanket. Our guns were ready loaded and each of us had his appointed place on the sledge. We would then drive towards the nearest forests or wooded gulleys where wolves generally had their lairs, and on approaching these one of the sportsmen would begin to pat the piglet or to pinch it gently. True to its kind, excitable and nervous, the piglet shrieked and squealed violently. Attracted by this noise, the wolves began to follow the sledges, at first at a considerable distance but then, as their numbers grew, they came ever closer until their green, luminous eyes could be seen like so many lights flickering in the dark.

It looked uncanny, and even somewhat terrifying if one did not have implicit faith in one's gun. Each of us, knowing exactly which was his sector, waited attentively for the pack to approach. The horse, though always chosen from among the most reliable and steady ones, showed signs of nervousness and began to increase its speed, snorting violently. The sight of the uncanny, green eyes over the grey, shallow surface of the track and – above all – the shrieks of the piglet, all this was enough to put to the test the nerves of any good horse. Of course we usually took one from the working stables, smaller, steadier and less hot-blooded; but our choice was not always lucky and more than one of these "ordinary" horses turned out to be as nervous and as thin-skinned as any thoroughbred.

Thus, with the piglet squeaking, the moon shining and the horse going at a good pace, the sportsmen had only to wait for the opportunity to get a good shot at the wolves as they approached the sledges. Generally there was not much time lost in waiting as the wolves closed in rapidly and became more audacious than one would expect them to be. The first shots would frighten them off for a time, especially if one of the pack had been hit. But the fall of one wolf did not seem to affect the rest of the pack for any length of time, the ranks closed in quickly and the attack began anew with increasing fury and tenacity.

Of course the driver had a difficult task, as it is not easy to keep a horse under control when wolves are about, and also when the moon hid behind clouds there was a problem in keeping to the track. The situation could become serious if the sledge left the track or if it stopped in the mounds of fresh snow through which the horse could not pull it, or – and this was far worse – if the sledge overturned in sliding over an unnoticed hump or snow-covered tree trunk. This thought frequently frightened me, as to scramble out of the snow is no easy task and to keep the snow out of the barrel of the gun is another vital problem. But fortunately such mishaps did not happen often, and the driver was chosen for his safe hands and level head. We had little cause to worry about an unexpected plunge into the snow and could give all our attention to the wolves.

If in the course of the night two or three wolves were shot – to be picked up next morning as it might not be safe to go back and pick them up there and then – the night's outing was considered a success and the suckling piglet, though perhaps a little hoarse after its exertions, was brought back safely to its anxious mother, none the worse for its sporting experiences.

Snowdrifts were always a nuisance, especially when we had decided to hunt wolves in the classical way – that is, with beaters and red flags. These snowdrifts were bad enough in the north of Russia, although there the dense forests and closely planted fir trees broke the force of the wind and offered some shelter to man and beast. In the south, around Louisino, the snow and wind swept over the country unhindered, and even the forests there did not stop the drifts efficiently, as the gaunt branches of leafless trees offered little opposition.

I remember one January when the snowfalls in the Kursk province were particularly heavy. The thermometer went lower and lower, the snow came down in masses day and night, and the snowdrifts never stopped forming. The efforts of the gamekeeper to trace the wolves and to ascertain where they had their favourite hunting grounds remained unsuccessful. All traces of man and beast were immediately covered by a soft and uniform layer of fresh snow, all roads were levelled out with the surrounding fields, and the villages were like islands in a sea of snow. Only the small peasant horses managed to plough their way through, pulling the flat, broad sledges which swayed and dived like flat-bottomed boats.

Afanasiy, the gamekeeper, was in despair, and we had nearly given up all hope of sighting a wolf. Then, one morning, there was the sun shining at last, the sky was blue and it was intensely cold. Afanasiy had left at dawn on his skis to look for the wolves, whose traces would now be easily seen. By noon he was back with the good news that four wolves were for certain in the northern end of the forest, and asked that by two o'clock we, the guns, should be there. He himself was taking the beaters and the red flags immediately to encircle the beat before our arrival.

It took us nearly an hour to get to the indicated place, which was only some three miles away, but the horses could barely make their way through the masses of fresh snow. The sledges dragged on the soft surface and there was no trace of a beaten track anywhere. The sun was brilliant, the shadow of our sledges blue, as if transparent and distant like the blue of the sky. No time was lost in arranging our stands; we were two guns only. I drew the first stand nearer the edge of the forest.

Noiselessly, with skis digging deep into the snow we followed Afanasiy. Cold, clear, not a breath of wind, the frost "hanging" in the air, as the Russian saying goes. No dark fir trees in this forest, not like in our northern ones, and everything dazzling white with a patch of rusty brown here and there – a stubborn dead leaf hanging on to an oak tree. I had reckoned with this whiteness and had put on a white shooting suit with several pullovers underneath, but I felt now that my grey fur-lined coat would have been welcome. However, white would not show up and wolves have sharp eyes.

I was standing against a birch, sparse brushwood all round me, a few large trees, and clusters of yellow reed-like grass still showing above the snow. To my right was Sasha, the other gun – I couldn't see him, but I knew exactly the direction. To my left, in one or two places, glaring bits of red – the line of red flags closing the flank of the beat. Perfect silence reigned everywhere, a silence full of sunshine, of glittering specks and deep blue shadows. I began to feel the cold creeping through my clothes: impossible to hold the gun. My thick knitted gloves felt as thin as gossamer: they stuck to the steel and my fingers ached and stiffened. The beaters were shouting now, and from right and left the noise grew. Now the entire line of the beat advanced slowly; and my hands ached and grew numb.

In desperation I put the gun over my arm and dug both hands deep into the slanting side pockets of my coat, trying to move my fingers there so as to bring life to them somehow. My breath froze into hoar-frost on my eyelashes and eyebrows. I buried my chin into the soft white bashlyk twisted round my throat and twitched my face to prevent my cheeks from freezing. But I dared not move. To stand still is the first rule the huntsman learns, for the quarry has sharper eyes than man and may be watching you from behind some bush long before you suspect its presence.

Suddenly, right in front of me, as if rising out of the snow, appeared a wolf – a large and beautiful animal. He stopped and looked round, listening to the approaching shouts of the beaters, evidently considering which way to turn to evade them. He was not yet in range of my gun and he stood facing me – the worst possible shot if I wanted to risk it. My hands were still in my pockets. I couldn't pull them out while the wolf was there watching. Finally, he made up his mind and stepped with high and light bounds, his proud head well up, his ears moving slightly. He came straight towards me: thirty strides, I counted in my mind, twenty-eight, twenty-six strides now separated us. Evidently he had not seen me. I dared not look at him direct for fear that our eyes would meet and he might recognise the human eye – and the danger. Twenty-five strides – I had to take hold of my gun; he turned his head slightly to the right, and with a rapid movement I pulled my hands out of my pockets, raised the gun and shot at his neck.

It was a heavy gun and nearly knocked me over. I stumbled and when I looked up I saw no trace of the wolf – only the white forest, the blue shadows long and deep, and I heard the excited shouts of the beaters ringing in my ears. Did I miss him? If so, I would have seen him get away – and I was positive he didn't. But where was he?

Petrified, I dared not move a muscle. The beaters were there, a few steps away. Sasha came up rapidly on skis. Afanasiy ran from the flank wiping the sweat off his brow. Where was the wolf? Who shot? Where did it go? "I don't know what happened," was my only answer. "I shot him there – right there, some twenty-three steps away." Suddenly shouts of joy – there he was, lying in the soft snow, on the very spot where I shot him, buried deep from his own weight. It was a happy moment, but I only begged to get back quickly to the sledges, to let me slip into the fur coat waiting there, to let me run on the skis – anything to get warm.

7

KAMENKA

For the next few years, our life followed a regular pattern. Each spring we spent a few weeks with my mother in Waldensee, and every summer we went as usual to Louisino for the best of the shooting season. There were frequent visits to Petersburg, but Kamenka was the centre of our family life, and it was there that we really felt at home.

Sasha was working hard to improve the Kamenka estate. As I already said, his service at the Imperial Chancellery did not amount to much. He directed all his attention to Kamenka, which was suffering from several years of neglect. In 1905, when revolts and riots spread all over Russia, peace continued to reign in the area round Kamenka, and Sasha enjoyed shooting there to his heart's delight. The work, however, was very poorly done – but he was too young to judge. The manager at that time was an Austrian, Paulson, who did not know a word of Russian and who had to have an interpreter when he needed to speak to the peasants or workmen. The interpreter and Paulson himself were both lovers of wine, and spent their summer evenings drinking bottle after bottle under the huge lime tree in front of the house.

The manager at the time of our marriage was Baron Constantin Fersen, but he seemed to make mistake upon mistake – in spite of being quite good at shooting – and so after a few months he left, together with his fat and virtuous wife. After him we got Gustav Woelke, who stayed with us until the war. He did not know anything about forestry but he was a conscientious worker and knew a good deal about agriculture in those parts. Sasha started studying forestry himself, and took advice from our old friend Kravchinsky who was head of the large Forestry School at Lissino. New forestry plans were made in 1908 or 1909, all under the supervision of Kravchinsky, and all irrigation works were started on the basis of these plans. Every year we put so many thousand roubles into irrigation. This was Sasha's favourite work and he spent hours over the plans, and hours trotting about on moors and marshes marking out ditches and seeing after the work.

Many hundreds of acres of the estate were made up of peat bogs. A landowner blessed with the possession of large stretches of peat bog is not, as a rule, very pleased with this blessing. Sasha was interested in their irrigation and drainage. I was attracted to them in a more romantic way. In my childhood, a small peat bog on my father's estate at Waldensee had become my favourite haunt where I fled when my governess became too vehement in her scolding. It was there, in this small, very secluded bit of peaty paradise that I stalked my first moorhens with bow and arrows, and shot my first squirrels with the old Montecristo rifle. But the main attraction of the bog lay in the colours and the silence that reigned there – a silence like that of falling snow, a soft, complete silence and the sensation that it will never end. The dark colour of the soil, the still brown water in the ditches, the pale pink and light green moss, soft and thick, the slender blades of the moor grass with cotton-wool fluffs at the points, and the dwarf pines crouching on humps of peat with strange entangled roots sticking out – all this made a mysterious picture lovely at all moments of the day.

At Kamenka, the many peat bogs figured on the estate maps in their pretty greenish innocence and they added to the overall acreage of the estate, but we often sighed and wondered whether we could ever make use of them.

Sasha started by draining those that lay nearest to the timber-floating canals which we had dug through our estate. (Sasha had also purchased a saw-mill at Tosno, with the idea of floating wood to Tosno and of sawing it there into boards to be sold on the open market.) The main drainage ditches were not less than three yards wide on the top and had at first to be cleaned every year as the soil, saturated with water, gave way after having been frozen to a considerable depth throughout the winter. But the work was well worth while, the satisfaction being more in our minds than in our pockets as we could not hope to reap any material benefits for many years.

However, our hopes were high from the very start, for even after the first year the drained districts showed a great improvement in the growth of the pines – the only trees that ventured so far into the boggy areas. The frail, undersized, round-topped trees gave new shoots of a couple of inches the very first spring, and four or five years later many had turned into well-growing pines with delicate reddish-brown bark and a crown of feathery needles.

It was encouraging too to notice how the birch and spruce began to take root in the newly reclaimed soil in places where they never could have existed before. After a year or two we could ride safely along the ditches and began to make lovely plans for the installation of peat-cutting, paper pulp and turpentine plants – plans which shone brightly when a new railway line was scheduled to pass through our estate, touching three of the largest bogs. But these alluring pictures were short-lived; the revolution put a quick end to them – as to all of the great and fascinating plans we had made for the improvement of the estate.

However, independently from economic considerations, for me the peat bogs had maintained the attraction they had had in my childhood. It was the same charm of the reigning silence but now the spaces were wider, where only the ptarmigan dwelt and where occasionally elk took refuge from the persecution of the "elk-fly", which stayed in the forest and would not come out into the open. But the elk could roam only on the edge of the bogs as the ground was too soft to support them. The sound of one's own steps was deadened by the soft damp moss that gave way under foot and made progress slow and very tiring. Nothing moved, nothing seemed to grow, everything was at a standstill – one had a sensation of timelessness.

I think the charm of the peat bogs is felt, perhaps unconsciously, by the people who spend their lives near them. At least it must have been so in former days, for there are numbers of stories and fairy tales about the bog spirits. The amusing feature is that in these folk tales the all-powerful king of the forests, the "Leshii", never seems to have any power over the bog spirits, and when, for example, he wants to send his enemy to death in the bogs, he has to ask the bog spirits – the "Kuli-baba" and others – to help him. These Kuli-baba are humorous beings and love playing tricks on people to lure them into the bogs. In daytime they make people lose consciousness by spreading strong intoxicating smells from various plants; in the night they lead men astray by making use of little lights, leading their prey towards the "windows", the violently green grassy patches which are the gates to the underground realm of all bog spirits. (These windows were spots where the process of soil formation had not been completed and the surface of the water was covered by a very thin layer of grass. Such openings were very dangerous, being often very deep.) The villagers were very cautious when they spoke about the bog "inhabitants" and they avoided going near the big bogs – except during the cranberry-picking season.

This cranberry-picking season starts towards the end of September and runs into October. For many small villages lost in the large forest areas this is a time of work and of rejoicing too. Entire villages set out and camp on the edge of the great moors; huts made of branches form a real settlement, camp fires flare up and loud chatter and singing break the usual silence of the place. The cranberries grow in a very generous way: where they have taken root they simply cover the ground,

their fine and delicate little plants trail on the soft green and
pink moss and the dark red berries look as if they had been
scattered out of a basket on to a dainty coloured carpet. They
are easy to see, easy to pick, they don't crush and there is no
temptation to eat them as they are still very sour. They become
sweet only after good hard frosts or, better still, after having
lain under a cover of snow for months.

This sudden intrusion of human life on the bogs gave me
much pleasure, although I usually disliked the noise and presence of people in the forests. Perhaps I knew that it would not
last long and this passing picture was cheering with the loud
singing, the calling and laughter of the children. Everyone was
busy, hurrying to make the best of a fine day; everyone carried
baskets or bags full of the bright clean berries. I never could
quite get used to buying berries in sacks – simple potato sacks,
but this was the accepted way of packing and transporting the
cranberries. The sacks were emptied out into large barrels kept
in the cellars and the berries remained fresh until the end of
May and even June, in fact until the wild strawberries were
beginning to ripen.

As I looked at the lively picture I could well imagine that the
fear of the Kuli-baba and other spirits had vanished from the
minds of the pickers, even in the night when they sat round their
camp fires. Surely the Kuli-baba sat then hidden and frightened in their underground realm, listening perhaps through
their "windows" and waiting for the silence to return.

Riding home from the lively scene I too waited for the
silence to return, for this was the greatest charm of the bogs
– a charm I had felt as a child and felt now as a married woman
when I sought peace from worries and cares and those doubts
which arise so easily in the heart of everyone.

During the winter of 1908–1909 Vladimir grew a lot, but he
certainly did not improve in looks! The nose remained that of
a puppy dachshund and the lack of eyebrows was noticeable.
His hair was desperately straight and straggly – but apart from
all that he was a dear, full of life and fun, with an awful lot of

101

will and decision and a very kind heart – giving in easily to kind persuasion and sharing his biscuits with others. But he made sure that his nurse and the maids knew what he wanted and what he did not.

In April we all went again to Kamenka and Vladimir was delighted to trample about in the mud, to dig up the last hillocks of snow, to play with the dogs and to chase the hens. For May 1st, Sasha's birthday, I made him a surprise and dressed Vladimir up in a lovely English sailor suit with long trousers. Vladimir was thrilled and proud of wearing long trousers and his father was very proud too: the boy looked a good three or four years, tall and sure of movement, whereas in fact he was not yet two.

One small worry at that time was that Vladimir's niania was becoming more and more difficult. She hated living in the country, and the language she used in front of our son when in a temper was too much – especially as he was very quick in picking up expressions and started to repeat her words loudly and clearly. When we came to town at the end of May this niania was asked to leave. A new niania came, and we had two days of terrific scenes with Vladimir. However, new impressions in town pacified him; the new niania was mild, kind and did absolutely all he wanted – and spoilt him terribly. From the start he insisted on going off to sleep with her hand slipped into his cot – he grabbed it firmly and she sat for ages not daring to move. If she drew her hand away before he was sound asleep, he called out "Niania, where is your hand?" and she obediently resumed her very uncomfortable position.

But this small upset was soon overshadowed by a great and unexpected blow. On June 1st we left for Waldensee with the intention of spending two months there before going to Louisino. My father arrived in Waldensee on the same day, from Geneva – and was delighted with Vladimir, calling him always "Vladimir le Grand" as he really was tall then. Father was very happy to have us all in Waldensee, happy that my brother Kolya had got a good post as Second Secretary at the Legation in Stockholm, happy to be back in his beloved Waldensee. We played tennis with Father every day and had pleasant rides in the afternoon. It did not last long. On June 9th, Father took the ten o'clock evening train to Petersburg where he wanted to spend three or four days on business. At 10.34 when the train was approaching the station of Walk, Father had a stroke; he was taken out of the train at the station and a doctor was called – but it was too late.

There had been a thunderstorm that evening and as a precaution we had disconnected the telephone in Waldensee. Mother had gone in advance two days before and was spending the night at Peterhof, in the summer villa of Uncle Timashev. They tried to telephone to us from the station, but as the servants had forgotten to re-connect the telephone no message got through to us until our neighbour, Konrad Knieriem, having been informed, arrived at twelve o'clock to break the news.

Konrad Knieriem was a great help – he took Vladimir, the new niania and Elsa the nursery maid to his house, Murmoise, where I knew they would be safe and well looked after. We left for Walk by the two o'clock train. I need not dwell on these days which were so difficult to grasp and understand. Father had always been so much the head of the house, the head of the family and a wonderfully warm-hearted father to me.

That summer was very hot, but despite the heat we decided to go to Louisino, taking Old Niania with us to help with Vladimir. Old Niania was delighted to be in a real Russian country place, with the white church just outside the garden, the long straggling village across the dried-out pond and the old park with its magnificent trees, especially the lime trees which were then alive with buzzing bees. The young niania was delighted with all the lovely fruit we had that year, and ate so many apples that she grew fat and could not get into her clothes any more; they had to be re-arranged for her before we left.

Vladimir's Kursk grandmother loved him but she was very strict and he had to obey her on the spot. Sometimes it worked

– but very often it did not! Vladimir used to walk with his niania (Old Niania could not go so far) through the park gates on to the high-road, because there were some water-filled ruts there which attracted his interest. One day, coming home from shooting, we met him at the gates and when I lifted him into the carriage he immediately started telling me that he had seen our village priest all drunk, lying in the road. I was horrified of course and tried to divert his attention from this unsuitable subject, but he obviously guessed my manoeuvre and cheerfully continued to chatter on this same topic. The story was repeated to his grandmother and to all inmates of the house, and he kept up that story – as a good joke – until we went back to Petersburg.

In August and September the shooting was excellent, with snipe, wild duck and quails in quantity. Sasha and I spent the days out shooting and came back at sunset very tired, very hot and very dirty from the black earth dust.

We all returned to Petersburg at the end of October. My mother had arranged for me a little flat attached to hers, as we had decided to give up our own.

Christmas was sad without Father, but for Vladimir's sake Mother had a tree as usual and we all enjoyed his happy little face as he ran from one toy to another. After Christmas Mother left for abroad with both my sisters, and we took Vladimir to Kamenka. It was a very cold winter and I took great care about Vladimir's walks, not to be out too long at a time. Unfortunately I had now to change Vladimir's niania; she had never handled a new-born baby, and our second child was due to arrive. Very reluctantly I let her go as she was a very clean and very kind woman – nice with the other servants and very soft – perhaps too soft – with Vladimir. When we returned to town I looked for a new niania, found one very highly recommended and took her immediately. She seemed very efficient and handled Vladimir very well, but somehow I did not like her. There were times when she sang and talked very loudly – too boisterous for a woman with grown-up daughters.

One day Miss Cummins came down to me and said she had just discovered a number of empty vodka bottles in the nursery. What a surprise! Apparently Miss Cummins had found on the table in the nursery a silver goblet she did not recognise; she lifted it up to have a look at it and spilt some vodka – much to her dismay. The niania was out that afternoon and Miss Cummins, who had offered to take Vladimir out for his afternoon walk, was waiting for the little maid, Varia, to dress him. Varia knew about the vodka and pulled out from underneath the niania's bed a basket with the whole battery of vodka bottles.

Of course there was no question of keeping this niania or of trusting her with a new-born baby. She was sent away a few days later, and I was lucky to find then an English nanny, Miss Taylor, who proved to be a devoted and very nice person. At the time she could only stay with me temporarily as her father was ill and refused to let her leave Petersburg. Still, I was so glad to have her for the time being and in later years, when her father died, she came and stayed with us for good until we all had to leave in August 1918.

Our second son, Alexander, was born on the 27th March, 1910. When after a few days Vladimir was brought down to see me, he chatted happily but seemed to feel a little shy about his new brother. When I told him to pat him a little, Vladimir punched the baby's tummy and Alec responded with a dissatisfied grunt. "Ah!" exclaimed Vladimir, "he's real – and he grunts like a little pig." This grunt pleased him very much.

There is not much to tell about these first weeks of "two boys" – an idea to which I could not get used so easily. I remember one late afternoon when I was sitting in the armchair near the window when I suddenly saw the familiar triangle of wild geese flying north. How lovely they looked and how they made me long for the country! That spring I missed my favourite shooting – for capercailzie and woodcock. It could not be done with an ever hungry and very often howling baby Alec. I had never missed them since I was married, and longed now for the spring in our northern forests.

Miss Taylor took Alec in hand as soon as the nurse left. He had been born with quite a lot of hair and looked much neater than Vladimir had looked at that stage. But at the age of two weeks he started howling, really howling lustily, and he steadily went in for long daily howls until he was about one year old. It was quite an achievement. All the doctors agreed that he was perfectly in order and in good health, nothing was wrong and we would just have to put up with it. Miss Taylor and Miss Cummins loved him dearly, but he certainly gave them quite a difficult time.

Our arrival in Kamenka was always an event in the village – and even at the Tosno railway station. The only two porters – the dark one and the fair one – were waiting for us on the platform. They grabbed our numerous parcels and, flopping along in their long black coats, hurried us down the broad steps and through the station to the square. There, Ivan was waiting for us with two carriages, the big so-called "red victoria" with red velvet cushions – very heavy, very old-fashioned – and the lighter carriage, plain and modest. Three horses were harnessed to the first, two to the second. It took some time to pack us all in. The trunks went on a separate cart, but even the hand luggage amounted to quite a nice pile and had to be well roped and fixed for the three-hour journey. Then we all settled, well wrapped in coats sent from Kamenka, and Ivan started off with a flourish of his whip and a click of his tongue, throwing his three horses into a mad gallop – all bells ringing under the hooped wooden "duga" and on the collar of the central horse. I disliked this noisy display, but it was hard to stop Ivan: he was so proud of it, so certain that this was the only proper way of driving gentlemen, that I could not hurt his feelings by correcting him. And thus we drove for a good mile through the long-drawn-out village of Tosno, dogs barking, children staring, other carts pulling aside and local policemen saluting.

Once out of Tosno the pace slowed down, for we had a good 32 versts before us. We drove now at a regular trot, first through meadows, then through brushwood, and then through forest closing in upon us on both sides. Vladimir started by looking around, peeping out of all his wraps and shawls, then asked for biscuits and finally went off to sleep. After 16 versts we reached Lissino and stopped at the house of the good old couple Kravchinsky, who met us with open arms, admired Alec as a newcomer, allowed Vladimir to run about and slide on the polished floor of their large sitting room, and fed us with endless hors d'oeuvres, jams and dainties – all home made – while the large copper samovar cheered us with cups of tea.

Mr Kravchinsky, the head of the large forestry school at Lissino, was always keen to hear any new ideas, read new books, catch any whiff of fresh air from outside. After a good hour's rest and a very pleasant chat with him, we had to get back into the carriages and start on the second half of the journey. Generally by five o'clock we reached the "bad" road, the last five versts before Kamenka, when the carriages had to go very slowly, and the horses had to rest between each big effort, pulling the vehicles out of the deep ruts and holes. Sasha and I usually had our riding horses waiting for us here and rode on in advance while the children and the nurses had to be patient and sit in the carriages. I really disliked this part of the journey.

At last we came out of the forest into the open fields, then past the blacksmith's place and down the hill to the wooden bridge. The smith came out and waved his cap to us, his numerous children standing with wide open mouths under the crooked overhanging roof of the smithy leaning on two thick column-like posts. Then Ivan made the tired horses give one final effort, and the carriages thundered across the bridge and raced up the steep hill at full gallop. The farm buildings appeared, children with dirty faces came out to stare, dogs barked, farm workers stopped to look round as they led their horses to the working stables. The huge cowshed loomed against the red evening sky like an Indian temple, with its quaint double roof slightly bent in, giving it the impression of having upturned corners. The carriages swung round the lawn and stopped at the steps of the house, the horses steaming and snorting. The maids and the other servants were waiting on the steps to greet us, glad to welcome us and awaiting our orders.

I was still on my horse as I looked at this picture, so familiar and so amusing, and as usual I felt at a loss being expected to give orders, to decide something, to be efficient. I knew it was my duty, I tried to take it seriously, but inwardly I wanted to laugh and to forget that this "is the thing to be done", or that is "what should be decided". Why always so many prescribed things, even in the smallest details of one's life? Why not have a free laugh when one feels like it? As I caught myself having these thoughts, I realised that the dogs had started a fight, the maids had muddled up the parcels, Vladimir had run off to see his little hut near the lime trees, and even my black mare refused to stand still, impatient to get back to the stables. Yes, no time to laugh – I had to swing myself back into my part, my duty – off the saddle – and try to look efficient and decided.

At that particular time, when Alec made his first appearance at Kamenka, we had some crocuses near the steps and little white anemones under the trees near the lime avenue. It was a lovely spring, and a lovely day when we arrived. The new niania – a temporary replacement for Miss Taylor – was rather horrified at finding herself so terribly far from any town or even village. The long drive in the dark forests had impressed and terrified her. I dreaded the thought of her ill-humour, complaints and eventual departure. Still, when a short time after our arrival we heard songs from the road and a large group of villagers came up to the steps singing, the niania became more gracious and brought Alec out to where Vladimir was already standing with Sasha and myself. We were congratulated about the new baby, a second son being particularly appreciated. The village women had brought a plate or two with fresh eggs, some home-made cheese and cream. They stood in a semi-circle, their faces framed in the coloured kerchiefs tied under the chin, their hands folded over their striped aprons or twisting absentmindedly the ends of the kerchiefs. First they sang, and then they started to dance. They stamped away fiercely on the gravel, singing a wailing tune which had at times weird whirling parts and shrill high notes. Vladimir looked on in wonder, with dignity and seriousness, then waved his hands in thanks as the women stooped and bent low, bidding us good-night. We gave them silver coins and sent out some home-made drinks and white bread for them and the children, while the men – who lingered further on the road – received some vodka.

Yes, it was good to be back. The house was always open, the servants were always there. Sasha and I came to Kamenka on our own quite frequently, but only when the boys were with us did the household feel complete. Summer or winter, this was our real home.

The winter in Kamenka brought me a new experience: the excitement and danger of bear-hunting. Bears were no longer as numerous as they had been in former days, but they were still familiar wild animals, quite well liked – from a distance – and certainly not hated as were the wolves. To shoot a bear was considered the height of a sportsman's luck, and to be invited to a bear shoot was always regarded as a real favour.

The brown bear of Northern Russia and Siberia is exclusively a forest animal, dwelling only in large stretches of forest where villages and fields are scarce, like islands in a sea of trees, and where he can roam about for miles and miles without coming across a human being. This does not mean, though, that the bear always keeps away from human dwellings. There are certain times of year – towards autumn, for instance – when he seems to have a particularly good appetite, preparing the good layer of fat which will keep him warm during the winter sleep. The villagers fear him then, for he will come closer and will attack young cattle or sheep grazing in the forest glades. But I have never heard of bears attacking men, except in self-defence and especially when already wounded. Then, of course, he is a terrible animal, baffling by the rapidity of his movements and the incredible strength of his paws: I have seen a young birch tree, some twenty years old or so, fly into little chips as if under the blows of a sharp axe when a wounded bear stood up on his hind legs and went for it, mistaking it for his human enemy – the man who had wounded him in the head.

It seems strange that an animal whom nature has supplied with such impressive teeth and claws finds particular delight in dainty foods like honey and wild berries of all kinds. More than once we came across holes dug out under old roots showing signs of honey and wild honeycombs – and very evident signs of the bear's paws having done the digging. In other places one could see how a bear had pulled bilberries and whortleberries off the low bushes, broken shoots of wild raspberries, which grow in masses in these northern forests, or bent to the ground young mountain ashes in order to pluck the berries, which bears are apparently very fond of. It is quite wrong, though, to think that bears will not touch the meat of a dead animal, as is often told. On the contrary, he rather likes his meat to be a little "high". Thus when we wanted to make sure that a bear was roaming in certain parts of our forests, the gamekeepers would put the carcass of an old horse in some distant secluded thicket, and if a bear found it he would come back for his meals there regularly. Such delicacies as dead horses were put out for the bears in September and October so as to attract them to certain parts of the forests and to entice them to remain there for their winter sleep. "Border" bears as we called those that we supposed dwelt on the borders adjoining our neighbours' forests had a very good time in autumn as both sides tried to attract them, and the more "high" the meal, the greater was the chance of having the bear stay on that side. The competition between the gamekeepers was great, and each had his own definite ideas as to what the bear liked or disliked. There were gamekeepers specialising in tracking bears, finding their lairs under the snow, organising the shoots, and even sometimes bringing up bear cubs. Such specialists got a higher salary than other gamekeepers and were not easy to find.

For some time I was not allowed to stand alone for a bear shoot. Instead I accompanied Sasha and was allowed to shoot after his first shot, if the bear needed a second one. This had actually happened once and experts had judged then that my bullet had been placed as well as that of Sasha's first shot. Consequently he graciously said I could share with him in the honour of having taken this bear. It thus figured in my list as "half a bear" taken on December 14th near Kamenka. The time came, however, when I was considered a fully fledged bear hunter and was put on my own stand, the second in a line of four. Sidor the gamekeeper stood behind me with a spare gun – for my use, Sasha told me, but I suspect that Sidor had orders to use it himself if necessary.

And so there I was waiting for my opportunity, on a mild March morning with mountains of snow, a light frost, and grey mist drifting slowly through the forest. The beat started – a strange disturbance in the perfectly silent surroundings where I scarcely dared move. I listened to the growing noise of the beaters but all my attention was focused through my eyes. Then suddenly, fifty yards in front of me, the large and bulky figure of a bear appeared, coming towards me in clumsy bounds, heavy and swift at the same time, somewhat rolling in his gait. The head was slightly raised, the little bead-like eyes set closely together looked restlessly from side to side; I could follow their movements.

Sidor pushed my arm, slightly; my gun was ready, finger on the trigger. I only had to wait for the right moment to raise it to my shoulder. Now – the bear was near, he turned slightly sideways – and with a quick movement I raised the gun and pressed the trigger. A bang, I swayed back from the shock, and looked in vain for the bear somewhere to the left.

"He's down! Grand, marvellous!" called out Sidor. His voice struck me as being terribly loud, as loud as the shot, after the silence of the anticipation and the occasional whispers exchanged during the beat.

"Where is he?" I asked, bewildered, still looking in the direction the bear had been going.

"There, straight in front of us," said Sidor, pointing to a black form half hidden by small fir trees. Yes, there he was, my first bear, lying cuddled, his nose dug into the snow, poor beast, I hated to look at him and felt disgusted with myself. Such a beauty, so dark and so large too, and only a few minutes before he had been turning his little eyes so swiftly right and left. Why had I shot him?

"Well done, congratulations, a beauty . . . and one straight shot too!" The voices were all around me and my husband put his hand on my shoulder in appreciation. Sidor went back up the track, pointing out where the bear had come from and where he had turned showing me his flank. My gun suddenly felt so heavy on my arm and I leaned against a tree.

"Come and see your excellent hit," said Sasha. Sidor bent down and raised the bear's head, holding it by the ears. And then, all of a sudden, the little eyes turned again right and left: it must have been an illusion, I must have been dreaming!

"Let go, Sidor!" called Sasha sharply, pulling a Browning out of his pocket. A short dry pistol shot in the ear put a definite end to my first bear. I was horrified to have seen those small eyes again; this last semi-conscious movement of the eyes had marred the pleasure I felt at having made a fine, clean shot.

The next day we, the bear and I, were photographed together in front of the house. Strangely enough this photograph was later picked out by the correspondent of the *Illustrated London News* who had come to Russia in search of typical pictures of the country. In a special number devoted to Russia, three or four photographs of winter shooting taken on our Kamenka estate were published, and among them mine with my first bear. As I look now at this photograph, one of the few that I still have from home, I see in the sad expression with which I look down at the bear a reflection of the feelings that haunted me at the time – feelings of regret, doubt and nearly shame; but I do remember that I was quite proud too.

A few years later, when Vladimir was about nine, he had his first – and only – chance to shoot at a bear. I had taken him for a stroll in the forest in search of squirrels that he could shoot with his .22 Winchester rifle. My pointer Sport was with us. It was in early August, I think, and I was carrying my own gun in the hope of shooting some blackcock. When we came to a ride between the old forest and a young thicket of firs, birches and aspen, I sent Sport into the thicket. He disappeared into the undergrowth but soon dashed back whining, trembling and seeking refuge at my feet. As I tried to soothe him, Vladimir suddenly called out to me: "Look, Mother! What strange big paw marks on the clay!" Sure enough, on the damp clay of the ditch running along the ride were the clearly marked footprints of a bear. It was not a very big one, as my hand would have more or less covered a footprint. A few stray mountain ash berries lay scattered on the ground, and the lower branches of the young tree hung limp and half broken.

"It's a bear – he must be in this small bit of thicket," I said. "We will try to stop him getting back to the forest. You stand here and keep your rifle ready. Stand still and don't move on any account. Shoot only if the bear passes over there, showing you his side. Don't shoot if he is facing you: don't shoot, and don't move – just look at him and enjoy it."

The boy was rather overawed and nodded silently. I put him behind a very large tree trunk and set off at a trot on the soft meadow grass round the thicket. I ran as fast as I could, but the thicket stretched out quite a bit and when I reached the other end of it I was just in time to see the black form of a bear leap across the ditch on the edge of the big forest. It was a disappointment, but I must say that I was quite glad that the bear went away without a shot. While I was running round the thicket the thought had crossed my mind that it might not have been exactly wise to leave the boy – so young – all alone to face the possibility of quite serious danger.

I went back to Vladimir. He, too, had caught a glimpse of the bear at a distance. He was delighted at the adventure and certainly the thought of danger had not crossed his mind.

Living in the country, it was soon necessary that the boys should learn to ride. They started with a donkey, and then one day there was a new arrival, a Shetland pony who by some mis-understanding arrived in Kamenka without our knowing her name. Vladimir at once decided to call her "Mousy" because she trotted so fast, taking tiny steps and never stumbling.

There were very few varieties of ponies in Russia, and any-one wanting a pony for a small child generally had to import one from England. The harsh climate and the poor roads in our northern districts accounted for the very limited number of childre riding. There was no social side to this sport among children, for they rode alone or with some member of the fam-ily or a tutor. Altogether it was a sport limited more or less to one class only – that of the landowners' children, and few chances were open for others as riding stables were very scarce even in the large cities.

Children generally started riding bare-back in the park or on the estate. One of the favourite amusements was to help the village boys in rounding up the young horses in the meadows and rough pastures and bringing them back to the farms for watering. This exercise gave the children assurance and endur-ance, if not a classical seat. Proper tuition was given as a rule once the child felt at home on a horse.

The nearest approach to an indigenous child's pony was the Finnish cob, a very sturdy and quick little animal rather like a Welsh pony but faster and with more temperament. I planned to get one of these for Vladimir later on. In the meantime, we could not have found a nicer pony than Mousy! She was easy to catch in the paddock, she was always keen and quick, always good natured and ready to follow her old motherly friend, the donkey Maria Ivanovna – or Marivanna for short. This was a bit of a long name even when shortened, but Ivan the coachman had given it her out of sheer respect. The fact was that he had never seen a donkey before, as they are very rare in northern countries, and he had rather feared that this quaint animal with the long ears and the distressingly sad voice might be dangerous for the children and difficult to handle. When, to his surprise, he discovered that she was the most docile and gentle animal, he gave her all his attention and respect. He respected her mainly because of her grey hair, he said, and also for never being impatient; and so the worthy name of Marivanna was given to her.

Mousy and Marivanna became an inseparable pair. Wherever the donkey went, the pony followed, bridle or no bridle, and I would often see Vladimir aged six and Alec aged four riding together in the garden and in the meadows near the house. Marivanna, always duly saddled and bridled, carried Alec, while Mousy trotted alongside with nothing more on her back than the leg-dangling Vladimir. Of course Mousy trotted so much faster and invariably left the donkey behind, but before long she would insist on turning back and coming into line with her "aunt" as the boys called Marivanna. A great problem arose when Vladimir succeeded in making Mousy jump a ditch, whereas the aunt decidedly refused to take such risks – however hard Alec tried to urge her with his heels. Marivanna knew better. She stopped on the edge, quite unconcerned, hooves well dug into the turf, and seemed to beckon to Mousy to come back. Mousy turned round and jumped the ditch back again – much to Vladimir's delight.

Mousy was really Alec's pony as she had been a gift from his godfather. Although he was too small to ride her yet, he was very conscious of his rights and duties, and insisted on grooming her himself. But when it came to polishing her hooves – then old Ivan was adamant and would not allow it: it was much too messy a job, he said. Mousy, together with Ivan, always figured in Alec's bedtime prayers, particularly in winter when

115

Ivan coughed and Mousy limped sometimes on her rheumatic hind leg.

The boys' greatest delight was to finish their afternoon ride by fetching some biscuits for themselves and their mounts from the grown-ups' tea table. They rode up the steps, through the hall and into the dining room and round the table two or three times until both boys, the pony and the donkey had received the cakes and biscuits they liked. I think it was Marivanna who led the way, as Mousy was a little shy about entering the house up the steps; but once the aunt did it, then Mousy followed. Only the dogs seemed somewhat displeased with this visit – they regarded it as an intrusion for, after all, it was their right to be in the house and large animals were not admitted as a rule!

But I must not dwell on Mousy alone and forget the good and swift Ryzka, the cob that Vladimir rode when Alec was able to use Mousy. Ryzka was a light brown thirteen-hand Finnish working mare, strong, hardy, sure-footed and good-natured. Vladimir was really glad when he got Ryzka and was allowed to ride alone – as long as his governess knew where he was going. This daily exercise suited them both, and Ryzka soon began to be keen on taking ditches and small obstacles, so that when I rode with Vladimir she eagerly followed my big mare Shalunia and never gave any trouble. The one thing we always had to be careful about were the bridges: there were many ditches in the forests and there were so many bridges that it had been impossible for us to put them all straight, after years of lack of attention. So whenever we saw a bridge we carefully avoided using it as there was every chance of its being rotten and then, of course, the horses could fall through and break their legs. Even the main bridge across the little river was not to be trusted, and we used the ford instead. But in spring this ford was very deep and once or twice I had to put my feet up on to the neck of my tall Shalunia as she waded across – not a very elegant way to ride, but better than getting my boots in the water and riding with wet feet all day long.

By now it was 1912. Was this the last "normal" year of my life at home? Yes and no. Certainly things seemed to run the way they were expected to run and there was no sign of any changes on the horizon. I had the household and my two sons to look after. Sasha was very busy with his local self-government (Zemstvo) duties for the districts of Petersburg and Kursk and with his interests in managing Kamenka. I tried to share all these interests although he did not take me to the Zemstvo meetings and I took it for granted that this was a man's job and that there was nothing for me to do there. When at home he was as keen as ever on shooting and on running Kamenka. In Petersburg he was keener than before on the activities of his Lyceum Club (a club of former pupils of the Lyceum); here, too, I could not mix in and left it entirely to him. In the spring of 1912 we were both keen members of the Tauride tennis club and played there every day, so far as the weather allowed it.

Now that Kamenka had been put on a more or less reasonable track, Sasha turned his attention to the social work and took part not only in the Zemstvo work at Louisino, which he had been doing since leaving the Lyceum at the age of 21, but also in the Tsarskoe Selo Zemstvo. Thus, at the outbreak of the war he was in the Zemstvo of the Dmitriev district and the Zemstvo of the Kursk government, and also in those of the Tsarskoe Selo district, the St Petersburg government, the Novgorod district and the Novgorod government. In all these he had various special duties – on the roads committees, revision commissions, and any amount of others. He was also honorary Justice of the Peace and assistant to the Maréchal de la Noblesse of the Tsarskoe Selo district.

Sasha spent a lot of time going about from one Zemstvo meeting to another and scarcely ever spent more than a few weeks in the same place. He liked this work and was apparently much appreciated by the peasants who were members of the Zemstvo. They always supported him and in Kursk Sasha was regarded as a real "liberal" – if not a freemason!

We lived in town and in Kamenka alternately, while the children stayed in Kamenka. I was so used to Sasha's frequent absences that I never dreamed of being suspicious – I felt it would have been beneath my dignity to suspect him. Perhaps I was right in adopting this attitude – better to have that point of view than to develop a jealous nature. But the fact remained that I was often left alone.

By June 1st we sent the boys down to my mother's place, Waldensee, where I knew they would be happy and well looked after, and as Sasha wanted to go to his mother about the middle of June I decided to stay on in town with him until then. Perhaps these were the last quite happy years of my life: no worries and no suspicions to trouble my inner life, and though I did suffer from his total absence of interest and his absolute lack of any desire to share things with me, I put it all down to "fate" and to my having useless ideals of common interests or inner understanding. Life was smooth – why long for understanding and feelings in common? Probably all these aspirations were just a fantasy derived from too much reading – although I read the smallest number of novels I could, always feeling that they portrayed a life which was not for me – a life of sentimentality so acute and so beautiful at times. I was trying to do my duty, I was sure he was doing his too – so why worry? I was so young and so dreadfully naive and never could have suspected my nearest. Now, after fifty years, time has passed and brushed away these wounds and sores, and left me with no regrets except that I could have been much more understanding and helpful to Sasha who was so young too. But time was not on our side. In September 1913 came the birth of our third son Nicolas – an event which kept me busy in and around the nursery. Then, before we knew really what was happening, our lives were marching on into 1914 and the start of the Great War.

8

WARTIME

The arrival of the new baby, Nicolas, on September 12th was a welcome event in an otherwise sad year, for my mother had been taken ill during the winter and had died of pleurisy in March 1913. This was an unexpected blow for us all, especially for my two sisters Katya and Mary. Mary was very dependent on her mother, even though she had been away for a few months at a boarding school in England, an experience which she had loved. Katya now felt she must fill her mother's place and "take Mary in hand" – a dutiful decision but one which did not bring happiness to either of them. After a while Katya left home to study art in Munich, while Mary stayed on alone and unhappy in the Petersburg flat. We all tried to help her but it was not easy, and it was Old Niania who faithfully kept her company when the rest of us were unable to do so.

When the war broke out we were in Odessa for a holiday with Vladimir, Alec and little Nic who was now nearly one year old. Sasha had to leave at once to join the 1st Line Detachment of the Red Cross, in which he had already been appointed adjutant to the Commandant. My task was to go back home to Kamenka to await further news, and meanwhile to take charge of the estate in Sasha's absence.

It was a heavy burden to fall on my shoulders. There was so much to be seen to in running the Kamenka estate. Even the smallest details of management required so much time

– and so much patience. All the time I was aware of my lack of experience, especially in business matters. I remember, for example, the nightmare of my first business deal after Sasha had gone, and the effort it cost me to keep calm and strike a sound bargain.

"Another cup of tea? You will certainly like one in this damp weather," I hear myself saying for the tenth time to a fat, bearded timber merchant sitting in an armchair facing me as I sit at Sasha's desk.

I ring the bell as he answers, patting his glossy auburn beard: "Thank you, thank you, it would be wrong to refuse. Tea is a good thing for the body and for the soul." It is the third time I have had the teapot refilled and fresh tea brought in.

The merchant came at one o'clock, as we were finishing luncheon; it was about three now and he had been steadily drinking tea, munching biscuits – aloud – and talking about the weather, old-time customs in forestry, present-day difficulties with workmen, etc. My head was beginning to ache – he smoked appalling cigarettes and would not take those I offered him: they were too weak, he said. I had to keep up the conversation, for the real reason for his visit had not been approached yet and I had strict instructions from Sasha regarding the etiquette of such negotiations. The fact of the matter was that this fellow, a simple peasant who had made millions in the timber trade and who now owned large forests in our neighbourhood, bought timber for fuel from us every year but bargained in the most stubborn way when it came to fixing the prices. As a rule the business between him and Sasha would be concluded after a conference of several hours and I was prepared, therefore, to sit through the afternoon listening to his senseless talk, as I must definitely not be the first to approach the topic of the deal.

There he was now, the red-faced, glossy-bearded man, with cunning small eyes and rough short-fingered hands folded over a very bulging figure. "Another cup of tea does one good," he repeats, smacking his lips as if the drink were a Sunday treat.

"Don't you like tea? My wife has the samovar going all day long and she likes to drink a cup of tea at any time of the day." As I mumble something by way of an answer, he goes on as if strengthened by the new hot potion: "Yes, you are out a great deal, you are always in the forests, so the men tell me, you have no time for drinking tea as we like to do it . . ." Another smack of the fat red lips, another broad pat of the reddish beard. "A nice place you have here, and the number of books . . . do you read them all?"

"Yes, no, not quite . . . I am pretty busy now, and the timber season is just starting . . . You probably read a lot and . . ." I stop abruptly, sensing the ridiculous nature of my question and seeing the man's rather perplexed face.

"Yes, my son, the eldest, reads a lot, you know, but we old folks do not think much of reading – I mean my wife and I," he says.

"Indeed, it tires the eyes and . . ." I feel I am getting out of my depth and cannot keep up the conversation. A cold terror seizes me. Am I already out of the game? Will I be able to stick to my task? I must pick up my thoughts and keep my wits together; and in sheer desperation I light a cigarette.

The man looks at the ceiling with a sigh – I half feel a sneer in it, as he has probably noticed my nervous state and is rejoicing inwardly at having got me so far. The beast, I think. These cunning eyes, this cunning of the peasant who suddenly feels stronger than the master. I won't let him triumph. It's a question of sporting spirit and family honour. Braced by these reflections which run through my brain, I suddenly feel cool and rested.

"Another cup of tea? Will you have one? It is good in this damp weather," a smile, an inviting voice – as sweet as a "real lady" on a provincial stage – and inwardly a laugh at myself in this role.

We go on in this way until past four. We are saying our goodbyes, I am on the verge of ringing the bell for his horse to be brought to the door, when – as if casually – the man throws in: "By the way, how about your fuel wood? Will you have any for sale this year?"

At last he's come to the point. I stood the test of patience and must now stand the test of tenacity. For two more hours we talk, or rather he talks – all business, prices, questions of market, floating the timber, etcetera. I am a block, numb to all his most persuasive considerations, dull and stubborn, reciting over and over again all the prices for all the categories, following Sasha's instructions, written down in advance in my notebook. "My husband wants me to sell the wood at these prices," I repeat and am deaf to all his suggestions.

Exhausted, nervous, I bid him goodbye at six o'clock. What the man felt like, I did not care. I knew that I had won, but I was too tired to rejoice over my steadiness and rushed upstairs to the boys to forget these stupidly wasted hours of petty bargaining in their noisy presence.

The war continued. The news from the Front, reaching us as it did in the unchanged surroundings of Kamenka, seemed remote and almost unreal. But as the months went by, more and more of our foresters, gamekeepers and farm workers were recruited into the Army. The men from the neighbouring villages were taken also, and so it became increasingly difficult to find new workers to take their place. Fortunately there were a few old and trusted servants who for one reason or another did not go off to the war, and they helped me greatly with their knowledge of the work to be done as well as with their devotion and patience.

It was during the war years that I learned fully to appreciate Izmail, the Tartar who had been Sasha's childhood friend on the family estate and later his faithful servant. Small, wiry, with dark eyes, high cheek bones and a fine set mouth, Izmail was very different from our northern peasants. His position as foreman of the estate farm at Kamenka was not easy, for as a Tartar and non-Christian he was not easily accepted as a head to be obeyed. But somehow he succeeded in making himself generally respected – if not exactly loved. I think his quick temper

blazing up into regular rages frightened our more placid north-
erners and they kept out of his way for the sake of peace.

"Izmail must do this, Izmail will know how to fix that . . ."
was the first thing to say when something went wrong, in the
house or on the farm. And this, too, was what I thought when
I had some new ideas about improvements to be made. In our
isolated position we really needed a man who had imagination
and could see to things without having to ride the 30 versts to
the nearest town. And in fact, Izmail was very inventive and
was never more happy than when he had some unusual task
put before him. To fix some new equipment in the mill, to
build a greenhouse, to grow some unusual vegetables, to lay on
water in the cowsheds or put a new bathroom in the house: for
all these and many other tasks Izmail always found time, was
always eager, keen and resourceful.

He had the reputation also of being fearless. It was only his
weak chest that had prevented him from joining the Army. He
was the only person on the farm who could tackle the fierce
bull we had at the time, or who could coax my really dangerous
Caucasian wolfhound, Topka, back into his kennel when he
got loose by accident and the whole village ran for shelter on
hearing that Topka was at liberty.

My eldest two boys had the greatest respect for Izmail, and
a little awe too, I think, for he never spoke much nor played
with them but quietly answered their questions, put in a little joke and never allowed them to interfere on the farm or
with the agricultural machines which are always an attraction
to boys. But I knew he had an eye on them and that I could
rely upon him in case of emergency. A little incident confirm-
ing these feelings remains well engraved in my memory. One
autumn evening, returning home after an absence of two days
in Petersburg, I found Izmail waiting for me at the gate – an
unusual place for him to be. I stopped the carriage and asked
him anxiously what had happened, for there had been rumours
of robbers roaming about the country and I had only left home
very reluctantly on urgent business.

"Everything is all right, my Lady – only I wanted to warn you about Master Vladimir. He is all right, but there might be some difficulties about him and I just wanted to say that he is all right, and a nice straight boy too." This puzzled me but I did not put any more questions and thanked Izmail, feeling quite certain that there was some problem where I'd have to be careful in judging the boy – a bit of a handful at the time. How thankful I was for this timely warning when approaching Vladimir on the following day; had I only listened to the accounts of his governess and nurse, I certainly would have adopted the wrong attitude, but with Izmail's words ringing in my ears I soon came to an understanding with the boy. Apparently, exasperated by these governesses during my absence, Vladimir had run away early in the morning having decided to join his father at the Front, but hungry and cold by the end of the day he had returned at sunset and staged a swoon, partly to cover his failure and partly to give his governesses a good fright as they "bored him stiff", which I well believed in spite of all their excellent qualities. The boy had simply outgrown them and wanted a man's hand to guide him. And Izmail had understood this, so that the boy – reviving from his extremely well-staged swoon – would speak only to Izmail and to no one else.

With an inquisitive brain and very deft hands, Izmail had learnt to repair watches and soon became the watchmaker of the district. In early spring he was always over-burdened with work and sat up late into the night repairing the watches and clocks for all the peasants who helped float the timber down the swollen streams from their villages scores of miles away. The watches had to be repaired quickly before the peasants returned home upstream a few weeks later.

Izmail was also our miller and mechanic for all agricultural machines. When a strategic railway line was being built through our estate in 1915, Izmail and I sat for hours over catalogues and books learning the workings of a sawmill, because I found out that sawing boards on the spot would be most advantageous. A few weeks later our old steam engine puffed cheer-fully away at the end of the park, running now not only the mill but also a brand new sawing mill.

There was one great problem in Izmail's life: he was a Tartar and a Mohammedan and no Russian priest could marry him to the Russian girl who had joined him from the estate where he had lived as a boy. When his first son was born, Izmail asked me to be his godmother, to which I willingly agreed – much to the indignation of the villagers and servants but to the great satisfaction of the kind red-bearded priest.

When with the revolution we were deprived of our estates, houses and capital and I was trying in vain to get out of the country, Izmail frequently came up to Petersburg in spite of the long journey and brought me what he could spare: a little rye flour, some potatoes, dry mushrooms or vegetables. Being the miller and the only expert with agricultural machines, he had been left in peace in the cottage on the estate and could carry on his work. It was to him that I went, on foot, when I felt like seeing the old home which, though "nationalised", had not yet been definitely taken from me. But I could not have stayed there alone, and so Izmail and Katya did their best to make me comfortable in their cottage and they were not afraid of the local Communists who might object to my coming.

During the war years I came to know the people of our vil-lages, to understand something of their lives, and not to take them so much for granted as we unthinkingly did in former years. When out in the snow with my skis on my feet, my gun hanging from my shoulder, barrels downwards to avoid snow entering them when passing under trees, I would look across to the village, which could scarcely be seen in the deep snow. The peasants' houses formed a patchwork of squares, each with a column of smoke rising slowly into the frosty sky. And I knew that under each one of these the life of a family was centred. In one hut, Piotr carried out his little business enter-prise selling matches, salt, petrol and flour; while next door old Katya worked at her sewing, and Stepan was surely curled round on the stove fast asleep, with the good excuse that the snow was too deep for any lumber work. And across the road one of the three old women, who were each and all known as "the one-eyed baba", sat at home to keep the fire going whilst the other two sawed firewood at the back of their woodshed. They had one son between them and they shared him in the same way that they shared the one good eye between them – or so it seemed to me. I found myself wondering if all these people felt at peace with the world, in the midst of the dead white silence. Even the local mongrels were silent now, curled somewhere in hayloft or cowshed trying to keep warm.

Yes, life in our northern parts was hard for the villagers, especially in winter. During the war, with so many men taken for the Army, more work had to be done by the women and children. In the country, the children attended school for three or four years at the most and by the age of twelve or thirteen they began regular work as apprentices or helping their parents at home.

The first problem of course was to keep warm – and as the big masonry stoves required a lot of wood and were not so easy to light, it was for the children to help in preparing the small kindling wood. They went with their little sledges into the forests and collected bundles of wood, stacked these in the yard and broke the branches and twigs into small bits before taking them inside the house. They had to pull the bark off the birch logs to prepare the best kindling material one could have; they chopped short logs into chips and gave a helping hand in sawing up the larger logs.

There was, too, the question of getting water. The wells and rivers being frozen, the ice had first to be broken with an axe and the water carried to houses and stables in buckets, along a path soon covered with a coating of slippery ice. On Saturday, the day when all the family had their bath, the amount of water needed was prodigious even though the baths were taken communally – first the men and boys, then the women and girls. And the need for wood was prodigious too, when the

huge stove of the bath-house had to be made red-hot in order
to make the room really hot as well as the bath water. It took
a good day's work to prepare for the Saturday bath, but the
results were extremely worthwhile and the clean and scrubbed
family emerged out of the bath-house as red as lobsters and
hungry for their supper. You could not fail to know it was
Saturday when you saw the steaming, smoking bathhouses
standing in a row near the river, brook or pond of any village
in northern and central Russia.

In the north the forestry work was mostly done in winter,
when men and boys felled the trees, cut them into logs, sleepers or firewood and loaded them on to sledges. Very often the
mothers and sisters worked there too carrying the branches
into stacks, sorting them out, and watching over the bonfires.
The family would leave the village at first light and spend the
whole day in the forest in the cold and snow. The big fire kindled at once on arrival would keep the kettle boiling, cook
the meal and warm the family and the horse too. It was often
so cold that the men's beards and fur caps, and the women's
hair peering out from under the heavy woollen shawls, were
all white and stiff with hoarfrost, and the small shaggy horses
looked like hedgehogs with their long hair frozen into spikes.
Men, women, boys and girls all wore the same yellow sheepskin coats tightly fitting at the top and gathered into wide
sort of skirts at the waist with a sashlike belt of bright colour
twisted round it. The clumsy felt boots reaching to the knees
were very warm and comfortable but being rather wide at the
top they were usually filled round the edge with hay to prevent
the snow from entering. When dressed like this the children
looked like little bears, clumsy and heavy as they rolled about
and gaily shaking off the snow from their sheepskins which
never needed any brushing.

In these same northern parts of Russia the winter's work
ended for men and boys with the great floating season of the
spring. The timber massed by them on the edges of streams and
canals was now rolled down the banks into the water – with

much noise and great splashing – for with the melting snow every stream became a powerful river with surging grey and muddy water. All along the twisting current the big logs had to be kept clear of the banks, where they would stick fast between trees, roots and boulders, half-flooded, half-submerged. Using long poles with a strong iron hook at the end, the men and boys pushed these logs into the middle of the stream and kept a close watch in case one log stuck across should prevent the others from moving on. When this happened, in no time at all great walls of wood rose in the river and with terrific noise log after log climbed on the back of the other, ice blocks mingling with them, and before long the water – unable to flow on freely – flooded the surrounding country. It was a most dangerous task then to break up such a barrage and only skilled and experienced men undertook it. Some of the men accompanied the timber right down to the final barrage where the wild floating came to an end and where the timber was fished out and loaded on to large flat-bottomed barges. These were then taken in tow, three or four together, by a tug boat and brought into port for further shipping abroad or for loading on to railway trucks. It was a busy season for the villagers, with no time to be lost, as all the work had to be finished before the water level fell and the great rivers became once again gurgling brooks or still, shallow canals. But it was also a happy time when people of different villages met, and when a cup of tea with friends was most welcome after the day's wet work.

The summer months brought different work and different problems. A rainy June could be a great nuisance, for haymaking was a matter of importance. The peasants walked about with morbid faces, the landowners became ill-humoured, and the estate managers became the most bad-tempered of all as they cursed the workmen for being seemingly too slow whenever the sun put in a half-hearted appearance.

Such wet June days would have been utterly dismal if the evenings had not compensated for all the nervousness of the day. These evenings are connected in my memory – apart from the desperate fights against mosquitoes – with the exhilarating smell of wet earth and strong uncut grass, with the scent of orchid-like forest flowers, of lilies of the valley, of hawthorn along the hedges. And the smell of clover rose sweet and strong, penetrating the soft white mists through which I rode back home at nine or ten o'clock at night, lost in dreams, listening to the song of the crickets and the persistent call of the landrail coming from those far-stretching clover fields.

In the distance I heard a measured, rhythmic throbbing, a dull knocking, and the wailing monotonous sound of an accordion. These sounds, and the smell of burning fresh green branches, became stronger as I approached the bridge. The smoke bit my eyes, and black figures moved aside in front of my horse as it stepped on to the wooden bridge. The throbbing sound stopped short and the accordion alone continued some vague tune. With all the mud around, the boards of the bridge provided the only clean place where the young people of the village could dance at night, forgetting for a while the sodden fields and wet hay. To keep mosquitoes away they made great fires all round the bridge and danced, ghost-like, in the thick smoke. My horse took fright and broke into a gallop, through the mud and up the drive to the left, while the wailing music and the throbbing of the dance started anew behind me in their uniform, slow rhythm.

Sometimes the weather would go to the opposite extreme and we would be faced with a very hot summer without any rain. In spite of the boggy and marshy soil the danger of forest fires was always great in these conditions because of the dry grass, the heather and the dry ferns. Even the moss dried rapidly and was a good conductor of fire. A match carelessly thrown before being extinguished, a camp fire not carefully put out, these were sufficient to start a fire that could cause great havoc. As the land was flat and the forests stretched over thousands of acres with scarcely any breaks – here and there a brook, now and then an open glade – it was very difficult to locate a fire once the smoke had spread over the district.

There was a very hot summer in 1917, and forest fires started breaking out all the time. Was it carelessness by youths doing the work of men gone to the Front? Was it deliberate intent on the part of the revolutionary-minded? We did not know. But it was clear that the older men and I must be constantly on the watch, keeping track of the fires as best we could and deciding what measures could most effectively be taken. These old and trusted gamekeepers reported to my house each lunch-time; they came, coughing and with blackened faces and bloodshot eyes from the biting smoke. And each had the same story to report and the same request – that I should come myself to see, and to decide. And I would promise to go with Ivan Pavlovich the next morning early, and with Ivan Ivanovich the same day after lunch, and with Piotr the following day. And so it went on day after day. I rode out early in the morning on my faithful black mare Shalunia, so safe and sure-footed, alert and attentive and not easily approached by a stranger. After a quick lunch it was Zmeika's turn to be saddled; she was light and quick but more difficult to handle, was frightened of the dense smoke and was less sure of her steps on boggy ground. I was out often until sunset, tying Zmeika up in some sheltered and safe place while I tried to locate a new fire or check up on the progress of one that was dying down, to see whether the treacherous smouldering under old roots had not flared up again. It was a tiring and worrying time. I could rely on my gamekeepers, but what about the villagers hired for the day? Were they honestly helping to put the fires out? Were some not ready to let a flare-up go unnoticed? I began to wonder.

And then a day came when every gamekeeper had something urgent to report and I had to be in three places during that afternoon, all in different directions and several miles away. I did not know what to do. I had just returned from my morning survey and felt that a cup of good black coffee was the best thing I could have at the moment. Lunch was quickly over and the coffee came as a blessing, even though it seemed also to taste smoky to me. I was just trying to map out my afternoon rides when Vladimir, then just about ten years old, came up to me and suggested that he might perhaps help me out. I think it was the first time that he understood the seriousness of the situation and realised that he might have other responsibilities than those of the schoolroom to carry. He wanted to help me and I felt it was right to avail myself of this help.

I explained to him that a fire extinguished two days ago in a peat bog might be smouldering still, and would need a careful check-up all around. Quarter of an hour later the boy was ready with instructions and a rough map, for it was not easy to find the way in these forests and with the smoke. We left together. He was riding his trustworthy Finnish cob Ryzka, very quick and sure-footed, and reliable when left alone tied to a tree. He had to ride some three miles on the road, then walk into the forest for a mile along the ride and then into the thicket towards the burnt-out place and skirt it carefully, watching for any possible sign of smoke. At the gate we separated as I had to ride in the opposite direction.

When I returned after sunset, Vladimir met me on the steps. "Everything seemed all right at first," he said, but then he told me that as he skirted the place he noticed a thin streak of smoke round a burnt-out bush. He realised that the roots might be smouldering and, going closer and poking at the spot, he discovered red coals glimmering. Afraid of letting it have too much air he covered the place over, marked it with a stick, went to cut himself fresh branches and returned to beat it hard, stamping out the least little spark that he could notice. "I had my high marsh boots on," he said, "so I was not afraid of stamping!"

I thought it was quite an efficient way of dealing with the task and was very surprised when he announced that he had marked the spot with sticks so as to be able to find it again tomorrow – this was really much more thoughtful than I had believed he could be. During the next few days he kept watch on this fire and on one or two others which were not difficult to locate – and certainly helped me a great deal by taking this care off my shoulders.

Finally a spell of wet weather put an end to my anxieties about the fires – but not about the attitudes of our workers. Revolutionary ideas were catching on. The good old servants stayed loyal, but there were others not so well known to us personally who disappeared suddenly and without warning. On the whole there was no ill-will. In one case only did I feel the sting of malice and betrayal.

This was in the case of a seventeen-year-old boy, Vanka, a stray orphan whom Sasha had picked up on some road in Poland two years previously. It was in the depths of winter, the Russians were retreating before the advancing Germans, the boy was in rags and barefoot. Sasha gave the order to take him up into one of the Red Cross vehicles and to look after him. The boy remained with the unit and when at Christmas Sasha joined us in Petersburg for a short leave, he brought Vanka with him.

Vanka remained in the house. He helped in the kitchen first and then, as there was no proper work for him there, he was sent to Kamenka and entrusted to Ivan the coachman. The reports I got were not satisfactory: whenever I came to Kamenka, Ivan had to complain about Vanka's laziness and bad work in the stables. He was put to work in various jobs, with the carpenter and with the blacksmith, with the cattle man and finally as an odd-job boy around the house when I was there and could keep an eye on him. But Vanka was just no good – lazy and a liar and totally unreliable.

When the revolution started, we were in Petersburg and Vanka was bringing milk from the country every second day. The trains had stopped, he could not return to the country at once and so remained in our house. But he soon vanished and a few days later sent a message that he had enlisted in the Red Militia. When I told my maid this, she crossed herself reverently saying, "God be thanked for it". Astonished, I asked her why she felt so strongly about it, and Masha then told me that on one of the days when rioting soldiers were attacking officers in the street (two were killed a couple of yards from our entrance door) and two of our officer friends had taken refuge in our house, Vanka boasted in the kitchen that he had told the "revolutionaries" in the street that our flat was a hiding place for officers and firearms. The servants had lived in terror all that day, but knowing that it would be unsafe for anyone to leave the flat had decided that "fate is fate" and that it would be better not to worry us.

A few weeks after his disappearance a workman turned up in the servants' quarters and gave us a message from Vanka. The poor boy had been caught stealing and was condemned to be shot: the message contained his thanks for what we had done for him and a pathetic "forgive me". This was a sad end to an unfortunate and troublesome youth.

Vanka had been a stranger in our parts, and he did not have the strong local roots which sustained our other servants and kept them steady through the war years. I came more and more to respect the value of our local customs and superstitions, even when on occasions they made my task in managing the estate even harder than usual. One day I was sitting groaning over some dairy accounts when Ivan the coachman was shown into the study. He stood there, cap in hand, high felt boots just brushed from the snow, and indicating by his serious look that all was not well.

"My Lady, excuse me, but we must sell the new horse," he announced with a dignified assurance allowing no doubts.

"Sell the new horse? But why? Have you tried it again this morning? Is it ill?" I could not see why the horse I had bought only the day before – upon Ivan's special advice, and after due tests – should now be sold without having been used. The animal had given entire satisfaction when we drove home, the long 30 versts drive from the station; it had shown no signs of fatigue, had looked fit and ready to go on although we had driven rather fast.

"It won't do – it doesn't suit us," replied Ivan looking steadily at the ceiling.

133

Ivan had something on his mind, it was clear, but I could not imagine what it was. "I can't make it out, Ivan. Tell me what the matter is. I will sell it if you explain what it's all about."

"The horse can't stay in our stables. 'He' won't have him," whispered Ivan looking furtively around. Now I understood. "He" – in other words the spirit of the stables – did not approve of our new purchase. Was it the colour, I wondered? Every stable or farm is said to have favourite colours – those that please the local spirit. No, the horse was light brown and Ivan had said this colour would be suitable. What was it that had gone wrong? Apparently the horse had been in a dreadful lather because "He" had been sitting on the horse's back and "torturing" it all night long.

I went with Ivan to the stables. We found the sturdy, well-built brown horse eating peacefully as if nothing had happened. But its coat certainly showed signs of the lather it had been in.

It would have been no use at all to try to persuade Ivan to change his mind. However loath I was, I had to sell the horse – and that at a moment when we really needed it very much and had little time to look for another. Gazing at the ceiling and spitting (with due respect to my presence) into the corner, Ivan remained steady in his certainty that the horse did not please the spirit and therefore it must go, or evil would befall the stables and us.

Ivan the coachman was not the only one at Kamenka to believe in the power of the local spirits. There was another Ivan, our oldest game-keeper – Ivan Ivanovich. He had been a gamekeeper on the estate long before Sasha bought it, and he was the first to teach us the names of the most distant parts of the estate, the local legends and stories attached to streams or moors, or disused sandpits, or lonely abandoned charcoal-burners' huts. Once launched on these subjects he could go on for hours, his speech became rapid, often in whispers and he used such a selection of local expressions that it took me quite some time to understand him. He had his own names for certain districts of the forests, for thickets or mossy parts on the bogs, as well as for the weather. I often regret now that I never thought of writing them down – it was such a colourful and descriptive sort of speech.

When I first knew him, Ivan Ivanovich was already in his fifties. He was tall and thin and slightly stooping; his long measured strides were swingy as if he were always walking on the soft boggy ground of our forests. Clean shaven with greyish hair and very bushy eyebrows, clear grey eyes, weather-beaten skin and a deep low voice – this is how I still see him in my mind. He had been a sergeant in the artillery of the Guard and had retained the habit of standing to attention when talking to us. He also used military expressions when addressing us and had the soldier's manner of giving short, precise answers. His clothes were always neat, well patched, and his boots were his pride: they were made of particularly soft leather, reached far above the knees and were, according to him, entirely waterproof, having been made to order by some former military shoemaker.

At first I knew him only as the gamekeeper of the wildest district of our estate and as he lived in the village near it – some seven miles from our house – I saw him less often than the other keepers. But after the war broke out and I needed help and advice with the management of the whole place with its extensive forestry work, I learned to appreciate this man more than ever. I could trust him entirely; he was quiet and reserved and never complained of the others or tried to put himself forward. Like the other keepers he used to come twice a week to bring me the report on the work that had been done in his district, to receive money for the workmen and to get orders for the following week. If I had any spare time I could not resist the temptation of going for a day's shooting with him. It was he who had initiated me in the stalking of elk in autumn and in the approaching of capercailzie in early spring, and I felt that our long shooting rambles had made us firm friends.

Ivan Ivanovich was glad to get away from the lumber work routine, for he was a passionate hunter. His weak point was that he got so excited in the sport that he made me quite nervous too. I remember the trembling of his hand when he pointed out a capercailzie in the dark pine trees at dawn or the silhouette of an elk in the thicket in the early mornings of a misty September day. Those shooting trips of ours usually involved a night spent in the open, and it was then that he told and re-told the strangest of stories. Were these stories true? True in the sense of being in tune with the understanding and the feelings of the country people, those who had lived in close contact with nature for generations and generations. Most likely they were legends handed down among these people whose life was spent close to these great forests and vast bogs. Old Ivan could not have invented them. Where could he have found all the material for these colourful stories? Not in his peasant's life, not in his life as a soldier, nor in his experience as a gamekeeper. They must have been deep-rooted folk tales, handed down from earliest pre-Christian times. There must be a sort of intuition, akin to the instinct of animals but harmonised by the human spirit with the strong religious feelings which still prevailed amongst the older country people like Ivan. Faith and fear were mixed together.

And yet, for me, these superstitious feelings were not inborn and I could walk or ride alone over the endless stretches of moors and feel only a sense of peacefulness and harmony, as I watched the swarms of gnats dancing in the evening sunlight. Looking back, this is the picture that I always see. I am riding my black mare Shalunia, who steps carefully along the ditch in which the dark moor water trembles at our passage. On either side are clusters of dwarf pines, here and there a contorted small birch, and the slow rustle of high dry reeds and grass, with grey-green moss hanging like drooping whiskers from the lean branches of a few stray fir trees. Thick green leaves of white moor flowers stand proudly along the banks of the ditch and oval, long-legged water spiders rush in queer zigzags on the chocolate-coloured water.

I am riding straight towards the setting sun which almost blinds me. My eyes are half-closed and I trust the horse to pick out the way. There is no path – just the slightly raised edge of the ditch. It is quiet, almost dead quiet all round – no crickets, no birds but for a few stray grey-tits in the lonely fir trees. The sloshy steps of my horse resound loudly but the sound dies off immediately in the damp and heavily scented air.

In the stillness of the air I feel the symphony of scents and colours, one which reveals the very soul of this landscape. Not a breath of wind disturbs its harmony. The smell of the dry moor bushes, their small flowers looking like tiny stars, is almost too strong for me and seems even to affect my horse who starts snorting repeatedly. No wonder Ivan Ivanovich said that the forest spirit leads his victims into the moors by making them lose consciousness through the smell of these bushes.

The ground gets too soft, the horse stumbles and sinks in above the knees. I dismount and lead Shalunia to a tree where she can wait for me safely chained (a rope halter was not strong enough to keep her safe). I can still hear the click of the chain around the glossy neck; this sound is insepara-ble from the recollection of all my long, favourite rides. The ground gets softer still – the ditch has gradually disappeared. It is my turn now to pull with difficulty my heavily booted legs out of the black peat. The smells grow more intense with the advancing evening. In front of me the sky is ablaze, all golden red, the horizon line straight like that of the sea, firm, unbroken, endless. Two or three tall pines rise against the sun; they serve me as a landmark. At their foot must be the moor lake traced on the map of our estate and mentioned to me by Ivan Ivanovich, but never yet seen by either my husband or myself.

The trees grow nearer; I reach them finally after crossing a bright green patch of swamp, a former "window", and before me glitters in deep orange-brown and metal-blue tints the smooth, unruffled surface of the lake.

I stop and gaze at this lake that was my goal. Not a sound anywhere, a dead land of dark brown and rusty red flooded by the golden red light. To my right I see a deep and narrow furrow in the ground, like the trace of a canoe drawn over the soft peat – it shows the place where a thirsty elk has crawled to the edge of the lake. Its hoofs, working like oars, have thrown up tufts of the soft, long and pale green moss.

My thoughts are far away from everyday interests and cares and dwell on the beauty of the moment; there is the glorious light alive over the silent moor; there is the richness of the strong scents rising from the moor towards this light. Great joy and gratitude for this wonderful moment fill my heart. It is worth living if one can experience such rare moments of deep joy. In front of me the unattained light in all its glory; behind me the dark outline of the forests to which I must now make my way back. Back, too, must go my thoughts to the cares and duties of everyday life.

Reluctantly I leave the lake and follow my own footprints left in the green and pink moor moss. Back to the waiting Shalunia and a slow ride through the forests, eastwards, looking back over my shoulder into the sunset glow which remains in and over the moors. I reach home around midnight in the transparent pale light of the northern night.

9

THE REVOLUTION COMES

Around Christmas, 1916, Sasha had obtained his commission as lieutenant in the Guards Mounted Artillery, and I came up to Petersburg with the boys to celebrate the event. We were aware of a great deal of unrest, both in the government, where the ministers were changing every few weeks, and also in the Army, where the veteran soldiers especially were being influenced by Bolshevik propaganda. But I fear we did not take these warnings very seriously. Life went on much as usual: there were luncheons, concerts, dinners and dances. When I look back upon that Christmas – the last that we were destined to spend in happiness – it seems incredible that it was the prelude to such a disaster.

Sasha was on leave during January and February and, together with other friends back from the Front, we gladly pushed aside all worries and went on leading the usual life of the winter season which lasted until Lent, when balls and parties would stop and be replaced by theatres and smaller, more intimate parties. But we often hesitated when making plans for the future, catching each other on the sentence: "Yes . . . if all goes well . . . if it is possible . . . ."

It was a cold and very snowy February. In Petersburg the shops began to be short of food supplies because of the disorganisation of railway communications. As well as being the centre of government, the capital was also the centre for military supplies and reserves in manpower; no wonder that the railway lines were overloaded. All food had to be brought from the centre of Russia, and there was only the oldest line connecting Petersburg and Moscow, really the artery of the country. There were only two or three other lines which could be used for supplies: the Windavo-Rybinsk one from Vitebsk and the south, the Warsaw line which had been blocked since the penetration of the Germans into Poland, and the Baltic line from Riga and Reval which could not be regarded as an important supply line.

Thus, the capital was short of bread, of sugar and of lard – the very essential elements in the people's diet. Fish was plentiful coming from Archangel in the north, from Lake Ladoga and the Finnish Gulf, and potatoes could be got in the immediate vicinity of the capital – but this was not enough to keep the people satisfied. Every day long queues grew from early morning in front of the bakeries and butchers' shops, patient queues which seemed at first to cover all their troubles with the answer: "Well, it's wartime – what do you expect!" But there were disturbing voices which we did not hear but which made their way among the people, scattering doubt, discontent, ill-will, and which were working steadily and according to a well-fixed plan. It was enough for one of the agents of the subversive parties to approach one queue and to murmur something about people freezing in the blizzard waiting for a small piece of bread while the rich – the capitalists – were finding time to amuse themselves going to theatres or restaurants, and enough to point out a passing elegant sleigh drawn by a high-stepping trotter or a closed carriage with coachman and footman on the box and women hiding their faces in furs peeping through the frozen windows – enough to provoke grumbles of dissatisfaction, murmurs of anger, sharp words of criticism. We felt it in the air, we knew that something was brewing, but what can a single individual do? The officers of the Guard regiments knew of the pernicious propaganda carried on among the ranks and many of them sensed the danger of it, but the majority of those in charge were so taken up by the war, the front line, the drill of the reserves, etc., that they did not realise how much that propaganda was actually undermining the people at home as well as the soldiers in the trenches. It was like some evil disease which was creeping through the country.

We noticed symptoms, we noticed the evil spirit growing in the masses, but we did not act, we simply did not know how to act, from which end to tackle the problem. The best the average man or woman could do was to carry on his work and duties as well as possible, to be as just and correct as possible in all dealings with the people. Personally, I did not see the problems very clearly, perhaps not clearly at all; I had a fear and disgust of the revolutionary movement, having clearly in mind the uprisings of 1904 and 1905, but I was far from realising the depth of the discontent now brewing under cover. Outwardly, everything was still so calm and the police seemed firmly in control. Of course, my talks with the people in the country, in the villages, had opened my eyes a little. People in the country are wont to speak more openly and freely, and during the long hours spent with the gamekeepers in the forests there were frequent open-hearted talks, when difficult questions were put to me and I was often at a loss to find the proper answer.

I think it was about the last Sunday in February of 1917 when Sasha and I were invited to shoot bear and lynx with some friends outside Petersburg. On our way to the Nikolayevsky station we heard firing and were told it was unsafe to continue, as the bread riots had become so serious that the soldiers had been called out. We returned, thinking little of the incident, but the next morning, when we were again prevented from going to the station, Sasha and I walked out in our shooting clothes to reconnoitre. We were approaching the big barracks near the Nikolayevsky station when the gates were thrown open and hundreds of soldiers, without caps or belts, poured out into the streets. They had mutinied; and as Sasha was wearing his officer's uniform underneath his shooting coat we thought it better to return home.

It was lucky that we did. Hardly had we arrived when we heard shouts outside the house and one of our friends rushed in. He told us that he had been pursued by mutineers who were after his sword. Luckily they had not attempted to follow him into the house, but we saw that we were up against realities – indeed, although we did not realise it, the revolution had begun.

The military riots continued and gained force, for although the police were loyal there was no competent central authority to combat the revolutionaries. Many officers were attacked. In fact it was impossible to go out in uniform. The hopes of non-revolutionaries centred round the Duma, which although of little authority was the only national body in existence. One morning we heard shooting and realised there was no question of leaving the house just then. We saw from our windows crowds of men and women drifting, it seemed, through the streets; a few shouts here and there, calls of "to the Duma" and one had the feeling that the Duma was to be the wizard who'd straighten things out, who'd find a solution to the questions which weighed on these crowds. They looked so grey, so slow, so sinister in their uniformity; they were cold, the women huddled themselves up into large kerchiefs over their coats, the men had frozen whiskers and let the earflaps of their Finnish fur caps flop about loosely over their ears. Was it the revolution again? Like 1905? It did look grim with this slowly moving grey crowd of set faces, a silent or rather inarticulate crowd, for one could only hear a sort of muttering, growling sound like an underground rumbling. That day the children did not go out for their usual walk before lunch with Miss Taylor; both Miss Taylor and I decided that it might not be quite safe.

And then came those hurried days, full of events which seemed to fall upon us out of the heavy snow-laden sky. The streets were crowded all day and night, shots were heard here and there, rumours contradicted one another. We telephoned our friends, we went out avoiding the crowds, the servants reported that this or that could not be got, luncheons and dinners were all mixed up, with friends dropping in unexpectedly – unable to proceed through the streets barred by the crowds. And then came the thunderbolt – the abdication of the Emperor, the refusal of his brother to take up the government, and the formation of a provisional government. It was a sunny, clear cold day with blue skies and everywhere shouts of "Freedom, freedom" with red ribbons on the coat lapels, on the caps – and amid all this the horrifying sight of soldiers hurrying, running, with unbuttoned coats, with torn epaulettes, with caps pushed on the back of the head – no cars, no sledges, only from time to time a military car with a red fanion and with soldiers on the running boards or lying along the radiator, rifle or pistol in hand, and people pressing aside: "Let it pass – going to the Duma – the new government – the new Ministers . . ." murmured here and there.

That evening we sat late into the night by the fire in the study, talking. Talking? . . . No, rather exchanging sentences, opinions, saying trivial things because the events were so tremendous, so overwhelming, that we could not find words to express them. Two friends had dropped in – I was glad for Sasha, for I knew how he felt about the Emperor's abdication and I realised that he knew more than I did about the probable repercussions in the country and – what was more important at the time – in the Army. I think all three of them had no illusions as to the seriousness of the moment, all three were landowners and as such were in close contact with the essential part of the population – the peasants. Sasha saw things in a very dark light, and it was something of a relief when another friend, Nikolai Rodzianko, arrived to bring a more cheering note in our little circle. He was a few years younger, but had been closely connected with politics through his father who was president of the Duma; he had great confidence in the liberal elements of Russian society and very great confidence in his own opinions. On this occasion it was actually helpful and reassuring and for once I did not feel like pulling his leg about his aplomb and undoubting knowledge of things.

The men smoked an awful lot, drank cups and cups of tea and we talked late into the night. We felt as though we were standing on the edge of a precipice, and there was a blankness in our minds due partly to sentimental attachment to the monarchy and, to a great extent, to the conviction that there was nothing that could take its place. Nikolai Rodzianko went on explaining things to us, making a broad outline of what the "bloodless revolution" could achieve, about the inner situation in the Duma and the prospects of its individual members. He had a quick brain but drove rather superficially over the problems, easily losing countenance when pressed for a concise or direct answer. It was baffling to us all; we had lost our footing on the soil we knew and we could not imagine from where help could come – help for us landowners. The optimistic description of the Duma committees working out some sort of a system for the country did not sound very reliable, for the men at the head of these committees were new to the task, new to the very thought of governing.

The next day we stayed at home, not really able to grasp what was happening, not able to realise the immensity of the events unrolling before our eyes. Everything one said seemed so futile, so childish, so naive – if not blankly stupid. Again, "Freedom" was the word; "Freedom" written on the walls, on improvised banners, in the scraps of newspapers issued that day. And the sun shone so brightly on the crisp white snow, from the clear blue sky and the red ribbons looked so gay as if suddenly the revolution had acquired a brighter face, a hopeful face, and the word "freedom" sounded so full of promise to all these crowds moving briskly now, chattering cheerfully, even vivaciously, and smiles were on many faces. I remember going out with the children and Miss Taylor who was not at all sure that it was safe to do so. We went together only in our quiet residential streets, the children rather enjoying the sight of the red bows everywhere – but Alec taking the thing seriously and putting many difficult questions about the fall of the Tsar, about the revolution and the undisciplined soldiers.

Politically, events were moving faster and faster: the monarchy was to be given up for good, the Allies were to be supported in the struggle against Germany, a Provisional Government was being formed to take the country in hand, the peasants were to be coaxed into orderly work – because of the war – and industry was to carry on with the production of army supplies of all kinds. It is then, I think, that the member of the Provisional Government responsible for the administration of the Army issued the first decree of that government – the really disastrous one – releasing the soldiers from their bond of obedience to officers. The effect was like that of lightning: the same evening soldiers attacked officers in the streets, in the barracks, tearing off their epaulettes, seizing their swords, molesting them and finally killing them if they offered the least resistance. The "bloodless" revolution was beginning to take on another aspect and a more threatening tone.

The next day house searches for officers, weapons and hidden treasures began; we had our first experience when some six soldiers appeared on the threshold declaring their intention to search our house. There was nothing to be done but to let them in. Fortunately they were still shy beginners and seemed lost in the large house and intimidated by the presence of men whom they obviously suspected of being officers. I accompanied the soldiers as they wandered singly through the rooms and when they approached the nurseries I told them that these were the children's rooms, whereupon they politely turned back saying, "We don't want to disturb the children." The servants peeped in, very disturbed and at a loss, and Old Niania shook her head and said to me afterwards, "This is not the right freedom if these dirty soldiers in their mud-covered boots walk through the gentlemen's houses – it's plain disorder!"

After the first weeks of total disorganisation and scare for us "privileged classes" or rather the "bourgeois", as the left press now termed everyone who was not a workman or a peasant, life was outwardly settling into some kind of pattern. Everyone had one main care – that of securing food for the family. Supplies were coming through very irregularly although the railways were still working after a fashion; it felt as if the trains continued to run from sheer habit and inertia for all authority in every field of life had lost its basis and support in the law. War materials were still being sent to the Front, but when the trains returned they were full of soldiers removing themselves freely and of their own accord from the fighting. Meat, sugar and flour were becoming more and more scarce in the capital and this is when horse meat first appeared on the market, and when bread was made from a mixture of flour and chaff and sometimes potatoes. But some restaurants were still open, the theatres prospered, and it was perhaps this contrast that made our life seem so weird and unreal since the outbreak of the revolution.

As soon as it was possible to take the children to Kamenka, Miss Taylor and I did so, for with the approaching summer there would be plenty to eat in the country. Sasha went to Krasnoye Selo to join the 2nd Guards Mounted Artillery Battery – a unit which had remained loyal and might shortly be sent to the Front – and I was once more in charge of things at Kamenka. There was a lot of work to do that summer and I did not have much time to be with my boys. The nursery and schoolroom were in the reliable hands of Miss Taylor and Miss Baker, who kept to their usual daily routine despite the unsettled times; and in this they were helped and supported by the faithful Elsa, our nursery maid.

Elsa was a Lettish country girl, who had lived with her widowed mother near Waldensee until she came to us as a nursery maid at the age of eighteen, when Alec was just a few months old. Small, fair, with a slightly blank expression and a very quiet voice, she seemed altogether a mouse-type girl. At first she spoke no Russian but she soon learned it and spoke very correctly. She was very clean, and I felt quite happy to know that she was near the children and no nurse ever complained about her. She was quiet, obedient, and clean – but very forgetful and absent-minded. We wondered what little Elsa could be thinking about.

All her spare time she spent reading. She had to buy her own books as they were in Lettish – a language no one in the house knew. Little by little her library must have become quite extensive – to judge from the weight of her trunk. When the children travelled she travelled too, and the problem of Elsa's luggage soon became a standing joke. Our travel preparations were quite complicated enough already; the carts for taking things to the station were ordered in advance and the servants saw to the things being taken down in time. But Elsa's trunk had always to be taken first, as it was so heavy that it had to be placed at the bottom of the cart – and three men could barely carry it downstairs. When I asked Elsa what made her trunk such a heavy weight she told me, blushing, "Only my books, Madam!" Somehow I had not the heart to put a limit to such praiseworthy interests and we continued travelling with the monstrous trunk.

In the summer of 1917, we none of us had any idea of the things that lay ahead. It was enough to get through the hot summer, with its forest fires and other problems, and with the news from the world around us becoming ever more threatening and dismal. We did not know that this was to be our last summer at home in Kamenka.

We had reached September, the weather was still good, but the nights were longer and one felt the autumn approaching. At Kamenka the men were bringing in the last harvests. Every grown man was needed to lend a hand in the fields, including our coachman Ivan, and so when I needed to go to Petersburg on business I drove myself to the station in a small four-wheeled carriage, taking the twelve-year-old Adamka along as a groom to look after the horse. The road was very bad in some parts, and I had rented some stables in the village of Tosno so that our horses did not have to return the same day. Adamka was to take the horse to the stables and wait there for my return.

The business kept me two days in Petersburg. Sasha was there too and promised to follow me to Kamenka shortly. Meanwhile I wired the time of my arrival to Tosno station, and Adamka was there with the carriage to meet me. I must say I did ask him how he managed to harness the horse as he was a very small boy, and he admitted that the innkeeper had helped him to put on the collar and to fix the hoop in the shafts. If only the horse were a little smaller, he said, he would have been able to manage quite well. Off we went, and on the way home Adamka told me that lots of refugees from our neighbouring villages had been arriving at the station.

"Refugees?" I asked, "What refugees? Who are they? Where are they going? Why are they running away? . . ." I said, unable to understand what could have happened.

"Oh, they are just peasants, peasants from the villages, you know. There are robbers plundering the villages – wild Caucasian people who go all over the countryside and take the cattle, and kill people," said Adamka in his clear piping voice.

Just then we had to give way to three heavily laden carts coming towards us. And, in fact, I recognised one of the peasants – a man from a village some five or six miles from our house. I called out to him: "Tell me, Piotr, where are you going like that with your whole household?"

"Escaping, we did not dare stay on longer – the Wild Division is loose and is plundering the country. Hurry on, my Lady, they were saying around our places that the next village would be yours."

What a cheerful prospect, I could not make the horse hurry too much, because the last few miles of the road were the worst. Generally I had my riding horse out to meet me but, not knowing when I would be back, I had not ordered it for today. So, armed with much patience and faith that things might still be all right, I drove slowly along the bad road with the horse barely able to get the little carriage out of one big rut before it dropped into the next. Even Adamka had become quite glum. His family lived on our estate but they were already fugitives from Poland – so he knew what it meant to have to escape, to run away.

At last we got over the little hill, the forest cleared, before us lay our fields and at the far end of this clearing one could just see the tips of the tall spruce and pines of the garden. As we came down the hill and across the dried-out brook a little figure on horseback appeared on the road. It was Vladimir who, having seen us coming, cleared the ditch beside the road and came galloping along the edge of the field. As he came up to us I noticed that he had his .22 Winchester rifle strapped on his back.

"Yes, so far everything is all right, Mother. I am out on duty watching this road, so I can't ride back with you. Sidor is to relieve me before sunset." I felt that the boy was proud of the grown-up task that had been given him, and I did not want to interfere with the arrangements without knowing how things stood – but I did not feel reassured. After giving Vladimir strict instructions to turn back immediately if he saw the dreaded Wild Division men, and to ride home along the forest edge so as to avoid their possible pursuit, I drove on with a heavy heart. On approaching the old smithy I was glad to see Ivan the coachman coming down the other road, and I asked him for news.

"Well, we are all right for the present, but I hear it's pretty bad all along the river Tosno and also near Lissino – I thought you might not get through. I have been keeping watch on this road and Sidor is on the Kudrovo one. Bad times, and we have so few men!"

I thanked Ivan for keeping watch and said I would return for more news after having seen how things were in the house. As I stopped the carriage at the front steps, Miss Taylor came out of the front door with a hatchet in her hand – and a rueful smile on her face. "Good evening, Madam, you see I am ready for any guests! But it is just as well that you have arrived, for we are entirely at a loss." I went into the house and was met by Miss Baker with the two small boys. She was very pale and the children very excited, telling me together and at the tops of their voices all the news and terrors shortly to be expected. It all sounded rather bad. Miss Baker begged me to take them straight to the station to catch some evening train for Petersburg; but I finally persuaded her that it would be impossible. Darkness would set in within an hour, the roads would be dangerous, and I wanted to stay here anyhow as I thought it wrong to abandon everything in sheer fright. But I agreed that Miss Taylor and Miss Baker should go with Elsa and the children to catch a train early in the morning, so as to be in Petersburg by about noon. They could then inform Sasha of the situation and he could decide what should be done.

I went out as promised and checked up the watch for the night. Two men would guard the farm buildings while the third one got some sleep. Vladimir and I would see to the defence of the house. After the children's dinner I took Vladimir aside to give him his instructions, as I did not want to frighten the little ones. He was to keep his rifle fully loaded and a supply of cartridges near his bed and, in case of alarm, to keep a watch from the upstairs windows looking north and west; he was not to shoot unless I gave him a signal; we both had whistles. I undertook the watch downstairs. Before bed-time I tried to keep the children occupied with their usual games while the nurses and maids packed trunks and cases, and the housekeeper prepared a big provision basket – the essential supplies for the long carriage trip and train journey. Soon I noticed that Alec looked flushed; he complained of a headache and it was obvious that he was beginning to run a high temperature. No wonder – the excitement of the last few days had encouraged his particular capacity for producing a temperature at inconvenient moments. He tossed about in his bed all night, and there was no question of taking him on the journey next morning. So our plans were changed: the two other boys would go as planned, and Alec would stay behind with me.

I had spent the night dressed and with lighted lamps, burning low, in three "strategic" points. Sports guns with reserve ammunition were placed in the different rooms, and I had my two Brownings in my pockets. It was a strange night, trying to keep watch and worrying about Alec. From time to time I was so tired that I dropped off to sleep, counting upon my Samoyed to wake me with his bark in case of danger. At four in the morning the coachman Ivan tapped at the window – as agreed – to tell me that he was now taking the watch on the road. He said that refugees were still passing and that a man from a distant village had said the Wild Division men were now combing the villages on the banks of the river Tosno. Poor Ivan was in great anxiety for his own village and his relations there, but as his wife and children were with us in Kamenka he did not feel he had to go to the rescue of his village.

Early in the morning the boys left, Alec remaining with me – still feverish but sleeping less restlessly. I was very worried about the little carriage alone on the road, where it might well be intercepted by the brigands, and the day seemed to drag on in gloom and anxiety. Alec was better towards evening, his usual good appetite returned and he really enjoyed being alone with me, being pampered and made a fuss of – he was an important person and he always liked to be treated as such. I knew Sasha could not come before late in the evening, as the horses would have to rest for a number of hours after having brought their load to the station. But as the evening wore on and Sasha did not turn up, I realised I would have to face another night without him. Alec was sound asleep and snoring, the night watches outside were organised and the house remained in my care.

This time I did not feel like sleeping – the strain was too acute – and I settled in an armchair with a biography of Beethoven to read, in the hope that this would take my thoughts entirely into another world. The Samoyed, Tiavkin, was at my feet, it was quite cosy really but a wind had arisen and I was not sure I would hear someone breaking in on the other side of the house. Every hour or so I went round checking all the windows. Everything was quiet, until at about 5 o'clock in the morning I was suddenly roused out of my reading by a loud snort of a horse right under my window. "There they are!" flashed through my mind, as I knew that the dreaded brigands were all mounted. I reproached Tiavkin in my thoughts, for although he growled he did not seem to be very excited, and was clearly leaving the next move to me. Lowering the light of my lamp I crept on all fours towards the window, so that my shadow would not be seen from outside, for the curtains were not very thick and we had no shutters. On reaching the window I stopped when another loud snort and stamping of horses hoofs resounded right there. I crept along the wall to the other window so as to have a better side view and not to show myself at once, and lifted with infinite care and trembling hands a tiny corner of the curtain. It was still dark, but in the faint light of the approaching dawn I could discern a dark shape in front of the first window. A low shape, too low for a horse – what could it be? I waited – hours it seemed to me – and the shape moved to approach my window, a low shape, shaggy, riderless – and then I understood; it was Alec's pony, Mousy, who must have got out of the paddock and had come to the windows to receive her accustomed titbits! "Mousy" I said; Tiavkin wagged his tail in agreement and put his front paws on the low window-sill. Mousy gave a slight neigh and I laughed aloud, laughed with relief and laughed at myself – still on all fours talking to dear old Mousy.

Thus ended the second night of my watch without any further excitements. In the morning the news came that much havoc had been done along the river Tosno and that the robbers were now taking a rest there as their horses needed to be fed – and the men had drunk too much. Alec woke up fit and well and very pleased with himself, and by noon Sasha had arrived with our friend Alphonse Riesenkampf as a support if need be, and a whole arsenal of guns and ammunition. Sasha had been absent from town the previous day when the family had arrived there, and in spite of frantic telephone calls and searches by Miss Baker and Vladimir he could not be traced and came home unconcerned for dinner when it was too late to catch the train. So he and Alphonse took the first train in the morning. On their way from the station they met a peasant who warned them to be careful at a certain cross-roads, and added that two wild-looking men on horseback had asked him the way to our place, but he had given them false directions. The men believed him and rode away. So for the present we were safe – but for how long?

The following night I slept soundly while the men kept watch and the next morning we all left together in two carriages and had an uneventful journey to the station. There we heard that the whole band of robbers had got so totally drunk that they were overcome in their sleep by the peasants and delivered to the local authorities. Fortunately these local authorities were courageous enough to hold the men, which was already an unusually lucky circumstance as the police did not exist any longer and the newly formed militia was very vague as to its duties and preferred to avoid any definite action.

Thus ended for us the Wild Division episode. It put an end to our family life in Kamenka, for after that I did not take the children there again. I went there frequently alone for a few days at a time to carry on the work – but even that was to stop a few months later when Kamenka was nationalised at the end of December 1917.

10

REVOLUTION

At the end of October 1917, the Provisional Government that had been established in March was overthrown after a few days' street fighting, and the Bolshevik Party with Lenin at its head seized power in Petrograd. Very uncertain at first of their own strength, of their hold over the people and of their effectiveness as a government, they found it safer to establish their headquarters not in the centre of the city but on its outskirts. They chose the Smolny Institute, which offered them many advantages. Its buildings were vast, its walls were strong and it was close to the Neva; it could easily be turned into a sort of fortress in case of emergency. This complex of buildings dated from the eighteenth century, having been first a private palace, and then a monastery, but it was generally known now as a large boarding school for young girls of the nobility. This school, or institute, existed right up to 1917, and closed down – as far as I remember – only in the summer of that year. The cathedral of Smolny, towering above the large square buildings, was one of the largest in Petersburg and was held in great reverence as a shrine. It was in these surroundings that the newly self-appointed government started its career.

Along with most of the population of Petrograd, we had great doubts as to the chances this Bolshevik government had of remaining in power, and our attitude – that of the non-proletarian classes – was to hope that with their shortage of adequately trained men they would be unable to run the government machine. We rather expected to see the new regime collapse through its own inexperience. This was wishful thinking, of course: the preceding few months should have shown us how, in their struggle against the Provisional Government, the Bolsheviks had been quick to act and had not hesitated to adopt ruthless and drastic measures when they deemed it useful. Now, after only three weeks of their rule, the name "Smolny" had begun to acquire a sinister sound as all the people who were arrested – and there were a great many arrests right from the start – were taken to Smolny for interrogation or trial, and many of them did not return.

The real terror of the revolution had not yet swept over the country, but we felt instinctively that we were being driven towards some entirely unknown destiny and that the future could only be a very unpleasant one. And yet there was nothing that we could do. Our best men were at the Front, trying in vain to stop the disintegration of the Army, trying to keep the pledge given to the Allies – to fight the Germans. There was no centre round which we could gather, no leader to guide us. The "we" as used here included not only the upper classes but more or less all people with a semblance of education, who at the time were generally called "bourgeois" – without any real class distinction. Deprived of our customary backgrounds we lived now as best we could, each according to his code of honour, and following his own ideas and ambitions as far as it was possible to have any; in fact it was an altogether egotistical existence. Strangely enough there was a certain lurid attraction in this complete disorganisation where everyone depended only upon his own self, his ingenuity, his courage, and frequently also upon his sense of humour or sporting spirit. Maybe in saying this I am expressing the feelings of those who were still young at the time and who had been smiled upon by fortune until then.

Anyhow, to a great extent such was my state of mind on that particular dark November morning when the door bell rang in my town house where I was alone at the time – Sasha and the children being in the south. Sasha was endeavouring to keep close to his regiment, and could combine this with a visit to his mother. He had heard that conditions of life in the south were easier than in the north and had decided to send the boys, under the care of their faithful nurse Miss Taylor and their governess Miss Baker, down to Louisino to visit their grandmother. As things turned out, they never reached Louisino. On arrival in Kursk they were informed that conditions on the estate had deteriorated to such an extent that their grandmother had taken refuge in the town of Kursk. So the children spent the winter in her hotel in the town, which cannot have been a very easy arrangement for anyone. Added to this, Miss Baker spent the winter making friends with an officer in a British armoured car unit which for some reason spent several months in Kursk, and finally she departed for England to get married. Fortunately Miss Taylor did not permit herself such ideas and with her usual devotion brought the children safely back to me in the spring.

In the meantime, I remained alone in the north in order to carry on as long as possible the management of Kamenka, and to keep an eye too on our property in town. With the rapidly progressing nationalisation of estates, and the consequent dwindling of incomes, life promised to become more and more difficult for families such as ours – and the damp November weather did nothing to improve my spirits. Thus, when the bell rang and our good friend Alphonse Riesenkampf entered my sitting room, I felt greatly relieved and cheered by the feeling that I would not be alone with my thoughts and worries.

"Hullo, so you have not gone to the country as you intended? Has anything happened?" he added, using this sentence which had become so current among us of late.

"No, so far not," I replied, touching the wood of the table and forgetting that Alphonse was indignant about superstitions in general. "I could not get any answer from the district authorities regarding some business in Kamenka, and so

I decided to wait until tomorrow when a definite answer was promised me."

"Shouldn't I come then and help you squeeze an answer out of those authorities whoever they are? Besides, I have never been to those new offices of theirs and can't help wondering how the whole bunch of people deal with business matters when they've never done it before."

"Yes, it's quite funny seeing them at work. But I am not quite sure that it is safe for you as a man to go there. Often a woman can obtain much more from people, by putting silly questions and then, when people are sure that she is 'just a silly woman', suggesting the solutions she wants to obtain."

"Well, I feel we must go somewhere and do something on this beastly dark and damp day," said Alphonse. "I could not stay at home with my brother looking more gloomy every day and Father – well, you know . . . I am so much younger and it makes me feel depressed."

Alphonse's father, General Riesenkampf, was a very old man. He was always called "the General" by friends and even by relations. He had retired many years ago and had taken no part in the last war, and was thus not in immediate danger of arrest as a military leader. Besides he was too old to try to leave Petrograd, and his sons had stayed on to keep him company.

"I am ready to go out right away. Just give me time to get my hat and coat. But where shall we go?" I asked.

"I have it! Why not take the bull by the horns? Why not go straight to Smolny and see the working of the show at the very centre?" Alphonse was delighted with his idea.

But, go to Smolny? The very name made us good "bourgeois" shiver. It was now synonymous with arrests, interrogation and imprisonment . . . a rather gruesome picture. And yet, after all, why not go and have a look at it?

So we went. First on foot, then by tram, we reached the imposing white block of buildings which had been the Smolny Institute for Young Girls of the Nobility. This name brought back pictures of young girls in their old-fashioned uniform, brought up according to the strictest rules of bygone days. I recalled these girls being brought in old-fashioned closed carriages to the matinees at the ballet or at the French theatre where classical plays were given on Sunday afternoons for the young. I always looked with compassion at these uniformed girls in dull-coloured dresses with short sleeves and white starched capes tied with bright bows, being herded by uniformed *dames de classes* – sort of grey shepherd dogs. Everything about them was prim, well behaved and demure. And now – this Smolny was the seat of the brand-new revolutionary government, at the time a mere three weeks old.

As we approached the gates we noticed that some kind of pass or permit had to be shown to the soldiers on duty. This was perplexing: what were we to do? We mixed with the considerable number of people who were now assembled at the gate and as the guard called out: "Who are the typists and secretaries summoned?" Alphonse nudged me and we stepped forward with the others, pushing on with the crowd and somehow getting through without any further questions. We were both ready and eager to play the game and knew each other well enough to guess and support any fancy that might occur to either of us.

Whilst crossing the spacious court we decided that the aim of our visit would be to obtain a permit to carry arms for each of us, and a travel permit to the Caucasus for Alphonse. This settled, we entered the main building. Field guns and an anti-aircraft gun adorned the entrance instead of the former dignified and liveried porter.

We entered the lofty hall, dimly lit, the air thick with tobacco smoke, with the smell of soldiers' boots and of crowded humanity in general. A detachment of sailors, rifles in hand, was on guard duty, looking quite impressive. Two machine guns were mounted right and left of the entrance, wooden barriers barred the hall in various directions and soldiers or Red guards were posted at the exits. The heterogeneous crowd moved slowly and apparently aimlessly through the space left free between the barriers.

More passes were required to penetrate further into the building. We told a dishevelled youth busily writing at a small desk that we wanted passes and instructions for obtaining travel permits. The youth looked at us blankly through his pince-nez, then handed us two slips of paper and suggested that any further information could be obtained "inside".

Now we were actually "inside" and ready to explore the place. It looked extraordinarily deserted and very gloomy. The crowd was only in the hall apparently. How different it must have been here just a few months ago when the merry laughter of young girls resounded on these spacious stairs, in these wide stone passages running along the entire length of the building.

On the first landing a woman had established a stall with a choice of Communist literature; she offered us the "latest speech of Lenin", the "new regulations for this and that", and so on. We bought a bunch of these unattractive pamphlets and Alphonse stuck them in the outside pocket of his great-coat, the titles well in evidence – "to make a good impression", he said.

Not a soul in the passages of the first floor. Only a grubby little fox terrier met us here, wagging his stumpy tail with some curiosity, and accompanied us as we continued our exploration.

There did not seem to be any possibility of getting the information we wanted, for neither the soldier on guard, nor the woman on the landing, nor any of the men who occasionally passed us could give us any directions. This suited us very well indeed and we decided to enter all the rooms as we came to them, thus taking the opportunity of seeing more of the place. Opening the first door on the left, where the inscription "Dame de Classe" still glared at us in all its reserved severity, we found ourselves in the private den of some high official who apparently had only just gone out, as a cigarette balanced on the edge of a large table was still sending up a fine column of smoke. Papers, maps, cigarette boxes, teacups, lumps of sugar, papers everywhere and a military cap – lay all mixed up on the numerous tables, while the slim silhouette of a machine gun adorned the window. Spare belts of ammunition were slung over the back of the only chair to be seen. It was stuffy but cold in the room; no wonder the man had needed so many cups of tea to keep him warm. As we were closing the door the fox terrier slipped in and we left him there to keep the high official company on his return.

It felt damp and cold in these endless passages, classrooms and dormitories, the doors of which we now opened one after the other. Everywhere the same picture: crowds of girls typing feverishly – some in most inconvenient positions – kneeling in front of boxes or balancing on piles of books; men smoking and dictating, or arguing with one another, and delving in the piles of paper which surrounded them like walls built up on the floor and on endless tables. In every room two machine guns were pointing out of the windows and piles of ammunition boxes, rifles and revolvers lay on and under the tables. Altogether we came to the conclusion that there were incredible numbers of tables but scarcely any chairs, and all the big and bulky cupboards were permanently open as they could not hold the masses of papers, loose and in bundles, which now lay scattered on the floor.

Our stereotyped questions about permits received invariably in reply the advice to "Have a look at the end of the passage". However, these ends of passages never gave us what we wanted. At one of them we found a regular first-aid post with a smiling nurse in white and no patients – and this quiet white room struck us as the only normal picture in this topsy-turvy place. At one of the other "ends" we were nearly knocked down by a man apparently practising riding a bicycle in his spare time. Round the corner, at another "end", we came to a large glass door with a militia man, in civilian clothes but with rifle in hand, standing on guard. He looked so good-natured in his floppy dark coat, his flat fur cap and his drooping moustache that we tried to coax him into letting us through. He remained firm, however, and when we insisted he took a step closer and whispered: "I would let you pass Sir, but they say Lenin himself is there – so I can't!" How strange this "Sir" sounded to us, like a word belonging to another world, to history already. Alphonse smiled understandingly and slipped a coin into the hand of the man who, looking furtively around, took off his cap and bowing low thanked "the lady and gentleman for their kindness". It was comic and pathetic at the same time to hear these words on the very doorstep of Lenin's apartments and from the mouth of one of the dreaded Red Militia.

However, another "end of passage" proved more promising for, as we approached it, the smell of cooking beckoned to us. It was well after our usual lunch hour and, following the smell, we arrived at the glass door of a large dining hall with rows of unpainted wooden tables and benches. A long low counter separated the dining hall proper from the improvised kitchen where monumental kettles were steaming lustily. A plate, a mug and a spoon were handed out in exchange for tickets bought at the door; a few steps further on the plate was filled with a large helping of boiled potatoes and salt fish, the mug with a liquid representing tea. We took our food, our tea, with two sweets instead of sugar, and found empty seats at the end of one of the tables. A sailor, a peasant and a workman – as far as we could judge – had already taken their seats there. We could not have chosen three more typical representatives of the new regime.

The boiled potatoes had no salt, the fish was much too salted, but by mixing the two we managed to get a dish which could be eaten by people who were as hungry as ourselves. Our companions looked at us in steady silence, apparently wondering where to place us. What struck me first was that they all ate with their caps on – a thing one never saw in Russia before, even in the remotest and most forlorn village. The peasant, as I noticed, had at first removed his cap, but on looking round, he shyly put it back on his long straggly hair and looked down into his plate eating with evident and audible appetite. The other two did not seem to enjoy the salt fish and the sailor finally pushed his plate away with an impatient gesture murmuring something about "uneatable stuff". Alphonse looked at him with an innocent smile saying "I wonder whether comrade Lenin and his friends get the same food? I had hoped in fact to meet them here."

"They have no time to waste on waiting in the public dining hall!" replied the sailor with reserved dignity and a somewhat superior tone.

"And I have seen good salmon and a plate of white buns being carried in to them," put in the workman with a grin and casting a knowing glance at the door.

"Surely it could not have been for them, comrade?" exclaimed Alphonse indignantly. "They can't make a difference between themselves and the people; there are no privileges any more – all have been abolished!"

"Privileges or no privileges, good food is more pleasant than bad food," muttered the workman shrugging his shoulders.

"But where is our dearly acquired equality, the greatest achievement of the revolution? It was for this equality that our Cronstadt sailors fought so hard, isn't it so, comrade?" said Alphonse, turning to the sailor.

"And didn't we fight for it! But they – the men at the top – know best where equality is at the right place," proclaimed the sailor sententiously.

"Yes – the ones at the top – they surely know that equality is not always equal, that one piece of land of the same size is still not equal to another – never . . ." said the peasant gloomily, shaking his head.

Nobody could contradict this great truth and the topic of conversation was dropped – much to my relief I admit. We then spoke about the Smolny building and discovered that the peasant and the workman were in the same plight as ourselves and had not been able to discover the offices dealing with their business. We parted good friends and the peasant even lifted his cap saying good-bye.

Finally, after many more passages and classrooms we arrived at another "Dame de Classe" door and found that the bearded inmate of this room was the man who issued travel permits. He seemed, however, to be very vague as to the area under the control of his government and was quite unable to determine whether a journey to the Caucasus could be made through Soviet territory or not. To cut his doubts short Alphonse simply dictated him the names of the main railway junctions on the way south and finally suggested that a permit for the "entire Empire" would be the simplest solution. The bearded man willingly agreed and started writing it down when he suddenly realised that the "Empire" had fallen and decided that the word "Republic" would do better.

Upon the advice of this man we went in search of the Commandant of Smolny for it was he alone apparently who could grant permits for firearms. This information did not appeal to us particularly, but neither of us wanted to admit a certain feeling of fear at the idea of having to appear before the very Commandant himself. The title alone was scaring, for some of our people had been brought before this Commandant to be sent on to prison. Still – once we had got so far we had to see it through – and we set off in search of the Commandant.

His office was not difficult to find – everyone seemed to know well enough where it was. The same picture met us as we entered the narrow room: two machine guns on the window sills, papers and files on the tables, but the place was cleaner than the other offices we had seen. A newspaper serving as a lampshade dimmed the light.

A tall, good-looking and extremely young sailor met us. He was the dreaded Commandant of the place, and the beaming smile on his tanned face made me think that he was still thrilled at finding himself in this exalted position. We told him in a few words what we wanted and without the slightest hesitation he agreed to grant us the permits, never asking even for our identity papers or for any further explanations. He must be in a particularly good mood this afternoon, I thought. Seeing that things went so smoothly, I decided to ask for a permit not only for my Browning pistol and one shot gun, as I had intended, but for all the firearms I still had at home, both in town and in the country. Thus, when the Commandant took a slip of paper on which the permission was already typed and where only the name of the holder and the make of the firearms had to be filled in, I showered upon him the names of all the guns I had in mind. Bewildered, he said:

"Look here, comrade, it will be much easier if I put on your permit simply 'all firearms' – don't you think so? Then you can use a different one every day – just as you feel inclined," he added with a loud laugh. "But where on earth is my pen again!" he exclaimed rummaging about in the drawers of the desk. "Hullo, Sidorov, where did you see my pen last? I hope it has not been stolen again! Really, this is too much for anyone's patience! . . ."

"Stolen? Do such things ever happen here?" asked Alphonse with feigned indignation. My heart sank – why does he always try this risky game, I thought.

"Don't they? Fancy, only yesterday my own teapot was stolen and a few days ago an unopened pound of sugar I had obtained with great difficulty," replied the Commandant, not noticing the sarcasm in Alphonse's question.

"How very difficult it must be then to be the Commandant of this place!" I added with warm sympathy.

"Yes, comrade, it is a hard task – and the responsibilities alone . . ." He was filling in the slips of paper, signing them with a pen which Sidorov had produced from the next room, and blotting the papers with a good bang of the fist. "There, that's done. And now you can walk about in safety with your whole arsenal. Should you want anything else, please come to me again, I'll be very glad to help you."

Thanking him for his amiability we left this young Commandant of Smolny, with his beaming smile and laughing eyes which were so little in keeping with the dismal aspect of the place and the more than dismal reputation of Smolny in 1917. There was something uncanny in this contrast – it struck us so deeply that we hurried to leave Smolny, unable now to enjoy any further investigations. The fun we had had in roaming about seemed all of a sudden wrong. We quickly made our way towards the hall and, supplied with passes and permits, walked out of the stronghold unmolested. The machine guns pointed over our heads, the large guns by the big door looked menacingly into the dusk, and armed men came and went; it was gloomy, threatening. We crossed the big court and were glad to be out in the dimly lit street, in the tram crowded with people, in the daily surroundings we were getting used to by now.

It was in another tram in Moscow some years later that I finally lost the firearms permit, which was stolen out of my pocket as I was trying to hang on with both hands and keep my balance amidst the crowd. I had cherished that permit as a souvenir and also for its usefulness: many times it had helped me board a train with my gun when I went on my last shooting expeditions; and I was really upset when I felt in my pocket and found it had gone.

With the Smolny adventure behind us, we came back to the realities of our daily lives. When Sasha returned from Kursk for a few days he found me endeavouring to keep the work going in Kamenka, and negotiating anxiously in town with the engineering company that was constructing the new Petrograd–Pavlovsk –Novgorod railway line. The company was continuing to buy from us (Kamenka had not yet been "nationalised" and the land and timber were still ours to sell), and I was trying to get payment from them for what they had taken so far. Winter was approaching and, whatever we decided to do, this money would be useful.

Christmas 1917 promised to be a very dismal one, for I was alone again in our big town house, Sasha having returned to the south to join his mother and the three boys. Not wanting to sit day in, day out in the dismal, silent home and glad to be of use to someone, I worked on a refugee committee for Baltic people. But the work there was progressing wearily, and we expected any day the closing down of the committee as it was not a State or Bolshevik organisation. Still, as long as it dragged on its anaemic existence I went there conscientiously every day and offered my services for any about-town errands. Such errands were much disliked by the other people on the committee who dreaded the cold, long and tiring walks through snow-covered, unswept streets.

Chatting one day with some of my colleagues about the approaching Christmas, I mentioned the fact that I simply could not imagine this great day without a real Christmas tree and – however childish it might sound – I was determined to have one, even though it would be for myself alone. The problem, however, was where to get hold of a tree since all private shops were closed and the sale of trees on the languishing markets had been prohibited. Should I fetch one myself from Kamenka? Rather a long way to go, and anyway I was sent out on a number of errands that day which kept me busy until the evening, when I returned home without dropping in at the committee's office. The next morning, Christmas Eve, the snow was falling thick and fast; no wind, a mass of large white flakes falling steadily and silently and blurring the view like a thick curtain. I waited for the snow to stop but as it did not seem to change by noon I decided that, snow or no snow, I would get myself some sort of Christmas tree. The nearest tram line took me quite far out of town and, once near the park which lay at the end of the line, I was sure to find some sort of wood. I was lucky in getting into the tramcar, which was usually over-crowded. This was an encouraging start. I got to the wood, found a very small fir tree and was back home before dark, pleased and happy.

Barely had I got into dry clothes when the door bell rang – an unusual occurrence and a dreaded one in these days of house searches, police visits, or other unpleasant visitors.

Cautiously I opened the door to find two unknown little girls, neatly dressed, red-cheeked and covered with snow smiling shyly at me. The bigger one was holding in her arms a nice large Christmas tree. Timidly they asked me for my name and the elder then said: "we went to get a tree for ourselves and Mother thought that you might like to have one too, so here it is." And she put the tree down in front of me. "How very, very kind," I exclaimed, "but who is your mother? I am sorry but I don't know you."

"Mother works at the Baltic Committee. She said you were alone and your children were away. So my sister and I thought we could get two trees instead of one and we found two nice ones."

I thanked them as warmly as I could and they trotted off, hurrying to get home before it got quite dark. I remained with my new tree smelling of frost and forest and snow, and the picture of the smiling childish faces in my mind. "If only my boys were here" was my natural thought – but I knew they were probably better in the south, further from the centre of the revolution and in a part of the country still well supplied with food.

That same evening I decorated the large tree with the silver stars and beads and the few candles remaining from last year's happy family Christmas. The vision of my own little boys perhaps doing the same thing hundreds of miles away did not leave me. Will they have presents? Will their father see to it all? These and many other sad thoughts brought tears into my eyes. But the sight of the tree, the memory of the kind little girls who had brought it here, gave me courage.

I had put the tree in my study where the wood fire (logs I had carefully preserved for this occasion) burned cheerfully, and I was preparing to light the candles when the entrance door bell rang. Hesitatingly, full of apprehension, I went to the door. Could it really be a house-search? Today, this great and holy day? No – a low and well-known whistle from outside the door dispelled my fears. I opened the door and there was Alphonse together with his father, the General. They too felt lonely at home, they said, and had decided to come and cheer my loneliness. I was very much touched by this kind thought, especially as the General went out so seldom, and the recollection of this Christmas Eve which I had expected to be so dreary becomes bright in my memory thanks to these good friends. We sat near the fire in the study, drinking a bottle or two of good wine which I had found in my father's cellar and eating some almonds and raisins, which I had managed to secure – the traditional Christmas food.

The General seemed to enjoy the evening; he talked about the past, and spoke too with the ardour of a young man about the future of his own country – Poland – a topic which he rarely mentioned in conversation. As his eyes brightened and his speech quickened I felt that the pent-up feelings of a life-time were breaking out. We, the young ones, sat listening intently, holding our breath, following the words which sketched the outline of a picture greatly cherished but usually hidden.

The Christmas candles had burnt down long ago, and the fire was dying when the General and his son left, leaving me alone in the empty house but with the grateful memory of these happy hours. Thus strengthened and comforted, I was able to bear the next blow which fell. One dreary day in late December, I received word that our dear Kamenka had been nationalised – just taken from us, without much ado and without any indemnity, with effect from December 20th, 1917. I was thankful that the news did not reach me until after Christmas.

One month later I faced the unpleasant prospect of going to Lissino in order to appear before the "Lissino District Rural Committee" as it was grandly called on the note summoning me. Translated from the beautifully illiterate Russian, the note ran as follows:-

Lissino District Rural (Zemski) Committee No. 43
30th January 1918.

To: Citizeness Eedita Feoderovna Sologub
This is to notify you that the Lissino District Rural
Committee request you to inform them whether you wish
to be present at the disposing of your estate in
accordance with the laws of the Russian Republic. We
request you to attend in person or answer by letter.

p.p. the Chairman of the Rural Committee
. . . . . . (signed) Member of the Executive

I decided that to "attend in person" would be the better course
of action. As I saw it, my task was twofold: first, to secure
some continuing means of existence for the people in my service until the 20th December 1917, left now in the middle of
winter without salary and some without homes; and secondly,
to maintain for myself the right to dispose of the house and its
contents, as according to the information I had through my
servants the house itself seemed still to be left to me.

The next morning it was dark and so bitterly cold, even in
the house, that I dressed in my warmest shooting clothes and
put on my big fur-lined travelling coat before drinking the cup
of watery tea that Masha brought me. Masha was my maid, and
the only servant who had remained with me in town. I was glad
of her presence in the large and otherwise empty flat.

At Tosno, Ivan was waiting at the station entrance – short
coat, floppy fur cap, moustache and eyebrows – all in icicles.

"I have Zmeika here – she goes well with the small sledge.
I thought it better to take the small one – for the present
times . . ."

I knew what he meant – not so noticeable, a sledge like all
the others, like that of well-to-do peasants – probably Ivan was
right. Anyhow, what a pleasure to see Ivan – and Zmeika, my
favourite young horse, the one I had broken in only the previous summer and that I had ridden in turn with my old Shalunia.
She trotted quite well, I noticed. Ivan had a good hand with
young horses: he did not rush them or treat them roughly,
and they could trust him to be even-tempered. The cold was

intense: Ivan shivered and rubbed his hands and stamped his feet. I wished he had his long thick coat on – but he could not – it was a coachman's livery coat, and that wouldn't have done.

On the way he told me all the news from Kamenka and gave me an idea of what I could or should try to arrange for all the servants. They had to be allowed to keep their lodgings until autumn; they must each have a horse and a cow, some pigs and hens, and each had to get the use of part of my fields and meadows to keep them going until they had either settled in their own farms (some of the men had their own house and plot of land in the neighbouring villages), or had found some other means of existence. With Ivan's help, my mind became more clear, and I felt as though I had enough courage to face the committee. I knew then what I wanted to ask for that would really help the people who depended on us for so many years.

At Lissino the dear old friends Kravchinsky and his wife received me with the usual warm welcome and hot tea, buns, jam and even cream. Only they had both grown so old! He did not joke with me as he used to, he did not start eagerly the political discussions over which we frequently had spent two or three hours on end. He merely waved his hand in despair – he was losing his last illusions about the better life to be brought to our country by the revolution. At one o'clock Ivan fetched me and we drove to the village school where the committee was to meet.

In spite of the intense cold, peasants were standing about outside the building – talking, stamping their feet, rubbing their hands. Some stood in the doorway, some on the steps, and I realised then that they were part of the crowd which simply had not been able to squeeze in. This promised to be quite an ordeal, I thought, both morally and physically – for I knew what a gathering of peasants in a closed space would mean, especially in winter with their clothes thawing off little by little . . .

Someone made a way for me through the crowd. I got a seat at the side of a long narrow table where twelve men were already seated – the committee, apparently. I knew only two members of this committee: one was the president of it – a German by origin – who was the deputy director of the Forestry School of Lissino, and the other was a young sailor – the Finnish type so often found in those parts – a boy from our village and a former swineherd on our estate.

No one got up, no one greeted me. The president mumbled something – he was obviously ill at ease, nervous, and did not know how he should behave; he fumbled in a pile of papers. Scarcely had I taken the seat when the young sailor, Andrei Kirpu, hastily stood up and turning to me said:

"Comrade Sollohub, why did you not come sooner to wind up the business of your estate Kamenka? Pray render account to the National Committee."

"I have no account to render and I do not see why I should have come to Kamenka. No one asked me about any winding up of business – since my estate was taken without any warning."

"But you should have come before – when summoned."

"I never have been summoned – nor asked to come. This is the first notice I have had; it comes from your committee – and here I am." Turning to the president I asked him whether any other summons or notices had ever been sent to me. He replied that there were none to his knowledge – he looked embarrassed. The sailor, still standing, looked at the other ten members as if waiting for their support – but all remained silent.

"I am sorry," I continued, "but apparently no other summons was ever sent, as you see."

"Well – perhaps not exactly a summons," said Kirpu reluctantly, "but your former employees, foresters, gamekeepers – they have written asking you to come . . ."

"Oh, that is another question. It is entirely my private business what my servants write to me or what I write to them. I do not think it concerns anyone else and not your national committee."

Kirpu sat down, the committee growled and coughed; the president took up more papers and uttered something about proceeding – and Kirpu left me in peace throughout the rest of the meeting.

The president started reading some regulations, stumbling over the entirely new terminology and evidently getting lost in it. I did not listen – it was useless as no one could follow the muddle. Looking round me I realised that I was the only one of my kind in this crowd – the only landowner and a woman besides. The place was packed. I heard the breathing of the public right up behind my back, I heard the snorts, sniffs, coughs and frequent remarks which were not really aggressive but somewhat sour, bitter, growly.

Soon I found a moment to state my case – the problem of my servants first. When I had finished talking, someone in the public shouted unpleasant remarks about "those slaves of for- mer masters"; other voices picked it up, adding "serves them right" and "let them fend for themselves now", and a general hostile murmur spread through the place. I felt extremely ill at ease; after all, I had set my heart on getting something for my servants, and I hated the thought that because of me their lives would be made unendurable.

The president, wishing to restore order, sat ringing his bell – a procedure which apparently pleased the public very much, as I noticed how the necks were craned and the people at the back jostled those in the front, eager to see what was happen- ing with the bell. At any rate the desired effect was obtained, the crowd quietened down and the discussions continued. The committee refused by unintelligible grunts or silent shaking of heads all my suggestions regarding the servants; I continued to insist and it really looked as if these discussions could go on for ever.

Someone on the committee finally had the good idea of moving on to the next question on the agenda – the question of

The engagement photograph of Edith to Count Alexander Sollohub
in the summer of 1906. She was 20, he was 22. Edith was not looking
forward to the responsibilities of marriage.

Kamenka, the country house of Count Alexander (Sasha) Sollohub, bought in 1903, used by Sasha and Edith as their family home until "nationalised" by the revolutionary authorities in December 1917. No photograph remains, but this sketch was later made from memory by one of their sons.

Count Alexander Sollohub standing beside two elk brought down "with a right and a left", i.e. using both barrels of the gun. The horse and groom in the photograph had been sent into the forest to bring the elk home. November 1906.

The children's pony Mousy harnessed to a sledge for Vladimir and Alec. Kamenka 1914.

Vladimir leading Mousy with Alec astride the pony's back. Kamenka 1914.

Edith's prowess with the gun was demonstrated in a 1915 bear hunt attended by the Japanese Ambassador in the imperial forest near Kamenka. The other men in the photograph were imperial forestry employees.

Photograph of Count Alexander taken in 1916 in army uniform, before his first posting to the Front. Edith was left to run the Kamenka estate.

In the war years, Edith was often in charge of the Kamenka estate. In this 1916 photograph she was supervising the sale of timber stock-piled in the forest.

A traditional "lineika" used for travelling on rough tracks through the forest. 1917.

what would be left to me of my property. This was an interesting topic – I felt all were on tiptoes to see the show. Apparently I still had the right to the main house and all it contained in the way of personal belongings. But then the question was put: "Shall we allow the citizen Sollohub to enter her house which is now sealed by the National Committee of Lissino?"

Again the murmurs all around, grunts and growls, until one clear voice from the public called out: "No – no – she can't be allowed into the house – she'll go against the people – she'll shoot at us."

"Yes – she'll shoot, she'll shoot – she'll go against the people – no – she can't be allowed into the house – she'll shoot . . ." This was a marvellous idea which seemed to have caught the fancy of the public, as everyone now took it up. I was so surprised at first and then so amused that I did not realise the unpleasant attitude of the crowd. Spontaneously I got up and said: "I thank you very much for the high opinion you have of my shooting – but I think it would not yet be worth while my starting to shoot at you – especially alone . . ."

A strange silence fell over the crowd after these words. Did these people see the ridiculousness of what they had got excited about? Or were they thinking of my words "not yet", which meant a lot to me, as I felt keenly the readiness to shoot but knew that common sense dictated otherwise? I really enjoyed this instant of sudden quiet – of taking stock – of temporary respite; it was an encouragement for me.

The committee was at a loss – especially the president who was looking down with concentrated interest into the files of papers. Then, in quick succession, he put forward some other questions regarding my private property, such as which horse to leave me, which cow, how much hay, etc. The old water-barrel horse was to be mine – but I protested, having got into the sport now, and insisted on having Zmeika who would be no use to a peasant. "No, no, no . . ." went the voices.

Finally, after three hours of discussion I turned to the president to tell him that it was time for me to go as I had to catch a train. I also told him that my claims and desires were now known to the committee and that I hoped this committee would discuss the problems further and would let me know the conclusions arrived at.

Again one of the men made a way for me through the pressing crowd. I hated this walk through the live alley – beards and shaggy hair and intent looks, the kerchiefs and thick woollen shawls of the women giving a gay patch of colour here and there. The air was thick, fog-like, no wonder there was one continuous coughing going on all the time – the smell was appalling. At the porch my devoted Ivan was waiting with the sledge and we drove off, the crowd forming a semi-circle in front of the school building.

I thanked God it was over; only then did I realise – or allow myself to realise – the unpleasant and dangerous moments I had been facing during these three hours. It had been a horrid experience but also a useful one in that it taught me something about the unsteadiness of a crowd.

The cup of tea, the friendly smiles and kind words of the Kravchinsky couple raised my spirits – here were people who were still my friends. An hour later Ivan came again for me. He was beaming.

"My Lady – I went back to the assembly – and scarcely had you left when all the questions were read over again and all your suggestions accepted. We get the lodgings and the use of fields and meadows – and each gets a horse and a cow – and Your Ladyship has the house and can go there whenever she likes – the keys are here at the committee and can be fetched any day – and Your Ladyship gets Zmeika too, not the old grey!"

He simply unpacked before me this mass of good news and was beaming as I had never seen him beam before. His expression was my reward for those ghastly three hours.

The return journey lived up to the unpleasantness of the earlier part of the day. The cold increased and the wind grew into a proper gale. We got to the station at seven, just in time for the train which was due to leave at seven-fifteen. I was sorry to see Ivan so frozen, and sad to say goodbye to him. However, he seemed to be quite cheered by the decision of the committee and I was glad that he would bring the good news to the other men.

The train stood at the side platform – no lights in any of the carriages, windows broken all along the train, and snow and ice trodden down in thick layers on the floor of the corridors and compartments, preventing the doors from closing. I felt my way into a semi-open compartment and sat down in a corner, trying to find shelter from the wind which blew through in all directions. I must have been alone in the whole carriage for I did not hear a sound. By seven-thirty there seemed to be more movement around the station – somebody shouted some orders – the engine puffed more energetically – it looked as if there was a chance of our starting. Another ten minutes and we were actually off. It got colder and colder. The train moved slowly and soon stopped altogether, after travelling a mere three or four miles. It waited some time for no apparent reason, then somewhere a voice shouted: "Hullo, why do we stop here?" and from somewhere at the head of the train another voice answered: "No steam – the wood is too damp – but don't worry, we'll get going soon." The shortage of coal and suitable timber was so great even then that freshly cut wood was being carted hastily to the stations all along the line and used right away by passing trains.

We moved on and went smoothly as far as Sablino. Here a crowd of young men climbed in with shouts and laughter, passed through my open compartment and settled with shouts and jokes at the other end of the carriage. They sounded as if they had had a good drink.

We started again, and the noise of the young men grew louder and louder. They joked and fought and rushed about, playing hide and seek apparently, and then they started betting whether they'd find other passengers on the train. I decided it would be safer to be on the open platform at the rear of the carriage from where I could easily jump off – it would not be difficult with the slow speed at which we were advancing. Noiselessly, in my felt boots, I crept out there and stood leaning out over the steps. We stopped every mile – or so it seemed – and stopped for long periods. The noise inside did not subside – it grew more and more unpleasant. It was past nine now, and we were still very far from Petrograd when normally the whole journey took an hour and fifteen minutes at the most.

Suddenly I heard steps approaching my end of the carriage. Three or four men came out, and one of them caught sight of me while the others were wrestling on the other side of the platform.

"Hullo, comrade, there you are – the passenger! How are you, youngster? Not too cold?"

What luck – he mistook me for a boy, probably because of my high grey fur cap which was rather like the military caps worn during the war. In a gruff voice, hiding my face in the depths of my bashlyk and fur collar, I answered: "Not so bad – one pulls along – the wind does blow a little."

"Come in and join us – it will be warmer all together. Come…"

"No, thank you – that's all right – I may get out at Pulkovo, or before that if we stop again in the fields near . . ."

"As you like – but don't freeze to an icicle here – mind," and giving me a good slap on the shoulder he turned round and joined his companions who, with curses and much stamping of feet, were going back into the carriage, "to try to get warm" as they said.

Gone – what a blessing – but for how long? Twice again they came, with noise and jokes – twice the same man asked me whether I was still alive and I grunted some unintelligible reply. Fortunately the noisy crowd left the train at Obukhovo, a suburban station, and finally – at about one o'clock in the morning – we reached Petrograd.

The railway station was empty – curfew hour had passed long ago. Together with the three or four other passengers who came off the train, I was mercilessly pushed out of the station and the big gates were closed and locked behind us. In vain I had asked two railway guards to let me stay somewhere in the station, as it was forbidden to go about the streets at this hour of the night. They only shrugged their shoulders and answered that it was equally forbidden for anyone to stay at the station.

Here I was, in the streets with scarcely any lights, lit by the whiteness of the snow but swept by the gale which blew the crisp snow powder into whirls. The other passengers had slunk along the walls in the opposite direction – into the suburbs apparently. I had to get home alone – a good forty minutes' walk – in streets where only the Cheka patrols and a few militia watchmen were expected to move at this hour.

How I went, how I found strength to run in my heavy fur coat, I will never know. But I remember that I ran more or less all the time, hiding under gateways and on door steps when I thought I saw some figures in the distance, running again when the street seemed clear. My heavy travelling coat reaching to my heels and not made for walking seemed to weigh a ton – but I had to keep running. Twice I stopped short at cross-roads hearing steps in the distance; once I dodged behind an upturned van and saw a patrol of three men with rifles pass along the other street. Finally I reached home, let myself in and only then did I feel the terrific strain. I fell down on my bed, hot, exhausted, unable to move.

The Rural Committee of Lissino kept its word, I am glad to say. All was done as I had asked – my house was at my disposal to stay in when I wanted – and Zmeika went to Ivan as I had neither food nor means to keep her. Encouraged by this, I felt there might be a hope of getting some things out of the house in Kamenka – things that I particularly cared for such as certain pictures, books, souvenirs, and also clothes which represented now quite an important value. But I knew I would have to get special permission from the central authorities.

Time after time I went to all the authorities I could think of, both in Tsarskoe, which was our district town, and in

Petrograd. I needed an official "paper" – this word alone still having a magic effect in the provinces. Finally, I discovered that the permission I wanted could only be given by the Commissariat for Agriculture. I went there and without further hesitation asked the man who was apparently a hall porter, or perhaps a reception clerk, to let me see the Commissar himself. A secretary, shaggy and without a collar, came out to speak to me and – of course – told me to go to other places and other authorities. But I declared that all these steps had already been taken by me without result, and that I would now have to speak to the Commissar himself. Finally I was shown into his office.

A middle-aged man in the Sunday-best outfit of a well-to-do peasant or cattle dealer, with a red beard and small grey eyes, greeted me with a slight nod.

"Your name, comrade?"

"Countess Sollohub," I said, for at the time I still felt it would show lack of courage to omit the title which we would have used in ordinary times.

The man frowned, and noted something on the pad on his right. I told him in a few words what I wanted.

"After all," he said, shrugging his shoulders, "your estate is nationalised, but if you still have the house at your disposal – what else do you want?"

I insisted that, being unable to live in this house since I had not been left any of the means of livelihood which would have made it possible for me to stay there, I wanted to take out my personal belongings and those of my family. The man asked me what exactly I wanted to remove, but as I began counting up the things he kept interrupting me with the words: ". . . No, you cannot take those things, they might be of use to the people."

At last I lost patience and said, when he stopped me yet again: "All right – if you look upon it like that, then everything could be useful to the people – except my pocket handkerchiefs."

He looked at me angrily at first, then smiled and said: "I see – all right – we will consider the matter – come again next week." Somehow I suddenly felt that the man was really going to try to do something for me.

When I came again the hall porter let me in as soon as he had announced me – although there were at least seven or eight people in the waiting room when I arrived. This looked a little like the old "bourgeois" ways – and it amused me very much.

The Commissar greeted me like an old friend. He said that he had not been able to get an official permission for me yet, but that he had received the verbal promise and hoped that the matter would be settled by the end of the following week.

"And by the way – when you come to me don't go up the big staircase into the general waiting room, take the little staircase to the right and come straight in – no need to wait – you know."

This was really a step forward in my dealings with the Bolshevik and I felt quite proud of this little bit of success. At my next call, I used the direct way as advised – and the Commissar received me with a satisfied smile.

"I have secured the official agreement of my colleagues – there it is," and he showed me a statement. "We must only inform the local district before you make use of this permission – otherwise misunderstandings might arise. But may I ask you – do you plan to remain here in Petrograd? I understand you have a family – have you possibilities of earning anything?"

I told him in a few words about my family, describing the children and avoiding any mention of my husband being an army officer.

"You have three boys – small ones? What will you do now to bring them up? How will you manage if all your property is nationalised?"

This sounded all terribly un-Bolshevik and just simply human. I was extremely puzzled, but the answer came straight out of me as it was the answer I gave to myself when these questions arose in my own mind.

"I don't know yet what I'll do. I don't see yet how I can manage to exist. But I feel confident that we have not received a good education in vain, we have not inherited an old culture to forget it all at a critical moment. These are values which no one can take from us, and it is for us now to show that our money and leisure were not just spent on enjoying ourselves – we got something better out of them and now we have to prove it."

It was a long speech – but somehow I felt that this man would understand, and I was glad of the opportunity to speak to a Bolshevik just as I felt and thought. The man got up. He took my hand and shook it heartily with both his.

"It is good to hear you say this. I wish there were more people thinking like that. Perhaps – if ever you change your viewpoint and think of working with us – please count upon me." We parted in the "bourgeois" style, with a handshake and no "comrade".

Poor fellow, he did not know how precarious his own position was, how little he could have helped me – if I ever had wanted to ask for his help. I never saw him again; a few days after my visit he was forced to resign – or was simply removed. Probably he had a train of thought which did not quite fit into the spirit of the Bolsheviks.

The house remained closed for more than a year. Then, in the autumn of 1919, when the White Army of Judenich took Tsarskoe Selo and tried to cut through the Petrograd–Moscow railway line at Tosno, Red troops were sent into that area and some were quartered in Kamenka. After their stay there was nothing to be done but to abandon it altogether. They had taken all they could carry away, they had burned most of the furniture, and when I asked Izmail what had become of our library, he said "They tore the pages out to use as cigarette paper or to make balls to play with. But there were some thick books – leather ones (our collection of Freemasonry books evidently) – those they used for the open fire-place. They were too lazy to get the wood outside."

That was the end of a once dear and much-loved home.

11

SEPARATION

The only cheering thing about the spring of 1918 was the return of Sasha and the boys from the south. How good it was to see their faces and hear their cheerful voices. The boys had all grown a good deal – Vladimir especially – and my first thought when I saw them was: "How shall we feed them all now that Kamenka is no longer ours?"

Soon after their return, as I was sitting in my study deep in thought, I heard a commotion in the hall.

"Ivan Ivanovich has come from Kamenka," shouted Vladimir with excitement, rushing into the room. "I have just seen him in the pantry; may I go and talk with him?"

"Wait, we'll go together," I said, wondering why the old gamekeeper had come to town now that he was not in our service any more. And there he was, tall and gaunt, cap in hand, his greyish hair well brushed off his high forehead, the clear blue eyes shining from under the bushy eyebrows. I was so glad to see him, his familiar figure, and he too looked pleased – smiling as he stroked paternally the fair hair of my boy who was showering upon him question after question.

"Yes, little master, Ryzka is not in your stables any more. She is in the village, and the pony and the donkey have also gone away."

"The pony is mine!" piped Alec, by now a most decided little man extremely conscious of his property rights. "Coachman

Ivan looks after my pony and must not give it away to strangers!"

"You don't know anything, Alec, it's the revolution now and the revolutionaries take away things from us when we have estates," said Vladimir sternly.

The discussion was threatening to become stormy as the inveterate feeling of ownership stored in Alec could not be easily moulded to the moods of fate and revolution. I left the boys to discuss the matter with Miss Taylor, and took Ivan Ivanovich into the study to hear from him all the news of Kamenka, however sad it might be.

In his picturesque and hurried speech he gave me an account of all recent developments there. I knew it was useless to ask any questions about our forests, about the game, but I could not separate myself or him from either of them. Had he not been the first to teach me the art of stalking a capercailzie at night in early spring? Was he not our best expert in raising a bear from the lair? Had I not learned from him endless numbers of stories about forest ghosts and goblins and spirits? As he stood now mentioning all the familiar names of meadows and brooks, of bogs and forest districts, I thought I saw them all again, just as I used to when we made our way through endless moors and thickets, when he strode with his long swinging step next to my horse showing me the way to some felling districts.

"Yes, I see, Ivan Ivanovich, all these meadows are to remain untouched this year, not cleared," I said, thinking of those meadows when I crossed them on skis with him early last winter, when I still believed in a meagre chance of keeping up the work and holding on to the place a little longer. It seemed such a distant past now, this life of work in the country. It seemed all years and years ago – and yet a few months only had passed since then.

"I keep an account secretly of all felling done in my district, my Lady," Ivan Ivanovich was saying now. "Don't worry about that, and when you come back you will know right away where things have changed and forests been cut. It will be easier for you then to put things in order again."

"Thank you, thank you so much. But be careful, don't run any risks, you might get into trouble. And who knows when we'll come back . . .?"

"The young masters will surely return," he replied, but his "surely" did not sound convincing and in his eyes I could read a hesitation, a doubt.

We then talked about his family and his face lit up ecstatically when I mentioned his son who was younger than Vladimir and somewhat delicate. "Yes, they are all right . . . they will pull through . . . they are at home in the village . . ." I was surprised at his seemingly carefree tone as he spoke about them and their future. He had generally shown such preoccupation and anxiety about their future for, having married late in life, he feared he would not live long enough to see them grow up. I was wondering half-consciously at his optimistic tone when he stopped abruptly and cleared his throat in a manner that brought me back to the present.

"May I ask you a question, my Lady?" he said, hesitating a little.

"Of course, Ivan Ivanovich, what is it?"

"Have all your estates and houses been taken from you, and taken for good?"

"Yes, I fear so. This town house now belongs to the municipality, we are told, and I don't know how long we'll be allowed to stay here."

"And the money in the banks has been taken first, has it not?"

"You are right. Nothing is left but what you see here in this house."

"I thought as much. Besides, the Count can't stay here – and he can't join 'them', the new government?"

"Of course he can't. I myself don't know where he is at the moment. He was here recently, but it is not safe for him to stay."

"What then are you going to do, all alone with the three little boys?"

"God alone knows, and only He can show me the way. I can't see it yet."

"Well, I have been thinking of it all these last weeks and I dream every night about it – and walking through my Veretinskaya dacha [the wildest district of the Kamenka estate and Ivan's favourite] I thought that this can't go on. Something must be done. So I came here. I did not tell them at home that I was going to town, no, the village people are cunning and they would guess at once that I was going to you. So off I walked in the night to the more distant station where people don't know me and . . . and I want now to ask you to take my savings from the savings bank. Here is my booklet, there are three thousand roubles there . . . it might help you for the start with the children, you know . . ."

It is difficult to describe what I felt. A lump stuck in my throat. I knew I was meeting one of those rare moments in life when a kind deed comes straight from a warm and under-standing heart – a kind deed which means a great sacrifice. I could not accept this sacrifice, but it was difficult to know how to refuse.

I tried to argue, to find the right explanation for my refusal. Finally Ivan Ivanovich gave in when I said:

"You have thought of my children, Ivan Ivanovich; let me think now of yours and for their sake ask you to keep your sav-ings. They are still very young and you may not be able to earn much now. I will never forget the help you wanted to give me – and God will help us both."

He had tears in his eyes as he left. My heart ached to see him go, to see him give a last pat to both bigger boys as they said goodbye in the hall. I knew I might never see him again but his kind deed would be always present in my mind. It was an expe-rience for which one remains grateful throughout one's life.

By summer 1918 the food problem had become really acute. Transport was still badly disorganised and official food distribution was inefficient and inadequate. So the hungry eyes of my boys quickly became my main worry. I could not bear to watch their disgusted faces as they tried to chew the so-called bread containing such unexpected additions as field peas, maize or straw. Even then one could get only a few ounces a day.

Something had to be done about this immediate predicament and some temporary solution had to be found. "Temporary" seemed to be the general attitude to everything at that time. In spite of all that had happened so far, we still clung to the belief that the power of the Bolsheviks would collapse and that sanity, law and order would be restored. I do not know what our feelings and actions would have been if we had known the Bolshevik regime was there to stay.

To get away from Petrograd seemed to be the best way towards a temporary improvement. I thought it might be a little easier to get food if we moved out of town. Miss Taylor and I took the boys to Tsarskoe Selo where we rented a villa for the summer season. I hoped that there we might be able to secure more easily the kind of food needed for growing boys. At Kamenka they had been accustomed to a plentiful supply of milk and butter, eggs and poultry – as well as meat and game from our shooting expeditions. But, alas, life in the suburbs offered us none of these.

Where else could we go? Petrograd was more or less a besieged town at that time, the Bolsheviks unsure of their hold on other parts of Russia and fearing imminent attacks from outside. The British Navy was in the Finnish Gulf and was constantly being mentioned with most uncomplimentary epithets in the Bolshevik "appeals to the people". There were also references in the press to "counter-revolutionary bands" in the south, which made us prick up our ears and kindled hopes that some kind of resistance in the south was gathering strength. But the south was very far away and it was difficult to get any definite news.

Meanwhile, should I perhaps try to secure some food by shooting, since I still had my firearms permit? Yes, this was a possible temporary solution and one which appealed to my sporting spirit. Alphonse and a friend of his were planning a shooting trip to Lake Ladoga. I had only seen the lake once, having crossed it by the passenger steamer which used to leave Petersburg every morning to steam up the Neva and then across the lake to the mouth of the river Svir. The impressions left by this seven-hour journey, by the stretches of reeds, the wide powerful Svir, the constant flocks of wild duck, geese and other water fowl – all this had fired my imagination and I could not resist the chance to try my luck shooting on the lake.

Alphonse and his friend had had the idea that we should join one of the cooperative organisations which were then cropping up, and suggest delivering to the organisation any game that we might shoot – a tempting proposition because of the food shortage – and in exchange the organisation was to help us in securing the necessary shooting and travel permits. Very soon a co-operative was found, with, as its president, a former butler of one of our uncles. Everything worked beautifully. The butler was only too pleased to give his gracious patronage, and secured for all three of us the required permits.

A long and restful trip all up the Neva with the impressive and gloomy fortress of Schlüsselburg at the entrance to the lake, some large barges, a few tugs, but scarcely any steamers or other boats. Then throughout the afternoon, the crossing of the lake, first following the southern shores – low marshy land with very few villages in sight, and from time to time a glimpse of the important canal that runs parallel to the shore and which was built to allow the passage of barges in winter and also when navigation on the lake is rendered difficult because of violent storms. By four o'clock we were far from the shore and soon all traces of land disappeared. For some hours at least we could forget the worries and dangers which had become our daily companions and we spoke lazily of the colours around us as the sun came low on the horizon, of the game we hoped to find the next day, and instinctively avoided any mention of the future.

Through half-open eyes I scanned lazily the surface of the lake, no land to be seen anywhere. But there, towards the north-east, one – no, two – straight lines on the water. I gazed at them too lazy to make any conjectures – lines, two lines, that was all. Alphonse raised his head, resting it on his hand; we heard some orders called out by the old captain who had sat placidly until then on the bridge behind us.

What could they be, these two lines? We both wondered. The steamer altered course towards them – some movement could be discerned on the nearest line, on its rising upper structure. "They are submarines!" said Alphonse, puzzled and laughing at his own words.

"Submarines in the lake? Too ridiculous – it is utterly impossible," I replied, but my eyes too could make out the unmistakable shape. They were grey, nearly silvery in this evening light, and we could discern figures moving on deck. Rising suddenly to his feet, Alphonse turned towards the captain's bridge. "I'll find out who they are and why we have come near them," he said. I lay still, looking at the two forms through half-closed eyes. It was so hard to abandon the realm of peace and quiet I had lived in those past hours. And the sun was still as glorious, the lake as silvery . . .

"They are Soviet submarines who take refuge here from the British naval units in the Finnish Gulf," reported Alphonse. "I had heard about some naval units having scampered away when the British ships appeared, but I admit, I only thought of smaller units slipping up the Neva – not submarines. We have been ordered to approach. The captain fears a search on board . . . Let's hope the search party won't be too thorough and won't ask too many awkward questions."

We stayed on deck. A small group of men on the nearest submarine signalled, our crew answered; some orders were given by the old captain who looked flustered and wiped his bald head with a handkerchief. Were we slowing down? Was a boat to be lowered? We waited – and the steamer went on, gliding past the two ships. Men on board the nearest submarine exchanged a few words with our crew, others were busy washing their linen – they looked so very harmless as we slipped away.

"Thank God," murmured Alphonse, "they let us go on without a search. The captain must have given them the proper answers!"

How relieved we felt as the dreaded shapes vanished in the evening light – but the feeling of peace and distance from daily worries had also vanished. Involuntarily my thoughts again hovered around permits and identity papers, guns and bulging cartridge bags; I dwelled on possible difficulties on arrival at our destination, on the checking of permits, on the altered attitude of the peasants in whose house we must stay for a couple of days. The feeling of being tracked – not individually, but as a class – was there again with all the unnerving thoughts it entailed.

The sun had set, we saw land now to our right – in an hour or two we would reach our destination, face the problem of getting safely through – but we also thought of tomorrow, of the sport we hoped to get – we were young and could switch easily from one world of thought to another.

On the first day I had as guide and gamekeeper a man whom I had just seen for a moment on the evening of our arrival. He was not exactly prepossessing, I thought. Dark eyed and with a scanty beard, the cap drawn deep over the forehead and a much darned ragged coat hanging on his bony shoulders, he looked gloomy and morose and certainly he was not talkative. Alphonse had seemed reluctant to let me go with this man, but it turned out that he owned the better and safer canoe, so I had to take him because of the canoe. Of course I soon forgot the man, as duck rose up in plenty and I was kept very busy all the time. By midday we had a good bag and reached our rendezvous for a picnic lunch on the island in good time. The breeze had freshened and rather low clouds were now hurrying from the west. After a quick meal and a rest we decided to move on. The low cloud was now running fast and the sky was darkening. We proceeded in the direction of the home village. It had got grey and murky, the wind seemed to blow harder and it had got colder too. As we approached the edge of the reeds a gust of wind startled me, and I noticed a shadow on my guide's face as he pulled his cap deeper over his ears.

"Where shall we cross the Svir?" I asked now, wondering a little about this crossing. The Svir had seemed a big expanse of swiftly running water as we crossed it that morning and I had a feeling that conditions were becoming worse.

"We'll have to try here, some fifty yards further, and we'll have to hurry for it will be getting dark much earlier today." These words did not cheer me particularly and when we swung out of the protection of the rushes into the open I certainly did not feel very courageous. "You'd better leave the gun now and take the rudder. Point across, on a slant, with the waves . . ." he added, giving a swift glance at the water running high now in the river.

It was a nasty crossing; I shall never forget it. The waves were running fast, the wind was blowing very hard and the canoe seemed to dance quite aimlessly on this angry stretch of leaden-coloured, blackish water. I held as fast as I could on to my rudder, with the sickening feeling that it was doing no good in these waves and was more often out of the water than in it. My hands became numb, the spray of the white crested waves showered over us and the canoe danced in a most vagrant and terrifying manner. "Hold on tight," called out my guide, "keep the boat steady half across the waves!" Of course I had to do my best, but it was not easy and it seemed that we did not make any progress as each oncoming wave threw us back yards again. How long it took us to cross the river I really cannot tell, but it was getting dark when we finally reached the opposite wall of rushes and diving into them found at last a respite from the wind. "Thank God!" said my guide, crossing himself and wiping his forehead. "It was not easy!"

Certainly, it was not easy, and I felt my limbs like wooden clogs now, cold, lifeless and terribly clumsy. And it was cold – or was it because of the wet clothes which seemed now to cling to my body? "Shall we get on towards the village or towards the island first?" I asked, just to say something and to hear a comforting word. "We can't get to the village tonight, it is too late. The island is nearer . . ." and my guide pushed now through the reeds and I sat doing nothing. It grew quite dark, I grew colder and more numb and indifferent until a bright spot of light beckoned between the reeds. "Look, a fire!" I called out, happy at the sight of a fire which meant warmth. "Yes, that is the island and they have made a fire there to guide us," answered my guide and his voice too sounded warmer. We pulled on, the fire grew bigger and at last we reached the island where Alphonse was waiting anxiously for us. The tea brought life into my numb body, the fire cheered me and I slept like a log, dug in up to my neck under the only haystack on the island.

After the excitement of this expedition I was glad to spend the final day of our visit on dry land, letting the men go out in the canoes while I stayed with the women of the village. The wife of my guide had suggested my going for mushrooms in the big forests looming at the edge of the fields, and as I loved looking for mushrooms in new places I willingly agreed.

We set out in the morning as soon as the men had left, and walked the two miles across the fields chatting about local life and conditions in the country. I took care to avoid mentioning anything political – anything that could be connected with the revolution, and the woman seemed entirely engrossed in her village interests.

After a good two hours' search for mushrooms in one of the most magnificent fir forests I ever saw, where daylight penetrated reluctantly as if not to disturb the seclusion of the semi-darkness under the trees, we decided that it was time to have a rest and perhaps some tea. By this time we had been joined by another older woman and a young girl with rosy cheeks and bright, laughing eyes. The girl was making fun of the two other women, teasing them about having forgotten

190

the best places for mushrooms and boasting about her two full baskets, which she could barely drag along.

I returned with the women to the village and we were given tea and some excellent rye pancakes filled with potato purée and taken hot out of the oven. It made me think of my old Niania who was from the far north and who could make delicious pancakes and buns out of the simplest rye flour with sour milk and a little butter.

A year later it was this guide who agreed to try to take me illegally across the border towards Finland, when I was trying to get out of Russia to join my children. Money was not worth much at the time and I had offered to leave him one of my guns as payment. He accepted the offer willingly, and was to take me across the Svir in his canoe. There I was to land on a sandbank which ran north among the reeds for a distance of about twelve miles and at the end of it I would have to wade through shallow water to avoid a village – which meant wading by night – until I reached a sandy cliff which marked the Finnish border. It was not exactly an easy task but with the prospect of reaching my children all tasks seemed feasible and I readily agreed to this plan. However, a week before the escape this guide came to Petrograd to tell me that he could not undertake to help me, because a strong garrison of Red Army soldiers had been posted in the village at the end of the sandbank, and there was no chance for me to get past their posts into Finland. I thanked him warmly for his warning and especially for the trouble he had taken in coming all the way to Petrograd. A good selection of cartridges was the most welcome pay he could have, and we parted great friends – never to meet again.

But in summer 1918, my boys were still in Petrograd and getting hungrier every day. What was I to do? Kamenka was no longer there. What about Waldensee, which still belonged to my two sisters? Cossacks had been quartered there during the war, and Mary, who had left Petersburg in 1916, found that much damage had been done but that some of the rooms were still usable. Here perhaps was a ray of hope. Since the signing of the Brest-Litovsk Treaty the war with Germany had come to an end and German troops occupied all of Poland and the Baltic Provinces, relatively close to Petrograd. Perhaps if I could get the boys to the newly independent Baltic States, food would surely be more plentiful there?

I made enquiries and was soon on the scent of something promising. Large numbers of people had fled eastwards from the Baltic Provinces during the war and, now that the fighting had stopped, these refugees all wanted to get back to their homes and relatives who had remained behind. The Bolsheviks were doing all they could in 1918 to help with this repatriation, because for them it would mean fewer mouths to feed.

For once, the inevitable hurdle of "documents" did not prove too formidable. A friendly talk with the chairman of our House Committee in Petrograd produced quite satisfactory "certificates" to the effect that all my children and myself had been born in the province of Estonia. This was not entirely true, but our family connections with the Baltic were sufficiently strong to give my assertions a ring of authenticity. The only sad part about it was that Miss Taylor, as a British citizen with no possible claim to Baltic citizenship, would not be able to accompany us and I would have to look for new and untried people to help me with my sons. The Baltic Committee, largely composed of Baltic gentry only too glad to help out their own kind, received my application favourably. Three over-loaded trains of refugees had left Petrograd already, and we were promised places in the fourth train.

This is how we found ourselves, one clear and sunny morning in the first days of September, in a shed in the goods yard of the Baltic Station. I had with me the three boys, one tutor, one governess, a cook and Elsa the devoted maid. Sasha was not coming with us. Having returned from the north where he had been most of the summer, he was going to try to make his way to the south where he hoped to be of some use to those "counter-revolutionary bands" about which we had heard.

We were in for a long wait at the Baltic Station. The goods train we were to board was not yet at the station, and we learned it would not be ready until some time in the afternoon. So we wandered off in search of food and surprisingly enough managed to get a good lunch by the standards of that time. A restaurant next to the station had kept intact its red plush, gold and crystal decorations, waiters in their traditional garb, heavy silver dishes and there was really an almost pre-war atmosphere about it. Only the fact that the steak was horse meat reminded us of the unsavoury reality.

We returned to the goods yard and sat on our luggage until well into the afternoon. We looked at the people going with us, and noticed that as well as German, Lettish and Estonian refugees speaking to each other in their own languages, there was a good deal of Russian being spoken by "refugees" of a somewhat different kind – such as ourselves. It was surprising how many people among our acquaintance had suddenly remembered their Baltic origins!

As the sun went down it became colder in the goods yard, and I realised that we had not packed any winter clothes – so difficult was it to believe that we might not be coming back. As there was no sign yet of our train, I let Elsa hurry back to our flat and return with some pullovers and the boys' overcoats.

Finally, late in the evening silence was called for and the elected leader of our train-load made an announcement. Apparently the goods station Commissar would not let the train be assembled, in spite of all the official papers being in order, unless he was given 10,000 roubles. There must therefore be a collection taken to raise this sum, and members of the "train committee" would come round and collect the roubles in their hats. The Commissar must have been an honest man, by his standards, for after the money had been collected the train did eventually turn up, and we could at last load the sleepy children into the moderately clean cattle trucks which were to become our home on wheels for the next three days.

Other commissars were to be faced all along the line – station commissars, district commissars, security commissars and every other kind of commissar imaginable. Every station and every commissar meant a new negotiation, another bargain to be struck, another delay of many hours as money was again collected or confirmation requested from the Cheka or the railway authorities in Petrograd. Some of the commissars quite rightly thought that there was a most unusual proportion of "bourgeois" faces and able-bodied young men in this lot of refugees, so they wanted either to derive some profit from the situation or make sure of extra official cover, on top of all the permits we already had, before letting the train proceed further down the line.

Changing engines was a further problem. At times an engine was to go to a certain station only and, once there, there would be no other engine to take over; so the engine driver had to be coaxed or bribed into taking us a bit further until another one could be found. As for fuel, several times the train stopped and eager volunteers from amongst the passengers would form a chain to transfer wood from the nearby forests where it lay ready cut and piled but not yet transported to the railway sidings. Other passengers meanwhile would stand about and watch, while some would pick berries or mushrooms – or simply lie in the fresh grass and talk. What surprising things came out in these talks. Most of the younger men were talking of their plans to make their way through German-occupied Poland back into the Ukraine and the south, eager to liberate Russia from Bolshevik control. They were full of a spirit of adventure and were already enjoying the feeling of freedom that we all felt as the train neared the Soviet frontier.

It took three days for our train to travel from Petrograd to the demarcation line at Pskov – a distance of less than 200 miles. It was evening when we reached the Soviet frontier post at Toroshino – a few shacks in an open field, with the inevitable commissars in leather jackets and their rough looking henchmen with machine gun belts worn diagonally across their chests. This was perhaps the worst moment of the journey, when the long hours of waiting were particularly painful and the threat of being turned back especially unnerving. But then a few whistles were blown, a bell rang, the Bolshevik guards receded from us as the train crossed a few hundred yards of no-man's land and entered the brightly lit German-occupied Pskov Station.

How strange suddenly to see again those trim and disciplined soldiers, clean-shaven, all buttons buttoned, standing sentry duty or guiding our sleepy crowd to the checkpoints; officers calmly giving orders to soldiers who saluted and clicked the heels of their boots. They were still supposed to be our enemies (we were hoping for a victory of the Allies in the West which would deliver us from the shameful Brest-Litovsk Treaty) – yet it was an unquestionable joy to see proper troops once more, after the uncouth revolutionary militia on the other side.

At 3 a.m. we finally reached "Lager Deutschland", a transit camp where we would be kept in quarantine for the next two weeks for the required formalities of de-lousing, sorting out according to destinations and successive vaccinations against smallpox, typhoid and cholera. The camp was in the grounds of a large, recently built agricultural college set in a pine forest. We were assigned in groups of 16–20 to dormitory huts with double-tiered sleeping bunks, which were a great improvement on life in the cattle trucks – but not exactly comfortable all the same. However, food seemed abundant, and wine could be obtained by slipping under the barbed-wire fence around the park and going shopping in the picturesque old town of Pskov. There was no hot water in the camp, but warm "coffee" was supplied every morning. Real coffee was something that the Germans could no longer obtain, and the tasteless black liquid given out was used by many of the men for shaving rather than drinking. It certainly produced a most unusual looking lather.

Fortunately the cramped living conditions did not worry any of us too much, probably because we were all so glad to be over the frontier, and a general spirit of friendliness prevailed. My boys made a number of new friendships, developing in particular a great admiration for young Count Muraviev-Amursky – already a Colonel at 24, after four years' war service – who was now heading for Kiev to take up arms against the Reds. No less admired by them was Count Adlerberg, who owned an extensive collection of tin soldiers and was a great expert on all European military uniforms. There was also an enormously powerful fellow called Ettlinger who had such muscles in his arms that he could not reach his own neck, and had to have it washed for him every morning by his frail, sylph-like blonde wife – much to everyone's amusement and delight.

Then came the day of liberation with a few speeches, greetings, thanks, reciprocal good wishes – from which any political references were tactfully avoided by both sides. We were now on our own, free to move, free to breathe, free from searches and free from constant document checks.

I had decided to go first to Dorpat, an old university town in Estonia, where we had family connections and could stay among friends while deciding whether to make for Waldensee. On our arrival by train in Dorpat early in the morning, we were met by friends who took us to the restaurant of a local club for breakfast. "Look, Mother, look!" cried Alec, staring open-mouthed at cakes – yes, really beautiful creamy and sugary cakes – a sight long forgotten in Petrograd. White bread and butter was in abundance, and it is not surprising that this breakfast remained for ever a milestone in the memories of my boys.

We took a house in the quiet Pepplerstrasse, no. 3, near a church, and with a fairly large garden behind it. At the entrance to the garden we found, surprisingly, a German sentry on duty. Was this unexpected honour meant for us? No, we soon learned that it was for a larger house at the end of the garden, the residence of the garrison commander, General Eichhorn. He was a kindly old man, who saluted us as he drove past and sometimes gave sweets to the children.

What wonderful sunny late summer days, what a wonderful sensation to sleep in peace and not fear the ominous bell or knock at the door! What a picturesque life it was in German-occupied Dorpat! A military band played for an hour every morning in the main square, amidst the medieval houses and with the population promenading around. The children enjoyed themselves and I think Vladimir was old enough to share my sense of relief that, so far, our plans had worked out well. He was fascinated by this little town, by the different elements that went to make it up. At the head of society there were the "Baltic Barons", descendants of the Teutonic knights, Protestant and German speaking, but with unswerving personal allegiance to the Emperor of Russia for whom their large families provided generations of officers and diplomats. Then there were the townspeople, also German speaking, who had been settled in these Baltic towns for many centuries. Coming into the towns from outside were the Estonian speaking country people, and others speaking Lettish, like our own dear Elsa. And finally there was Russian, the language of the officials, the civil servants and the larger merchants; yet all these different languages and cultures seemed to be able to exist in harmony. Vladimir was developing a strong interest in history and in the workings of society, and impressed his new tutor with the breadth of his vision. "He will make a good diplomat," I found myself thinking. But for which country? Would he ever be able to go back to his own? . . .

Yes, soon enough the practical problems caught up with us. It was wonderful to have freedom but food and other necessities had to be bought, and the supply of money I had been able to bring with me was dwindling. Reluctantly I decided that I must go back to Petrograd to sell things from the flat and so raise enough money to tide us over to better days, when things would be once more "normal", when this temporary bad dream would come to an end.

An unexpected difficulty was the reluctance of the German authorities to grant permits for a return to Soviet Russia.

They were perhaps influenced by the fact that Communist ideas were spreading more virulently than they had expected, and they perhaps wanted to discourage contact with the Soviet-occupied territory. But still, my case was clear-cut and my references such that I could scarcely be suspected of being a carrier of Communist propaganda. My request was forwarded by the authorities in Dorpat to the Armee Oberkommando VIII. Every morning for the next few weeks, my daily walk with the boys would take us to the army headquarters to see if the longed-for reply had arrived.

It was late October when it finally came through, and I knew I had to tear myself away for what I felt would be an unpleasant job – but one which should be quickly over. I did not suspect, when kissing my three boys goodbye and assuring them that I would be back after two weeks, that it would in fact be more than two years before I saw them again. On November 11th, 1918, an armistice was signed in the West, the German troops began to withdraw, and there began a new struggle which brought back warfare in the Baltic States and left me separated from my boys by a closed and cruel frontier.

12

ALONE IN PETROGRAD

I had come back to Petrograd in the hope of saving something, selling whatever possible, so as to provide for the existence of my children. I knew very soon that I had failed and that my efforts were utterly in vain. Once I had seen that all thought of raising money had to be abandoned, and once Sasha had left in November to join the White Army – or whatever units he could find that might still be carrying on the fight in the south – I decided that I, too, must try to leave.

To get out of this city of madness, out into a free country and rejoin my children – these were my only thoughts and they turned unceasingly round in my head. What a fool I had been to come back, to re-enter of my own free will the tightening circle from which it was now almost impossible to escape, and from which every one of my friends and acquaintances still in Petrograd were endeavouring to flee. But by now the frontiers were closed and did not offer the slightest crack through which to escape.

Legally there was apparently no possible way out, as the simplest request for a passport in my own name would have brought immediate arrest. I was about to send in my petition for a passport, accompanied by the required doctor's certificate, when a kind soul stopped me just in time – on the very day I was going to the Commissariat of Foreign Affairs with these papers in my pocket. I was warned that mutual friends of ours, elderly people, had just been arrested a day or two before, after having sent in their petition for a passport – and they were not the only ones. Evidently the desire alone to go abroad aroused the suspicions of the authorities and therefore this legal way of leaving the country seemed to be barred.

I was thus obliged to look for unofficial or illegal ways of leaving Communist Russia, and for some weeks I did not meet with any success – until one day, when definite help was promised me by the Danish Red Cross.

The Danish Red Cross was at the time the only foreign official organisation remaining in Petrograd, and the relief work it carried out on a large scale was worthy of the greatest admiration. Hundreds of daily rations of milk, sugar, hot soup, etc. were distributed to mothers and children at the headquarters.

As I knew several people working there it had been possible to talk matters over very frankly and I had been told to be ready to leave at a moment's notice. All I knew was that we were to cross into Finland – a very short journey – and what next? I really did not trouble myself about it. Every second day I was to call for possible instructions. This was my purpose as I pushed the door open one morning as usual – and a soldier appeared on the threshold. I stepped back, but too late – the man took me by the arm and made me enter. I knew that I was arrested or, rather, that I had fallen into a trap of the Cheka, and my first feeling was that of anger for having fallen into it so easily, and I blamed myself for such stupid carelessness.

"What do you come here for?" asked a Commissar in the entrance hall.

"I come here often for some milk and soup for children," I boldly replied, looking round at a large number of women and children sitting around in the hall.

"All right. Wait for further orders," was the reply.

I waited, we all waited – for seven hours. Men with and without revolvers and rifles, men in uniform and men in civilian clothes came up and down the stairs, in and out of the building; women in large numbers came in and our group grew to more than a hundred people – as far as I could judge. Children began to cry, lonely and terrified as many had come without their parents; mothers begged to be allowed to go home where their children had remained locked up alone in the house for the time of the mother's absence. I remember especially a young woman, one whom I knew slightly, who had a baby of a few months that she was nursing herself. She had left the baby at home, a few houses away, and had the keys with her as her husband worked on the outskirts of the town until late in the evening. She was in despair about the child and suffered great discomfort herself as the feeding time came and went. With tears in her eyes she begged the soldiers to let her see a Commissar who might understand the situation and let her go home – under escort if necessary – and allow her to fetch the child. The soldiers shook their heads, looked at each other in doubt – but did not dare move. When she approached some of the uniformed men passing through the hall, they pushed her aside and told her to wait, her turn would come, other business was more important . . . and so on. It was heart-rending to see her anguish and despair.

I stood near the door where the crowd was less dense, as people feared standing in a draught. Suddenly a man's voice shouted from the top of the stairs that women who had come for food supplies could be released. There was a rush for the door, I was pushed forward by the crowd and was one of the first three to get past the Commissar who, holding the knob of the door, asked again the reason for my call. "For milk and food for the children," I repeated, and he opened the door without a word.

I was out in the street and free again – I felt like shaking myself like a dog let off the leash. It was getting dark, the day had seemed endless. I ran home, thankful that neither my name nor my address had been taken down by the Commissars.

All the evening I thought of the poor nursing mother, hoping that she had got out too. Three days later I met her husband at the house of friends. He told me that mother and baby were safe and well, although on the day of the arrest his wife had returned home only at midnight. A counter-order had been sent down just after I had slipped through, and the doors were closed again for another six hours. Only eight or nine women had succeeded in getting out the first time, and I was one of them. The counter-order was given as the personal documents of the women present were to be verified, and a proof of their call for provisions had to be produced. I really had been lucky that I had not been questioned more closely.

The word "arrested" was, I think, one of those we invariably linked with the names of friends and it sounded quite normal at the time. Friends were always either threatened with arrest, or had just escaped arrest – or were indeed arrested. The ways and means of escaping were remarkable and the record of such escapes would fill many thrilling volumes. But my memory was never good enough to keep track of all the lucky escapes over which, despite the seriousness of our plight, we often rejoiced and laughed amongst ourselves.

The former officers were of course those whose position was the most difficult. I remember amongst others a young officer, Count Andrey T., who had no identity papers and carried on an illegal existence month after month. No one had the right to spend the night in any house without having registered with the "house commissar" or "house commandant". Andrey could not register at any house without risk of arrest, either as a "suspect" for being an officer, or as an "enemy of the people" for being titled, or as a "deserter" for not having joined the Red Army. How he managed it I never knew, but he seemed to dodge arrests with great skill and presence of mind. We frequently met at the house of his aunt – an elderly woman, the wife of a well-known general and mother of several high-ranking army officers.

This aunt, Madame R, still lived in her private house, in the rooms she used to occupy in normal times. Most people by then had withdrawn into as few rooms as possible, closing the rest of their house because of the impossibility of heating and the absence of servants. But Madame R. remained surrounded by all her magnificent furniture and works of art, and the tea table was laid as if it were well supplied with the usual cakes and fruit – instead of meagre pieces of black bread and an occasional plate of water biscuits. She had been arrested, then released, and house-searches were frequent – but her spirit was undaunted. She did not seem to worry over the fate of her husband and sons who had all been obliged to flee the country, and she even succeeded in seeing the funny side of things, laughing heartily with the young people – her daughter-in-law and numerous nephews and nieces who were always sure of a warm welcome. I can still hear her voice greeting me one day with the words:

"You don't know, ma chère, what an amusing evening we had yesterday – c'était un peu désagréable un moment – but we laughed so much afterwards! Imagine, Andrey was here for a cup of tea in the evening when suddenly the bell rang and Ivan announces the Cheka – ces horreurs! Andrey était merveilleux! He walked out through the side door into the hall just as the search party came in here, right behind their backs. Then he slipped into the front hall where the two men left on watch were gaping at the stuffed bear shot by Paul. And then – he slipped into the lift, hid under the seat, and pressed the button. You know how the old lift always sighs when it starts – well, the two men on watch were terrified – they evidently thought that the bear was coming alive – and they backed away without noticing the lift moving. J'aurais voulu les voir!"

At this moment the door opened and Andrey himself came in, with a smile on his fine face.

"I hear my lift experiences are being told. Ma tante, you exaggerate surely – it was a natural thing to do in the circumstances. But if you knew how my legs ached after spending all that time squeezed under the seat in the lift . . . I am sure that my father's gout can't be worse."

"My dear boy, you play with fire, you will get burnt one day – can't you really go away after all?" said the aunt.

"No, I am afraid I can't go yet. I can't leave sister Betty alone – she must get away first . . ."

"Yes, I know, we hope to be able to arrange things for her, there is a possibility . . . But where are you going now, Andrey?"

"Dear aunt, I must be home before eleven, before the last plank is lifted."

"Plank? What plank? Some new invention of yours?"

"Not exactly, but I spent the last two nights on one of the timber barges along the Palace Quay – a very good address!" he added laughing.

"How did you manage to get there – on the barges? Cela doit être infecte!"

"Well, it is not exactly comfortable, nor does it smell only of timber. But I can stretch out and really sleep. The owner is one of our village men – from the Novgorod place – I met him on the quay, we talked about things and came to this arrangement. He is a nice chap and keeps watch for me. I can't spend more than three nights there though, or I might get him into trouble – the people from the neighbouring barge were away but are due back and they might see me coming and going, you know . . ."

"God bless you, my boy," said the aunt, making the sign of the cross over Andrey, "and come again soon. Look for the signal – the curtain in my salon." We all knew this curtain across the third window from the corner: when it was tightly drawn, it meant safety; when it was pushed aside, however slightly, it meant danger.

The last I heard of Andrey was that, one evening when the house of his brother-in-law was being searched, he got out of the window of the pantry and made his way on the ledges to the drainpipe and down it into the street. He got through all right that time, but apparently a few days later he was caught during a street "round-up" and was never heard of again. His sister got out of Russia with the aunt – under assumed names and with faked passports – as foreign citizens. They were among the lucky ones. In the course of time the Cheka and other Soviet functionaries became better organised and trained, gained in experience too and our situation became more and more difficult. Many friends lost their lives crossing the border into Finland or the Baltic States. Many were caught in these attempts and were put in prison or exiled to Siberia or some distant province. Many simply disappeared and no trace of them could ever be found.

By Christmas it was clear to me that there was no way, at present, to escape. On Christmas Eve I was alone – and this was hard, very hard. Needless to say my thoughts wandered to the boys, as I wondered where they were and how they were, and thousands more questions. No news from them since the middle of November – it seemed very long. When and how could I join them? So many, many uncertainties and difficulties grew up around me day after day. The house empty, bleak, terribly silent – and everything so black around me. I looked wistfully at the furniture of the various rooms, at the Italian pictures on the walls, the Gobelins and Japanese tapestries. It had taken decades to assemble all these works of art. Already it was almost impossible to imagine that these rooms had been full of laughter, that music had sounded from the grand piano, and the rooms had been warm and well-lit which now stood cold and dim and dusty.

It was December 24th by the newly reformed calendar, but the Russian Church did not recognise the new dates and therefore the celebration of Christmas in most churches was to take place thirteen days later. However, the Catholic churches were celebrating Christmas now and I decided to get a small tree and make my study look festive, with a few white wax candles on the tree and one silver star at its point.

A real winter gale was blowing as I left the house some time after 10 o'clock to go to the midnight mass at St Catherine – the large Catholic church on the Nevsky. The streets were only dimly lit by one lantern here, another there – no carriages, no sleighs – here and there a hurrying dark figure disappearing rapidly in the darkness. It was a long walk, and I hurried through the snow hiding my face in my high fur collar and endeavouring to keep my hands warm. The less familiar streets looked even darker and certainly more terrifying; this was the right setting to remind me of all the cases of robbery, which were becoming very frequent at the time. It all looked so empty and dead – it was hard to believe that there were people behind these silent walls, behind the dark blank windows, and dark entrance doors against which the snow had drifted high – as if no one ever went in or out of them.

Figures began to appear, hurrying in the same direction; I guessed they were also bound for the church – and I felt less lost in this black stillness. Figures going up the broad steps, stamping the snow off their felt boots, shaking it off their coats and caps – a few words of greeting between friends – Polish talk mostly, with here and there some other Slav language. The doors of the church swung open and bright light streamed out – light from many candles, from a Christmas tree – light spread over human faces tired and worn but full of inner quiet. Another world – a world of peace.

Midnight mass had begun, music, singing, people kneeling and praying in the flickering light of the candles. A crowd lost in prayer – prayer, a word despised now by the new rulers, a word laughed at and hated by them. For once I was happy in a crowd – happy because this crowd had forgotten selfish motives, put aside hatred and bitterness, and felt the presence of God in light and peace – in spite of all the evil, hatred and brutality outside.

Mass finished and the crowd moved reluctantly towards the doors. A gust of biting cold wind made us shrink into the protecting fur of coats and caps. Night everywhere, muffled steps in the soft snow, people streaming out of the church and hurrying away, first in groups and then singly – all were silent, as if afraid of losing the bit of light and happiness we had all just experienced.

In the lonely streets again a feeling of terror seized me. I saw two women who were going in the same direction on the other side of the street. I crossed and asked whether I might join them. A muffled voice, a vague answer – and I said thank you in Polish. "Ah, you also come from the church?" was the quick reply. "Yes, it was a beautiful mass," I answered. One woman murmured something – the other nodded her head covered by a thick shawl over a fur cap. "Yes – a beautiful mass – how happy we are to have that still . . ." We walked on in silence as far as my street corner. They had at least another half hour's walk before them.

"God's blessing be with you – and happy Christmas," said my companions, and they disappeared in the white darkness of the drifting snow. And so it was, that that Christmas Eve remains in my memory as a quaint contrast of dark and light – if I can put it in these simple words – of oppressing darkness and misery and of vivid light of inner simple faith. The light side of the picture prevails – why? I don't know – probably because inner joys last when dangers are forgotten.

I was alone in the apartment, except for Masha, my former maid, who had chosen to stay on. She had a friend in the neighbourhood, a black-whiskered chauffeur, and together they made a living out of selling illicit alcohol. (He supplied her with motor fuel and she distilled it in some primitive way to make an evil-smelling strong drink.) I was alone to handle all the new problems which cropped up daily, often urgent, often unexpected and without any precedent. Every day there were new Communist "decrees" and ordinances. A "Communist Commandant" was appointed for each apartment block. I knew that I must face an interview with the Commandant of our particular block, that I must control my real feelings and appear calm and indifferent in his presence. Thus, summoning up my courage and conscious that I must do all in my power to keep the flat as a home for my family, I went down the three flights of stairs and across the yard to the small door which had been pointed out to me as the dwelling of the new Communist House Commandant. I knocked at the door, which was immediately opened by a small boy of about twelve. In the back of the room sat an older man bent over a pair of boots that he was polishing vigorously.

"Could I speak to the House Commandant?" I asked the boy.

The man turned round abruptly, and I gazed in amazed recognition at the red beard, and the beaming smile.

"Edinka! Countess! Yes, here I am now, times have changed . . . Yes, I am the Commandant . . . who would have thought it . . .?" and he stood there with his broad smile and a strange sorrowful expression in the eyes of old Ivan, my father's former coachman.

I was so taken aback that I could not think what to say, how to address him. In a few words he told me how he had been appointed by the "new authorities" because his daughter-in-law knew them all (I quickly noted this for it meant I must keep well out of the way of that daughter in-law) and he wound up by saying, "Times have changed, no carriages to drive, no horses to care for, I can just as well be a Communist and be in the old house!"

This was an unexpected conclusion but Ivan was here, Ivan could not have changed much and I could talk to him – probably – without fear. Cautiously I sketched out the situation, avoided mentioning my husband, who as an officer would evidently be "suspect" and it was better for us both that Ivan should know nothing. Ivan only nodded his head, ordered his boy to note down what I wanted and what my problems were, frowned and stroked his beard, repeating: "We will see to it . . . we'll manage . . ." But this first meeting was inevitably somewhat strained, and I left soon fearing some stranger might call. As Ivan opened the door for me, he patted my shoulder and smiling childishly from under his bushy eyebrows said swiftly, "Come to me whenever you want help – I'll find the way to wriggle out!"

How relieved I felt and what an utterly unexpected surprise it had been to see old Ivan, in this exalted position, after all the years that I had lost sight of him. Was it too much to hope that he would remain, as before, a devoted old friend?

Ivan kept his word and helped me in a quiet, unnoticeable way throughout the year and a half that I remained in my house in Petrograd. He was really my "guardian angel", helpful and clever in getting me on the right side of the "new law". And this he did even though he was illiterate; it was his little son who had to read out aloud every new decree, every new ordinance which came out, for the old man to ponder over. But by the time I had read the paper and came down to ask him for advice, Ivan had already found an answer to the new difficulties.

Thus, one morning, instructions were issued according to which so many square yards per head were allowed as living space, the surplus being put at the disposal of the municipal authorities. In many well-to-do houses of the residential quarters, entire families of factory workers, or groups of soldiers and sailors, had already been billeted upon the owners who were strictly assigned their own small "living space". Worried by this prospect, as three rooms only were occupied in my sixteen-room apartment, I went for advice to Ivan. He met me with a knowing smile which meant "I know what you have come for!" and added that he had just worked out a plan for me and was already carrying it out. Pointing to his boy who was bending over house books and papers, Ivan said in a triumphant tone: "You see – Vaska is copying out of the house-book the names of suitable people who died here in the course of the last few years. You see – I will say they are alive and all live in your house. They are registered now as your tenants. Will that do? . . ."

I was aghast, and then I understood. "Dear Ivan, but this is marvellous! Shall I learn their names?"

"No, you go home and put some sort of bed in all the rooms, and then hang up here a skirt and there a pair of trousers – well, you know, to show someone lives there – and if the authorities turn up, I will talk to them, that will be better . . ."

As I thanked him effusively, he gave me one of his broad placid smiles and said: "There it is, you'll have to live with the dead souls, they are not bad people – And very quiet tenants."

They certainly were – and I never knew their names; but in putting down coats and trousers, hats and shoes, stray brushes and shawls near the bedsteads arranged all over the place, I pictured to myself who these dead souls were and soon imagined their names and occupations as I thanked them in my thoughts for the good turn they were doing me. True to his word, Ivan did all the necessary introductions when Communist search parties appeared – searching for people hiding, for money, jewels, firearms, photographic cameras, and anything else which might momentarily interest the individuals making the search. Ivan walked in with the head of the search party and rattled off by heart name after name of my "tenants" as he led the way from room to room. I was always referred to by Ivan as the "hostess" and as being the wife of "a very good Red Air Force man now in Moscow". Once or twice I heard him explain the absence of my tenants, saying that several of them worked in a night shift in a factory, while others had been sent to the provinces on a government job, and someone was having a baby in hospital. So it all worked to perfection: the house search went its very unpleasant way, opening cupboards, pulling out drawers, unlocking boxes, throwing clothes out of cupboards to see whether weapons were hidden in the depths of these enormous old-fashioned linen and clothes cupboards. And after four or five hours of search they would walk away with a sleepy Ivan talking ponderously and patiently, unperturbed, unruffled, probably having to accompany the search party to some other part of the building. What I marvelled at was Ivan's readiness on the spot with suitable answers, something one would least expect from an elderly man who had spent his working life as a coachman and who could not even read or write.

Another instance of Ivan's helpfulness concerns the hiding of my guns. Since 1917 I had been hiding our sports guns and our collection of old guns in the house, in spite of decrees ordering the delivery of all arms to the authorities. A couple of sports guns had been taken by the peasants when Kamenka was "nationalised". The better guns, which were in the special care of Sidor the gamekeeper, had been hidden by him and the Kamenka coachman Ivan, who together had taken the guns to Ivan's own *izba* in the next village some six miles away and had dug them into the ground under the floor. Still, there remained seventeen guns in our town house, and about as many pistols and revolvers – an impressive arsenal as there was plenty of ammunition for the modern weapons. But I simply could not bring myself to deliver all these good clean weapons into the hands of the Bolsheviks; I felt it would be disloyal to let them go where they might be used against innocent people, or anyhow pass through the hands of people I despised. So I kept them, hiding them in a wall cupboard which was very unobtrusive in a passage and which I papered over myself, papering the whole wall of this passage.

In the end, when things were going from bad to worse I found I could not stand the strain of the "secret", especially as the discovery during the frequent house searches would have brought disaster not only upon myself but upon the people around me, such as my maid Masha, and the old invalid lady to whom I had let a room, and also to Ivan who would have to answer if my stock were discovered. Unbearable thought.

One day, tired and worried, I went down to look for Ivan in his little flat near the stables. He was alone at home and we could talk undisturbed. I told him the exact number of weapons I had: so many modern guns, so many old guns, so many pistols and so many rounds of ammunition. Ivan listened patiently, shaking his head as I spoke.

"A bit of an arsenal," he finally muttered. "We'll have to see what can be done. Give them up? We'd be asked why we did not do so before. They probably should disappear," he concluded.

"I am so sorry, Ivan, to give you so much trouble with this question. But you see, how could I give up these guns we used for sport, these old guns which have served gentlemen in the old days, how could I give them up to these Bolsheviks – and who knows for what purpose they might use them?"

Ivan continued to shake his head. "No, those dirty hands are not used to good noble weapons, no . . . they would not even know how to use them properly . . ." Inwardly I had to laugh, for here was a Communist official expressing a very definite and uncomplimentary view about his leaders. "Well," he added after a few minutes, "I know what we'll do: we'll dig them in in your old coach house, right here near the stables, the door next to the back stairs, no carrying about anywhere. We'll do it tonight, before house-search time. You oil them well, wrap them up in paper and rags not to get rusty, for one day perhaps you or the Count can fetch them. That's the best. My son will dig a deep hole under the floor – the floorboards and beams can be easily moved, they are loose and old. Go now and prepare it all. God bless you – Edinka," he added as he always did when a little disturbed.

Dear old Ivan. I rushed back home, collected the necessary rags, hunted up the last bottles of "Newarks" oil we had always used to clean our guns, and settled down to the job. By night-fall all the guns, wrapped up like Egyptian mummies, lay on the floor of the secret wall-cupboard. I kept them well out of sight as a safety measure in case of an unexpected, special house-search. Ivan turned up at the appointed time accompanied by his son. We crept down the stairs, each carrying the most he could, and after two or three journeys we had the whole lot in the carriage house without having met a soul on the stairs. The door was locked from inside, a small light was lit on a ledge above the gaping hole and we laid down the guns one by one on a thick litter of newspapers, covered them up with more newspapers and shovelled the soft, dry earth back in its place. The floor beams were not so easy to roll back as they were heavy and we had to avoid all noise, but this job was also successfully completed. I gave a last glance at the tomb where the old friends lay – better to rot in the soil than be used by unworthy hands – and we slipped out into the dark courtyard. Not a soul. I went up the stairs feeling my way and murmuring my thanks to good and devoted Ivan. Do the guns lie there still? Who knows?

Once more, Ivan had been ready to help and protect me. And Ivan's devotion did not end with my departure from home at the end of 1919. Five years later, when I was working in Paris, I had news of him again. I was working for the head of the American International Reference Service in Paris, who for some reason needed to go to Russia, so I gave him my old address in Petrograd and the name and description of Ivan. On his return, my American friend gave me a full account of his visit to Ivan, who apparently was very uncommunicative at first until the American gave a description of myself and of my three boys, and Ivan was able to believe that he really was a friend of ours. Ivan asked for permission to call at the hotel the next day. When he turned up there, the American had to tell him in detail everything I was doing and how I earned a living for all of us – and finally, on taking his leave, Ivan produced from the inner pocket of his jacket a double sheet of white paper on which were scribbled in pencil a list of "things found in her house when the Communists took possession of it". And Ivan explained, "I thought she would like to know what there was remaining there – not much, you know – still, if she came back . . ."

Poor Ivan, he had tears in his eyes, said my American friend, and when they shook hands Ivan kissed the American's hand, saying "for her". It was hard never to be able to write a few words to Ivan to thank him, but I did not dare to do so, for a letter from abroad would be noticed by everyone and might put him in an awkward position. I still have the list – in his son's clumsy handwriting – a list of such incongruous and useless things, probably the little remaining that had not been disposed of by Masha and her friends.

Apart from the house searches, the main problem for everyone was how to obtain food. All available supplies went first to the

Army, the Red militia and party workers, and only the remainder was distributed to the civilian population under a ration system which provided the barest essentials. My position was more fortunate than some, for I was still in touch with some of my former servants in the country, who brought me supplies of potatoes and rye flour so that I never went really hungry. I came to rely on the occasional visitor from Kamenka: either Ivan Ivanovich or Ivan Pavlovich would come, or it could be Ivan the coachman – or even Izmail. I appreciated all the more the devotion of these men, for it meant a long trip for them – a day's journey at times when the roads were bad or when they had to walk all the way from Kamenka to the railway station at Tosno twenty miles away.

There was no butter, no fat whatsoever, in our rations. People exchanged carpets, clothes, any household articles for a tiny lump of butter or lard. I would sometimes get some of this treasured substance from another of our former servants, a Lettish girl called Elsa, who for a number of years had been kitchen maid helping the chef in my mother's household. This girl was ambitious, learned all she could from the chefs, then followed some courses and finally was able to take independent posts as a professional cook. With the war and the revolution I had quite lost track of her, when one day she turned up when I was alone in our town house and asked me to let her and her mother have the use of our former coachman's room. Of course I agreed with pleasure and Elsa, thanking me profusely, said that she would pay for the room in kind as she was now a "bag-woman", which was the name given during the revolution to women – and men, too – who carried on a barter traffic between town and country, taking supplies of clothes, cotton, needles and bits of material to outlying villages and bringing from there sugar, flour, butter and any other country produce.

Elsa explained that she had abandoned cooking since there were no "masters" any more requiring professional cooks, and had turned towards the adventurous and risky trade of a bag-woman. Risky and adventurous it was, for the authorities persecuted these traders; police or militia posts were stationed at all important railway junctions and bag-traders were mercilessly stripped of everything when caught. Besides, it needed a lot of skill and imagination to get a railway ticket for any distance beyond the suburbs, for it meant finding the bribable railway officials who would agree to producing the long-distance permits, and having found them it was important to keep them "warm" and under control so as not to be betrayed at some later date. Elsa had apparently found the right way with these people, and from time to time she appeared in my house bringing a little sugar, some tea, a pound or two of semolina, or a small piece of lard.

One day Elsa asked me to come down to her room to see the way she had packed these goods and had managed to get them through in spite of the strict inspections on the way and the endless controls in the train. As I came in she showed me a bright quilted jacket lying on the bed. I lifted it and it felt very heavy and clumsy, and she explained that every little square of the quilting was filled with sugar; similarly quilted was her coat, which she had already partly drained in order to give me and others some of the sugar. The baskets she had were a sort of double weave to hide cottons and even reels which she took down to the villages; the large milk can standing on the floor was only half filled with milk, for the bottom was lined with butter. She explained to me that milk could be brought in freely as it counted as perishable goods (like vegetables too) and therefore the cans were not examined and could slip through undisturbed. Later I heard that this trick had been discovered by the search parties, who would pour the milk out on to the pavement if they suspected there was butter in the can.

Of course Elsa's help was very much appreciated by me, but as the civil war spread more and more it became ever more complicated to find a way into the country and Elsa's trips were more dangerous than ever. Sometimes she did not return for weeks and weeks on end, and her mother began to pine away worrying about her. Conditions of life in Petrograd were also growing worse: no private trade of any kind was allowed, our so-called rations were laughably small, especially those of the lowest category to which I, one of the "bourgeois", belonged – often limited to a quarter of a pound of black bread per week.

Before one of her long-lasting trips, Elsa had come up to me to ask what I would appreciate most in the way of food, and I had said that a little bit of butter would be extremely welcome as I had not tasted any fat for a month or more. Elsa promised to do her best. When finally she turned up again after an absence of six weeks, she looked haggard and exhausted having been obliged to wander partly on foot, partly getting lifts from peasants and always threatened by inspections and possible arrest. But she was smiling now and asked me to come to her room. As I entered my eyes were immediately attracted towards two nice large, round cabbage heads lying on her bed. "This is what I brought you, Madam," Elsa was saying triumphantly, "look at these lovely cabbages." I thanked her a lot, as fresh vegetables were also a delicacy now. But she laughed more heartily and said, "Look into them, for there is the real treasure," and moving the leaves apart she disclosed a neat little ball of butter forming the heart of each cabbage. It was a surprise and a great success, for not only was I overjoyed at the idea of having some butter, but the happy smile of Elsa and the chuckle of her mother were a joy in themselves.

One day near the Nikolayevsky station, I met a peasant whose face seemed familiar to me. He looked at me hesitatingly, then taking off his fur cap greeted me: "Good morning, Countess." This was a compromise between the new way of greeting and the old traditional one. Of course I recognised him now – Piotr Matreshinko, one of our most assiduous beaters during the autumn shoots.

"How do you do, Piotr. How are you all getting along?"

"Thanks. So-so. Times are difficult."

"Yes, times are difficult, that's right. But you should be rather pleased with the new arrangements?"

"Well, of course, the new arrangements are not so bad perhaps; time will show though."

"Surely, time will show. How do you like Communism? Does it suit the village?"

"Well, Communism is not so bad as long as there are things to be taken. But when everything has been taken – we won't need Communism any more."

I laughed inwardly at the candid frankness of the man who evidently had my property in mind when he spoke of "things to be taken". We parted cordially, and a few weeks later, when Izmail came to me with a little food from the country, I told him of my chance encounter with Piotr.

"Oh, he is a cunning one," said Izmail. "When it came to the distribution of your cattle and agricultural equipment, he introduced an unknown cousin of his who was to share his house with him and who thus should have the right to claim a cow and other things. But then, once Piotr had got it all, the cousin was dismissed and his share remained in the hands of Piotr." Izmail laughed a knowing laugh – and I will always think of Piotr's appreciation of Communism as being very characteristic of the Russian peasants at that time.

Once I had accepted the unwelcome fact that escape from Petrograd would not be possible for some months (especially during the cold of the winter), I began to ask myself how I should occupy my time. There was work to be had in the state service, but many of us could not bring ourselves to work for a regime opposed to all our ideas of justice and right. The choice of independent occupations was very limited since all commercial and industrial activities had come under the complete control of the state, all enterprise was nationalised and any private trade was thus "illegal".

I was just turning these problems over in my mind when a friend, a Red Cross nurse, dropped in to ask me to help her bring back from the office some food supplies she had received there as payment in kind. She had a small sledge with her and we managed to get the heavy load of pumpkins safely home. The friend then insisted on my sharing her ration of rye bread "in payment for the work" as she jokingly put it. Here was an idea – why not earn my living by driving a sledge, by joining the transportation business? It would suit me to perfection since it was an independent occupation, and it would leave me free to choose my own hours and places, and keep me free from too close contact with other people.

Without wasting any time, I sent a message to my old game-keeper Ivan Ivanovich and a week later he came to my house with a nice, comfortable country sledge.

"Here is the sledge you ordered, my Lady. It must be right – I polished the runners and they run easily," he said, lifting the sledge for me to admire his work.

"It looks excellent, just what I wanted to have. Thank you so much, Ivan Ivanovich. It is a fine sledge and of birch wood too."

"May I ask – is my Lady going to use it at once? I might carry what is needed – I can take the evening train home."

"No, thank you – it is not for today . . . it is for me to earn my living with," and I saw his eyes getting round with aston-ishment. "Well, I have no money left and am going to take luggage from the station to private addresses – something like a porter, you know?"

A look of dismay, then of deep sorrow came into his face. He looked away and murmured:

"So this is what we have come to . . . with their rights and liberties . . . shame on Russia." Then turning to me quickly he said: "God speed – and don't overwork yourself, my Lady – I had better go now . . ." He went, and the sledge was lean-ing against the wall with its smell of fresh birch wood, and I felt that Kamenka's friendly presence was still with me. The next morning I set out on my first attempt in the career I had chosen.

The Nikolayevsky railway station, which was the main station for the line connecting Petrograd with Moscow and central Russia, was the nearest to the centre of the town, so I walked off there cheerfully pulling my sledge behind me. In front of the station a small group of luggage drivers had already assembled. I must say, the looks of my new colleagues rather terrified me. They seemed to be the very outcasts of society – queer looking individuals, men and half-grown boys, ragged, dirty, long-armed and slouching, growling abuse or shouting at each other, occasionally coming to blows. They made me think of a pack of snarling dogs. I am afraid I would not have withstood for long their evil side-glances in my direction, but at that moment a long distance train came in and as the passengers with luggage appeared on the steps, the crowd I had been looking at rushed with howls and gesticulations at these victims of their professional appetite. I stood well out of the way, waiting for some lucky passenger who might be able to escape this attack.

From a side gate came a tall soldier with two boxes and a square basket and, catching sight of me, he beckoned me to approach. As I helped him tie the things on the sledge and asked him where they had to be taken, he looked at me attentively and, having given the address, added: "I suppose I'll have to make use of the services of a member of the intelligentsia today," and smiled ironically. I did not answer but was amused at this remark.

Off we went, the man striding along the pavement with his hands in the pockets of his short leather jacket, and I on the road – dragging the heavily laden sledge, walking as fast as I could in my thick felt boots. Fortunately my shooting coat was light, but the high grey astrakhan cap and the bashlyk on my shoulders soon felt much too warm. The way was long, a good walk across the town, through the snow lying deep in the unswept streets – and the pace was more a trot than a walk. I did my best to keep up with the man, and when we finally arrived at the given address the soldier paid me the fare I had asked and, smiling gently, added a three-rouble note "for driving so fast".

I was so proud of my first earnings – and of my first tip – that I took it easy for the rest of the day and allowed myself the luxury of a real dinner at an "illegal" private restaurant. But I did not spend that three-rouble note which I kept as a souvenir of my first success in my new career.

However, not all excursions to the station in search of clients were as successful as my first experience. I remember one day standing over two hours in the blizzard, with snow drifting along the streets, whirling in clouds in the open square, the wind howling dismally and cutting my face. And no passenger appeared for me; the few who came were immediately snatched off by the rushing, gibbering crowd of luggage drivers – like dogs or monkeys dashing for a good morsel, I always thought.

Suddenly I felt a slap on my shoulder: "Hullo, youngster, will you undertake a job for me?" I turned round to see the face of an old man, long-bearded, black-eyed, crooked-nosed. He looked at me in some surprise. "Oh, I thought you were a boy! However, the job may suit you anyhow. A little wood is to be driven from a shed across the yard to another place – that's all. Will you come? It's right here near the station."

"All right, but what will you pay?" – I was trying to be business-like.

"Don't worry, I'll be generous and the work is but a trifle, about one cubic metre of fuel wood to drag across. Ten roubles will be a real present for it."

Tired of standing in the cold, I agreed and followed the old man. We reached his house in five minutes and here I found that first I was expected to climb into the loft, to throw the wood down from there, then to drag it across the yard and carry it upstairs to the third floor. And besides, there was much more than one cubic metre – all scattered about the loft. Still, I had agreed, it was late afternoon and no more long distance trains would be coming in – and the work would warm me up. So I started with set teeth – I was dismally cold – and two hours later, when the large stack of wood was piled up in the stuffy entrance hall and kitchen of the old man's flat, I received my ten roubles and went off as hot as after two hours of tennis on a July afternoon.

I ran home, my soaked gloves freezing stiff now in the severe cold, and I laughed heartily at myself for having made such a bad bargain. The next day, however, I could scarcely move being so stiff . . . and the ten roubles were enough to buy just two buns!

At times, when the rage of the Cheka seemed to ebb down a little, we found our good spirits quickly enough and turned to our favourite pastimes with renewed energy. Some people, for instance, played bridge with a perfect rage, forgetting time, hunger, fright. In my case it was my longing for music which reappeared, and I was only too happy to discover that an old colonel, whom I had met at the house of some friends, still managed to play the piano and even to keep his room warm enough for the instrument not to go out of tune. We arranged to practise together and for some time I went regularly to him twice a week with my violin.

These evenings have left a deep impression upon my memory. We played for hours, practising old things, picking up new music. When I was tired, the colonel – who really played extremely well – would let me choose what I would like to hear and would play some Chopin, or Beethoven, or Liszt. Sitting then in the big armchair in the poorly lit room, near a small iron stove, I listened and listened to tunes so well known to me that they felt like old friends. The colonel's orderly (who had remained with his master even though the institution of orderlies had been altogether abolished as unworthy of a revolutionary country) prepared the tea on a large round table and proudly brought in warm biscuits he had managed to make out of rye flour, potato peelings and water.

After tea I packed my violin into thick blankets, tied it with the music books on my sledge – and trotted home through the deserted dark streets, my heart full of joy and of music. The colonel's health was not good and so he could not accompany me home – and anyway I enjoyed these lonely walks home when the mood of the sleeping streets seemed so different from the harsh reality of the daylight hours. These evenings seem now like bright spots in the dreary picture of those hard years.

Little by little my reputation as a transportation agent spread among friends – and strangers – and I received daily so many private orders that trips to the station in search of customers were no longer necessary. Some of the requests addressed to me were most amusing, while some were almost impossible. Once I was asked to move the entire contents of a four-roomed flat, including sideboards, chests-of-drawers, etc. Another time the widow of a well-known admiral asked me to take her boxes and luggage from her flat to that of some friends, insisting on my taking all the six or seven trunks at one time – so that she need pay for one trip only. It was physically impossible to do this, but I was so amused at her insistence – and parsimony – that I agreed to do so on the condition that she would sit on the top of these trunks "to keep the balance" as I explained to her. I could just picture myself with the dignified and very stiff old lady with highly powdered nose, a lorgnon in her right hand and a miniature portrait of her late husband adorning her jacket, perched on a pyramid of trunks on top of my small sledge. She finally refused my suggestion with sour politeness, having realised that I was joking.

Having become something of a specialist by now, I began to enjoy undertaking the delivery of "illegal" goods such as typewriters, sewing machines, etc. In order not to be stopped by the Cheka I had to take certain precautions. Besides the usual ropes, I would take a rug or blanket, a big pillow and an iron kettle. I would then wrap up the typewriter so skilfully into a parcel with the pillow sticking out on one side and the kettle fixed on the top, that the bundle looked exactly like the luggage of any peasant woman going off on a journey by train. I was never stopped although I frequently passed Cheka agents combing the streets.

Transportation of food-stuffs was as a rule quite pleasant, as the fee was frequently paid in kind and this meant so much less hunting for food. However, I remember one journey of that kind which was most unpleasant – except for the comic side which made me laugh at the same time.

I had been asked to take some horse meat from a cooperative organisation to a school. On approaching the store rooms of the cooperative organisation I was struck by the most unpleasant smell of the place, and when the bags of horse meat were carried out and put on my sledge I knew where the smell came from. Nothing to be done, I thought, and as I am a horse myself and run in front of the sledge, the smell will not disturb me too much. Off I went quite cheerfully, though apprehensive of any payment in kind this time.

Scarcely had I come out into the street when a kind of forlorn fox-terrier who was busy gnawing a bone by the roadside looked up, sniffed the air, abandoned his bone and dashed after me and my sledge. Poor little beast, I thought, one of those thousands of abandoned dogs roaming about the town – and I smiled at it with sympathy. But the smile was wasted on it – all its senses, all its attention, were concentrated in the black, shiny nose which sniffed and sniffed the air at the back of my sledge.

When I looked back again to see whether my companion had abandoned me, I saw two black noses sniffing the air and I laughed at the funny picture they made. Evidently these two dogs awakened the interest of all the other dogs we met, and soon enough I found my sledge being followed and surrounded by a pack of the most disreputable looking dogs – all breeds, all colours, all sniffing violently, all lean and mangy. I began to be rather anxious about the safety of my load and the increasing snarls and growls made me think that sooner or later some of the more enterprising creatures would not be content with sniffing but would bring their teeth into action. I stopped once or twice and tried to scatter the crowd by swinging my spare rope in a circle round me. The effect was good as none of the dogs had spirit enough to oppose me – they were all so scared, so much beaten, so starved that they darted aside with their tails between their legs. But the moment I resumed my course, the whole pack reassembled and renewed its concert of sniffs and growls. We must have looked a very comic procession, but I was glad when I reached at last my destination with the load untouched. I felt sorry for the children, whose faces must have worn a different expression from the faces of the dogs, when the time came for those children to sniff the dinner that I had brought them. But perhaps they were too hungry to care?

Some people, if they saw a horse falling in the streets, would wait for it to die, and then run to cut meat from the carcass. Such was the plight of horses in Petrograd in 1919. I like to believe that, in the same way that some people have a way with plants – "green fingers" as it is called – so too there can be a mysterious connection between a human and an animal. I felt that I had a special way with animals; I felt it particularly as a child and later also as a married woman dealing with the horses and dogs in the country. My attention turned now towards the horses to be seen in the streets of Petrograd, whose sufferings were so hopeless and cruel. The city was by now on the brink of famine: we all had the smallest possible rations to live on, and even the black market in illegal goods was highly insufficient and badly organised. People, especially the old and the very young, walked like shadows in the streets and frequently some peasant woman would stop one, offering some coffee or lard hidden carefully under her apron, illegal goods carried across the border from Finland. All this was bad enough for humans, and few people had thoughts to spare for the half-starved horses who were falling like flies in the snow-covered streets of the town. Not a day passed without my having seen two or three collapsing in their shafts.

One day, unable to bear any longer the sight of a miserable animal endeavouring to rise to its feet, hampered by the harness and beaten pitilessly by his driver, I came up to the man and said to him with an assurance I had never had before: "Let me raise the horse, I know the trick!" The man looked at me with an evil smile but stopped beating the horse, probably ready to rest. "You? Lift the horse to its feet? – We'll see that! . .." and he laughed with a sneer.

I patted the horse's nose and spoke closely into its face, wondering what I could do to help it. The first thing was to loosen the strap across its back, and in spite of the man's sneers I managed to do this. By then the horse had quietened down, its breathing was more regular, I took it by the bridle and spoke soothingly close to its head, ashamed of the man hearing my endearing words. The horse seemed to understand, and as I began to lift the bridle and collar it gave a jerk and stood up on its knotted trembling legs. I tightened the strap, gave a final pat and walked away, leaving the man muttering something into his beard. A few seconds later I heard the regular, slow and muffled sound of my horse pulling the sledge with its load of wood.

This first attempt gave me courage and from then on I never hesitated to approach a horse in difficulties. I did not always succeed, but it was worth trying and often both horse and driver seemed grateful for my help. Once I saw a sledge with a heavy load trying to get up the raised approaches of a vaulted bridge over one of the canals. The snow had been driven into drifts along the sides, and the middle of the road was covered with a bluish surface of ice. The horse was a relatively well-fed beast – not all of its ribs were showing, and the sinews of its neck did not stand out too starkly. The man was shouting, swinging his short whip, but was also leaning his shoulder against the curved front of the sledge trying to help push it off the icy spot. The horse's legs could not grip the ice and were sliding apart in all directions. It looked hopeless, but why not try? As I approached, the man stopped shouting, the horse stood still. "Can I help your horse?"

"You, Miss? Your help won't be of much use," answered the man, but with quite a friendly smile. "Look at the ice. The horse sees it and he won't pull – he knows it's useless – he is a clever, cunning old horse, I know him."

I was patting the flank, then the head of the animal, talking softly to it, and wondering what to do. Just then I noticed an axe stuck under the seat of the sledge.

"Let me have the axe . . . and pull the horse back, just a little . . . I'll roughen the ice. He is a clever horse, he'll understand that it's less slippery . . . let me try."

A minute later I was chopping at the ice, making the surface irregular, the man looking on and smiling, the horse looking on too and perhaps smiling in his own way. People passing turned round and smiled, and I began to laugh about the picture myself.

"Now, this must do the trick. Come on Vanka!" I said, throwing down the axe and pulling by the bridle. The horse put his feet hesitatingly on the roughened surface as if to test it, and having a more secure foothold he suddenly gave a pull and dragged the load up the short slope with the man running and shouting encouragements on one side and me clinging to the shaft on the other. We stopped on the top of the bridge, red, hot and pleased.

"Here is your axe," I said, "and really your Vanka is a clever one – how he tested his footing before he pulled. Good luck to you both!"

The man touched his cap. "Goodbye, Miss, and thank you. Vanka and I won't forget your help. Well, I certainly never expected it from a girl like you."

It was a nice day full of smiles.

But there were also some very unpleasant days when the most abusive language was showered on me for interfering. However, with the sight of a miserable horse half-sitting on its haunches with head turned sideways and receiving volleys of blows from an irate peasant, I could remain deaf to the abuse and concentrate on the horse. I still remember exactly the spot where this happened: right near the famous circus Ciniselli where as children we had so often admired the well-schooled, well-fed and well-groomed performing horses. And here was a poor and shaggy beast giving its last effort and receiving only blows and abuse. I dashed forward raising my arm and calling "Stop, have pity on the horse!" What met my words went far beyond all my knowledge of evil language, but I thought only of the horse and as the curses increased so the blows hesitated and stopped. I seized the horse's head, trying to bring it into a normal position, but a side strap had caught in the shaft and had to be loosened. As I loosened the strap the poor beast let itself go and flopped down exhausted. I was downright frightened that it was going to breathe its last then and there, and the shouts of "So that's your help! The horse is finished" rang like thunder in my ears.

The poor beast did look very low; I knelt on the snow and patted its head and spoke something while the man swore and wiped his forehead in evident distress. I began to lose faith in my art of "lifting horses", and I just prayed for God's help – it all looked so dismal, so sad, so utterly miserable: the grey, cold winter day, the unswept streets, the hungry looking people – yes, hungry, and I knew that they would eat my poor horse the moment it really had breathed its last! I had seen it often enough. It made me shudder, I prayed so intensely and I talked so warmly to my horse that hope crept back into my heart. And as I knelt holding up the limp head I felt a movement, a shudder, an effort; the head rose, the front legs gathered under the body in an attempt to rise. I can't remember what I did – what straps I undid or fastened, but the horse stood up . . . and the man who had stopped swearing suddenly uttered some inarticulate sounds, picked up the reins and gently urged on his horse as it began to pull the sledge. I thought I had seen a miracle and I was happy.

13

GOODBYE TO THE PAST

After the hungry winter of 1919, the spring and summer brought little relief to those of us still unable to get away.

It was the only complete summer I ever spent in Petersburg, and I think it must have been the drabbest summer that city ever had. The weather was bad: plenty of rain and fog, very little sunshine. The government had transferred its seat to Moscow, the port was closed to foreign trade, the city was cut off from the outside world, and the majority of industrial and commercial enterprises had closed down. Houses were closed, abandoned, the smashed windows open to rain and wind. The wooden paving blocks of the streets had been partly taken up in winter and used as fuel for heating, and the blocks that were left were now loose and swam about in the middle of the streets after it had rained, or served as toys to the skinny street children playing listlessly in the pale sunshine. And the main worry on all faces was – food, where to find food.

The "wandering milk-queues" were a specialty of Petrograd at the time – at least they cropped up in great numbers then, and I never came across any in other places. They roamed about often until noon through drizzly rain in empty streets. They roamed in search of a milkman who was supposed to come sometimes to this or that street corner. These "wandering queues" were a quaint sight and would have made one laugh if it had not been so tragic and sad to see haggard people, often holding children by the hand, wandering in this way.

Such a queue would often form at dawn, at some spot in the street where, to a casual observer, there would be no reason to start one. Why should the queue start here and not twenty yards further on? But the reason was always the same: a milkman had stopped his cart here yesterday – and so there was a chance that he would return today. Soon enough, more and more people would join the queue, and discussions would begin about a better spot for waiting. If the more enterprising element of the queue took the upper hand, the first person in the line was forced to move and to lead the crowd as directed towards a supposedly better place. With shouts of "left, left, the corner opposite the post office . . ." or "stop here, I saw him here two days ago . . ." the queue would make its ragged way forward, accompanied as a rule by a number of uncomplimentary remarks about the "leader". If the leader had a strong character he would not stand for these remarks, he would reply and lose his temper, but he would stick to his rightful prerogatives as head of the queue. Often arguments grew very hot, and the shouting finally drew the attention of patrolling soldiers – either militia or Cheka – and the whole queue was then dispersed, its members scampering away like rabbits.

Similar queues formed also for vegetable carts, but less frequently, as few peasants had managed to keep a horse which had strength enough to drag a cart to town. As the vegetable carts were so very unreliable, the queues for them formed rarely, did not keep together long – people just hoped for the best and "did a little standing". Frequently, when money was very short, barter arrangements were made – but surreptiously and with many cautious side glances, as they were strictly forbidden.

The normal daily queues at the government shops where rations were expected to be distributed and sometimes really were handed out – these looked dull and glum when compared to the wandering ones. There was no excitement, no sport in them; they were a habit now, each member of the queue knew the others only too well (especially from the back) and all were tired, all were dumb – even the women seemed to have lost their capacity for gossip. Fortunately I never had to stand in this sort of queue as my former maid, Masha, used to fetch my rations with hers. These, together with the flour and potatoes which reached us from time to time from Kamenka, were adequate according to the standard of the time. But rye flour cooked in water, or boiled potatoes every day for weeks and months on end did prove a little meagre and monotonous, and one day I decided to liven up my menu, if I could, by a trip out of town for some sort of green vegetables.

I went by tram to the Islands – the big parks, now deserted – at the estuary of the Neva. There, along the overgrown and untrimmed hedges, near the abandoned villas and on the edge of the woods where as children we used to gather the first anemones of spring, I found an untouched wilderness of nettles. The younger shoots were quickly gathered into my basket and it was a triumph when Masha produced a remarkable soup out of them – with a little rye flour to give more substance and some caraway seeds for flavour.

After this success I grew more ambitious and decided to get some fish for a real meal, or at least for an "ookha" – the traditional Russian fish soup. Somewhere among our summer and sports things I found the necessary tackle, some hooks and an old fishing rod of my father's. It was a real joy to put everything straight as in the good old days. Then the bait had to be found – not so easy as I did not even know what kind of fish I could hope to catch from the quay of the Neva – a most unusual place for anyone to fish from. Deciding that a "neutral" bait would be best, I packed my day's ration of black bread, caught a few flies on the kitchen window and set out towards evening with my fishing rod on my shoulder, making straight for the quay of the Neva. The few people I met looked a little surprised, some smiled, others had a scowl; a soldier produced a joke about "bourgeois", but I did not care.

It was not easy to find a proper spot from which to fish – barges were moored all along the quay, and drains made some parts impossible to stop at. Finally I turned left along the Fontanka and soon settled down on some steps leading from the granite quay to the water's edge. The Summer Garden was silhouetted in black against the red evening sky of a glorious sunset; the air was mild and warm and a little misty. The water looked black and oily and my bait seemed to sleep on this motionless heavy water. I waited, waited, the sky grew duller, the air cooler – it was so quiet and unreal, with these large houses now lifeless, their broad quays silent, the gardens abandoned and my cork quite still on the black water. Somehow a feeling of terror, of emptiness, of unreality seized me. I could not stand any longer the contrast of impressions in my mind – this deadly silence overshadowing the pictures of the past, so lively, bright, colourful – on this same quay, in these same houses, in these same gardens where I knew every tree. I quickly reeled in my line and walked up the steps to the street. On the granite balustrade at the top of the steps an old man was leaning. His eyes were dreamy and vague, he looked unreal too – so thin, so pale. As I passed him he smiled faintly and murmured: "No luck today? Even the fish have become cautious and afraid. Better not disturb them – poor things!"

I did not try fishing any more.

On August 6th, 1919, it was Vladimir's birthday. I knew it, I felt it – and I tried not to think about it. It was a sunny day after a period of rainy, cold weather. I had forgotten about the seasons, and when a real summer day suddenly looked through my bedroom window, it felt strange to put on an old summer frock and to walk into the sunlit streets. I walked to the quay of the Neva. The Neva was blue today, the quay as elegant and grand as ever, but, as on my fishing trip, I noticed how empty and silent it seemed without the sound of hoofs and carriages.

In my own childhood I had loved these sounds, they were like music accompanying my walks: hoofs of single horses pulling private carriages, hoofs of trotters which I knew by the sound and which I was tempted to identify by looking round as they approached; but it was bad manners to look round, so I had to be patient until the carriage passed us and gave me the joy of a quick glimpse of the fine stepping horse. Or the sound of a pair, when I played a game with myself, guessing whether it would be a Victoria belonging to some young couple, or a landau taking children out for a drive, or a coupé occupied by some old lady or gentleman. And what fun when there was the sound of hoofs alone – no wheels – it must be a rider! Anyone I knew? The excitement and curiosity of seeing if I could recognise both the rider and the horse . . .

Now the quay was quite dead. No horses, not even any cabs or carts. And as I strode along this quay thinking of my boy, wondering where and how he was celebrating his birthday, it brought a freezing feeling to my heart when I realised that for almost a year I had had no news from the children and had not been able to send them a word – neither letter nor telegram. It was one of my saddest walks.

For my friends the Riesenkampfs it was also a time of sadness and difficult decisions. Antoine and Alphonse were worried about their father, the old general, who had fallen ill that winter and for whom there was no hope of recovery as even the necessary medicines could not be secured. His sons had stayed on in Petrograd because of him, but they were without identity papers and constantly on the run from the authorities. Their father was becoming weaker and close to death. I remember how he apologised for being in his dressing gown, for not rising to greet me. The house was watched, the sons could not approach it, but I succeeded in passing unmolested and served thus as a link between the sons and the father.

One day I went with Alphonse to a house where he had been offered shelter for a couple of days. It was a large building with offices on three floors and two private flats at the top. Alphonse was to come before the offices closed so that he could go up the stairs unnoticed, mixing with the business crowd going in and out. The owner of the flat was going away for a few days, and on leaving the house herself she would tell the hall porter (a militant Communist) that she proposed to be absent for a day or two. When I left Alphonse, a few doors away from the house, he asked me to ring him up that same evening at ten o'clock to give news of his father.

I called on the old General, found that the news was reasonably reassuring, and returned home in good time. At about ten o'clock I telephoned the flat where Alphonse was staying but there was no answer to my call. I wondered what could have happened, as the flat was small and he would have surely heard the telephone bell. Worried and anxious I rang up an hour later – still no reply. What could have happened? Had he fallen into a trap? One of the Cheka's favourite ways of trapping people was by occupying a flat and then laying hands on any visitor who came to the door. But if this were the case the occupiers would probably have answered my telephone call too, trying to find out who was ringing up. No, they might also have refrained from answering, so as not to arouse suspicion. I was lost in these different conjectures, for more than one of our friends had vanished, simply disappeared, in some mysterious way – and the thought was obviously distressing. It was a sleepless night.

Next morning I was still uncertain what to do, when the door bell rang. I rushed to the door, and heard Alphonse's whistled signal behind it; what a burden can roll off one's mind in a fraction of a second! And there was Alphonse, somewhat haggard looking but smiling.

"I gave you a fright last night? And how is Father?"

"Slightly better, temperature falling. But what happened?"

"Well, your telephone call came at a very awkward moment. This is what happened. I got into the flat all right, as people were still walking up and down the stairs. My friend gave me

233

instructions about the key and left the house, intending to inform the hall porter of her absence. I was reading in the drawing room, making use of the last evening light when just before ten I heard steps coming up the stairs. As you know the only other flat on the top landing is unoccupied. Well, the steps halted in front of my door. There was a pause and I heard the jingling of keys – and then, one by one, twelve keys were tried in the lock of the door! And after each failure I could hear a disgruntled voice muttering some oath accompanied by a spit. You can imagine what thoughts raced through my brain during these few minutes. The first thing I noticed, with relief, was that on locking the door after my friend I had put the key into my pocket – as otherwise its presence in the lock would have given me away immediately. But I also noticed that I had not bolted the door, so that it would open the moment the right key was found. I knew it must be the hall porter who had decided to have a private view of the flat in the absence of the owner. But what was I to do? No use trying to hide, for the flat was small. No use trying to make a run for it down the stairs, because the house door at the bottom would be locked by this time."

"What an awful position! So what did you do?"

"I waited – not exactly patiently – but cold-bloodedly, resolving to knock the man unconscious if necessary. I felt cold sweat running down my neck, and my hair standing up on end – and look, if it has not turned grey on the temple?" added Alphonse with a cheerful laugh, bending his head to show me.

"Yes, it certainly has a strong streak of grey now" – strikingly grey for the young face, I thought. "And it is a real miracle that the man failed after all."

"Yes, a miracle indeed. And you know, your first telephone call encouraged him, since the fact that it remained unanswered only proved to him that the flat was really empty."

"I am glad I did not ring up too soon the second time," I said.

"Well, it remained unanswered too, as the man, having used up his supply of keys, went downstairs swearing and cursing and returned with another bundle – and the game started anew. That's when my other temple went grey", said Alphonse turning his head and laughing.

But I saw more than the grey hair; I noticed the haggard face, the tired eyes, the shadow that passed over his face at the thought of having to look for a fresh hiding place the following night. It is difficult to give an idea of the nervous strain and the moral depression felt by a man who is tracked, who has never for one moment the feeling of safety, who can run at any time into a militia squad checking the identity papers of people in the streets, in trams, in trains, at the markets. It was not long after this that the old General died. One of his last worries had been the fate of his sword, the St George's sword won during the Turkish war of 1877. He could not bear the thought of it falling into the hands of the Bolsheviks to be soiled by those who did not recognise the honour of the old army. As house-searches were always a threatening danger, he finally asked his sons to throw the sword into the river in front of his windows. In the dead of night, Alphonse carried out this order a few days before his father's death.

Somehow we seemed to feel in advance when our turn to be searched would come. Our strained nerves warned us – and on such days I conscientiously checked all of the hiding places before it got dark. Thinking back now, I quite admire my gift in camouflaging arrangements. There was the secret wall cupboard in the passage, with wallpaper stuck across the door. And there was a second secret cupboard in one of the rooms with panelled walls. A large carved sofa was pushed across in front of it, and along the top of the cupboard door I nailed a dark oak shelf on which some vases with artificial flowers looked very artistic – and in very bad taste. For symmetry a similar arrangement was put close to the other end of the sofa, and the place looked so innocent that I felt quite pleased with my work.

One late afternoon, as I was examining for the tenth time the wallpaper stuck across the door of the first secret cupboard, I heard the entrance door bell ring. It sounded more urgent than the usual ringing of friends and I dreaded some unpleasant surprise. Cautiously I opened and saw to my great relief the old servant of the Riesenkampfs laden with parcels. Yes, it was their turn to be searched. For, as the old General had feared, his house was being threatened with immediate "nationalisation". Both brothers and the faithful servant Jan packed frantically and, making use of my hiding places, carried to me all they could. By nine o'clock in the evening my secret wall-cupboards were stacked full and we could not help being amused at the quaint collection of things there: pictures, a few rare books, field-glasses, silver trophies, house linen and clothes, and fourteen cameras – all forbidden goods! I did feel a little terrified when I thought of the consequences of a possible discovery of these stocks but we all helped each other as best we could and I was glad to be able to help my friends. The most curious box in the collection contained twelve sets – complete to the last pair of silk stockings – of footmen's liveries! Alphonse assured me that these liveries, which had belonged to his uncle the ambassador, were of great value at the present time and could be marvellously exchanged for provisions from the country. I made a note in my mind to ask Elsa, the bag-woman, if this could really be true.

Three weeks later their house was taken and, with their father dead, Antoine and Alphonse were at last free to leave Petrograd as and how they could. Their best chance was to use their family ties with Poland, under a scheme of "repatriation" similar to the way my boys and I had been "repatriated" to Estonia some fifteen months before. If only I had known my good luck and stayed there. But perhaps here was a second chance? By now I had learned quite a lot of Polish, and with luck I might be able to pass as a Polish refugee too.

So, in December 1919, there seemed to appear at last a real chance of escaping from Russia. Until then all my researches had been in vain and, with the onset of winter, I had almost given up hope. Then one day, about the middle of December, I received a short letter from a friend, Countess Krasinska, who was in Moscow with a number of other Polish hostages. She invited and urged me to come to them as soon as possible, as her husband had some important questions to talk over with me. I guessed immediately that this meant something about my escape from Russia, as these friends knew well enough that this was my only goal and desire. As all letters were likely to be censored, we could never write openly what we thought.

At the Nikolayevsky station where I went immediately to enquire about trains, I was told that no private people were allowed to travel unless there was an especially important reason – government service, or illness or death of near relations. What was I to do? On my way home I thought of Elsa, the bag-woman, who always managed to get a ticket for her provision-hunting expeditions, and I went straight to her for advice. Elsa understood the situation immediately and said that she would try to get me the permit and all necessary papers through a friend of hers working on the Petrograd–Moscow railway line. She warned me that I would have to pay a considerable sum to this friend who ran great risks in helping people but who was in need of money for her large family. I thought of the few thousand roubles I had saved, and wondered if they would be enough.

The next evening Elsa appeared mysteriously at eight o'clock and suggested that we should go to this friend at once. We walked a long way beyond the Nikolayevsky station, through goods yards and customs houses and found the friend, a pleasant young woman, busy in a small office. She was alone, on duty for the night, and she said we would not be disturbed. We talked the matter over and she promised to send me the ticket with a return permit. The ticket would be accompanied by a telegram from Moscow stating that my father was dangerously ill and that my presence was urgently needed. On the basis of this telegram the railway authorities would let me through. The arrangement would cost me five thousand roubles. She would accept a part payment, if we would bring the rest as soon as possible.

I was very pleased with such a speedy settlement of the matter, but how could I find the money? Here again, Elsa was able to help. By this time even quite modest household goods had some value, if one knew where to find a buyer. We gathered together what money we could, and we made the long walk again on another evening with the rest of the payment.

By January 2nd, 1920, I had the ticket, the return permit and the telegram duly sent from Moscow. I left the same evening. It was freezing hard and in apprehension of the unheated railway carriage I had dressed as warmly as I could, wearing my shooting coat and cap and my brother's boots – the only ones I still possessed. How grateful I was to him for leaving behind these strong waterproof hunting boots when he went to England. The journey was far from being comfortable although I was in the best First Class carriage (thanks to Elsa who arranged matters with a porter). The crowd there was to a certain extent clean and not too rough. Some engineers who filled the compartment played cards throughout the night and smoked without opening the door. The windows were nailed fast for the winter season. I began to regret my thick clothing as the air became unbearably stuffy.

Once in Moscow, I went straight to my friends who were lodged in a large apartment arranged temporarily as a hostel for the hostages waiting to be sent off. Count Krasinski was one of the main Polish hostages waiting to be exchanged for some Communists being sent out of Poland. He was travelling with his wife, his son of 15, and an old aunt. By chance, he also had the passport of a former maid of theirs who had left some weeks before. Having received a travelling passport she had left her old passport – still valid – with the Krasinskis. They suggested the following plan to me: that I should take this passport and be put on the list of Polish hostages as a niece of

Count Krasinski – under an assumed name. The details on the passport, including the age given and the description, vague as usual, could be adapted to me, and fortunately no photographs were required. This was a brilliant idea; I agreed with joy and gratitude, and in three days everything was fixed. It was decided that I would be registered straight away as one of the Polish hostages waiting in Petrograd. I felt I had to return there to see to my flat and to try to secure what money I could by selling things in the few days left to me. Thus I planned to return to Petrograd now on my present travel permit, and to leave again – using my new name – with the next train of Polish hostages. Antoine Riesenkampf had already left the country in this way, and I was confident of success. And Alphonse, too, had said he hoped to do the same.

In the meantime I had to obtain a ticket for my return journey from Moscow to Petrograd. Armed with my travel permit, I was certain that I would have no difficulty. However, when I went to buy the ticket I was told that the return permit had to be certified by the Moscow Cheka and only then could I get a railway ticket.

To go to the Cheka was always unpleasant – even on harmless errands – and I was worried that my name might arouse suspicion. The Sollohub family name was known in Moscow, where some cousins had owned one of the largest private houses. But it was unavoidable and reluctantly I entered the ominous building which I disliked even passing in the street. Luckily I still had with me the telegram calling me to Moscow. When I showed my papers, the man, peeping out of a small guichet asked me:

"What has happened then to your father?"

"He died," I answered quickly, realising that if he were still alive I might have to give his address – and this would complicate matters.

"All right – then bring a death certificate signed by a municipal doctor," and a wooden shutter closed the window with a bang.

What was I to do now? Find a dead father – and find a doctor too, a municipal doctor who would certify the death of my imaginary father? How could I hope to find one or the other, or both? This did make a strain on my imagination. I decided to go and see Aunt Lelly, in the hope that she might be able to help me.

Aunt Lelly – Elisaveta Vladimirovna Sabourov – was Sasha's aunt, his father's sister, and a kind and helpful person. Fortunately she had come home from work early that day and was at home when I called. She immediately gave me the address of her own doctor, an old friend, and who might also be a municipal doctor. I ran to him – he too was at home and received me at once, a nice quiet grey-bearded man with a fine face. I told him my story and asked him whether he knew of some old man who had died within the last week or ten days at most. The doctor looked in his book and found the right deceased – a man of sixty, who had died five days before – and a carpenter by profession. All this worked perfectly. The doctor made out a certificate – kindly changing the first name of the carpenter from Athanasiy to Fyodor – (my father's name was Fyodor as was indicated in my passport) – and wrote some complicated Latin name specifying the nature of the fatal illness. It turned out that the doctor was the head of one of the large Moscow hospitals and had at his disposal all necessary and imposing seals which he applied to the certificate.

The next morning I appeared again at the Cheka with all papers as required. The man looked at them, at the doctor's certificate – at me as I stood there with a face suitable for the sad circumstances.

"Your father died – that's all right. He was a carpenter? And you are married?" he asked, raising his eyebrows.

"Yes, Father was a carpenter – a very good one too. When I married I went to Petrograd."

"And you have to go back to Petrograd now? Why?"

"I have my house there and my work."

"What work have you?"

"I am a musician," I answered and prepared to produce my membership card of the Musical Syndicate.

"All right, all right – that will do . . ." A stamp on my permit and pop down again came the wooden shutter.

How grateful I was to the unknown old carpenter who had adopted me after his death – he does not know perhaps of this good deed to his credit. The next afternoon I was back in Petrograd.

It is with a heavy heart that I think of the last week or ten days I spent at home – in the last real home I ever had. They were hectic and miserable, those dark January days. The cold and dreary winter weather, constant snowstorms and howling winds, the chilly unheated rooms – except my own, kept warm like a den – all this left on me a deep and mournful impression. The removal of all odds and ends I could dispose of, the burning of correspondence – my parents', my husband's, my own; the opening of all hiding places, and the anxiety every night of possible house-searches. It was endlessly dreary and sad – this conscious putting an end to the past of a family, this destruction with my own hands of a home arranged with so much love by my parents, the home that I had known all my life. It is all blurred in my memory – and perhaps it is better that way.

Masha was very helpful; and Elsa, the bag-woman, trotted up and down the back stairs mysteriously hiding in her coat "goods" she was planning to take to her customers in the villages, in exchange for foodstuffs. As I did all the work my mind was in a haze – it was impossible to think that these were my last days, my last hours in the dear old home, that I would never again see the portraits of my parents, or the paintings Mother brought home from Italy, or the sketches she did herself. And my father's library, his writings, his correspondence – even the toys of my children – everything hurt as I prepared to leave them.

I could not dwell on these thoughts. There was so little time left that I had to persevere and finish the work as best I could, for my name – the new one, Miss Maria Adamczewska,

Polish citizen – was on the list of Polish hostages who would leave on January 14th for Moscow, where it was expected that we should join without delay the hostage train leaving for the Polish border. Thus, I was to meet my adopted aunt and uncle at the railway station in Moscow and continue the journey with them straight away.

My train was due to leave at eleven in the morning. We set out, Masha and I, pulling a sledge on which my two suitcases and a fur coat were loaded. It was cold and grey, and yet every street, every house looked like old friends to me as they vanished behind me – and were gone for ever.

I had given Masha the address of Aunt Lelly in Moscow and had told her that I was going there in the hope of finding work. It was not safe to speak of what I was really doing, nor about the combination of passports, for Masha was getting more and more pro-Bolshevik since her friendship with the black-whiskered chauffeur and their business cooperation.

At the station I met several people I knew, Poles who were leaving with the same train. Alphonse was not there; he had already left for Moscow by an earlier train, but it was likely that he would rejoin us on the hostage train out of Moscow. It was easier really without him there, for I had to learn to live with my new identity and play a part to suit it, and at present I felt a stranger even to myself.

It seemed to last hours as I sat in my corner seat waiting for the train to leave. Little groups stood in front of our carriage – the faces of those staying behind, tears here and there, a joke sometimes, a gay laugh from the younger ones. They all seemed to have friends, relations, someone to see them off. I was alone, quite alone, for I had had to send Masha away fearing that the way she addressed me might betray my real identity.

At last the train started. There were handkerchiefs waving, and handkerchiefs wiping tears from the faces of those remaining, as they watched our train draw out of the station. Slowly we moved on, first through the suburbs, then through little bits of country and more suburban places, all so familiar to me from the train and all so quiet now under the thick white cover of snow. Petersburg had gone – we had left it behind; for me and for the majority of my travelling companions it meant leaving a home, perhaps a family, a bit of one's own life – and leaving it for ever.

Very soon, I became acquainted with a few people in our compartment, and the long journey, which lasted this time almost 30 hours instead of the usual eleven or twelve, turned out not to be too tedious or depressing. Once or twice Soviet control officials passed through our carriage but the leading hostage knew how to manage them and we arrived without any serious incident. Having to play a part I had to think of everything I said and all my attention was centred on the attitude I needed to adopt – it was still very new to me.

We arrived in Moscow towards evening on the following day. At the station I was met by my so-called uncle who – alas! – instead of boarding the train as many other Polish hostages did, had come to take me off the train because at the last minute he and all his family had been refused permission to go. It was a great blow. And there was Alphonse getting into the train that I had just left. It was a sad hour we spent at the scantily-lit station, shivering in the cold and looking at all these friends going – going towards freedom and a human existence. Only an hour ago I had been so sure of being one of them, and I had never thought of having to stay in Moscow. It was a stroke of the worst bad luck. "A delay of a week or two," said my new uncle – but it became a delay of five months.

Not all of those who boarded the train in high spirits came happily across into Poland. A dozen men and women, all with well-known names, were sent back by the Soviets from the very frontier – when they had been within a few yards of the border. Among them was Alphonse who, like me, had to stay on in Moscow and await a second chance.

14

IMPRISONMENT

On the very first night that I spent with the Krasinskis, in the Moscow lodging which served as a temporary home for the Polish hostages, there was an unexpected house-search which began at 11 o'clock and lasted a good hour. Stunned as I was by the blow of learning that we could not yet leave Russia, and saddened by the memory of the final break-up of my home in Petersburg, a kind of numbness overtook me as I watched this all-too-familiar sight.

The hostel was large and at that moment almost empty, for most people had left for Poland on the train. The furniture was sparse and certainly not comfortable. I was to share a room with an old lady, for me an adoptive great-aunt, who received me as warmly as if I had really been a part of the family. We had a most precarious installation: two iron bedsteads with bumpy mattresses, a table and two chairs, one of them serving as a washstand. By and by we managed to make the room look more comfortable by using papers as tablecloths, and covering our beds with our fur coats. Unfortunately our mattresses already contained some unwelcome inhabitants; how I shudder at this recollection now, at the feeling of the bed-bugs crawling in one's bed – but at the time I became hardened to it little by little and learned to enjoy hunting for them as if it were some kind of new sport. The more adventurous ones would crawl along the wall – in broad daylight – and it was my daily sport to crush them and so ornament the white-washed walls with their corpses.

Gradually the hostel filled up again with people, who being released from provincial prisons came here to await their turn to be sent home to Poland. Whole families arrived, with babies and servants, men and women from the most different social backgrounds, all moved by the one desire of getting away, back home to normal life again.

But the promised repatriation was now delayed, and delayed not by a matter of days but more of weeks, or even months. As we became accustomed little by little to the fact that we must wait here at the hostel for an indefinite period, we all seemed to get into a sort of everyday routine of life. The youngsters, a cheerful group of eight to ten boys between sixteen and twenty-two, were rather a problem and caused a lot of headaches to Count Krasinski. There was no regular work or occupation for them, they had no money and yet they always managed to get cigarettes and to go to the films. Business seemed to prosper among them and as this business could only be "speculation", the creeping disease of the time, the older responsible people felt very ill at ease. This "speculation" fever attacked young and old and took an infinite variety of forms – beginning with the sale and re-sale of foodstuffs in small quantities, from hand to hand, and ending with the sale of jewels, gold, securities, even of land. These latter forms were the most "speculative" since all private ownership of securities and land had been abolished, and only those people with a strong faith in their lucky hand would enter into deals connected with these goods. Naturally the danger of being caught in such transactions was very great, no one seemed ever quite certain of the loyalty or honesty of the other party, and speculative prices rose higher since the operation entailed more serious risks.

The Cheka had as one of its main tasks the struggle against speculation. Thus, these youngsters, anxious to secure some pocket money and keen on risks and complicated mysterious deals, were an easy prey to any "agents provocateurs". Count

Krasinski could only warn repeatedly the leaders of this group, and at the same time endeavour to keep his own son Andrzej, a tall thin boy of fifteen, away from them. I fear the warnings were not always effective and, as I heard later, several of these boys paid with their lives for their attempts at speculation – while others in the group, totally innocent, were nevertheless suspected and suffered the same fate.

Among these boys at the hostel was one who certainly did not seem to take the slightest interest in business and who probably kept with the group simply because circumstances had put all these boys into the confined space of the hostel and had deprived them of the framework of normal life and work. This boy, nineteen or twenty years old, was an alert, quick-speaking and quick-thinking individual. The large grey eyes with long dark eyelashes were the only redeeming feature in an otherwise ungainly, square face. Small, squat and somewhat clumsy in his movements, he seemed to be in a permanent haste and whenever I asked him where he was rushing to, he smiled a cheerful smile and answered: "Did I rush? So sorry, I did not mean to." He had one consuming interest and that was a passion for grammar, for any grammar. His regret was that he did not know many languages and could not, therefore, compare at his ease the various grammars. It seemed to me at the time a most incomprehensible passion, but he was always stopping me for information on English grammar in particular and finally I suggested giving him English lessons. He was delighted, beamed all over his kind square face but then suddenly the smile dropped:

"No, I can't accept your kind offer," he said in his somewhat old fashioned correct way. "I can't accept it however much I would have loved to."

Finally he admitted that as he could not pay for the lessons he did not like to take my time. Very soon we found a solution: I gave him English lessons, he gave me Latin; we both worked hard and wrote exercises and verbs. As there is nothing so enervating as waiting and waiting, we were both glad to have something to do. He was a good teacher and I made good progress. In the long run, this study of Latin helped to get me out of the Cheka prison. The boy was not so lucky. The last I saw of him was when we were marched off to the Lubyanka and he waved to me as he disappeared behind the wooden partition of the reception room. I heard later that he never got out, but was shot, together with several of the other youngsters who had been accused of "speculating".

Meanwhile, our days of waiting continued. The winter was particularly severe, and we were lucky that, thanks to the care of the Committee of hostages, the hostel was kept warm and there was enough food for everyone. But the state of uncertainty as to our departure weighed heavily on our minds, as the list of candidates for the next train was the result of hard struggles with the Soviet representatives who suspected everything and everybody. Difficulties seemed to arise everywhere. The distribution of food to Polish prisoners in the different camps and prisons of Moscow would suddenly be checked, and the arrest of Polish hostages already released would occur at intervals. The tension grew and we soon noticed that among the throng of people who came for information or for food, there were some queer-looking individuals, who tried to draw people into conversation, to provoke some political discussion or to tempt them into some illegal business transaction. We felt there was something in the air and I remember going through all my letters, notes, scraps of paper, destroying all notes with addresses or names on them, hiding photos, sewing money into the linings of coats and taking out of the hostel, to Aunt Lelly, the few jewels that I still possessed.

January had passed and we were well into February, the days were colder still, the air grey and misty and heavy with frost; and still the Soviet authorities would not let us go, the papers were not returned, we were kept at bay and under the constant menace of arrest. Suffering was all round us: friends hiding from the Cheka spies; Cheka people walking unrecognised among us; friends helping one another; friend betraying friend; furtive glances everywhere; torrents of words and promises; bleak, sullen silence where one expected sympathy.

One year and four months had passed now since I last heard from my children. Where were they? Who looked after them? If they had lived so long without me, couldn't they live on in the same way? Could I be of any use to them? I was alone, utterly alone and how should I bring up three boys – if I ever managed to reach them?

These thoughts had been torturing me for months. I was tired out, I had no answer to these questions, no answer but faith in God's help – His help to them, the younger generation. Help to them who are helpless and unconscious still of what happens round them. But must this help go necessarily through me? Were there not many people more adapted to the task of guiding the children, more conscious of where the right way lies? I was never sure enough what should be done, while many others seemed to know so well. If I should ever find them, would I really be the right guide? My doubts grew stronger and my helplessness crushed me. Thoughts whirled and whirled round in my brain and always brought me to the conclusion: I cannot be of use, I cannot see the way.

I was walking through the streets of Moscow, the cold bit my fingers, my face, it crept through the cloth shooting jacket I wore, through the thick white pullover, it made my arms so numb – they didn't feel anything, I wished my head were as numb – why not my whole body? . . . And vivid descriptions of people freezing to death came to my mind: they'd go off to sleep, they didn't suffer, they just walked across the white snowy plain . . . .

Yes, to go away in such a quiet manner and not be a nuisance to anyone – that was the thing to do. Only the children ought to be told that I was no more and that they should not wait for me. Alphonse could take them a message. He might be leaving soon. I turned down the street where Alphonse was staying. I found him and explained, but my story was as vague as my thoughts. Alphonse got angry, then tried to persuade me otherwise, talked, begged, what was the use of it? He may have been right – but I was no good. I could not listen to him and I went away, a little sadder still, having met with reason but not with understanding.

The broad streets of Moscow faded into the grey and heavy mist which grew raw and thick as the frost increased. I would walk west, I'd probably come out of town before dusk, forests couldn't be far – I would have liked to have seen a forest again – I always loved them and under their shelter I'd feel at home.

The cold took me again by the shoulders – a hard grip it seemed, my face was stiff, but my ears were under the soft bash-lyk wound round my neck and raised up to the edge of my fur cap – just as I used to have it in Kamenka. My eyelashes stuck together from my freezing breath, the snow creaked under my feet.

I must have been far away already, the streets looked deserted, people looked like shadows, faces hidden, just hurrying, lonely figures. A light touch on my sleeve stopped me abruptly. Who was it? What strange eyes in so haggard a face.

"Excuse me, please, am I soon in the centre of Moscow?" asked a deep and hollow voice with a strong German accent.

"No – I think it is far from here," I answered mechanically in German. The man looked startled and a sudden ray of joy lit up his features and gave life to those vague eyes.

"You know German, you can help me. I come on foot from far, far away, I just gathered my last strength to come out of the forests and find some food and shelter in Moscow. Where can I get a piece of bread, and warm myself near a fire?"

He had fled the forests, he – a stranger – probably just as far from his people as I was from my children, and in a foreign country too. He had fled the forests in search of a warm fire, and a piece of bread. He wanted to live – why? What for? He had the courage to want to live, even here where everything was strange to him, where he was not wanted. I looked at him and wondered: was life truly so worth living?

"Come, I'll show you the way," I replied, and we walked up the long deserted street, back into the heart of the town. I did lead him to shelter – and did he not lead me back to life?

Back in the hostel, the long low passage running from the entrance hall to the kitchen was crowded with people, the thick heavy air full of smoke, of smells of damp fur coats, of peasant boots – of humanity. A din of voices, a giggle here from a group of youngsters, a low sob from some worn-out mother seated on one of the narrow benches lining the walls, squeals from tired babies, and loud discussions with angry words exchanged between the men. The glass door of the hall opened and closed with a screech, people came and went, patches of melting snow covered the muddy floor. Nervous strain, irritability, despair and blank submission – all mixed here in the passage, all side by side, day after day. And yet the will to live, to survive and see better times, was present in them all.

Count Krasinski was busy as usual, walking from group to group, noting names and giving orders; he rarely lost patience, and if he became angry it was only for a minute. Some of the men sitting on the benches were looking at him, as if to spy on his words. Who knew whether they were real emigrants, Polish hostages, or whether they were not perhaps agents of the Cheka? These nondescript individuals who said that they had come from the Urals or the shores of the White Sea, from Siberia or the Caucasus – had they perhaps come from down the road, from the Lubyanka headquarters, to see what the Polish hostages did and said, what they sent to the prisons, to their people still in jail, and what messages they may have received from their country? Count Krasinski knew it well – his fixed smile, his nervous rubbing of his hands, betrayed his anxiety; but he was polite to everyone and tried to pacify all dissatisfaction, all impatient protests and anxious requests.

His wife, my adoptive aunt, flitted about the place and saw to everything at once. She distributed food to those who had arrived and saw to the parcels of food to be sent to the various prisons. She received the provisions that were brought in, and talked to anxious mothers who asked advice and expected help. She kept an eye on her own lanky boy who stood smoking in a corner laughing and joking with other youngsters; her look was nervous, she felt worried about the boy and his set of friends – but what could she do? She looked at her husband, noticed his nervously rubbing hands and went up to him with some trifling remark and a whispered word of encouragement. She had a smile for the old great-aunt who reluctantly sipped at the daily ration of cabbage soup, and she kindly tapped the shoulder of Stasia, a young relative of hers who had recently arrived, who had lost all the energy she may have once possessed and who wept for her lost life, her lost studies, her lost boyfriends. As I sat on the pile of books leaning against the warm stove I was tempted to weep too, but I was brought back to good sense by the sight of my uncle and aunt who had found the energy and courage to go on day after day with the same smile, the same readiness to help others, the same endurance. Was it merely the instinct of self-preservation? Or was it also a sense of responsibility – a sense of duty imposed upon them by fate, as representatives of a certain class before their various countrymen?

The days passed, the windows were dim with steam, the frost outside was so severe, and the smoke rose high and straight from the chimneys on the house across the street. I sat in our little room, next to the hall, trying to keep cheerful and helped by the old great-aunt whose courage never failed. I watched her haggard profile as she tried with stiff and chilblained hands to darn some linen or to sew on some buttons. How helpless these poor hands looked, hands so fine, so gentle and hesitating in their movements. She talked to me about the past, about members of her family, about her life in Paris and about the clothes she used to buy there and which she still had with her now. "But it is so difficult to darn this chemise – it tears when I try to push the thick needle and cotton through it," she would say, with a smile like an excuse lighting up her transparent face as she wrapped her once fashionable black coat more firmly around her shoulders.

From time to time Alphonse would come to the hostel. At once I recognise his quick and cautious knock on our door: the great-aunt says "Come in," greets him cordially and then finds an excuse to leave the room, saying: "I know you have your plans of escape to discuss – you are young and can make plans, old aunts can't be of any help there." And when she leaves, in spite of our protests, we hurriedly exchange news, discuss chances of escape, new possibilities of finding some sort of safety for Alphonse. He is known to the authorities as a "valuable" hostage. Once already he and some others have been turned back from the frontier of Poland, returned to Moscow and kept under close watch – to be exchanged another time for more important Communists, it was said. But already some of these men have been arrested and thrown into prison. Alphonse has avoided arrest so far; he has managed to find shelter at night in a nursing home where one of the doctors is a Pole. The doctor lets him in through the entrance door while all the servants are at supper, and lets him out again through some garden gate early in the morning. But how long could this go on, how long could the doctor run the risk of his being noticed?

One day, tired and worn out, Alphonse told me that the second order for his arrest had been signed two days before by the Cheka head, and that this order had been destroyed – as the first one had – by a Polish girl who was a secretary in the Cheka. Alphonse did not even know her. She was a Communist, but above all else she was a Pole, and she had tried to save her compatriots when asked for help. But how often would she be able to play this game? This disappearance of orders was sure to be traced one day. The situation was becoming more and more difficult. We tried to be cheerful, we made plans to meet elsewhere in the future as our hostage home was too closely watched for him to slip through unnoticed – but the uncertainty of it all made us feel like hunted animals.

Meanwhile, the relations between Poland and the Soviets were becoming more and more strained, and the attitude of the Soviet authorities towards all Poles in Moscow grew accordingly less and less conciliatory. Travel permits were refused, personal documents were always found to be incorrect, all kinds of new restrictions were introduced and no promise today could be considered valid tomorrow. Poles continued to arrive from the provinces, and Count Krasinski and the other men at the head of the Polish Committee of hostages continued to apply for their repatriation to Poland, but without success. Our hostel continued to be crowded: from early morning till late at night people came in and out, and more and more frequently suspicious individuals mixed in the crowd and lingered for hours in the large passage which served as a reception room. We all felt that we were watched and we all had little hope of getting away easily or soon. Count Krasinski had warned his family to be prepared for the worst – namely, arrest – which he considered very possible and imminent. We had already removed all letters, photographs, and addresses of friends from our luggage. I had repeatedly spoken to my adoptive aunt and uncle, to their son Andrzej, their niece Stasia, and to the old great-aunt, about my imaginary relationship to them so as to make sure that in a case of emergency my identity should not be divulged. I lived in fear of such an emergency and was far from being certain that these youngsters like Andrzej and Stasia would remember my camouflage and would not address me by my real name.

Thus, when on March 20th we were roused by loud knocks on the entrance door at five o'clock in the morning, we were not taken by surprise. Loud stamping in the hall, doors opened and closed, orders shouted – it was like a house search on a large scale. Our door was opened and we were ordered, the old aunt and I, to dress quickly. As soon as we were ready a soldier took us into one of the large rooms where all inhabitants of the hostel were assembling. Sentries were posted at the doors. We sat there waiting for our turn to be called for the examination of our luggage. No fires anywhere, and a penetrating cold; the air thick with the smell of soldiers' boots and of humanity in general.

My uncle and aunt, accompanying the soldiers, were showing them the rooms, giving explanations about everyone and everything. Both were pale, tired, nervous – but still they smiled to any of us whom they passed, they gave a word of encouragement to those who looked particularly distressed. Aunt Netta thought of everything – she found a moment to put a kettle on the spirit lamp and received permission to bring us tea; she got the soldiers to bring her several loaves of black bread and lard and she saw that everyone had something to eat.

The dear old great-aunt sat there on the edge of a chair holding her black astrakhan coat tight across her shoulders. She did not move and her fixed stare made us feel very concerned about her – was she aware of what was happening? Was the nervous shock too much for her already strained nerves? Could something be done for her? One of the hostages – a doctor – tried to talk to her, but her only reaction was a nod, a quaint smile and a hurriedly repeated "Thank you, thank you, I am very well indeed." We had to leave her alone in the hope that by and by she would recover her consciousness.

Some of the people in the room tried to joke, but the jokes fell flat; others dozed, their heads on their arms; the youngsters, pale, silent, sat in one corner and did not seem to have much to say to one another. Some of the people here had already been in prison, some had only recently been released; they all knew the dread of the cell walls, the lack of air and sun, the horror of the interrogations – all these mental and physical sufferings. Almost all the men in the room could tell a long and sad tale about their experiences and as I looked at them in the hard light of the dawning winter morning, I could well see how much older than their years they all looked – how tired and worn out.

Aunt Netta, accompanied by a soldier, came in now and beckoned me to follow her. My room was to be searched. Two men plunged their hands into my bags and began pulling things out. Everything was examined, felt, shaken, all books and papers looked through. When they saw the piles of my exercise books, they became quite interested. When I said they were Latin exercises, they were at first very suspicious, as they could not quite understand why a girl should be learning Latin. Then one of the men said: "Ah, you are surely going in for medical studies? That is good." How grateful I was to him for putting the words into my mouth. I agreed at once, and started to talk about the very difficult examination in Latin that I had to prepare for. This explanation seemed to be entirely satisfactory and after that they scarcely looked any further at my things.

By the time the search was over it was past nine o'clock and people began to call as usual at the hostel. The soldiers at the door let them in but would not let them out again – and five or six people were thus caught in the Cheka trap.

It had been said at first that only the men would be taken to the Cheka for further examination. Then the commanding Commissar ordered us, the women, to get ready too and to follow the men, "Probably only for a few hours". They watched us pack our bags, as we thought it safer to prepare for the likelihood of a longer stay at the Cheka. I was touched at the time by the thoughtfulness of several of the men when they knew that we were going too: one of them put a mug in my bag, another slipped in a spoon, others gave their advice to take a change of clothes and warm things if we had any.

Apparently the impression made by my great-aunt's strange behaviour was so strong that the Commissar took it upon himself to tell her that she need not go. "Il parait que je suis trop vieille," she was repeating time after time with a pathetic smile. She seemed to recover a little and as we were leaving she patted me on the shoulder saying, "Bon courage, je garderai vos choses, ma chérie." I see her standing there in the hall, together with the old, quaint and wild-looking cook who was also told to stay – such a contrast of old women and both so lost, so helpless like children.

At the last minute Aunt Netta pushed a large loaf of black bread and a good piece of lard into my bag and insisted on my

255

taking my thick fur coat with me – how I thanked her for this advice during the following weeks!

At about ten o'clock we were all assembled in the hall and passage and, surrounded by guards with revolvers or rifles in their hands, we wound our way downstairs and into the street. It must have been a curious sight, these thirty people walking in pairs with suitcases and bags, surrounded by soldiers and Communists with guns levelled. Moscow was used to such processions but generally these mass arrests were made at local markets where only the poor and destitute were rounded up, whereas the majority of us still wore clothes which spoke of better times and our general behaviour and appearance still set us apart from the usual "bag" of the Communists' beats. Many a furtive look of sympathy and compassion accompanied us as we approached the Lubyanka, the building of the Cheka not many minutes' walk from our hostel. "We are going to prison," I repeated to myself, and somehow there was a very strange feeling of shame more than of fear connected with these words; the traditional concept of "prison" as a shameful place was still stronger than the newer habit of knowing that our friends and relations were being sent there.

Arriving at the Cheka, we were shown into a small room, previously some sort of shop, where we were individually searched after having given our names and stated our ages and occupations. There were wooden benches, large posters, a kind of desk at the far end and then wooden partitions past which we were being taken, one by one. Aunt Netta was called and I saw her disappear; then Stasia – all pale, trembling, her eyes full of tears. Then my name – Maria Adamczewska – and I moved forward. Again questions, my bag opened, things taken out, a receipt for them handed to me. My prayer book, a needle case, scissors, a ring and two small brooches, a penknife and a pencil. I had another pencil somewhere which they did not find; neither did they find my watch, which I had not thought to hide on purpose but which passed unnoticed under the thick cuff of my flannel blouse. Then I too had to pass through the narrow door where a man scrutinised carefully the papers I had, compared them with some he held, and handed me over to a guard. Then came the walk along the endless and dreary corridors, passages, stairs, with many sentries posted at doors, past grimy yards, barred windows, dim lights. An ominous silence reigned everywhere. Finally we reached the office of the head or commandant of the Cheka prison. Here again a minute search, again the repeated order to deliver any jewellery in my possession, again the same questions about name, age, etc. I felt quite bewildered and stupefied by these repeated searches and when a man – the clerk in the commandant's office, I think – thrust towards me a parcel of food left for me by my aunt, I nearly forgot my part and found myself saying, "What aunt?" Seeing the man's astonished face I realised my blunder and hurriedly took the parcel which the ever-thoughtful Aunt Netta had left for me.

This moment of hesitation, and the astonished face of the clerk, were a timely reminder that from now on I was Maria Adamczewska, the niece of Count Krasinski, the Polish girl who prepares her Latin examination for future medical studies, the orphan whose mother had been French, which explained why her Polish was not perfect – all these details which involved a great responsibility towards the family who, out of friendship and true kind-heartedness, had tried to help me. Neither they nor I must forget my story for an instant.

"I am Miss Maria Adamczewska," I hear myself saying to half a dozen unknown women looking at me from different parts of the poorly lit, square-shaped room into which I have just been pushed by the Cheka guard. And as I say these words, I hear the prison warden turning the key in the lock behind me. I am replying to the question put to me by two of the inmates of the cell sitting on their bedsteads near the door. I launch into this introduction of myself as quickly as possible, knowing that I have to live the part whatever may happen.

The other women in the cell were too busy to put questions as I entered – one was arranging her hair, one was shuffling some playing cards, two more were sleeping and lazily turned their heads in my direction. And these two heads were so ridiculously similar in type, so unmistakably French and seemed so incongruously out of place here that I could not help feeling amused and cheered. They reminded me of the Swiss governess, Mimi, who had taught me French when I was very young.

Well, these two quasi "Mimis" rose quickly enough when they recognised in me a new companion and the questions they showered upon me in broken Russian were so numerous and incoherent that I found it simpler to answer them in French. Their joy and surprise were too amusing – the flow of questions redoubled, this time in French, until the elderly woman who had first asked me my name, intervened.

"Let the poor child breathe," she said, taking me gently by the shoulder, "she must get settled first and find her way in our life here."

"Evidemment, mais certainement, la pauvre petite – toute seule aussi une étrangère, tout comme nous . . ." and they sat up on their beds looking now exactly like two little birds with their black beady eyes, pointed noses and short movements.

Meanwhile the elderly woman had shown me a bedstead that was free and on which I put down my belongings.

"Mine is the next bed; if ever you want anything, just tell me, my child, and I will try to help you as much as I can," she whispered to me.

Unfortunately, I cannot remember the name of this kind old lady who guided my first steps in prison life. I know that she was the wife of a professor, that she and her husband had been arrested together a few months before, and that she had had no news of him since. During my stay in this cell she always found a kind word for me, a warm smile, and every night she came up to my bed and tucked me in gently under my fur coat, which was my mattress, blanket and pillow all in one.

However, not all the inmates of the room were so pleasant to me. One young woman with a mass of curly black hair, fiery eyes and a highly curvaceous figure was looking at me with a critical eye, apparently displeased with the friendly reception I had met with.

"May I ask why you speak French so fluently?" she now addressed me in a rather arrogant manner.

"My mother was French and I have spoken this language since my babyhood," was my reply.

"You said you were a Polish hostage. Why then are you in Russia?" was the next question.

"My mother died and I remained with the relatives of my father, an uncle and aunt who are Polish hostages too. They lived here for years and brought me up." My story was developing along the right lines. My fear now was that, as I got further and further into imaginary details, I might not be able to keep track of them and might very well contradict myself in future. In fact, more than once during those weeks in prison I lay on my bed repeating over and over again my adoptive biography, making myself familiar with it and working it into a plausible and logical story.

Fortunately, the unpleasant curly woman was much too pre- occupied with her own self to dwell longer on the insignificant little newcomer that I was, and she quickly turned to her improvised looking-glass to arrange her curls and to blacken her eyebrows with a little spit, humming a music-hall tune and dangling her black-stockinged legs as she sat on the edge of her bed.

The person with the playing-cards seated on her bed at the far end of the room was exceedingly fat – an enormous round heap of clothes and flesh. She peered at me with a good-natured smile and with friendly blue eyes blinking slowly – something between an owl and a walrus. She was speaking to me now in a soft, drawling voice:

"I fear you won't find it very pleasant here – maybe you want me to tell you your fortune – you see, we have our own cards here – they are not allowed in fact, but we made them ourselves with empty cigarette cartons."

"Thanks, I really don't think I would like my fortune told – I fear it will not be very cheerful and I would rather not think about it," I said.

"As you like as you like – but come, Anastasia Petrovna," said the fat woman rising slowly from her couch and rolling towards the table in the centre of the room, "I think I can tell your fortune pretty well today – I have had dreams, and this means that I will be good at it."

"Yes, that's splendid, you may be able to tell me today if the black-haired jockey thinks about me still – and whether Commissar X is taking steps to get me out of this place," called out Anastasia Petrovna, the curly woman, jumping up from her bed and settling down, cigarette between her teeth, on one of the three stools near the table.

The French birds were twittering again, sighing and bemoaning their fate, fussing over their beds, slipping into queer looking bedjackets-cum-dressing-gowns and other nondescript garments, arranging each other's hair into small, rather unappetising looking ringlets hanging over the forehead.

Something stirred in the darkest corner of the room where, as I now discovered, another inmate was lying apparently asleep. As my eyes got used to the poor light of the room, I began to discern the features of this companion – hard-cut features in a sallow face with pale, hard eyes. The woman now moved slowly towards the light over the table, a book in her hand. The two fortune-tellers cast a side glance at the approaching figure and shuffled their cards together.

"The jockey still thinks of you – but I will tell you no more today – things are not clear about the other man and, besides, it is not for everyone's ears," added the fat woman, raising her voice.

"You are very difficult and ill-humoured," said the sallow-faced woman with a sour smile. "I cannot read in my dark corner, and I cannot sleep all day long as you like to do."

"I like sleeping," was the quick answer of the fat one, "and if I am not sleeping I like playing cards – won't you have a game with me?" and she prepared to deal out.

"No, thank you, I prefer to read," was the dignified reply of the sallow one, while Anastasia Petrovna made faces behind her back.

"Don't pay any attention to these skirmishes – they never get on well together and besides, you had better keep away from the woman with the book," whispered the elderly woman in my ear, "she is the 'eye' of the authorities for our cell."

I was very grateful for this information, coming from someone I felt I could trust. It would not have occurred to me to look for a spy amongst us prisoners, although stories about such spies were often told. This one, however, did not seem to be a very successful spy, since everybody had learned to shun her and mistrust her, and all conversations dropped at her approach. Even Anastasia Petrovna would suddenly break off in the midst of colourful descriptions of her pastimes with the jockey, or the rope-dancer, or the Commissar X, when she noticed the attentive gaze of the "sallow-faced". A pirouette on the high heels, a hard puff at her cigarette, a lighthearted whistle or a muttered curse would make an abrupt end to the story.

The sallow-faced one tried to approach me with a few innocent-seeming questions, and with suggestions about books – she was the only one allowed to get books from the prison library – but I gave such stupid flat replies and apparently made such a successful blank face that she gave up all attempts with a short shrug of her angular shoulders.

The routine of the day was not complicated. We were awakened at seven-thirty, if I remember rightly, and were marched off into a bathroom along the passages, one soldier leading, another following behind us. The bathroom had no door, there was one cold water tap over a filthy wash-basin, a bath tub which was evidently not for use, and ten minutes for seven of us to wash. The soldiers seemed to find these ten minutes too long and kept on hurrying us all the time, pushing aside those who tried to secure some privacy for their companions by standing in the doorway. Great care was taken that we should never meet any other group of prisoners on our wanderings through the passages.

Between eight and nine we had breakfast – some hot water was allowed for making tea, a small piece of rye bread was given to each of us to last the day, and sometimes a lemon drop sweet instead of sugar. At ten, the commandant of the Lubyanka prison, Popov, came on an inspection round, and accepted petitions from the prisoners. At noon we had a meal, and this was repeated at seven. It consisted of cabbage soup followed by porridge. Two stalwart, husky, flaxen-haired women, the so-called "Lettish mares" (the majority of the Cheka wardens at the time were Letts), pushed a kind of trolley along the passages and distributed soup in wooden bowls while two armed men kept watch either side of the open cell door. A few minutes after the soup procession had rattled away, the "kasha" porridge trolley approached. The wooden bowls were used for both courses and then returned for use by other prisoners further along the passage. The edges always showed traces of previous meals – cabbage leaves, bits of porridge – for the bowls were seldom washed. In the evening another jug of hot water was pushed in, we were taken out for the third and last wander through the passages (no washing was allowed in the evening), and at nine or ten at night the lights were dimmed and we had to be in bed.

Day and night we were watched through a small round hole made in the door, and the sensation that this one eye might at any time be looking at us made us feel distinctly uncomfortable. The wardens wore soft felt boots so that their steps could not be heard when they approached the door from outside. From time to time they opened the door to call out an order or to make some remark. Thus I remember that once, as I was trying to explain to my companions the differences between a shotgun and a rifle, the door was opened abruptly and the warden shouted gruffly: "Conversations about guns and bullets are forbidden here." I was pretty scared, I confess, and wondered whether my knowledge of such "forbidden" matters would earn me a bad mark. As a rule, loud conversations or singing and laughter were rapidly suppressed.

Shortly after my first meal in the cell, a warden brought me a long questionnaire which I had to fill in. This was a very arduous task for it had to be plausible and to fit with information I had already given. Unfortunately the questions referred not only to myself but to my parents and my grandparents and there seemed to be lots of questions for which I was not prepared. I would have to remember exactly all dates and names that I mentioned, so as to make no mistake if I were to give the same data again. Slowly, I wrote my story down, giving as few names as I possibly could, making my father a Polish doctor who died in 1900, my mother a French governess who lived many years in Russia and died before the war, myself a girl of twenty-four preparing to be a medical student. What I dreaded most was that my adoptive aunt or uncle might be asked similar questions about me and that their answers would differ from mine. A discrepancy in such data would lead to the discovery of my real name and this would have proved fatal – both for them and for myself. This fear haunted me not only in the weeks I spent in prison but all the time that I remained under Bolshevik rule, for the Krasinskis were kept in prison long after I had been released, and any incident which could bring me again into the hands of the Cheka would revive this danger.

On the second day of my imprisonment I was ordered to follow a guard, leaving my things behind. "You are going to be photographed," said my companions. They were right. After endless passages, stairs, halls and passages again, I found myself in a very ramshackle photographer's studio under the roof. A chair stood in front of the camera and a peg with a large number was fixed above the chair. No Versailles background with fountains painted in misty blue, no gilt armchair, no cardboard boats, no potted palms – nothing of the usual outfit of an old-fashioned studio. This was a business-like place. I sat down, glanced over my head at my number and looked into the camera with as insipid an expression as I could produce, hoping that the photograph of "Miss Maria Adamczewska" would never resemble anybody in real life.

As I came back to my cellmates, I found them all agog: the little French parrots were leaving. The twittering, jibbering, feverish packing that went on was too funny for words, and the exclamations – lost on the warden and my companions but much appreciated by me seemed to syncopate with the orders to be quiet.

"Alors, au revoir, les amies, on se reverra bien une fois – on va nous mettre en liberté sûrement – et nous penserons à vous – au revoir, la petite," turning to me, "nous parlerons à votre consul et . . ." The door was banged with a crash behind them and we heard more twittering and rough voices telling them to "shut up".

It was a comic scene, but these two little parrots would certainly have passed entirely out of my memory had I not met them four years later in Paris. I was coming out of a tram at the Etoile, when suddenly a woman grasped me by the arm, whilst another exclaimed joyously: "Tiens, voilà la petite qui était en prison avec nous . . ." much to the astonishment of the public round us. The two realised the impression these words had created and laughingly added: "Yes, we all have been in prison together, imprisoned by the Bolsheviks, and it was no fun – je vous le promets." Friendly smiles and murmurs were the reply. One little parrot hanging on to each of my arms, I had to go with them and we landed in a café-tabac in the Avenue Wagram where I had to drink at least a coffee – having refused "cassis, pernod" and I don't know what other favourite drinks of my newly found friends. They told me their story, they told me their names – I forget them all; but what touched me deeply was that they still remembered me as "Mademoiselle Maria" and I did not disillusion them.

A few days after their departure from the Lubyanka prison cell I, too, had to leave our other cellmates – the elderly friend who had looked after me so well, the boisterous and adventurous Anastasia Petrovna, the fortune-teller balancing with difficulty her thirty- stone body on the three-legged stool, and also the sallow-faced spy. I was ordered to gather my things and to "follow", which I did full of apprehension. I felt sure that in my case a change could scarcely be for the better, and I was right, for an hour later I was trudging my way to the Butyrki prison.

I was taken down first to the inner courtyard of the Lubyanka, where groups of prisoners with bags and baskets were lined up against the walls. They stood with thin, pale faces, tightly closed lips and restless anxious eyes. Beneath a brilliant blue sky uniformed officials were splashing through the slushy snow, giving words of command and reading out lists of names. A few steps to my left, the tearful Stasia stared at me with vacant eyes from her pale, puffy face. Had she sufficient presence of mind not to betray herself, myself and the others? These thoughts troubled my mind and my heart sank.

"Maria Adamczewska . . ." I heard the official call out.

"Present," I replied with an unnecessarily loud voice, stepping forward not daring to look round.

As I stooped to pick up my things I heard "Stasia Z . . ." being called and a minute later, together with another Polish girl – a mere child of fifteen, we were following the three guards who, rifles in hand, led us through vaults and yards into the crowded streets of Moscow.

We walked on the pavement; muddy snow, ankle-deep, splashes from passing sledges; pigeons fluttered up, and many inquiring, compassionate but furtive glances from passers-by followed us. I noticed the expressions of many poorly dressed people on whose faces I seemed to read the terror of an ordeal perhaps already experienced, perhaps still dreaded and awaited. The leading soldier took long strides and as we struggled to keep up, Stasia was already out of breath and the chubby little Polish girl was very red and on the verge of crying. My boots were heavy, the bag and the fur coat weighed me down, and I was glad when the guards took pity upon Stasia and her groans and stopped for a few minutes in a quiet deserted street. No questions were answered, we were not allowed to talk, and then we strode on and on further into the suburbs.

"This is the way to the Butyrki prison," murmured Stasia.

"Silence!" shouted the soldier at the back and pushed her with the butt end of his rifle.

"Butyrki" meant a lot to all of us who were in Moscow at that time: it meant a prison where people generally stayed a long time.

After more than an hour's walk we approached the dark and gloomy prison, skirting for a while its high blind walls and when the heavy iron gate closed behind us, I felt that we all became a little paler. The sound was so final, so grim, no resounding echo but a dull clap of metal on metal and a faint, high screech from the hinge.

Another search through our things was made: a very minute search carried out by women with kerchiefs on their heads, ugly remarks on their lips and rough, greedy movements as they plunged their hands into our bags and searched us personally too. Then we were handed over to a warden with his professional bunch of keys; I shivered, and Stasia groaned, breathing quickly. The air was heavy and damp, the lamps spread a dim light through vaulted passages and iron-railed halls which reminded me suddenly and incongruously of the Friedrichstrasse station in Berlin. We were led up the iron stairs; the walls were metal too, and it felt somehow as if we were climbing along the sides of safes in some huge bank. Stasia fainted on the stairs and was carried up by two soldiers. The warden opened the door of one of these 'safes' – a door which was actually as thick as those in a bank – and while the soldiers tried to help Stasia by giving her some water to drink, a man – apparently a prisoner on duty – whispered to me swiftly: "Are you Polish hostages too? Lots of them have been brought in here today. I had been with some of them in another prison. Bad luck! You are being put into the 'single' cell . . ." A soldier turned round frowning and the man slipped

Edith after a capercailzie shoot, with birds displayed on the game-keeper's garden fence. c. 1917.

Alexander (centre of group) home on leave in 1917, discussing the serious political situation with friends. The friend on the right of the picture is Alphonse Riesenkampf.

Photograph of Edith with her three sons Alec (7), Vladimir (10) and
Nicolas (3) in the spring of 1917.

Showing a different style of hunting after the revolution, Edith went out alone with a gun in search of food. It amused her in 1918 to be, as it were, a poacher on nationalised land.

One of the boats used in the hunting expedition on Lake Ladoga with Alphonse Riesenkampf. 1918.

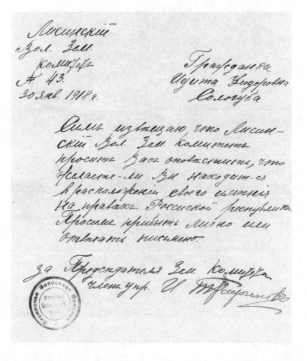

Letter dated 30 January 1918 from the Lissino District Rural Committee informing "citizeness Eedita Feodorovna Sologub" of a meeting to dispose of her estate according to the laws of the Russian Republic. She resolved to attend this meeting despite the possible dangers (see pp. 168–169).

away into the queer maze of open-work iron balustrades, stairs and pillars.

The door was locked and we were alone in the long narrow cell. The faint light of the ending day came in through the window high above our heads. Three narrow bedsteads of rough white boards with a thin layer of straw were raised just a few inches off the floor; there was very little free space between them. An iron table was fixed to the wall, and above it an electric lamp; an iron stove in one corner, a pail in the other. Cement walls, cement floor, water trickling in zigzags down the walls and forming pools on the already dirty floor. How could I be cheerful in these surroundings with the sobbing Stasia and the bewildered, trembling Polish girl?

We stayed ten days in this cell, and we were not once allowed out of it. Every morning the "cleaning deputation" as I called it, arrived with a broom, two soldiers to remove the pail, three soldiers with rifles and a warden with keys, all lined up in front of the open door. The broom was given to one of us, the floor had to be rapidly swept, the pools of water smudged into proper thick mud, and then the door was banged and locked until the ceremony was repeated the next morning. Our food was passed to us twice a day through a window in the door, and in the morning we got our ration of water, which consisted of a very small jug that had to last us twenty-four hours – for drinking and for washing. This shortage of water was perhaps the hardest privation we experienced at Butyrki. The lentil broth representing our twice-daily meals was black and lukewarm and more than once I discovered worms swimming about in it. Fortunately, we all had some black bread left in our bags and, though hard and dry, it saved us from suffering too much from hunger.

To pace up and down the cell was not easy unless both my companions lay on their beds – and this they did for the greater part of the day, Stasia crying, the girl humming some wailing, endless song. And I walked up and down, trying to keep warm, stamping the mud off my brother's big boots. Every now and then the little round hole in the door became alive, looked less black – it was the eye of the guard peeping in. The air was heavy, the window tightly shut. At night I lay tossing about on my boards, incapable of sleeping, for the dampness was worse so close to the floor, and I shivered in spite of my thick fur coat. The electric bulb glared down with its cold expressionless light.

Time went by so slowly. I drew horses on the walls with my short stubby pencil, marked every day the progress of the rivulets trickling down, watched for the eye of the guard, then nodded to him and asked about the weather and about his dinner. It is amusing to guess whether the eye was smiling or whether it was angry, whether the answer would be pleasant or an unintelligible grunt. One of the guards seemed to have a kinder heart and always gave a detailed description of the weather, sometimes stopping short when some suspect figure drew near. One day I played a joke on him; hiding the Polish girl in the corner near the door, I sat down gloomily on my bunk, Stasia moaning and groaning as usual on hers. I kept an eye on the watch-hole. There, the blue eye appeared and seemed now to run round the cell. It disappeared, to come back a few minutes later and dwell for quite a while stuck close to the opening. We two sighed and moaned. Finally, a voice asked from behind the door: "Where is the third girl?" I rose and, coming closer to the door, whispered: "The food has been so bad all these days, we were so hungry that we have eaten up the youngest of us three." The man laughed and walked away, but he was restless and a minute later steps approached again, another eye looked in, whispers could be heard behind the door. The little Polish girl chuckled and burst out into such a merry laugh that we all joined in and the guards behind the door coughed and muttered a joke. I fear that this was the only time we laughed in this cell.

Then came the last night at Butyrki. Soon after midnight, soldiers entered our cell ordering us to dress quickly and to pack up our things. The head of the Lubyanka prison was with them and stood stiff and silent in the doorway, the warden with the keys next to him and several armed men behind them. What a display for three girls! It really looked very imposing, I thought. Where could we be taken now? What a strange hour to move us from prison to prison – or would it be a camp? How quaint these men looked silhouetted against the dim light behind them. A few minutes later we passed through the heavy iron gate and, together with our guards, were squeezed into two open cars.

A swift ride through Moscow followed, first through gloomy deserted streets, then through the lively and still well-lit centre where crowds moved about in spite of the late hour. People looked round at us for there were no private cars, no taxis any more in Moscow; official cars running at this hour of night were generally Cheka cars – and everyone knew it well enough. I sat in front and enjoyed the brisk, clean air, the swiftness of the ride, and found myself asking the driver questions about the car – a powerful Benz – and about the speed he could reach on these slushy roads. He answered sullenly, looking round at me with slight astonishment, and I remembered then that I was a prisoner in the hands of the Cheka, and that my conversation must strike him as rather strange. After that I remained silent until we reached the Lubyanka buildings. What a pity to leave the car, and how bad the air would be inside . . . these thoughts seemed suddenly quite important, and I wondered at them and was ashamed at my lightheartedness. The commandant of the prison had disappeared, we walked up endless stairs, led and followed by several soldiers. On the landing of a small and badly lit staircase we were told to wait. A few minutes later the young Polish girl was called. Apparently we were to be questioned now – and Stasia and I watched helplessly as the little fifteen-year old went forward alone.

"I will not cry, I will not cry!" – this is what I was repeating to myself as I entered the interrogation room. The two girls who had been in before me had each come out with tears streaming down their faces and sobbing violently. It seemed to me essential that I should not cry; that I should not give these Bolsheviks the satisfaction of always making their victims cry. Too great an honour for these brutes, I thought.

The room was large and high, furnished like a study – but a study in poor taste. A large writing-desk in the far left corner, six or seven leather-backed chairs round it, an armchair in the middle. One lamp with a low green shade standing on the writing-desk, with its light falling directly on the one chair facing the armchair in which the president of the interrogation sat.

There were several men in the room: the president, a small, fair-haired, blue-eyed man with a pointed beard and a rather low voice, sat in the armchair making holes with his pencil in the sheet of blotting paper in front of him. He told me to take the chair facing him and gave me a quick but very scrutinising look with his piercing blue eyes. At his right and at his left the other men – six altogether, I think – had taken their places. They were mostly youngish men and all of a darker type – black curly hair prevailing.

After a few questions about myself, the reasons for my being at the hostages' hostel in Moscow, and the date of my arrival there, the president asked me what I knew about Polish political organisations in Russia. I denied all knowledge of the existence of such organisations and this was partly true, as my knowledge was limited to a very vague idea of something – somewhere. One of the men gave a sneering laugh; the others shrugged their shoulders.

"But your uncle and aunt seemed always to have a lot to do and to see a lot of people – they must have had some good reason for it," said the president.

"Oh yes, they had an awful lot to do: Uncle had to establish the lists of hostages and get all the documents in order for them; and Aunt had to see to feeding them all and to the distribution of food parcels for those still in prison," I answered, knowing perfectly well that all this was known to them and of no interest whatever to the tribunal.

"Did you never receive any messages from Poland? Surely some news from there reached you quite regularly at the hostel?" said the president.

"I really don't know as I never got any letters myself and I don't remember hearing anything much about it."

"After all, you were living there – you must have heard something about news and letters," put in one of the younger men.

"I was there all the time, that's true, but I spent a great deal of my time over my studies in Latin – the exercises alone took many hours . . ."

"Yes," put in the president, "We know that you were preparing for the entrance examination for the medical courses – yes, we have your exercise books and we know your handwriting very well," he added with a smile.

"It's very bad handwriting, I fear, but you see that I worked hard on my Latin . . ."

"Try to remember: in spite of the Latin, have you never heard mentioned letters received from Poland? Some of the hostages at the hostel must have had letters."

"No . . . I have never heard of any news," I answered hesitatingly, an idea crossing my mind. "No, no news, but letters – yes, of course there were letters," and I stopped as if remembering details but in reality only to see and enjoy the expression of eager attention and satisfaction on the faces turned towards me.

"Well, that's right – you see, you remember letters. What did they say? Surely you'll remember that too," said the president.

"Oh, we were terribly disappointed for these letters were always the same – they just gave names and names of people to whom others were sending greetings – and, imagine, the rest of the letters were just blackened out, absolutely black – you know how it is done, by the censor, for I think these letters were sent over from the Commissariat of Foreign Affairs." And I looked blankly at the men, but secretly enjoyed their disappointment.

Certainly they did show a genuine disappointment, as they must evidently have hoped to get through me some facts to be used against the chief hostages. I had looked the stupid little goose ready to tell them what they were anxious to find out.

The president looked annoyed – and this was not exactly a pleasant result of my joke. He asked me now which of my two companions in the Butyrki prison had been writing letters in secret. Again I denied all knowledge of any letters being written. The men insisted – I denied. They pressed me, saying that the suspicions were not falling on me, but on one of the other two girls. One of the younger men pushed before me a closely written sheet of paper.

"Look at this – read this letter – it was sent out of your cell: one of your companions has written it."

"Yes," said the president, "it must be one of the two other girls for it is not your handwriting – we know yours."

"Read it, read," pressed the younger man.

"No, I am not a bit interested in it, and I am not in the habit of reading other people's letters," I answered with assumed dignity and showing my aloofness.

The young man shrugged his shoulders and turned to the president for support. The president looked down at his blotting paper where the hole was growing larger. He looked bored – and no wonder, for the case was so insignificant, and I had the impression that he was letting the other investigators practise their art of persuasion on me.

"Besides," said one of them, "You must know who wrote this letter as you were the only one to have a pencil – that we know," he said, stressing the last words with evident satisfaction.

"Yes, I was the only one to have a pencil and you know it because the guard could see me drawing lines on the wall to mark the places where the water flowed down . . ."

"And your pencil was red outside, was it not?" – this with a triumphant smile.

"Yes, you are right, it is red outside, you can see it if you want as I have it in the pocket of my coat out there on the landing. But the lead is black, whereas this letter here is written with an ink-pencil – it is blue."

This seemed to be an irrefutable argument and I wondered what he would say now.

The young man fumbled quickly in his pocket and produced a short bit of an ink-pencil and pushing it towards me said, "But look, here is an ink-pencil and it was found in your cell as you were leaving it – this is a proof."

"I never saw this pencil and if you knew of its existence all the time why then did you say that I alone had a pencil, and why did you speak about my pencil which is red outside? Was it worthwhile?"

This was a dangerous thing to say and to ask, and I was scared of what I had done – but it was too late. However, another of the men saved the pencil investigator by putting some question about my companions who, he thought, belonged to some Polish political organisation. Thus we were all brought back to this first question and I denied again all knowledge about any organisation of the kind among Poles.

However, the president returned to the letter-writing question and insisted on my "confessing" that one of my two companions had been writing letters in the cell. I denied again and again and the cross-examination threatened to draw into indefinite length. The president's name was Menzhynsky. His steel blue eyes showed no softness – and it did not surprise me to learn later that he became the Head of the Cheka in due course.

Then came a change of tactics. One of the other men, a sleek, well-fed, bulgy-eyed man of about forty, got up and putting his chair next to mine began to persuade me in a suave voice accompanied by smiles and gentle taps on my arm.

"You know, it is no use denying – so why continue? It is senseless to deny and as soon as you confess – well then, you can be set free – it is so simple."

"But I cannot confess when there is nothing to confess."

Menzhynsky put in here: "If you continue to deny that one of your companions wrote this letter, then we'll have to put you into a single cell, alone, until you confess."

"I am very sorry, but I cannot do it."

"Oh, look here, even if you are not sure which of your companions wrote it, just tell us which one you think it might be and you'll be free – not in the single cell which is not agreeable. Admit it – and it will be all over." The suave investigator was tapping my arm, I saw the smoke-yellowed stumpy fingers on my sleeve, I saw his bulgy brown eyes looking at me and his little brown beard quivering as he spoke, and I hated it all so much and felt so utterly disgusted that, losing my self-control I said:

"Anyhow, you don't believe what I say – it's no use repeating and do you really think that I am capable of such a low action as to accuse one of my companions just in order to get free?"

Menzhynsky smiled a fine smile, the sleek investigator walked away shrugging his shoulders, and I felt angry with myself at having shown them that I had lost patience and at having used a rather strong expression in Russian which escaped me in my anger. The men exchanged a few words.

"I regret, then, we have nothing more to discuss and you will go to a single cell until you change your mind," said the president while the other investigators nodded their approval.

They had not made me cry – at least that was something to be proud of. Getting up to go, I found myself waving my hand and saying as I reached the door: "I'm sorry but it can't be helped: single cell or not, it is no use crying – goodbye." Why I said it I don't know, and the broad smile I felt on my face must have struck the men as being rather senseless. Perhaps I was just very tired – and of course it had been a strain on my nerves.

The soldiers took me a long way through passages and halls and stairways and finally opened a door into the promised single cell. Dimly lit with the night electric light bulb, it looked grim enough. But I was tired and stretched out on the bare bunk and closed my eyes as if to sleep.

It was not a restful night, this first rather short night in the single cell. I lay rolled in my coat, staring into the blankness, thinking over and over again all I had been asked, all I had answered during the interrogation. And, as usual, the right answers came now to my mind so logically, so clearly, and I felt worried and miserable not to have found them at the time. And throughout the night I could hear steps in the passages, doors being opened and closed, murmurs of voices, and the sinister meaning of these movements made this solitary night the more unbearable.

Still, the morning came at last. The usual routine of the Lubyanka prison was well known to me: the tête-à-tête walk with the soldier to the bathroom-lavatory, the tea with a fruit-drop for breakfast, the visit of Popov and his stereotyped questions, all this passed like a dream, and by ten o'clock I found myself faced with a long day of utter blankness. What should I do? Sit on my bunk and stare at the opposite wall? No, I had to do something, and besides it was bitterly cold in this tiny cell. How large was it? And I walked round its four walls, counting my paces – thirteen. Not too bad. I counted again – the other way – the same. Then diagonally – and if I try a circle? Here was an occupation: walk and count the paces, walk backwards, start from the door to the bunk, or from each corner to the bunk. Quite a number of combinations could be found with a little imagination. I looked furtively at my wristwatch: half-an-hour had gone. Why not walk regularly one hour, then lie down for exactly one hour, and then start all over again? There would be something to look forward to – the end of an hour. I carried out this plan very conscientiously and the day passed much more quickly than I had expected and feared. The guard seemed to get interested in my scheme, for I saw frequently the hole in the door liven up with a pale eye, which I disliked intensely and I tried not to look at it.

Then steps were heard in the passage at an undue hour – not meal time nor at the time of the usual pilgrimage to the bathroom. This was most unpleasant, and it was a very deep sigh of relief that escaped me when the steps passed on. What I feared was anther interrogation, or a visit from some local officials, or a call to confront my aunt in some matter concerning Polish hostages. And then, if the details I gave did not coincide with my aunt's version – what would happen? She and her husband would be held responsible for having tried to smuggle me through – I preferred not to think any further. This thought of the risk they ran, because of me, haunted me all the time.

The day passed without any incident. The next morning I took up my plan again and started the regular hourly walks and rests. By two o'clock the sentry was apparently getting worried about me, for the pale eye simply stuck to the hole. At four o'clock, steps approached my door; it was my resting hour. I sat up, listening. The steps halted, the key turned, I felt cold and hot and weak. It was Popov, accompanied by a soldier, who came in.

"How are you? How do you feel?"

"Thank you, I feel all right," I answered, wondering what this visit and this question meant.

"Do you need anything? Have you some complaint?"

"No, nothing – it is not very warm, though . . ." I added, not knowing what to say.

"Hmm . . ." Apparently Popov was at the end of his repertoire of sympathetic questions on the well-being of his charges. "I thought . . . I did not know . . . whether you did not need something . . . you walked . . ."

So that was it, I understood now the reason for his unexpected call: the sentry had reported my strange behaviour of walking rapidly in strange zigzags, they had decided that I had gone queer in the head, and Popov had come to see how far I was still normal.

He turned abruptly and left.

About two hours later I heard steps again; again my key turned, again came the feeling of terror and helplessness. A prison warden entered this time, with the soldier, and told me to take my things and follow. We went up some stairs and along a passage; the leading man opened a door, let me in and closed it behind me without a word.

I was in a large room with two windows, seven or eight bunks along the walls, the white-washed windows all pink with the reflection of the sunset; it was of course a prison cell but there seemed something almost friendly about it. All the bunks but one were empty – and on this one a woman was sitting. I took one look at her and exclaimed in English:

"Hullo, what luck – you must be English!"

"Yes, that's right. And you are an Irish girl, are you not?"

"No, I'm sorry to disappoint you – I am a Polish girl, but I am so happy now to be in this cell with you."

She took me by the hand and said something about being glad too, and asked me how I guessed that she was English and how I came to speak such fluent English myself. We talked and talked and that night I fell asleep quite happy and so thankful to be with a friendly soul. The single cell had been a disturbing and unpleasant experience. I do not know why I was transferred from it so soon – the promised stay there "until you confess" had not been kept – but perhaps this had been something of an empty threat.

My new companion was a Miss Anne Maxwell, who had been arrested at the same time as her brother, months ago in Petersburg where they had their home. As far as I remember, they had some business in Russia – factories I believe. Miss Maxwell had been imprisoned first in Petersburg for some months, then transferred to Moscow. She did not know what had become of her brother.

For two days we two had this large cell to ourselves, but then our peace was disturbed by the arrival of a fat and talkative Polish woman who had owned a shop in Moscow and who later, when forced to close down the business, had opened an illicit café. She assured me that Popov had been a policeman under the Tsarist regime (and I must say he certainly looked like one), and that his name was really something quite different as he was a Lett. She knew him in the interim period when he was no longer a policeman and not yet a Cheka man, when he used to be a client at her café.

The same afternoon, there were more new arrivals in this part of the prison. Into our cell came a young Russian woman, married to a Frenchman who had been consul in Kiev first and then at Archangel, if I remember rightly. I think her name was Madame Marchand. She was extremely nervous and upset as she had not had any news of her husband since their arrest; all she knew was that he had been brought to Moscow too. She was indignant about the treatment of foreigners who should have had the right to diplomatic immunity, and she tried in vain to make Popov listen to her explanations.

In the cell next door to ours we could hear men's voices, and I seemed to recognise Polish speech. One voice sounded familiar. I listened intently and soon had no doubts – it was the voice of young Andrzej Krasinski, the fifteen-year-old son of my uncle and aunt. The door between our cells – or, rather, rooms, as the building had not originally been a prison – was boarded up on our side, and builder's rubble apparently used to fill the space between the actual door and the boards. However, at the bottom there was a rather broad chink about an inch wide from which bits of chalk and sand trickled out. A bunk, at present unoccupied, was pushed right across this door, and if I sat down on it I could hear the voices quite distinctly.

I decided to let Andrzej know of my presence, and at dusk the Polish woman with her ample skirts and big shawl sat down on the bunk and spread her skirts; Miss Maxwell stood in front of her, between her and the sentry's peep-hole, talking as if explaining something; and I crept on my stomach under the bunk and started scraping with a hairpin at the rubble through the chink. The voices beyond could be heard even more clearly now – it was Andrzej, there was no doubt. But I wondered who the two other men might be? Would they betray him and me, if I managed to make him hear me? No, after all, he was only a boy, it would not really be worth while betraying him – and the other men were Poles, too. I tapped resolutely three short knocks at the bottom of the door. The conversation beyond stopped abruptly – they had heard me. I put my mouth to the chink and whispered as loud as caution would allow:

"Andrzej, Andrzej – ty jestes? – Is that you?"

A slight rustling, a slight tapping and an excited whisper.

"Mamusia? Mother?"

"No, Maria, your cousin Marysenka-Edy," I whispered back, adding my own name – Edy – to make him understand, as he did not usually call me "Marysenka" and might now be at a loss in his excitement.

"You are there – and where is Mother? Have you seen her?"

"No, not since the day of the arrest. But how are you? Are you hungry?"

"I am all right – if only I knew where and how Mother is. Yes, I am a bit hungry – I have still plenty of lard but no bread to eat it with."

"I have plenty of bread, but no knife to cut a thin slice to push through to you . . ."

"Tst . . ." the Polish woman kicked me slightly. I crept speedily out at the other end of the bunk and sat next to her. Miss Maxwell continued to gesticulate and to tell us some long story. Shuffling steps could be heard along the passage . . . but they went on past.

I was extremely happy to have found Andrzej and from then on we had regularly a short conversation twice a day. He had a knife and passed it to me through the chink; I cut him slices of bread and, wrapping them in a pocket handkerchief, managed to push them through. In return he sent me slices of lard. The communication chink could be hidden behind some chips of mortar to lessen the chance of its being discovered.

I found out that Andrzej had not been taken for interrogation yet. I tried to give him courage, and told him that when the time came he must not be upset by accusations which might be showered on him and his parents, and he must play the silly and stupid boy who only thought of smoking and of going to the pictures. I don't know whether this advice helped him, but I am sure that he was happy to hear a friendly voice. When I left the cell I had time to ask Miss Maxwell to let Andrzej know that I was gone – and I think he got the message. When I saw him years later in Warsaw he told me that he was kept three months in prison and when released stayed on in Moscow until his parents were freed more than a year later.

Meanwhile, another woman was brought into our cell. She was a noisy creature and certainly not an improvement to our existence. Her rough bluish-black hair was closely curled and stood quaintly like a halo round her face – a face which was not one of those you would associate with a halo. She looked like a bird of prey, with beak and curved mouth, beady piercing eyes and sallow complexion. Her movements were quick, nervous, jerky, and her voice shrill and raucous. She told us that she was the wife of a Persian consular official somewhere in the south of Russia. As soon as she found out that another "diplomatic personality" – the wife of the French consul – was in the cell, she pounced on the poor young woman and never left her any peace. All day long she would relate her "diplomatic" experiences both before her arrest and since; she protested vehemently against improper treatment of "diplomats", appealed to all powers on earth to set her free, and – when in a more quiet mood – went round the cell offering us in turn to tell us our fortunes from the lines on our hands.

I steadily refused her fortune-telling offers, saying that I was terribly superstitious, but then she insisted, promising that she would limit herself to telling me my character. Well, I could not find any plausible excuse here and showed her my hand.

"Strange," she said looking at it intently. "You are so young and yet your lines show a life with many problems – great

280

difficulties largely overcome, I should say," and she turned the hand more to the light.

I became quite nervous now lest she should discover all my biography and I found myself denying emphatically all her suggestions. Fortunately, she did not seem to be too sure of her art, for shaking her head she added: "It is a strange hand for one so young: it shows a life full of eventfulness – but as you don't want me to tell you the future, I will be silent. Only it is puzzling that all this eventfulness is in your case shown so differently, as if already past – when at your age it can only be coming."

I thanked her, greatly relieved when she dropped my hand. I did not enjoy being at close quarters with this person, especially when, not satisfied with the short time allowed us every morning in the bathroom, she would start changing her clothes in the cell. She would strip off all the garments she had on, then hunt for parasites on herself and in the clothes before dressing again and announcing that she now felt much cleaner! It was so disgusting that I regularly pretended to sleep and turned my back on the appalling sight.

As I lay on my bunk trying to look sleepy so as not to have to join in the general conversation, I started to think of some plan of escape. I had one idea and I tried to work it out, although I knew it seemed far-fetched and pretty impossible. At least it kept my mind busy and away from harassing thoughts. During my stay in the first cell, the professor's wife had one day been taken under the escort of only one soldier to a dentist in the town. This was the only case I knew where someone had been taken outside the building. If I pretended to have toothache and got the permission to go, I would surely get some poor wretch of a soldier to guard me, and I would surely be taken to some modest dentist who would have an unpretentious entrance and no porter at the door. On the stairs of the dentist's house I would suddenly turn and go for the guard; I would knock him out by one drive into the jaw and one kick into the body – and perhaps a punch between the ribs as well. This would be sure to make him topple over and then I'd run for my life.

It seemed a good plan in my mind – and I started practising some strong right blows on my fur coat hung up on a nail I had discovered near the door. My room-mates laughed at me, but I assured them that I needed exercise and this kind of boxing was the only thing I could think of, since some of them did not like it if I paced up and down the room.

After a day or two, when my blows at the bottom of the collar (the jaw blow) and the kick on the level of the pocket were fairly accurate, I confided my plan to Miss Maxwell. She laughed heartily but she was not encouraging about my prospects of success. What prevented me from asking immediately for an appointment with a dentist was the horror I had of dentists in general, and the thought that I might pile on myself this new calamity if I could not escape from my guard in time! And in my more realistic moments the thought that my adopted aunt and uncle would have to suffer the consequences of my behaviour weighed heavily against any such plan.

Time goes very slowly in prison – at least this was my experience. People who have had months and months of imprisonment say that soon enough the months go by quite smoothly because the same thing happens week after week, day after day. But for me, after a few weeks at the Lubyanka prison I felt as if years had passed since that cold March morning when we had all been arrested at the Polish hostel. The monotony of each day was made worse for me by the fact that the windows, dim and blurred, covered with dull blue-white paint on the outside and black with dust on the inside, were never opened and let in so little daylight from their position high above our heads. I spent hours trying to penetrate the secret of these large grey surfaces behind which there must be light, air, sun, wind and rain. They were double windows and were nailed and stuck fast. Even the top part which had originally been meant to remain free for airing the room, was now nailed up. My companions did not seem to mind this and grumbled when I meekly suggested that a bit of fresh air would be pleasant; they feared the cold and draughts and did not understand my silent longing.

However, as time passed and we had reached the middle of April, the weather had grown so warm that the room became too stuffy even for my hardened companions. They sniffed, sighed, and finally decided that when the prison chief next passed on his daily round we would ask him to let us open the top window. Thus, when Popov entered our cell the next morning at ten for his usual visit, he was asked about the window.

Apparently it was an unusual request, for he hesitated a little, but then agreed. Under his supervision, the top window was opened about a hand's breadth and nails were driven into the frame to prevent it from opening more. Even this little slit into the world outside appeared to me as a great boon. By kneeling down in one corner of the cell I could see a bit of sky, and whenever I looked at it this little triangle of sky seemed to be blue – pale blue in the mornings, deeper at noon, opal towards evening. At night I could not look at it because my companions, being afraid of colds, reached up and shut the window carefully before going to bed.

The joy I had from looking at this triangle of blue is difficult to describe. It meant all the world to me – it was a blue patch shining outside and above the whole world, not above Moscow alone. It reminded me of Kamenka, of the countries I had travelled to, of my boys somewhere far away but beneath the same sky. It gave me new hope, and the patience to wait a little longer if I must; time passed more quickly now.

One day, about four in the afternoon, we heard an unusual commotion in the passages: loud steps, doors opened then locked. Finally our door was opened and two men walked in, followed by Popov and a guard. One of the men had an Armenian name; he was a clean-shaven, oriental-looking beau whose looks betrayed immediately great self-satisfaction and arrogance. The other man was insignificant, greyish and sallow-looking, one of the nondescript types of Russian men belonging to the outskirts of the intelligentsia. They were introduced by Popov as the "Commission of Interrogation" and we were invited to put before them any claims or complaints we might have.

No sooner said than all the women – even quiet little Miss Maxwell – surrounded the commissars. Of course, it was the Persian woman who monopolised all conversation, and her copious tears and vehement protests were quite a study of excited humanity. Her complaints were accompanied by compliments to the Cheka and its worthy representatives, by allusions to the personal charms of some leaders – evidently those present – and by fiery glances in their direction. Madame Marchand, sure of her rights, tried to put in a dignified word about wanting to see her husband; the Polish woman went on with a story which she began over and over again – not being listened to; and Miss Maxwell was only trying to find out whether her brother was in Moscow, in prison, or sent back to England.

As they all stood in a bunch in the middle of the room I looked at them, quite interested and amused really by this picture. My bunk was right next to the door which was open now, with two guards barring the entrance into the passage. Suddenly a low voice in a rather slow drawl coming from behind me said in Polish:

"And you, Panna Maria – don't you have anything to ask for?" I turned back with a jerk to find myself face to face with Menzhynsky, the big man at the Cheka, the president at my Interrogation. The piercing blue eyes were peering at me inquiringly – I remembered this look and was not reassured.

"Thank you – what can I ask for but a little sunshine and fresh air perhaps . . ."

"Don't be impatient – you have already been at the Interrogation; it is a big step, you know . . ."

"Oh yes, I am aware of it and I shall be patient."

He nodded in a friendly way with quite a pleasant smile which somehow seemed incongruous on the face of a Cheka man; for a moment there was something quite human about him. The other men were leaving now, and Menzhynsky withdrew into the passage without having spoken to anyone else in our cell – probably he was glad to have avoided the assault of questions, and the answers which must have been always much the same.

The excitement among my companions lasted into the evening: the possibilities of their demands and of the answers were discussed, weighed, considered. The Persian woman was furious, the French woman was hopeful, the Pole was depressed, the English woman philosophical. The Persian, in her aggressive mood, turned to me – glad to find some new object of criticism.

"And you, little quiet girl, you don't even condescend to ask, to put questions! Too grand, eh?"

"Why should I ask questions when I know I won't get the answers I want?"

"But she has been better off than all of us," put in the Polish woman, "she has spoken with Menzhynsky himself."

"What? You spoke to him? But he was not here – how could you? Nonsense!"

"As a matter of fact, he was at the door for a moment," I said, "and he asked me how I was." I thought this would be enough in the way of information.

"Oh, the little secret-maker. She knows Menzhynsky – that's what it is . . ." said the Persian with an ugly look at me.

How it made my blood boil to hear her speak – but I kept quiet, playing once again the little goose and pretending not to understand her insinuations. With a blank smile I added: "He was at the Interrogation, so I remembered his face with the yellow pointed beard."

The Persian shrugged her shoulders. Miss Maxwell gave me a friendly smile, and the conversation went back to the chances and possibilities of release.

Soon it was Easter Day, the church bells rang gaily all over Moscow, and the sun was shining brightly apparently for I could see my favourite triangle of blue sky and the whole grey window looked brighter and lighter. Our day was spent in the usual manner, but my companions were less talkative and less quarrelsome; perhaps the sound of the church bells called back to their memory pictures of other Easter Days – who knows?

At about four o'clock the door of our cell was opened at an unusual time and a warden came in, accompanied by some higher official of the prison. My heart sank as my name was called out; was I going to be transferred to another prison? Was it to be Butyrki again? Or was I to be sent to some provincial prison or labour camp?

"Collect your things and come along," was the order given. Whilst I packed my bag in feverish haste, hurried on by the official, my companions tried to question him about my destination, their own fate, and other such things. A rough order to keep quiet and not to speak to me (in case they might try to give me some message) did not look encouraging. A nod to the four women who were now looking anxiously at me, a parting smile from them, and the door was closed; most probably I would never again see any of these companions from these dreary, weary days.

Walking between the two men, carrying my bag and my fur coat, I passed through endless passages, stairs and halls and was finally pushed into a small room, apparently on the top floor of the building as I could see a stretch of roof through the window. A man was sitting at a desk to the right of the door and, standing stiffly with his back to the window, was Popov, the commandant of the prison. His long, thick moustache looked red against the light of the window.

"Do you know why you have been brought here?" he asked me.

"No, I have no idea," I answered, preparing for a new cross-examination and dreading that my identity had been found out or suspected.

"The authorities have decided to set you free to continue your Latin studies – on condition that you sign this paper,"

286

he said, and read aloud a short statement according to which I must promise not to leave Moscow without special permission from the Cheka, and must declare myself ready to appear before the Cheka without delay when summoned.

Was I really to be free again? Could it be true? Of course I could sign these conditions.

"Are you ready to sign?" came the question from Popov.

"Yes, please – of course . . ." and as he gave me the pen I laboriously signed my adopted name, Maria Adamczewska.

"You are free now," said Popov in a matter-of-fact tone. "The warden will show you the way."

The word "free" – was it possible? I was happy, so happy that even Popov seemed to me to be smiling, to be kind – and I grasped his hand with both of mine for a hearty shake. His face was a study! Even in the excitement of the moment I could not help noticing and appreciating it. I firmly believe that he was pleased at my spontaneous gesture – over which I now laughed inwardly – his red moustache moved, a glimmer of a smile played on his impassive face. He looked amused, astonished – apparently taken by surprise by this handshake; for half a second he was simply a human being and not the morose unbending Soviet official.

He looked away, and I felt I had done something against the etiquette, but this fleeting "weakness" in one of the hardest men of the Cheka will always remain vivid in my memory.

A few minutes later I found myself in the street – on a spring afternoon, the sun low over the roofs, the sparrows chirruping somewhere overhead, the snow melting in slushy heaps on the pavement, people hurrying along casting a side glance at me as I stood on the step of the dreaded building. The air was so clear, so exhilarating, so light – I felt strange and giddy and walked away slowly. Where I was going to I did not know, but away, away from this building, from this neighbourhood, away from the lengthening shadow of the Lubyanka.

15

RELEASE

My first thought as I left the Lubyanka prison was an instinctive urge to run, fast and ever faster, away from this building, away from all buildings and out into the freedom of the countryside. Of course, the countryside was far from where I stood and, besides, I could not have run or even walked very fast after those weeks of prison life and lack of fresh air. Where should I go then? It was Easter Sunday, and what better place to go than into a church, to sit and rest and gather my strength. I don't think it is possible to put into words what I felt in those first moments of freedom. I wonder whether real criminals would have felt the same unmitigated joy?

Down a side street to the right I knew there was a church. I reached it and entered – it was a time of day when no service was being held, and there was scarcely anybody there. The quiet dim light, the flickering candles, the silence, the bright flowers on the altar – all this helped me to find my balance and brought a feeling of deepest gratitude and clear joy. I came out of the church and decided to go to Aunt Lelly, my nearest and dearest of all the people I knew in Moscow.

However, I did not dare go there straight along the big thoroughfare; I still felt that someone might be following me, and decided therefore to go a roundabout way and to make use of quiet streets where I could see whether I was being followed. It was dusk by the time I arrived at my aunt's house, tired and worn out but reasonably sure that no one had followed me.

My cousins had gathered together for Easter Day. Aunt Lelly was wearing her silver grey dress of days gone by, Mary was also wearing some lighter dress because of Easter, and two elderly cousins, quite jolly and not pecking at each other (because of the great day, I suppose), were all assembled there at the supper table. And it was as festive a table as one could have hoped to see in those days of need and misery. There was the shallow basket with gaily coloured eggs resting on a carpet of freshly grown oats; the Easter cake – kulich – with a large pink paper peony, rose proudly above other biscuits and buns; and the typical white paskha, although small and displaying but a few modest raisins, was leaning strongly to one side having been partially eaten the previous night, after midnight mass.

What a joy it was to be with them all, to hear the familiar voices and to see these faces so full of sympathy. How many things we had to tell each other! How kind these dear elderly women were to me, how thoughtful in the smallest detail. All was bright, clear and kind – with Aunt Lelly's deep blue eyes, her fine smile and her charming manner guiding the conversation and increasing my joy and happiness. To stretch out between sheets in a regular bed was a great treat that night, and no thought of a house-search or its consequences crossed my mind. It was good and lovely – and I was dreadfully tired.

The next day it was Alphonse's turn to hear my story. We were sitting in Aunt Lelly's living room, talking over our experiences of the last weeks. I was still full of simple happiness at my release, and had not had time to turn my thoughts to the future. And at this moment, an even greater joy was bestowed upon me. Aunt Lelly's faithful maid Tonya brought in a letter addressed to me. A letter? And from Petersburg too? For a moment I dared not open it. Then as I tore the envelope a small slip of paper fell out and I read:

"All well and in good health. Address . . . Breitestrasse, Reval. Signed: W. Favre."

This was the first news I had had from the children since I left them over one year and seven months ago. The signature was that of their tutor, the address was unknown to me – apparently he had moved them from Dorpat to Reval. On another slip of paper, Masha was writing to me saying that the enclosed message had been brought to our town house by a peasant from Estonia: he did not give her any details about his journey, but told her that the tutor himself had handed him that slip of paper. The man also asked whether I was alive, as rumours had been circulating that I had been shot.

It was incredible to have here in my hands this smudgy bit of paper which meant so very much to me. They were all well – my boys; could I think of anything else now? I felt a great and deep feeling of endless gratitude to God for His help and protection. For days I could not think of anything else but this great joy. Somehow I had no doubts any more that I would find them again – however difficult it might be. Over the months that followed, this confidence did not leave me.

Meanwhile, of course, there were things to be done and many problems to be faced. First of all, I had to return to the Lubyanka to fetch my belongings which had been taken from me at the time of the arrest.

How very reluctantly I approached the Lubyanka building, one dull morning, a few days after my release. I was tempted to stop, turn back and leave my things unclaimed. But this might have attracted attention and anyhow some of the things had great sentimental value for me. I went in. The little reception room was crowded; people stood in a long winding queue. The small window in the wooden partition opened and closed with a dry click of a small shutter, and this seemed to be the only definite noise in the place. The murmur of voices, the shuffling of feet, the occasional cough and sneeze were all subdued and subdued, too, were all the faces. Had all these people already been in prison? Were they there for the same purpose as I? They all looked dull, lifeless, grey – even the young ones had faces with careworn, tired, worried expressions.

I had plenty of time to study these surroundings, for there were at least eighteen people between me and the clicking shutter. Suddenly, as I stood there, I saw a man looking at me – he was not in the queue – smiling and walking towards me. He looked unpleasantly at home and at his ease here.

"Hello, how are you? . . . Don't you recognise me? I am Sidorenko, the chauffeur."

"Of course, I know you now – what a surprise to see you here in Moscow . . ." I said, and my heart sank as I realised that this was Masha's friend, the chauffeur in Petersburg, the one who, together with Masha, produced the illicit booze and "speculated" on it. And now, to find him here of all places – in the Cheka where at any moment I might be called by my assumed name, where I would have to answer it . . . How could I get rid of him quickly before my turn came to appear before the window with the clicking shutter?

Quite unconcerned, Sidorenko was now telling me all he knew about Masha whom he had seen a month ago, still living in my house and "speculating" on a modest scale, he said. "And now I am here for good – I sometimes go to Petrograd on service trips."

"I hope you have a good job," I put in, to say something as I counted and counted again how many people still separated me from the clicking window.

"Yes, quite a good job. I am chauffeur here at the Cheka."

Here? At the Cheka! And at any moment I may be called for as Miss Maria Adamczewska . . . and he knows that it is a lie! I was simply terrified.

"You look tired," said Sidorenko, "You have difficulties in getting provisions? I might help you perhaps?"

"Oh no, thank you – I eat enough – only I had a bad cold and my neuralgia troubles me a lot, especially today," I replied, hoping that he might leave me, and for once really pleased to look tired and worn out.

"I am sorry – perhaps you had better go – I can stand in the queue for you," Sidorenko suggested now.

This made things worse than ever: what was I to do? Only four people were separating me now from the shutter and from the moment when my assumed name would be called out. I felt really faint now at the idea, and could not find anything suitable to say.

"Thanks . . . it is good of you to want to help me . . . but I am not so bad today; it is only difficult to speak, this whole side of the face aches . . ." and I touched my right cheek and temple, making a suitable grimace.

"Yes, yes, better not to speak. And I have to go now – if I want my dinner nice and warm. Goodbye, and if I see Masha I'll tell her that you are all right – only a bad cold?"

"Yes, do give her my love, say I am all right – thank you . . ." I nodded and smiled and waited anxiously to see him go. He bowed politely, touching his cap and turned to the door leading out into the street. It was fortunate that he went that way. I had feared a possible conversation between him and some colleagues just behind the wooden partition, had he gone through the other, inner door.

Some shuffling in the queue and I realised I was the next to approach the window. Sidorenko had gone just in time. "Maria Adamczewska . . ." All the things that had been taken from me were duly restored and I hurried out into the street, glad to feel my mother's little ring on my finger again, and glad to get away from the neighbourhood quickly so as to avoid the risk of another meeting with the chauffeur. Poor fellow, he had been really very nice and willing to help, and I remembered too the numerous occasions when, upon Masha's request, he had done many an odd job in my town house. Presumably one good thing would come out of this encounter: Masha would know that I was alive and might even get a message through to the boys. But meanwhile I must not meet Sidorenko again, or "Miss Maria Adamczewska's" true identity would surely be discovered.

Yes, this was one of my greatest worries: my identity papers were not in order. I knew it was dangerous, and so did my friends. The frequent nightly house-searches made it essential

292

to have all papers in order – I say "all", as it was not sufficient to have an identity card alone. The working card was the main document. One was expected to be registered as a "worker" of some sort, and receive accordingly a ration card of the category to which one belonged. Having no working card meant that I had no ration card and therefore no food, as legally I could only feed on the strength of that card. Thus, the very fact of my being alive was illegal, since it meant I must feed in some illicit way. I could still produce my Polish refugee papers and show the certificate given me at the Cheka stating that I had been imprisoned as a hostage. But this was not a valid enough paper to "feed" on, and as time went on I had to avoid as carefully as possible all contact with the authorities.

The generally adopted way to avoid contact with the authorities was, in daytime, to keep a sharp look out for any crowd, movement of crowd, any popular market – all were to be carefully avoided; at night, to change address as often as possible and to spend nights preferably in parts of the town where a house-search party had been active recently. The day programme was not so difficult, as I was always attentive to any activity or crowd movements in the town. The night problem was harder to solve, as it was impossible to keep track of the house-search parties; I had to take risks, and these risks were the more unpleasant as they involved the people in whose houses I spent the night.

At first, I stayed at my aunt's house but dreaded a house-search and possible complications with my Polish papers, which were now overdue and which could not be renewed because the Krasinskis and other Polish officials whom I knew were all still in prison. Besides, I was not at all sure that the elderly women – Aunt Lelly, my two old cousins and another old friend – would remember my assumed name and help me play my part in the event of a search. In their nervousness it was only too likely that they would refer to me by my real name, or commit some similar blunder which would compromise Aunt Lelly – not to speak of myself and my Polish friends.

It was thanks to Alphonse that a better place of refuge was arranged for me, albeit a temporary one. Alphonse knew I needed a good rest after the weeks in prison, and he was able to arrange for me a fortnight of quiet and peaceful nights at a nursing home where he himself had stayed earlier – not as a patient but also for refuge. The nursing home was in a large house, surrounded by a garden; the rooms were spacious, the meals could be served in the rooms, and the nurses were well trained in their remarkable skill of never being heard or seen.

In order to be admitted to this nursing home I had to pass a medical examination, but Alphonse who knew how I hated anything relating to doctors and nursing had talked matters over with his friend, the Polish head doctor. It was this doctor who at great personal risk helped his compatriots by admitting them as patients.

"What illness would you like to choose?" Alphonse had asked me when he suggested the nursing home plan.

"May I choose? That suits me better. A good rheumatic pain in the right shoulder or left knee would be best," I answered readily, especially as the rheumatism in the right shoulder had already once helped me out, and the left knee had really suffered years ago – after an overdose of hours on a capercailzie shoot in early spring.

"I'll leave it to the doctor to decide which limb is to be regarded as affected – he is a practical man and will know best," said Alphonse and left to settle the matter without delay. The next morning Alphonse came to fetch me, with instructions that I should have a noticeable limp as I approached the nursing home and that my handshake should appear stiff and uncomfortable.

"Am I to be ill in both limbs?" I asked.

"Yes, for the time being. Make sure you limp as you pass the porters – and don't speak Polish to me, nor to the doctor. One nurse can be trusted – I'll point her out to you if she is there – she is very reserved and careful, a dear elderly woman, rather severe looking but heart and soul with us. Beware of the assistant doctor – he is the 'eye' of the Communist Party in the place." With all these injunctions I would know how to act.

We were approaching the nursing home and I adopted my slight limp. A young nurse received us and showed the room reserved for me. It was a large and somewhat sombre room with a window and a glass door opening on the garden at the back of the house. The doctor's visit was announced for the early afternoon and in the meantime I was advised to rest. Fortunately, I had a book or two, and having limped out into the hall to see Alphonse off, I returned to settle into my part as an invalid.

At two-thirty the doctor, accompanied by an assistant doctor (the Communist "eye", I guessed), and an elderly nurse, came to see me. He knew, he said, about my complaints. I had to do some bending and walking, to answer his questions which he phrased very conveniently with an "Isn't it so?" which made it easy to answer "Yes", and it was decided that the right arm needed electric treatment twice a day, and that the left knee would probably benefit from some pills. I was to have my meals in my room but could go out undisturbed as long as my knee did not hurt me more – in fact, the doctor was all in favour of exercise for the knee. Everything was duly noted by the stern looking nurse, and with a sigh of relief I saw the party leave my room at last.

The nurse came back a minute later to tell me that the electric treatment could be given today just before supper, and that I should be back at that time. This was thoughtful of her, not to make me sit there all day long, and I thanked Alphonse in my thoughts for I felt sure he had spoken with the nurse about my desire to be free.

Thus I settled down to my everyday routine in the nursing home – a peaceful, quiet fortnight with an electric treatment of ten minutes twice a day, pills I need not swallow provided they disappeared gradually from their box, and regular meals served in my room by a cheerful apple-faced maid. The head doctor saw me twice, the stern nurse remained stern and matter-of-fact but gave me advice about the best time to go out or come in, and whenever I saw the assistant doctor I expressed my impatience to get well again, so as to be able to play my violin. (He could not know that I had left it behind in Petrograd.) At that time in Moscow music was encouraged by the authorities, and so this would be an acceptable way for me to earn my living. I made a good show of the stiff right arm whenever the nurses or maids were in my room, and produced a variety of grimaces when the assistant doctor gave me my electric treatment. The limp was conscientiously kept up for three or four days, until the elderly nurse thoughtfully hinted that my knee seemed to be much better. Altogether it was an extremely satisfactory arrangement and I really had a good rest – much needed after the weeks in prison.

Unfortunately, my stay at the nursing home could not be prolonged indefinitely. The head doctor had to be extremely cautious so as to avoid arousing any suspicion in the mind of the assistant; and, besides, this chance of finding help and peace should be open to others after me – perhaps they were more in need of it than I was. Thus, I had to leave after a fort-night, and I was sorry to leave without being able to thank the doctor for his invaluable – albeit not medical – help. He was always on his guard, and the nurse too. They never spoke to me otherwise than on strictly medical matters, they even tried to avoid me so as not to arouse the suspicion of the "house spy". It was with great regret that I left my quiet room with the windows looking out on the still sleeping garden – gaunt trees and yellow grass of a Moscow spring. But I was able to send the doctor and the nurse my warmest thanks through Alphonse, who met them from time to time at the house of some Polish friends.

The contrast between Moscow and Petrograd struck me more then ever in that spring of 1920. When I left Petrograd it was a dying city, lingering away, with no inner life, no impulse, no initiative. It just existed because it could not die all of a sudden, and lived on because it had not yet had time to decay. I wondered then whether it would ever come back to life. Moscow, on the contrary, was teeming with new activity, with the transfer of the government to the Kremlin and with government offices distributed throughout the town. Always more colourful than Petersburg, Moscow was now also more animated and busy; people could find work and occupation here – brains and hands were wanted and sought. The question was, though, could any of us agree to work for the Soviets, with the Soviets? And yet we had to work in order to live.

My aunt, my cousins and their friends all tried to find some compromise, some sort of work which would not make them exactly "loyal supporters" of the Soviet regime. Teaching, Red Cross work, scientific work gave some satisfaction in this respect. Lucky were those who had any artistic capacity or training; artists were at the time a privileged class – practically the only one outside the leading Communists and heads of the Party. Painters, musicians, actors – artists of all branches of art could make a living, could enjoy a certain freedom and could display their individuality – as long as no opposition to the regime could be traced.

The theatres were crowded and actors were excellent; the famous Moscow Dramatic Theatre of Stanislavsky carried on and was as highly appreciated as ever. The Conservatoire – the musical academy of Moscow – was crowded too; orchestras were formed everywhere, professionals and non-professionals alike were accepted and sought. Painters had a wide scope in all kinds of decorative paintings – but of course strictly on the Party lines. If they had any talent for "propaganda painting" they certainly must have found a rich field of activity. And the film industry grew into an important branch of Soviet artistic activity. Film actors and actresses had to participate in all the pageants arranged by the government to celebrate special occasions (such as the First of May, for instance). I knew girls belonging to the best families in Russia who took part in these pageants, where they soon were given leading roles thanks to their good looks and artistic taste. Being young, they were attracted by the glory and praise and were thus won for the Soviet cause without realising it themselves.

With music one remained somehow on safer ground; the individual political convictions of the performers did not play an important part, and many of my friends found in orchestras or in music teaching a refuge from immediate dangers which otherwise would have threatened them as members of the aristocracy or bourgeoisie. Before the revolution, our elderly cousin Sonya had devoted much of her time and leisure to music, and now without much difficulty she got a very good post at the Moscow Conservatoire and worked there with real enthusiasm and untiring energy. Sonya was staying at Aunt Lelly's house, and on the nights when we had supper together she told us with great vivacity about her work, the progress of her classes, the talent of her pupils. She was not only teaching; she was also collecting old folk songs, putting them into shape for duets and trios, transcribing them for various instruments. In spite of her years she was as full of enthusiasm and energy as a young girl.

Later I learned that this period of relative bliss did not last very long. The older people were discarded, and the younger artists were compelled to join the Communist Party. Those who refused were doomed to perish with hunger or to linger in prison or in some labour camp. But in 1920 the future was not known; artists could exist, and could even allow themselves certain luxuries as they were quite well paid.

Perhaps there was something in this for me? Should I borrow a violin and start to practise, in the hope of using this means to earn my living? Should I try to join an orchestra? Or would this only tie me down in Moscow, when what I really wanted to do was to get away and find my boys again? With the note received from their tutor, those first few words of news after eighteen months of silence, I felt sure and certain that my escape was more than ever my only and immediate task and I started making new plans, searching for new ways of getting out of the country. All day seemed to be spent in wandering through Moscow in search of someone who could advise, or someone who had connections on the railways, or who could perhaps be of use in getting new identity papers of the kind I might need at the given moment. For one thing was clear to me: since "Miss Maria Adamczewska" was forbidden to leave Moscow I must, as it were, leave her behind and find myself another name.

The spring was becoming warmer and the snow and ice had long since vanished. The sun shone brightly, the sky was blue. Despite the outward signs of suffering, the city's inner beauty radiated through. The man in the street looked hungry, the streets were dusty and dirty, the horses were thin and the few cars one saw were dented and with the paint coming off in patches. But the fine old buildings were there, the gaily coloured cupolas of the old churches glittering in the sunshine, the church bells ringing, the heavy doors open for anyone to come in for a moment's rest, respite, quiet. The large private houses of the aristocracy and wealthy merchant class were now occupied by Soviet institutions or municipal offices – but they still had outwardly their old look of comfort and warm welcome, and if one peeped in, there were the painted ceilings, the heavy curtains, the marble fireplaces just as they used to be.

The sunshine gave me renewed strength, and my mind was full of hope and plans for the future. It was with some reluctance, therefore, that I found myself one day walking with knapsack on my back and a heavy basket on my arm in the direction of the Butyrki prison, having been asked by my Polish friends to carry some food parcels to the Polish hostages still being held in that grim building. The thought of seeing again the dreary prison where the hours had dragged on like weeks made me shudder; but I knew there were other innocent prisoners there, others who suffered the same privations I had undergone, others who had perhaps nobody in Moscow to think of them and to send them food. We had received news of a Polish Catholic priest, arrested in Kiev, and now transferred to the Butyrki, who had by his example been a true moral help to all those who were imprisoned with him. The Polish Committee wanted to help him, and his story made me overcome my own dread of the sight of the prison that I knew only too well, and to volunteer to carry the parcels.

It was nice to be out, and I did not mind the long walk on this lovely May morning. But when I reached the dingy walls I felt my heart tremble as I approached the heavy iron gates. In fact, I was tempted to turn back and run away without knocking; only my pride pushed me on and I soon found myself standing in the line of people with baskets and parcels. This line was long; I waited in it for seven hours, not daring to leave my place. It was hard and exhausting, but we all waited, not daring to protest or even to ask why we advanced so slowly. The crowd looked gloomy: some people, women especially, looked scared and nervous, others seemed indifferent as if used to this waiting. Hushed conversations were carried on here and there, but as soon as a voice became louder a warden in uniform appeared and ordered silence. A few steps in front of me a young woman, apparently belonging to the upper classes, poorly but neatly dressed, stood leaning wearily against the wall. She had struck me by the pallor of her face and the anxious expression of her large blue eyes. She exchanged a few short and rapid sentences with her neighbours but did not seem inclined to gossip.

There were also many children waiting patiently in the line – unnaturally patient they looked to me. They were at times more communicative though and were relating the story of their father's or mother's or brother's arrest in tones of childish indifference. Old women sat on the ground, wiping stealthily a tear from time to time, munching a boiled potato or a crust of black bread. Young mothers were rocking their babies to sleep or trying to keep their toddlers quiet. The rooms were cold and damp, the air thick and heavy with the smell of sheepskin coats, of food and above all of unwashed humanity.

Slowly, step by step, we progressed and came nearer to the barred end of the passage where the parcels were delivered.

I dreaded the moment when it would be my turn to give the parcels, to name the prisoners they were intended for, to give my own name and address. I had a feeling that the wardens and women who ran the service would surely recognise me and would wonder why I should come now to help other prisoners, and I feared above all that the mention of a Catholic priest would make me the more suspect. But I had undertaken to deliver the parcels and I had to do it. With a faint feeling in my heart I approached the rough wooden wall. Its fresh boards still smelt of the forest, the golden resin trickled slowly in large transparent drops. I thought of the forest they came from, the forest awakening now in the spring, the capercailzie . . . My thoughts were abruptly interrupted by a loud sob, and harsh voices. I looked up and saw the young woman I had watched earlier, leaning now against these boards, her eyes still larger, her lips white. I heard her say in an entreating voice to the woman warder who was receiving the parcels behind the counter: "Please, I implore you, do try to find out where my husband is – I have looked for him in every prison in Moscow – I was here the other day – everywhere I am sent back with no reply – perhaps he may be here after all – do tell me . . ."

The woman behind the counter was shrugging her shoulders impatiently and, leaning forward, was shouting now: "How can I know where your husband is? Perhaps he was shot long ago, perhaps he will be shot tomorrow, perhaps he was shot only this morning? How can I know? When parcels are not accepted it means they are of no use any more, that's clear. For all I know your husband must have been shot, but it is none of our business to tell people who has been shot and where he was shot and when he was shot . . ." and on and on she went, juggling with this word "shot", throwing it at the young woman who stared at her aghast and speechless. And in the heat of this cruel game the woman warder forgot her duty – she mechanically took my parcels, looked absentmindedly at the attached labels, and never asked me for any details or my own name and address. I stepped aside, people pushed on from behind, the young woman was making her way towards the door and I lost sight of her in the crowd. The cruelty I had just witnessed made me forget my own exhaustion and fright. What useless, senseless cruelty of woman towards woman – why had it been necessary? And yet, ironically, this cruelty had saved and protected me. I hurried away, my thoughts and feelings in a turmoil, aware once more of the dark chaos which surrounded us now that all conditions of life were changed, all occupations upset, our way of living uprooted.

A few days later, with this memory still turning in my mind, I was walking one hot and dusty afternoon along the Nikolsky boulevard. A cart went by slowly, drawn by tired horses; a few unwashed urchins were making sand-castles out of the dried mud and dust in the gutter; a few passers-by, poorly dressed in "town" clothes, were being approached by two or three peasant women from the country probably hoping to sell their products underhand – a couple of eggs, or a little butter. The blue sky overhead and the brilliant sunshine looked hard-hearted in all their glory beside the misery and poverty of this little corner of the earth.

"Good morning, how are you, Miss Maria? Not left Moscow yet?"

I turned round with a jerk at the sound of the unknown voice addressing me by my assumed name. A tall, fair man was looking at me, smiling a rather forced smile, his hard pale eyes fixed on my face.

"Thank you, I am all right. Yes, I am still here . . ." I replied hesitatingly, trying to remember the face which I knew I had come across somewhere – casually perhaps.

"Not quite sure who I am?" said the man, evidently pleased with himself. "Well, you will remember me well enough if you think a little – we met not so long ago. I don't forget faces easily. Goodbye for the present."

He nodded and walked away down the boulevard. I did not dare look after him, there was something uncanny about him. Where had I seen this face looking at me with the same self-satisfied and sneering expression? And then suddenly I remembered: I saw in my mind the reception room of the Lubyanka prison; I saw the man standing at the door of the wooden partition calling out the names of those who passed him when taken into the interior of the prison. I remembered him calling out my assumed name – he had to call it twice because I did not react to it at first. Yes, I knew him now, and felt very little reassured at the thought that these men had such a well-trained memory for faces. It was a warning which made me realise how careful I had to be in my attempt to leave Moscow. There might be men of the Cheka posted at railway stations to keep an eye on all travellers leaving Moscow. In fact, I had been warned a few days ago by Polish friends to keep as far away as possible from the railway stations if I did not want to remind these Cheka people of my existence.

I wandered on, meditating over this encounter and little encouraged by it. With many a stealthy look over my shoulder I approached the house of my friends where I was to spend the next two or three nights. If everything was in order there I would come at dusk again with toothbrush and pyjamas hidden in the pockets of my old Burberry coat. I peeped into the courtyard – the two windows on the ground floor were open: this meant that Shurik and Nadya were at home and I could go in without hesitation.

They had not changed – Shurik and Nadya Rayevsky. In what way I expected them to change, I don't know. Still, everything was so different now – life had turned topsy-turvy since I saw them last in 1916. They were dear, devoted friends of ours in Petersburg and in Kamenka where they were frequent guests. They were always happy, content, making the best of everything. Shurik had been a friend of Sasha's at the Lyceum and we had many friends and interests in common. For them, too, the revolution had meant the end of their way of life and the loss of position and property. And yet, here in Moscow, Shurik and Nadya were making the best of things and were still as void of doubts and as sure of the right way to act, as if they had merely changed flats or had one more baby. How I envied them this inner balance, this certainty of being right and this common understanding between them. They did not ask themselves useless questions, and carefully avoided unnecessary problems. Shurik had always worked conscientiously for the Imperial government; it was natural to him to continue to work conscientiously. He had a family, they had to exist and there was not much choice in the way of careers – the employer was everywhere the same – the Soviets. Men were wanted everywhere more than ever, and Shurik had been able to adapt himself to the new situation. He took a regular job as an engineer (although he was absolutely unprepared for it) and received his pay partly in kind – enough to exist. He was always keen on music and he played in some orchestra several evenings a week – which made things easier as it helped to take his mind off the other job.

Nadya had two little baby girls to look after and did all the housework and some knitting and sewing for outside orders. They had a tiny flat on the Arbat – a busy thoroughfare of Moscow. Friends dropped in very willingly at their house – it was a restful atmosphere of no problems, of plain answers, of simple solutions. They even managed to play bridge once or twice a week quite regularly. They had the same measure for the value of things in general, and their life ran in the new surroundings practically as smoothly as it had run in the good old times.

In the very dark living-room of their ground floor apartment, Shurik would sit smoking cigarette after cigarette as he did before – only these cigarettes were of a poorer quality. Nadya would sit darning stockings and socks – she probably did that before too, only now the darning covered the whole sock which had neither shape nor colour left. Still, it was a sock and it was wearable. In the next room, the family bedroom, there were no windows. It was the bottom of a well between the walls of two adjacent houses and one could just squeeze through between the beds and cots to get to the kitchen. Here, too, no window and no room for anything more than the gas stove and an empty cupboard. Provisions were scarce and what Nadya could get hold of she hid carefully in some recess in the wall – a secret safe in case of house-searches.

Whenever one dropped in at the "Shuriki" one was sure of a warm welcome, a quiet atmosphere, a cup of tea and some cheering jokes – jokes about mutual friends of former days, jokes about current events, cautious jokes about the authorities of today. Somehow the Shuriki seemed to stand everything – a feature which Sasha had noticed in Shurik as a schoolboy, and Nadya was a model wife and his equal in this respect.

One day as I dropped in on a late afternoon in May, I had barely stepped over the threshold when an appalling smell of something very rotten made me stagger. Nadya at the door was smiling, a fork in her left hand, a checkered apron tied round her waist.

"What on earth is happening here, Nadya? Have you dead rats in the basement?"

"Oh, no! It's all right – it is Shurik's meat ration that he just brought home – it does smell a little, I must admit!" answered Nadya with a laugh.

"But you can't keep this meat in the house – you'll suffocate!"

"Come in, come, Edy!" Shurik called from the kitchen. "It will be ready very soon and you'll stay and have dinner with us."

"Yes, stay, please," urged Nadya. "It is so rare to have meat, and Shurik has produced a marvellous sauce of his own invention!"

I was aghast. "But Nadya, you don't mean to say that you are going to eat this smelly meat? It is impossible . . . you'll both die and before that you'll suffer agonies!" I wanted to warn her of the danger, for I saw how eager she was to get to this succulent dinner.

"You really mean it? You want us to throw away the meat? Oh, Edy – you are too funny for words – how can we? It is so rare to get any meat. What about the smell? . . . One gets used to it. Come in." I was horrified but did not want to hurt their feelings by running away immediately. Shurik appeared now with a flushed and excited face. "Come in – really you are too faddy, much too 'bourgeois' still. You'll see how appetising the gigot is with the sauce . . ."

I came into the living-room, dashed for the window and refused to move from it, while the Shuriki busied themselves over the promising gigot in the kitchen. The smell grew worse and worse, more penetrating, more appalling as it mixed with the smell of dubious grease. I could not stand it any longer.

"Goodbye, you two – bon appétit – and leave the window open. I'll come in two hours' time to see whether you are still alive." And I went out hurriedly, incapable for a long time of forgetting the smell which haunted me.

True to my word, I came two hours later, seeing in my imagination my two miserable friends writhing in agonies of pain. Instead, as I peeped in cautiously through the window, I saw two tired figures reclining in the two armchairs of the place – Nadya sleeping with her apron still tied round her waist, Shurik snoring lustily with his bony hands clasped over his stomach, with a blissful expression, a half-open mouth – and such a snore! I left them to enjoy their well-earned sleep after so narrow an escape, or so it seemed to me.

Thus, we were right in saying that the Shuriki could stand everything. But I fear that they must have been put to a hard test when a few years later Shurik was arrested and condemned to eight years of imprisonment for no other reason than that he had been a pupil of the Imperial Lyceum of St Petersburg, which was considered by the Soviets to have bred only the most stubborn conservatives and monarchists. By then Nadya had three little girls to keep, and I do not know exactly what happened to her. But I am sure that she will have kept up her courage and will have worked unflinchingly to bring up her children, never doubting a moment where her duty lay.

It was through a friend of Shurik's that luck came my way at last, and I was able to get some new identity papers. This friend had come in straight from his country place, and was telling us how devoted some of the old servants were to his family and how, every time he went there he was sure of the warmest welcome and always came back with gifts of flour, vegetables, butter, etc. The place itself had, of course, been taken and nationalised by then, but the former servants remained his friends. Speaking of one man in particular, he told us how resourceful and clever this man had been in his attempts to be helpful to the former masters. Thus, for instance, this man had once simply taken from a pile of papers in the district militia a dozen unused but already duly stamped identity forms, and had brought them to Moscow to his former master thinking they might come in useful. I jumped at this news and asked if by chance any of these forms were left. Yes, there were three forms remaining and it was arranged that this friend would bring a form to Shurik's house on the following day, and he would see to filling it out for me. This was really a bit of luck, and that night my imagination was kept busy reviving my various plans and ideas on how to escape, plans which depended on my acquiring some sort of "passport" – and this at last seemed within my reach.

The next day we all met as arranged, and after having pressed and ironed the paper – which had been buried in the garden, in a bottle – we put in all necessary data to suit my purpose. I was to be Evdokia Fyodorovna Salogubova. (I would have chosen another surname, but the friend had already started writing my own name before I realised what he was doing, and so we could only make a small variation of it from the original.) Of course, I was not married, I was the daughter of a French woman née Mercier; I was born in the province of Kaluga, near the village named Il'inskoe, and had been partly brought up on the estate of a Miss Valentinova. These true details were provided by the friend, and I noted down some more details for safety's sake. Apparently this old lady was about ninety and any reference to her could do her no harm now. I noted down some facts about the district from where the form came, and I even had a sketch of the estate, knew how large the farm and household were, the names of the more important neighbours, and knew the distance of the place from the railway station. Meanwhile Shurik, Nadya and the friend put various signatures on the form where required, and by the time they had finished it had quite an authentic looking air and they were well pleased with their efforts. This was really a great day for me and I thanked them with all my heart.

I could now start searching seriously for some possibility of escape. I was quite sure that an escape could only be attempted in summer when the weather would be good enough for me to walk for days and to sleep out of doors, if this were necessary. An escape from Russia in winter would be practically impossible. But the summers are short, and I knew that I had no time to lose.

The first question to be solved was: how to get out of Moscow? No railway tickets for any distance over 25 versts (17 miles) outside Moscow could be obtained without special authorisation of the Cheka. This authorisation had to be secured personally, and valid reasons for the journey had to be produced. I did not dare to attempt this approach, even with my new identity paper; I already knew too well what a good memory for faces the Cheka people had. Alternatively, I could walk out of this 25 verst limit and board a train beyond it – but Cheka controls were carried out all along the lines and an explanation for my appearing so far out of Moscow would have to be found. And there was a third way, safer than the others, which would be to go out with some organisation or with people influential enough to take me as a member of their "family", when a general authorisation could be obtained. I set to work to explore every alternative, to follow every lead however unlikely it might appear at first sight. In the weeks that followed I certainly found myself in some very curious situations – and probably had a few narrow escapes before finally one of my plans succeeded.

16

LEAVING MOSCOW

Imagination is, I believe, one of the gifts we have to be most thankful for in life. My own imagination has always been a true friend and valuable assistant. It may have got me into a lot of trouble in my childhood, and it did not have much scope for development during my married life – except during my lonely rides and wanderings through the forests and moors. But it really came into its own during the revolution. In the dark chaos surrounding me there appeared – often only half-formed the new ideas and concepts on which a new life was to be built. They surged up seemingly without connection, out of the dark, and it was my imagination that had to link them together, to place them, to carry me through the bewildering and unfamiliar events. It finally armed me with a sort of courage and presence of mind, gave a subtlety and ease of adaptation which taught me how to face new people and new circumstances without losing sight of my ultimate goal – to find a way of getting out of Russia. All my thoughts and desires were concentrated on my escape – however bizarre or outlandish the means of achieving that escape might be.

The most outlandish idea of all involved a possible trip to the Kirghiz steppes, to purchase ten thousand horses there for a government Commission. Through a friend of one of the Commissioners, my services had been offered as a secretary and as someone who knew something about horses.

"As I already told you, Miss," said the leader of this Commission, "we are all absolute novices in matters concerning horses, although we all agree that the normal horse has four legs and one tail . . ." A chuckle and some grunts from the other Commissioners showed their appreciation of the joke. "Thus, not being certain enough of carrying out our task to the entire satisfaction of the authorities, we would be glad to see you join us as secretary of the Commission and, in fact, as the technical adviser – since you know something about horses and riding."

I looked at the six elderly men sitting smoking in the light and sunny office. Six bearded men, whose complexion betrayed that they sat more often indoors than out. There were two bookish looking persons with gold-rimmed spectacles and blinking eyes, unsuccessful professors perhaps. There was one jovial man with a broad laugh and an equally broad stomach who clearly enjoyed a good meal. And there were three non-descript functionaries of non-descript age and non-descript character. I wondered whether these six gentlemen were those I might have to accompany on the proposed journey to the Caspian Sea and the Kirghiz steppes. They did not look capable of undertaking such a tiring and adventurous journey.

"I am indeed very flattered by the high opinion you have of my knowledge of horses. I fear I am far from being a specialist, although I have had to deal with horses and have ridden them from my early childhood. Of course, if I can be of use – and as I am free at present I would be pleased to join the Commission and am ready to go at any time." I hurriedly added this last sentence which burned my lips: ready to go at any time . . . my only wish and desire was to go.

The gentlemen all murmured something that sounded like thanks, with a kind of vague satisfaction. Would they express their approval of my choice of the 10,000 horses in the same vague way, I wondered – and I visualised the six in a row, in the sunburnt steppe, nodding approval to any old horse I chose!

"I am glad," said the leader, "that you are willing to go and to spend some three months in our company. We will have a second class railway carriage as headquarters, the necessary staff – by that I mean a cook and assistants – and our salary will be part in cash and part in payments in kind. Does this suit you?"

My future travelling companions now turned to discussing the route we were to take, the time it would take to come to the edge of the steppes, the chances of finding on the spot the required number of horses; and they consulted statistics and reports from various ministries. I ventured to say that roads being probably scant and not very good, we might best ride deeper inland and camp there, leaving the train to wait for our return. The idea of riding, however, did not seem to appeal to my companions and it was finally decided to leave this question to be resolved later. After a few more hesitating discussions and considerations of a very vague nature, the old men took their leave one after another with a sigh of relief, I believe. I remained, as the leader asked me to stay "to discuss the technical side of the question."

"Charming people, don't you think so? Petr Petrovich – you know, the professor of botany – is a very learned man, and Ivan Nikiforovich B . . . is one of Moscow's best lawyers. Yes, very pleasant men – I am sure you'll like their company. Only, of course, they are not quite suited for choosing horses, I admit that. But what can one do in the present circumstances? One learns new trades every day. The pay is excellent, the distance from Moscow is also not unpleasant . . . you see the point? Not too near the authorities – not a bad idea? . . ." and he smiled meaningfully at me.

Preparations for the journey started. All the details of permits and equipment had to be considered. But nothing firm was ever arranged, and the date of departure was always being put off. It seemed a pity to abandon this plan – it would have been a rare chance of seeing parts of Russia I had never been to. But escaping towards the south would be full of dangers, for I knew none of the local languages and nothing of local conditions. Finally I decided to be more realistic and think only of a move towards the west.

Tonya, my Aunt Lelly's faithful maid, had a distant cousin who was married to an engine driver. I spoke with Tonya, met this cousin and told her, without giving detailed reasons, that it was essential for me to get out of Moscow towards Smolensk (her husband worked on that line) but that I could not manage to obtain the official authorisation. The woman understood more or less that things were difficult for the former masters, and promised to talk to her husband about me and to see whether he could get me a free ticket as his niece.

A few days later Tonya told me that the engine driver would like to speak to me but, being very busy, he asked me to come out to his house in a western suburb of Moscow. I went there without delay and found the family crowded in two tiny rooms, with lots of children, pots and pans, a geranium on the window and no air. The engine driver was a bit awe-inspiring with his bushy eyebrows and gruff voice, and I was not sure that he liked the "bourgeois" very much. Still, he was quite amiable, and said that once a month he could get a free ticket for a member of his family. Such a ticket would take me to some station half-way to Smolensk (at any rate beyond the 25 verst limit). After that I would have to manage on my own. This seemed all right to me, and I thanked him for his kindness. Thus we decided that when his turn to ask for the free ticket came, he would let me know.

Pleased with this result, I started to work out my route and to study the maps for all possible details. Moreover, it was best to have some addresses of people on the way, so as to be able to name them if asked where I was going and why I was travelling. The authorities endeavoured to limit all unnecessary movement on the railway lines, and despite the general disorganisation of rail traffic there were always frequent checks and searches. Through friends and relations I very soon found the addresses of two families in Smolensk, called on their people in Moscow and could thus fix quite a little story explaining my reasons for undertaking the journey. I was already thinking about the next stage – the crossing of the Latvian border, which was not an easy thing to do, especially as I did not speak Lettish. However, this difficulty might not be too great as I found that with a little knowledge of the country one could often soothe down the rigidity of the Letts. It flattered them if they saw that outsiders knew places and people in their country, or admired their capital – Riga. Counting upon all this, and upon good luck before anything else, I already imagined myself approaching Riga, via Smolensk, and saw myself happily reunited with my boys in Reval.

However, some ten days after my call at the engine driver's house I learned that he could not get the free ticket for me this month, as his mother was obliged to use it for getting back to her village where she was wanted. I was distressed, but there was nothing to be done and I was promised that the next month I would be sure to get the ticket. Still, the delay was hard to bear. I preferred not to count upon this arrangement and went on with the other plans at which I had already been working.

I had learned from Mr North, the English chaplain still in Moscow, that a small group of English people were due to leave Moscow shortly and travel to Finland. There was no possibility of my going with them, but here were people with whom I could speak openly and their advice could be useful. I met them at the chaplain's house, where I went from time to time to hear news of Miss Maxwell who had been so kind to me in prison and who had still not been released. (She was eventually released in the late autumn of 1920, and reached England safely.) The English people listened with sympathy to me, and one of them suggested that I should try to get in touch with German prisoners of war who were being sent back to Germany after years spent in Siberia. These Germans were coming through Moscow where their registration had to be completed, and many of them – having married Russian women – were taking their families back with them. I could try to get smuggled through with one of these families. This was an idea that was worth following up.

A few days later I had found out where these Germans came for their food rations, and it was not difficult to get into conversation with them. I picked out one worthy, bearded Landeswehr-man, surely the father of a family, I thought, and it soon turned out that he had been some kind of artisan in the Baltic provinces. This put matters straight at once; he understood the situation and what it was that I was trying to do. His only regret was that his papers had already been sent in and registered, so that he could not add me to his family "as his sister Lise" – evacuated from the Baltics. But he was very willing to help me, and a day or two later introduced me to another soldier who might be able to arrange matters. Somehow, I did not like the face of this man, but I said to myself that I must not be choosy and I must trust to my luck.

Hans Felber was a Bavarian. He told me he had a girlfriend somewhere beyond the Volga, but that he could not take her away with him for some reason or other – I forget. Apparently he was very devoted to her and regretted that he could not write Russian well enough to send her a letter. Of course I volunteered to be the secretary, and produced a long and touching letter to his beloved Nastya who was never to forget her devoted Hans. After this secretarial work, which I had to do in the man's room, sitting on a camp bed with another man stretched out smoking at the other end of the room, Hans Felber said that he would see me home. Of course, I did not give my exact address, just the general direction, and we went off together. Very soon Felber slipped his arm through mine and began discussing the possibilities there might be of my going as his wife – if he could still add my name on the lists already established. Well, I had to stand the walking arm in arm through the streets of Moscow on a mellow spring evening, but I did not like it and hoped with all my heart that Felber's negotiations with his chiefs would fail. I was glad to reach the corner of a street not far from home where I could take leave of Felber, who promised to do all he could to get me on his passport. I was to come for an answer two days later.

When I called at the canteen at the fixed hour, Felber was already waiting for me at the door – with a disappointed face.

"Es geht nicht," were the first words he said: "und ich hab's doch so gehofft." I was sorry to meet with another failure, but I was really very glad not to have to go with Felber, whose attentions somehow did not suit me. So, after the necessary words of thanks and regret, I went away feeling quite relieved and cheerful. But I could not ignore the fact that spring had turned into summer and here I was, still in Moscow. I knew I must not waste any more time, but it was hard to keep on trying when at every turn I met with disappointment.

My cousin Sasha Shidlovskaya, Aunt Lelly's daughter, was giving lessons in French and English in Moscow where she had remained with one of her daughters, although her husband and the other children had escaped abroad. One day she announced to me that she had a pupil who might help me, since his father was a Jewish businessman. What the business was I don't know, but some people still managed to carry on some kind of transactions, making a little money and enjoying a certain amount of security and peace.

The flat I went to was on fairly modest lines, small, darkish and in no way sumptuous – but the family looked well fed and there must have been money enough to spare for the son's lessons. The father already knew what sort of help I needed. He suggested that he would register me as employed in the timber works of a friend of his whose work was mainly connected with the forests along the Dvina. I would get a permit and a rail ticket for some place on the river, and across on the other bank was Poland. It would be my job then to find some way of getting across. This arrangement suited me perfectly, and I asked if there was anything I could offer him to express my thanks. At first the man refused to speak about any payment, saying that he had such great respect for my cousin that he would gladly render a service to any of her relations or friends. But I preferred to face the question in a business light and insisted that I should at least try to find something he wanted. He suggested something about furs being very useful and difficult to find, but I told him that unfortunately all my good furs had been left in Petersburg, where they were "nationalised" at the furrier's who stored them for me during the summer.

Having set aside the fur question, he suggested something else – I think it was a gramophone, which I did not have either. Finally, he said that the best present he could give to the friend of his who was to be my employer and who would secure the papers would be a large bottle of brandy. This seemed more feasible and I promised to try and find him one. Wine had been sold out, drunk and spilt in huge quantities in 1917–18, and it was difficult to find any in 1920.

My future employer was due from Polotsk on the Dvina in a day or two, and it seemed there would be no difficulty in getting the necessary papers from him. Thus, not daring rejoice yet but feeling that perhaps there was another way opening for me towards "the west", I waited three days, hunting round in the meantime for the good bottle of brandy. This seemed to be nearly as difficult a task as getting out of Moscow and by the end of the three days I still had not found it.

When I called as arranged to meet my "employer" I found he had not arrived yet. Dismayed, I went to the businessman and told him this, whereupon he was energetic enough to arrange through the offices of the timber yard a blank billeting paper, to be ready for me the following day.

I went home to Aunt Lelly's house – and found there Alphonse waiting to see me. He looked worried and more pre-occupied than ever – not without reason, too. The Cheka were after him: they had been at the two places where he had spent nights during the past week, they were close upon his heels and he was planning to go away on foot and trust to his luck. To walk several hundred miles, alone and without proper papers, was a bit of a test for luck. The thought came to me at once that

Alphonse might be able to make use of my promised billetting paper, if I really got it and if it was blank.

Needless to say, it was not easy to persuade Alphonse to listen to this proposition – I had to put in a little imagination and said that the businessman would surely be able to get a second similar paper from the same source, that I could not have mine anyhow until I had found the bottle of brandy, which Alphonse would be better at ferreting out in any case. Finally, he set off in quest of the bottle and we were to meet again the next morning.

At ten, Alphonse appeared at my door with a bundle of vegetables and flowers – in the bundle the brandy was hiding. We found the businessman all beaming and he beamed still more when we put the bundle before him. The paper was there, all duly signed and stamped but with no name on it as yet. He was waiting for me to give him the exact details, but was now rather surprised and disconcerted when I asked if a man's name could be put down on the paper, and explained that Alphonse's need was more urgent than mine. Yes, he said, it would be all right for Alphonse to have this paper and he would try to get another one for me in a day or two.

Alphonse was put down on the paper as Fyodor Lomov, agent for the timber yards of Z __, sent to obtain timber in the area of Polotsk. Two hours later he was ready to leave, and we went together to the railway station. In his ragged soldier's coat, with a battered cap on his head and a coarse bag on his shoulders, he really fitted quite well into the crowd which boarded the train in a frantic onrush; his unshaven chin and untrimmed moustache completed the picture. Towering above the majority of peasants who were climbing in, he pushed his way through and waved goodbye to me out of the window.

It was sad to see a true and devoted friend go after the three years that we had helped each other in so many dangerous and unpleasant situations. But I was happy to know that he was out of Moscow. His last words to me were: "Au revoir – next week, I hope – and thank you." Would he get through all right? And would I be able to follow? We had arranged a very efficient code so that he could let me know where and how I could find him, either in Polotsk or by following him across into Poland. The terms we used for the code were all expressions used in the timber trade – we both knew them well from Kamenka days. We each had a slip of paper with these expressions noted down – so small a slip that it would always be easy to drop it, in an emergency.

I waited day after day for news, trying to keep up my spirits despite the fact that the businessman could not secure a second paper after all. At the end of two weeks a peasant from Polotsk called at my aunt's house and left a note there for me. It was Alphonse's letter, already from "across". He gave me – in our code – full instructions about the people I could talk to openly, the distances from Polotsk, the sum to be paid for being taken across the Dvina in a rowing boat. But all this information was of no use without the promised paper. I tried to be happy for Alphonse's sake and forget my own disappointment – but it was a bit hard.

My next attempt at securing travel papers was equally unsuccessful and rather more dangerous, both for my own safety and for that of my aunt. In the same apartment house as my aunt there lived the director of one of the consumers' cooperative organisations which had at the time a very wide field of action and assured the supplies of foodstuffs and clothes for the urban population. Such cooperatives sent their agents out into the country and were able to obtain for them permits and tickets as required. This man's wife was being given English lessons by my aunt, and they both understood my position and wanted to help me. The man's wife was able to register me as an agent for the cooperative organisation, and I began right away my daily duties. They were not complicated: every day I had to report to headquarters, ask for the orders of the director, and listen carefully to the instructions which he took care to give me in the hearing of other employees in the general office. The section for which I was supposed to work was the "lime-bark fibre" section, and a paper certifying that I was a selling agent was handed to me, to my great satisfaction. I now had at least some proper "document", with seals and signatures, and in due course I hoped to receive a travelling permit also.

However, my hopes were shattered once again. One evening the wife of my director came to my aunt in great distress to tell her that her husband had been arrested, that the entire organisation was being closed and that she was now expecting a house-search, and probable arrest too. The poor woman was in despair – she who had always appeared to us the picture of optimism was now absolutely downcast and helpless. She had been so proud that her husband had understood how to handle the Bolsheviks and now this disaster.

Of course, this meant an end to my plans – and it also meant speedy departure from my aunt's house too, as a search of the apartment upstairs might well mean a search of all other apartments in the building. My new "documents" would not bear the close scrutiny of the Cheka, and I must not put Aunt Lelly in any more danger than she was already. So, taking a knapsack with the most indispensable things, I set off without delay to the flat of Shurik and Nadya.

I found Shurik at home, just back from work, on a lovely warm evening of early summer. Nadya was not there; she had gone with her children and her sister to one of the small suburban resorts on the outskirts of Moscow, to one of the summer camps for children that were being set up by the Soviet authorities. Most of the children there were either orphans, or children whose parents could not provide for them, or children whose parents had abandoned them. Nadya's sister, Mary, cared for three children belonging to an older brother of theirs who, together with his wife, had fled abroad without being able to fetch their children away from the country where they had been staying with their grandmother. To have the children in this school camp meant, for Nadya and Mary, having them in the good country air all through the summer and having free board and lodging for themselves in return for

helping with the other children. It sounded a pleasant arrangement, and Shurik felt sure that I could join them there for a
night or two at least, without too many questions being asked.
He gave me the exact address and indicated how to get to the
house from the station. It would be safer to pass unnoticed
and without having to ask my way on arriving.

I set off without delay for the station, and took the suburban train as far as the station that Shurik had indicated. (No
travel permit was required for this short distance.) I found
the little "dacha", or wooden summer villa, right in the pine
forest. Straight sandy roads cut through the thick forest, and at
irregular intervals yellow, high-roofed wooden villas stood
half-hidden in the trees, surrounded by low fences. It reminded
me of summer holidays by the sea and I almost expected to see
the dunes and a glimpse of the sea at the end of the road.

The evening was lovely and warm, the pine trees had
burning red trunks in the light of the setting sun; the air was
heavy with the penetrating smell of resin, and the white moss
– "elk-moss" I think – was crisp under my feet. I loved the
place at once, and it certainly looked as peaceful and as remote
from the tormented world as one could wish it.

The villa where Nadya lived was one of the series which
had been taken from their owners, or "nationalised" for the
accommodation of schools or summer camps. The idea of
the Soviet government at the time was to set up day and boarding schools which would bring the education of the growing
generation entirely under government control; to eliminate as
much as possible the influence of the family, and to foster
a state of mind, an outlook upon life and aspirations which
would conform entirely with the Soviet ideal of the proletarian
dictatorship. But within this framework such things as music,
dancing and acting were much encouraged – in those early
days anyhow – and so it was not impossible for Nadya and
Mary to consider working there. They had succeeded in being
registered as nurses or teachers in this school, and at the same
time were able to live a more-or-less independent family life

on the top floor of the villa. The children got their midday meal with the others in the large central villa of the camp and brought home from there the evening rations and the morning bread. The two mothers had no other duties in the school but looking after the children in their villa and giving drawing and singing lessons as required. They lived quite happy and content; they had started a vegetable garden and kept two rabbits. Their energy and resourcefulness were admirable.

Both gave me the warmest welcome, and it was decided that I would stay the night, sharing the room with Nadya and her little girls; a few coats and blankets on the floor would do perfectly well for me. But later, Mary, who had gone for the evening paper, returned with a worried look on her face – something very unusual with her. When the children were safely in bed and we sat on the steps talking quietly in order not to wake them, Mary told us that the head of the school had spoken today of some inspection from the local Soviet – and had inferred that such inspections might start by a surprise visit at night. This struck me as rather unusual in a school for small children, and it was bad luck in view of my arrival. I said I would go and sleep in the forest, but the sisters protested, and it then occurred to me that I might find a corner on the roof of this villa which, like so many wooden country houses in Russia, had an incredible variety of roofs slanting one way and another, meeting at unexpected angles and forming strange geometrical shapes. It appeared that there was such a hidden corner on the roof just outside Nadya's window – a favourite place of her nephew, who had been strictly forbidden to climb there after a dangerous slip in rainy weather.

In the light of the young moon I found my way there and with blankets, coats and a pillow arranged myself a comfortable bed. In fact, I really preferred it to sharing a room with the family. This was the first of many nights on the roof, and in the three weeks I spent there only once was I driven speedily back into the house by a thunderstorm. My discovery in this school villa would have been disastrous for Nadya and Mary, but the place was so well hidden that I slept there with a quiet conscience. Every morning I crept in after a good look round, and appeared in the garden when the children were already at their lessons and at an hour when any friend or caller might have dropped in. Then I would make my way to the station, filling my knapsack with dry fir cones which would provide fuel for the samovar at Aunt Lelly's house. Charming though it was in the country, I had to return to the centre of Moscow almost every day to continue my search for a travel permit, coming back again each evening to the happy little crowd of cousins. Their school life did not weigh on them, the few lessons were not tiring, and Nadya and Mary were plucky and had their children to live for.

No one noticed me, or thought it strange that I should travel everyday with a knapsack full of fir cones. Little by little, people's clothes and way of dressing had lost any connection with current fashions in the rest of the world – or any semblance of smartness. People wore what they could, and carried what they must, and each individual acquired his own kind of charm. The majority of men were wearing out their military, or semi-military clothes, which had been duly deprived of all outward signs of rank. Some men from the "bourgeois" classes wore their country or sports clothes, others donned for greater safety a Russian shirt worn over the trousers like the peasants did, or a shirt with a soft collar omitting the tie, or rolling a scarf round the neck to hide the absence of a collar. All had some sort of cap, military, sporting, fur or felt, sometimes a felt hat of a fanciful shape – it was unthinkable at the time that any man could go about bare-headed.

Women still showed some vanity in their dress – the younger ones at least – but the different items of clothing had to be brought together from various quarters, and the strangest combinations of colours and materials could be found according to the individual's taste and imagination. On hot summer days some women wore their former evening dresses with trailing, frilly skirts and deep décolletés topped by some kind of shawl or former cushion cover. Others had sports clothes or home-made frocks of rough towelling material. Hats were generally limited to a variety of home-made caps sewn together out of odd bits of stuff, often clumsily stitched but giving a neat effect on the head as a rule. One thing though seemed still to be within reach of the majority of women – the wave of the hair; hairdressers' establishments were always crowded. And both men and women could boast of the most remarkable assortment of shoes – anything from a light dancing slipper to heavy soldier's boots, or the coarse sandals woven out of strips of bark and worn by the peasants of central Russia. Watching the ever-hurrying crowds in the streets of Moscow offered some very amusing sights and some very unexpected surprises.

In my search for a travel permit, I kept in touch with all of the former friends whom I could trust. Through the Polish girl Stasia, who had been with me in prison and had recently been released, I heard that a supply train was being sent to Vitebsk and further towards the Polish–Lithuanian frontiers. An engineer officer travelling with his wife and children on the train was a friend of the landlady where Stasia had a room – he might be approached. Why not try?

On my way to the shunting lines of the western station I tried to make a programme of suggestions to be made to this engineer, in what capacity I could be useful to him or his family on the train. But thoughts would not obey me that day – it was hot and sunny and even in town I felt the joy of real summer weather all round me. The station looked sleepy with lazy flies sticking on the empty benches; the engines puffed out faint columns of smoke which looked quite pretty when seen against the sun; the few trains lying in the sidings stretched out in the sun like long multi-coloured caterpillars; and the men who were supposed to be working at the station were moving in an even more leisurely way than usual: altogether a very restful picture to look at. Answers to my questions about the supply train were given in a friendly and good-humoured tone, and for once the world of Soviet Moscow seemed lazy and oblivious to all harassing worries.

Finally I found the train, and approached the carriage in which the engineers were quartered.

"Can I speak to Vsevolod Nikolayevich Titov?" I asked a broad, black-haired man in some sort of engineer officer's uniform who was climbing into the carriage with a large basket of strawberries in his hand. A warm sunshiny smell rose temptingly from these strawberries. The man stopped short at my question.

"Well, yes, that's me – but what do you want?"

What did I want, anyhow? To go on the train – this was the only thing I could remember. My programme of suggestions had melted in the sunshine. My mind felt just blank.

"I heard you wanted a secretary . . . for the journey . . . someone . . ." and my imagination refused to go further.

"Hm . . . Yes, I do want someone to help, with the family going too . . . I suppose you had better come in and talk with my wife – she knows better," and he threw over his shoulder the green stalks of the strawberries he had been eating all the time.

I climbed up the steps of the carriage and followed Titov to the compartment from which the loud shouting of children's voices could be heard.

"Kitty, here is someone who could come along with us – secretary, help, something . . ." he said to a woman reclining languidly on the seat of the First Class compartment, now their living room apparently. Kitty turned on me her large, bulgy dark eyes, beautiful in their way but not brimming with intelligence. Two little girls with pigtails and large flat faces also looked up at me first, then exchanged a knowing look. I suddenly felt like a new governess must feel when her future pupils see her for the first time – and my conscience reproached me violently for certain moments in my own childhood. But this look also inspired me: that's it, I'll be the governess, if it means that I'll be taken on the train.

Kitty was looking me up and down meanwhile.

"Mon cher, qui c'est?" she asked her husband, in a typical 'sauce Russe' from Nizhni-Novgorod as we used to call it.

"What did you say?" said Titov, still eating the strawberries, with both daughters helping him busily now and all three spitting the stalks right and left on to the floor.

"Ah . . . you don't listen properly. Madémouaséil – you want a post in my house?"

"Yes, I would be willing to go with you – I thought as a secretary although I don't know shorthand, I can't type, and I don't know any bookkeeping . . ." and I poured out all my deficiencies simply because I could not resist making these bulgy eyes roll and change their languid expression. They did change, getting rounder and rounder and finally showing some disapproval.

"Oh, but this is quite impossible then! You must know something."

"Well, I know French well, and German too . . ."

These words had a magic effect upon Kitty. "You know French? You can speak it fluently? And you would come with us on the train and teach my children? Vsevolod – this is splendid, she knows French well – I can freshen up mine . . . When will you come, Madémouaséil?"

"When do you leave? I must get my permit – unless Mr Titov could get it for me, that would be surely quicker . . ." and I waited anxiously for his reaction to this suggestion.

"Ah, Vsevolod, mon cher, you must get her the permit at once – if we leave in two days she'll never get it herself – toujours attendre, attendre, – vous savez?"

"Parfaitement, Madame, vous avez raison," and I answered with a long speech in French to see what effect it produced. The bulgy eyes melted in their exquisite surroundings, the broad mouth smiled and repeated "mais voui, mais voui . . ." and it was clear that my speech was not understood – but certainly not wasted! Titov himself looked at me with an expression as if I were a performing monkey and the little girls were awe-struck, and surely hated me in advance.

"Give me your name and other details – I am sending papers in today – I'll put yours in too. Get a photograph also – or we can add that later – I will see to it," Titov was saying and fumbling in the basket for the last large strawberry.

As he noted all data I was giving him, Kitty was recovering from her delight at having a good French teacher in the "house" and simply assailed me with questions. "What books shall we get? You know, it is so difficult to find any good books now, but I will manage to get all you need. A 'grammaire'? Des Poèmes? And you will read Zola to me? Ah, Zola is so charming, so witty – so 'amusant'! You like Zola? He is like Shakespeare of the English, so 'amusant'" – and she rolled her eyes round and round.

"I see you appreciate Shakespeare – I am so glad – I could read some to you, if you like," I was saying, thoroughly enjoying this literary conversation.

"What? You can read English – really? . . ." and she put her well-padded hand on Titov's arm: "Vsevolod, it is a real 'trésor' – she knows English: we must have her – she'll teach Serge – it is splendid . . ." and her eyes rolled towards me again.

Titov was yawning – the warm sunshine, the strawberries, the close air in the railway carriage. "Yes, yes," he was repeating, "You'll get your photograph – tomorrow? Can you come here tomorrow? Well, all right, tomorrow afternoon. We will settle the business side, send the papers and you can speak French with my wife . . . and – all right, you come . . ."

I took leave of the family with a general "au revoir" when, turning in the door, I was faced by a youngster of thirteen or fourteen with a pasty face and bulgy eyes like his mother. This must be Serge.

"Ah, Serge, mon cher, here is Madémouaséil – she will come with us and she will teach you English – but take off your cap, Serge," Kitty was saying from her corner couch. Serge looked with very little sympathy at me and I visualised a most unenviable task in the future. But I smiled at him and said in an unconcerned way:

"Teaching and learning are two horrid words on a hot summer day. Perhaps we'll go fishing 'in English' in the Dvina – there will be more fun in that." Serge looked amazed, then smiled broadly, and the little girls giggled.

"What an excellent idea – of course, English sport – sport in the first place and then Shakespeare – ah, Shakespeare . . ." said Serge's mother, while his father folded his hands over his bulgy stomach and fell somewhat noisily asleep.

I went the next day with the photograph, and full of hope that this time matters would work at last. For the photograph I had to make my face resemble as little as possible that of Miss Maria Adamczewska, already known to the Cheka. I parted my hair in the middle, wetted it well so as to make it look darker, twisted two knots over the ears and borrowed some cheap earrings from my aunt's maid. The resulting photograph certainly did make me look very different. Titov would get as an explanation that this is what I looked like some time ago and that I could not afford a new picture.

As I approached the train I saw myself already across the Dvina and walking towards freedom; I had two addresses of reliable people in Vitebsk, and one address in Polotsk; and in case they were still of some use I also had Alphonse's instructions in our "forestry" code. Then Serge came out to greet me, smiling in a friendly way and pulling off his cap.

"A pity, Madémouaséil, Miss . . . we are not leaving yet. I want so much to fish in the Dvina – they say the fish there are very big."

"Not going yet? What a pity! But we can wait – a little . . ." and I was trying to push aside thoughts of despair. Again a failure? I hurried in to see his mother, who was alone in the First Class compartment.

"Yes," she said, "The train is not leaving yet. We are to wait here – you don't mind? You can come every day, for the day; we will read a lot, and Vsevolod will arrange the salary – he will be here in ten minutes – Oh, it will be beautiful to hear French the way you speak it . . ." She rattled on and on, and I only tried not to show my disappointment. Titov really did turn up in ten minutes, and his words confirmed my fears.

"Madémouaséil, you don't need any photograph – we are not going yet and perhaps not at all. But we need you, and I'll pay you – so much in flour and sugar – and . . ." he went on telling me all I should have for my teaching.

Not going at all, perhaps! This was even worse than I thought. I played my part, thanked him for his offers, said I was willing to teach his children except for the fact that I had an aunt in Vitebsk who was expecting me to join her as soon as I could manage it. I said I knew of another train leaving shortly. This was not true but perhaps I could find one. I was getting desperate now, and only hoped that I would not do something silly in my haste. Meanwhile I left the Titovs with half-promises, half-regrets, and hoping they would not try to trace my whereabouts if I failed to return the next day.

I went to see Stasia to explain to her what had happened. She was also trying to leave Moscow and return to Poland, having, like me, given up any idea of waiting for the Krasinskis. She had heard, she said, of a train leaving for Mogilev shortly, with a group of musicians and actors being recruited at present by a man called Block at the Artists' Club. She was thinking of joining them in order to get on the train, and perhaps I would like to go too?

I did not relish the thought of travelling with Stasia, whose conversation did not interest me and who might not remember which name to call me by. It had been hard enough for her in prison to remember that I was Maria Adamczewska, and now I was Evdokia Fyodorovna Salogubova. Could I trust her not to give me away? Well, perhaps I must try it, for my boys' sake.

Somehow I had succeeded in barring out of my thoughts the hopeless, nagging worries about the boys. I knew there was little chance of having any more news from them. But there were times when I found it more difficult to keep cool about the situation and this was one of them. Soon it would be Vladimir's birthday. He would be thirteen. Only thirteen years since he was born, and how life had changed for us. Sitting there in Stasia's modest lodging I suddenly felt so acutely the contrast that I could not stand it a minute longer and got up and paced round the room. Stasia stopped for once her chatter about past boyfriends and looked at me in surprise.

"Where are you going? What is the matter?"

"Nothing in particular. Well, yes, there is something." Finally the feeling overcame me that I must talk to someone about my sons, that I must have a look at their beloved faces and without hesitation I took out of my pocket the old leather chess-board which I had used on shooting expeditions and in which I now kept a small photograph of my three boys in their English sailor suits, just as I remembered them two years before.

As I opened the red leather case, Stasia asked me jokingly, "Is this where you keep the photograph of your boyfriend?"

"No," I answered abruptly, "look at these boys – my sons."

Stasia made the funniest face I had ever seen on her. She stared at the picture. "Your sons????"

The fact was that until now Stasia had not known that I was married, let alone that I had three children. At the Polish hostel and in prison I had never talked about my real life, for I wanted her always to support my story that I was a Polish girl, twenty-four years old, who wanted to leave Russia in order to join her relations abroad. Through all our difficulties there I would not have trusted her with the truth.

"Your boys? You mean you are a married woman? And these are your children? Then you must be much older than twenty-four!"

I laughed inwardly – what a typical feminine remark.

"How good looking they are," exclaimed Stasia spontaneously, "and you must have a husband?"

"Yes, I have a husband – but I don't know where he is. The last time I saw him was in October 1918."

Once over the first blow of the surprise, good Stasia could not stop asking questions, to which I answered as scantily as I could for I knew how unreliable she was when it came to playing a part and keeping a secret. Still, it was a great relief to speak to someone about my sons, to tell small details of our life at home, to speak with pride of their achievements. We chatted cosily, but at the end I made her promise that she would keep the secret, that for all official purposes I was an unmarried girl who had worked as a governess and these boys had been my pupils – should a personal search be made at any time and this photograph be seen. She promised me to keep the secret sacredly, and I believe she managed to do it.

Stasia managed to get herself accepted for the actors' troupe she had heard about, even though she certainly could not act! She told me that the man I must see was a 'handsome young man' named Comrade Block. Scarcely daring to hope, I entered the large hall of the Artists' Club, which was situated in one of the former private houses which had been nationalised. Crowds of people were going in and coming out of it and I had some difficulty in finding an individual who would listen to my request.

"You want to see Comrade Block? There he is, near the window talking with two girls. Be brief if you have to ask him anything for he is very busy these days."

I approached Comrade Block, a dark-haired, dark-eyed young man, dressed with a certain elegance in a jacket, long black trousers and something like a tie round his neck. He was just taking leave of the two girls.

"May I speak to you? I won't be long," I said, noticing an impatient grimace on his face.

"All right, what do you want?"

"I heard through friends that you want musicians for your orchestra. I am a violinist and am looking for work at present."

"Indeed, I need three more violinists. Where have you played before, and where did you study?"

"I have never played in a large orchestra, but specialise in quartets and trios, and I was a pupil of Professor Nalbandian."

330

"Oh, I see! You were in his class at the Petersburg Conservatoire; I know some musicians from his class."

"No, I was a private pupil of his since my early childhood" – and as the man raised his eyebrows with a rather startled expression, I quickly added, "My parents were friends of Professor Nalbandian and this is why he taught me privately."

"I see. Well, of course we want only good violinists in our orchestra – it is of very high standing, with excellent musicians and a first-class conductor. But as a pupil of Professor Nalbandian you must be able to join it anyhow." He rubbed his small, well-padded hands and gave me a benevolent look. What a blessing, I thought, I'll be spared the dreaded test. In fact, not having played regularly for several years I was a bit shy about my achievements.

"By the way, our orchestra is not here, it is at Mogilev. Do you agree to go there?"

"Oh yes, very willingly," I answered with such apparent eagerness that Block looked at me with some surprise. I added quickly, "In fact, I have some relations there – two old aunts. I am all alone here – life is not easy and food scarce – I would be very glad, therefore, to be near my aunts."

"I am from Mogilev myself; what is the name of your aunts – I might know them?" put in Block, showing an amiable but, to me, unwelcome interest in my imaginary relations. Their name? . . . Anything would do, of course . . .

"They are the Misses Wedrov," I announced, "but you surely won't know them as they live on the outskirts very modestly and quietly; they are already very aged."

"Well, I am glad if you can join them. It is settled then. Tomorrow you bring me your papers and a passport photograph, and I will put you down on our list. In three days – if we get the Cheka authorisation – we leave all together. Have you understood?"

With a look that did not expect anything but a positive answer, Comrade Block was already turning away to answer some other individual.

Could it be true? How lucky I already had the photograph. When I handed Block my papers the next day, he gave a somewhat astonished look at the photograph and stuttered, "Hm . . . you say it was taken last year? You did not look your best then." My bashful smile was very appropriate to this indirect compliment, and it amused me inwardly to see how far I could go in playing the part of Miss Evdokia Fyodorovna Salogubova, the new little violinist that Block had 'discovered' at the Artists' Club.

Three or four long days passed in anxious expectation. I spent hours at the Club waiting for an answer from the Cheka, waiting for instructions, waiting for nothing in particular but having been ordered by Block to wait. The faces in the crowd grew more familiar. There was a new troupe of artistes being formed for the Mogilev municipal theatre, and certainly most of the people waiting looked more like actors than musicians. It turned out in the end that I was the only musician in the group. I kept well away from Stasia, for obvious reasons, and anyhow at this stage it would not do to admit that we knew one another. I could not wait with any peace of mind, as the dreadful question of whether I would have to go to the Cheka in person, or whether Block would get a collective travel permit, held me in suspense. Finally, we assembled one day at the Club soon after luncheon, Block took all our identity papers and photographs and went off to the Cheka, telling us to wait either for his return or for his telephone call summoning us to the Cheka.

We waited for three hours, and I felt myself under great strain. What was I to do if the order came to go personally for the permit? How could I get out of it without arousing suspicion? What if someone in the Cheka recognised me? It was too great a risk. I decided to simulate a sudden illness, to faint, to do something that would make it impossible for me to go with the others. Fortunately it was very hot and very stuffy that day; there was thunder in the air, and the crowded place could really make anyone feel rather faint. Losing no time, I began to fan my face with a book, to ask for drinks of water, to talk about taking an aspirin – so much so that some of my future colleagues began to pity me and to give their good advice. From this preparation to a real faint, the step would not be difficult – and I waited, keeping up the game.

At last Block appeared, tired out but very pleased, having obtained the collective authorisation. With a sweeping gesture meaning "You are free to go", he took leave of us, informing us that the departure was fixed for the next day, six o'clock in the evening at the small western station, and that we were to be there on time.

It was on a really warm, June evening that I left my aunt Lelly's house with a heavy heart. Would I ever see her again, with her clever eyes, her kind smile, her charming manners. But she had given me her blessing to leave, I knew her thoughts were with me and that – at last – it was time for me to go. My knapsack weighed heavily on my back, the coat thrown over the arm and a large bag, with food for the journey seemed to weigh tons as I made my way on foot through the dusty streets of Moscow. I reached the station well ahead of time, found without difficulty the train and the freight van reserved for our troupe – no First Class carriage this time. Climbing in without delay, I was grateful to get a place not too far from the door and yet deep enough into the interior of the van to be little seen from outside. I started arranging my place, with coat serving as mattress and blanket, and the knapsack as pillow. It was safer to keep busy inside, away from the eyes of whatever Cheka agents might be on the platform.

Block was pacing up and down the platform waiting for the arrival of his artistes. They came now, accompanied by droves of friends and with bundles, trunks and baskets. Laughter, chatter and even tears were plentiful and no wonder people stared at our van. Block fussed about, deciding where people were to put their luggage, who was to sleep on the top bunks and checking the names of his flock, list in hand. From time to time he would chat with a pretty girl, or talk to some of the railway officials, but his head was always turning towards the main entrance of the station – he was evidently expecting someone and was beginning to get anxious. Then, all of a sudden, he darted forward and plunged into a small crowd of people all apparently very jolly, gesticulating, shouting, laughing. The central figure of this crowd was a very large and jovial-looking elderly woman dressed in bright colours, with a flowery hat on her dyed blonde hair. A big bunch of flowers in one hand and bundles and parcels in the other, this leading lady – for such she must have been in her younger days – sailed through the crowd smiling right and left.

"Maria Ivanovna, at last, I was so anxious about you and was just going to delay a little the departure of the train so as to give you time – I am sure the station master would have waited," Block was saying now to this smiling apparition, helping her into the van.

"Golubchik, I would have flown over to Mogilev – if any aeroplane agreed to take my weighty person. I always keep my word, you will see that," she answered, wiping her forehead with a large pink handkerchief and pushing her rather complicated hat on one side. "Where shall I put my trunks? I have two of them – yes, large ones. Dasha, Dasha, here I am! And where is the food basket? Have you lost it? Where is it?" and with a high-pitched voice she flooded a poor shrivelled little old woman with questions, orders and advice. Dasha was evidently her servant and a relic of older, better days with her black silk cap and dark dress. Block looked rather distressed about the trunks, which he now pushed one way and another with the help of two other men.

"Golubchik, you don't know how to arrange things – you push the trunks about – and here, in the middle is the proper place for them. You don't agree with me? Well, I don't care. The middle is free, the trunks need room and this is where they'll stand. And I, Maria Ivanovna, will sit on them like a queen on her throne."

So saying, she spread her ample skirts and sat down on the larger trunk, pushed her maid Dasha onto the other and, fanning her red and beaming face with the bunch of flowers, exchanged jokes and farewells with a number of people who now all stood in the doorway. I liked this woman, she had character and an open and frank expression. As to Dasha, she was a real picture from the past – the dignified servant of a boisterous and famous lady. How far the lady had been famous I don't know, but apparently she was well known among the other actors on the train. One of them, a curly young man with a puffy face sitting on the next bunk to mine now leant over to me, saying in a whisper, "Isn't our Maria Ivanovna a gem? Always her true self – and with such temperament!" to which I nodded my fullest agreement as though I knew all about the lady in question and admired her as much as he did. Later on I heard that she really had been a good actress and had played at one of the best known theatres of Petersburg.

By the time all the travellers were aboard, there was little room left free in the windowless freight van. Faces peered from all sides out of the semi-darkness, all turned towards the door, smiling, joking, calling last farewells and injunctions to "behave well" . . . Scarves, handkerchiefs, hands waved cheerfully as the train began to move. We were off – leaving Moscow. In what circumstances would I ever see it again? Better not think of it, as at present the only circumstances I could picture would be as a prisoner of the Cheka – a most unwelcome and unpleasant thought.

A glorious evening sky with a red sunset and fine dusty mist over the city; church towers gleaming in this yellow light. It was all quite lovely – and how odd it was to have to wish never to see it again. I wanted to persuade myself that I was glad to leave, but somehow this gladness did not come spontaneously for I felt it was the end of something in my life, another break with the past. It was depressing to feel so utterly alone and to have to pretend to be someone I was not. Would I be able to play the game? Would I be careful enough not to lose my presence of mind – and Stasia likewise? Hundreds of questions were crowding into my thoughts as I looked out at the slowly disappearing silhouette of Moscow; then a pair of legs, dangling from the bunk overhead, moved suddenly and a funny head appeared bending between them.

"Hello, comrade," said the head. "Where are you from? What is your name and father's name, comrade? . . ." it said, in a broad Moscow accent.

My name? My father's name? Ah, yes, of course, the game had started. "I am Evdokia Fyodorovna . . ."

17

MOGILEV

How terribly long those first days in the train seemed to be. We advanced slowly, we stopped at every station for hours on end; often the train stopped in view of some signal box and just went off to sleep, with the engine driver snoozing on the steps of his cabin and the stoker lying down on the embankment for a quiet nap, his cap well drawn over his eyes.

It was perfect summer weather, the uncut meadows full of flowers, the fields still green with the growing corn; it all looked so familiar, so near and so normal that it was difficult to fit my thoughts into the new surroundings. My world was now limited by the four bare walls of the railway truck, or freight van, which I shared with twenty total strangers, and I had to be a stranger to myself too – playing a part, careful not to make a slip, weighing every word I said. Fortunately, my companions were so taken up with each other that they soon stopped noticing me. My blank and flat replies to their questions made them think me a "dull girl", and this success gave me courage. Only Comrade Block and the jovial Maria Ivanovna persevered in speaking to me – and I felt ashamed at having to discourage them, for obviously they were trying to be friendly to this "poor slow girl". Block probably felt it was his duty to get to know the people under his care and Maria Ivanovna, seated on her throne of trunks in front of me, just had to talk and to shed her kindness on someone.

"My dear, don't be so sad – you are sad to leave Moscow? I know, it is very hard to leave Moscow, but you will like Mogilev – you are young – young people find a smile everywhere . . ." She went on and on in one breath and her face beamed and her eyes twinkled, looking so small in the broad surface of her face. I nodded and smiled and was so slow to react – despairingly slow!

In the dim light of the van there were always two or three pairs of eyes looking at me – because there was nothing better for people to do than to look at each other. What would they ask me next? What should I answer if they asked about my musical career, my school, my family? I had to prepare answers and work out a plausible story – and keep to it, too. Play my part and never forget it! Maria Ivanovna's constant questions were a good training. When I became too dull or slow for her, she would turn on her box and talk to the two quaint girls stretched out on the top berth above me, or exchange jokes with the curly-headed young man who admired her so. She even managed to get a smile out of the dramatic artist with sinister eyebrows and angular nervous gestures. And in between these jokes and attempted conversations she showered orders upon her devoted maid, Dasha. Maids did not exist officially and evidently this one had been put on the list as a minor actress or as a "dresser".

"Dasha, pass me the rusks, please – have you lost the parcel? Where did you see it last? Don't fool about in my hat box, you'll crush the feathers of the summer hat – and the rusks can't be there!"

Dasha, red and flustered, moved round the pile of trunks and cases, plunging her hands into one box, opening another, closing the lids with great efforts, tying and fastening endless ropes, stays, strings.

"Dasha, you are a fool! They must be in the 'uzel' – if only you had a better memory we could put you on the stage as a fool!"

And, of course, the rusks *were* in the 'uzel' – that well-known bundle consisting of any kerchief or bedcover or blanket filled with any sort of last-minute goods and tied cross-ways by the corners. The 'uzel' is the national luggage in Russia – all shapes, all colours, almost limitless in capacity and so variable and supple and adaptable. You push in anything, you sit on it if you have to wait for a train at the station, you use it as a pillow if your hours of waiting grow too long, and you can squeeze it into any odd corner of a cart or sledge or railway carriage. Of course, you have to keep it with you, not leave it out of sight, for it can't be locked and honesty was not exactly commonplace on Russian railways. This was why Maria Ivanovna had kept all her luggage with her and now, chewing contentedly her rusks, she sat on her observation post atop the trunks and went on talking, talking and at the same time shrewdly observing the rest of us and no doubt deciding what we were worth. I had the impression that this jovial woman was firmly fixed to her seat like a doll on a musical box, revolving rapidly and easily and taking in everything that happened in this narrow little world of ours.

Everyone seemed to find in Maria Ivanovna a congenial soul, a good friend – even the giggling, whispering girls seated above me, and even the morose couple of middle-aged actors, sleepy, sour and depressed who occupied the furthest corner of the truck. Only when the giggling and shuffling on the bunk above me became too noticeable did Maria Ivanovna try to crane her neck, then to rise to see what was happening up there. But after fruitless attempts she'd sink back on her bundles, exhausted and muttering "Eh, goda, goda! . . ." Old age, old age – was her complaint, but whether it meant disapproval or envy of these younger girls was not entirely clear.

We had been told to take provisions for a two days' journey, and when the third day had come and gone people were hungry and began to complain. Poor Block rushed round at every station trying to lay hands on some supplies. He would return, sometimes with a sack of potatoes or a bag full of cabbage, often with empty hands. The fun began when it came to sharing these spoils! The first choice was given to Maria Ivanovna who always knew what to choose, and then came the bargaining of all the other members of our van and the bitter words of those who thought they had not been well treated.

At last, after six days of travelling we reached our goal, Mogilev. We were immediately marched off, carrying our own luggage if we could, to the centre of the town where the empty building of a boys' secondary school had been reserved for us. We were not the first to arrive: a number of "entertainment artistes", as we were called, were already there, and altogether we were to occupy two floors of the building, the classrooms having been turned into dormitories with wooden screens and hay sacks as beds. No blinds or curtains, no electric light; school benches and desks in profusion, a few maps on the walls. I shared one small classroom with Stasia, and the noisy Maria Ivanovna and her faithful attendant were our next-door neighbours – very noticeable, too, as they unpacked their numerous trunks and boxes, Maria Ivanovna shouting along the passage:

"My dear Block, where are the pegs to hang up my costumes? Where are the blinds? I can't undress with half Mogilev looking in at my windows!" And Block hastened to see what he could do, soothing the impatient lady, promising pegs, looking-glasses, curtains, candles – all for tomorrow. "I know your tomorrow" Maria Ivanovna laughed in reply, "No, no, you won't catch me on that. Get me the things *now,* while I arrange my salon!" and Block hurried downstairs and reappeared dragging curtains, curtain rods, chairs and candlesticks.

Dusk was falling. We sat on our beds, Stasia and I, listening to the boisterous lady next door – Stasia crying quietly as she so often did, an occasional sniff, a subdued moan betraying her state of mind. For once I made an effort to try to cheer her up. Here we were, I said, nearer to Poland, nearer to freedom. I was certainly not in the mood for tears, and my mind was already full of new thoughts and new plans to find a way to get to this freedom.

"Are we not going to eat something?" Stasia put in plaintively. "I won't be able to sleep on this hay-bag, anyhow – I must at least have some tea . . ."

This suited me well enough, and I suggested having a look round in the town for some sort of café. We found the main street, where we joined the crowd moving slowly along in front of the buildings, but there was no sign of shops, cafés or restaurants except for some forgotten signboards over empty or boarded-up premises. At a street corner an old peasant woman was selling bright red summer apples: a cheery sight, and quite a welcome supper, I decided. Stasia was not so keen, but as there was no alternative she bought some too and we made our way back to the school in the gathering dusk.

After this hungry first night the food situation improved, and we were given adequate daily rations or, rather, payment in kind. We were expected to prepare our meals ourselves, and this meant that most people were pottering about all day long in the kitchen of the school, where a small kitchen range was put at the disposal of our troupe. Glad to be able to avoid this crowd, I took my provisions and my kettle to some sheltered place on the shores of the river Dniepr and had a picnic there by myself, with occasionally a stray dog to keep me company. There was no one on the sandy beach, plenty of dry wood from the cluster of pine trees and a delightful view of the town with its white wall and old churches. The town people stayed at home in the middle of the day, but in the late afternoon this beach became a regular meeting place for all the town people and many of our troupe joined them too. Even the fat Maria Ivanovna managed to walk down sometimes and came back red and hot and tired, and full of remarkable stories about the beach life. I preferred to avoid these social gatherings although the other artistes insisted that they had a "grand time", while I explained that I needed some extra time for my violin practice at that hour of the day.

On my first day with the Mogilev Symphonic Orchestra – a very grand name for a rather modest body – I was given a violin from the local cultural centre, and to my great joy it turned out to be a very good instrument. It was lovely to hold such an instrument in my hands again, and the quality of its tone compensated to a large extent for the lesser quality of the music we had to play. I found myself among the first violins in an orchestra composed entirely of men except for me. Twenty-nine men and myself the only woman. This made my position far more conspicuous than I liked, but I was relieved to discover that at the gala performance for which we were rehearsing – a comedy to be staged at the Mogilev big theatre – the orchestra would be providing supporting music from a position out of sight of the audience. We were to rehearse together three times a week only, and the rest of the time I was free to practise on my own. But the weather was lovely and it was easy to be lazy.

At the next rehearsal of our orchestra, our conductor made what was to me a most unwelcome announcement. He announced to us pompously that we had to do our very best at the next few rehearsals as he had just received notice that we were to give a short recital – a selection of waltzes – before the comedy at the coming gala. This would mean that we would be performing on the stage – just what I had hoped to avoid. Something had to be done. At all costs my face must not become well known if I was to carry out my plans of escape. I had no firm plans as yet, but my stay in Mogilev must not last much longer – and meanwhile the Cheka eyes must not know me. These were the thoughts that occupied my head as my fingers played at the required wild tempo the waltz from "Faust", then the "Blue Danube", then "Songe d'Amour" and so on. It was a very hot summer day, and our red-haired conductor – who was also the local chemist – was red in the face too from his exertions.

Suddenly I noticed a little sturdy red-haired urchin of three or four, creeping up behind the conductor. He was dressed in a very short shirt only, and his quick beady eyes were fixed on one spot under the conductor's music stand. What trick was the little chap about to play on his father – and how could the rest of us keep serious when faced with this apparition? Quick and nimble, the half-naked little urchin reached the spot under the music stand, at the very feet of his father but hidden from him by the music books and was waving a drum stick as if conducting too. He was imitating the movements he had seen and did it so well that we had difficulty in keeping serious. I remember this hot July afternoon so well, the small room where we rehearsed, the red-haired conductor in shirt sleeves, the red-haired baby in sleeveless shirt, and the rest of us playing waltzes, waltzes, waltzes.

Two days later I bought some iodine, washed my pen-knife carefully and cut myself, more carefully still – but quite deep – on the index finger of my left hand, smeared the wound over and over with iodine, bandaged it and went off to see our conductor.

"I am very sorry, Sir, but I fear it will be impossible for me to play tonight at the rehearsal and tomorrow at the concert. Look, I have a bad cut on my finger – I hope it was right to put iodine on it? How quickly do you think it will heal?"

"Well, how very stupid of you – too bad – and how on earth did you do it? Could you not be more careful? Show me the finger."

I undid the bandage. The blood was still trickling, the finger looked pretty ugly with a deep cut across the very tip. The chemist-conductor shook his head, shrugged his shoulders and, tying up the finger in a professional way, said:

"You won't be able to play for at least a week – this is extremely unpleasant with our concert tomorrow – and you in the first violins."

It was unpleasant for me to have a finger that ached, but it was extremely pleasant to know that I need not appear on stage at the concert. I was glad to have slipped out of it so successfully, and on the day of the gala I peeped out from behind the curtains and watched the first rows of the audience where military and other uniformed Soviet officials and their womenfolk applauded, laughed and joked. My twenty-nine fellow musicians played their waltzes and the conductor got a good round of applause. The red-haired urchin must have been put on the chain at home by his father, to make sure that he did not try to appear in his abbreviated shirt.

I was lucky with my finger; it healed up without much difficulty, even though the conditions in which we lived were not very hygienic. Our washing installations in the school building were very primitive. There was one tap, over the sink in the kitchen, and here some thirty-two people came in turn for their morning wash, with gargling and toothbrushing going on uninterrupted while our coffee pots tried to boil on the small kitchen range.

This washing arrangement did not quite suit me and so I went to the beach along the Dniepr, somewhat out of town, where the clear, quiet waters looked so inviting that each morning, at six o'clock, I hurried through the cool and empty streets and down to the beach, undressed on the sands behind a small mound and had a most refreshing and pleasant swim. By half-past six I was back in my clothes, before a detachment of soldiers started drilling further along the beach and some women came down for water on the other bank.

One day, as I was thus enjoying my swim, I heard some splashing behind me and turning round I saw the back of a head with long fair curls floating around it, swimming in the opposite direction. Annoyed at another woman having had the same idea of a morning bathe, I turned my back on her and continued my swim.

When, five minutes later, I approached the bank and came nearer to my bathing companion, I discovered to my dismay that this person – seen from the front – was wearing a lean yellow beard to match the fair straggly hair lying on the shoulders. It gave me quite a shock, for this view of a Russian priest "au naturel" was a very novel sight and one I was not prepared for.

The priest stood in the water quite unconcerned about my presence, splashing his chest with his lean, lifeless hands. Perhaps he had not seen me? His seemingly short-sighted eyes were blinking like an owl, and he only looked up when he heard my splashing. There was a minute's hesitation – then he turned slowly round; and I crept quickly up the bank to dress.

We never met in the water again, but once in the street when he turned his head away.

One good thing about Mogilev, from my point of view, was that it was a very mixed population with both Orthodox and Catholic communities, as well as Jews, and of course now there were others who professed the new atheism. No one thought it unusual that I should be a Catholic or that I should want to go to Mass. Soon after my arrival in Mogilev I attended Mass in the large Catholic cathedral and discovered – to my amazement – that one of the two priests remaining there was someone that I had met before, in Petersburg before the war.

His name was Father Bialoglowy, and I had met him at the house of some friends who arranged from time to time religious-philosophic evenings. They generally asked their friends who were interested in such matters and invited two or three speakers each time – priests of various creeds, professors of philosophy, noted writers and so on. At one of these discussions I had been struck by the clear, logical and interesting opinions expressed by a very young Roman Catholic priest. I remembered his face quite clearly and thus I immediately recognised him again in spite of the years that had passed. I spoke to him at once after the Mass. Yes, he said, he remembered very well the evenings at our friends' house. He would be pleased to see me at his presbytery whenever I cared to come. I availed myself of this invitation, and spent many interesting hours over cups of tea and discussions of books, politics, and local history. Father Bialoglowy was certainly a well-read and serious scholar and an independent spirit. He was full of life, quick of decision and very energetic. Above all, for me, he was a friend in front of whom I could be my real self without fear of betrayal.

I told him of my plans and hopes of escaping across the lines into Poland. The Front had receded so far that there was no use trying to walk across from here. And where the Front was, further west, Father Bialoglowy did not know the local peasants. But he told me that if ever I found the Commissar K who was head of an important section in the XVIth Army Corps, I could safely ask him for help and advice mentioning the name of Father B. This should be sufficient, he told me, as they had been good friends at school and at university. I was thankful for this suggestion but never thought that the moment would come when this Commissar would save me from a very difficult – if not hopeless – situation.

I often wonder what may have become of Father Bialoglowy. He was a warm-hearted patriot of White Russia, and his interests were local ones. I do not think he was particularly pro-Polish, nor pro-Russian – and certainly not pro-Bolshevik. He may have dreamed of some kind of autonomy for his bit of country, but Mogilev has remained firmly under Soviet rule ever since I was there, and he must have been made to give up his dreams. I doubt that he even would have been allowed to continue his priestly duties; he was too keen, too independent, too stubborn to be left in peace by the Soviet authorities. He is one of the people to whom I am much indebted and whom I would have been happy to meet again in life – but it was not to be.

I got to know quite a few people in Mogilev during the four weeks that I was there. I had brought some introductions and addresses with me, and hoped through such contacts to keep myself informed of the news of military and political events, upon which my chances of escape might well depend. The Poles were at the time beginning to retreat towards Warsaw, and my anxiety grew rapidly as the Front receded away from where I was, making my escape more and more difficult and doubtful.

Among the people I called upon was the family of a Soviet functionary working in the Forestry Administration. He was an engineer by profession, had probably little sympathy with the Soviets but worked for them because he had to earn his living and to support his family. His wife had relations in Moscow and these had given my aunt the Mogilev address. The evenings I spent there were restful and pleasant, in spite of their two noisy children and in spite of an obvious reluctance on their part to listen to any plans or projects of escape. They were probably afraid of compromising themselves in some way, and of being later accused of disloyalty to the Soviet regime if I were caught by the Cheka. However, it was on their glass veranda with its red and white curtains, and around the tea table with the inevitable and furiously panting samovar, that I met people who later on turned out to be very helpful to me.

There was, amongst others, a Madame P, a rather good-looking woman, very elegant as far as this was possible in the circumstances of the moment. She had the nonchalant air of a real provincial "belle" and spoke French quite well – but with a rather strange accent that made me want to laugh. She was the wife of a high official in the Red Army, but did not seem to be very eager to mix in the society of Soviet officials – at least, this was the tone she adopted when talking to me. She discovered who I really was and that I was the cousin of a brilliant cavalry colonel for whom she seemed to have had a passionate admiration. This cousin of mine, Count Alexander Keller, was mentioned by her so frequently and described to the party in such glowing terms that I visualised him in an entirely new light – that of a provincial hero as seen by the provincial ladies. How amused he was when, years later in Paris, I told him of the deep impression he had made upon the ladies of the little town near his estate. He did not seem to remember any of them very clearly – and certainly not my Madame P, who was still so much under the spell of his charm. Anyhow, she and I parted great friends and I was given the assurance that if ever I needed support from official quarters Madame P would do all she could through her husband – "mon cher Leon". In fact, several weeks later I met Madame P again quite by chance at Baranowiczi; she and her husband were extremely kind and helpful and I was very thankful to both for their friendly attitude.

Another person I met at the same house was the family doctor, a nice old man with a big beard, gold-rimmed spectacles and a ready joke especially for his lady patients. He did not know very much about me except that I wanted to get to Poland. One day, in case it should be useful, he wrote a letter of recommendation for me to the Head Doctor of the Army Red Cross detachment quartered at Mogilev and waiting for a train to take them to the Front. It may not sound now a great deed to write such a letter, but at the time a letter of this nature was a document which could easily put the author of it into a very difficult position with the authorities. Most people were very cautious about putting anything in writing. But for me this letter worked wonders, allowing me in due course to join the Red Army and start on the next stage of my journey towards escape.

From time to time I had to pretend to visit those imaginary aunts of mine in the outer suburbs of Mogilev – the aunts I had first mentioned to Comrade Block and who more recently had figured in my imagined plans of escape. I talked about them in the hearing of other artistes at the school where we lived and slept, and mentioned the possibility of spending a night or two with my old aunts, to help them with some housework. In this way my absence from the school would not arouse suspicion for a day or two at least.

In reality, when I trudged off in the early evening to visit my so-called aunts, I was going to spend an hour or two with another family whose address I had been given by Polish friends in Moscow. I remember a small white-washed house at the end of an unpaved and dusty street. A green gate, a shady garden, apples lying on the ground, cheerful red-cheeked and wax-white summer apples like those at home, a hedge at the bottom of the lawn – and fields beyond. And in the house clean white floors, embroidered table cloths, gaily coloured rustic plates on a rough unvarnished sideboard. Peace reigned in this house, cleanliness everywhere, faces smiling, Polish songs, Polish speech, Polish pictures and the Czestochowa

Madonna in a place of honour. There was a grandmother, a mother, an earnest young man and his little sister. Stas was the young man's name, and he was the only one to go much out of the house. He seemed to be the only link with the outside world, and when Stas came in from town all eyes would turn on him – with anxiety, with hope and expectation. Are they coming? Where are they – the Polish Army? What are they doing? Can it really be so long?

Hopes were ebbing and flowing, according to the news, but faith in the final liberation never seemed to abandon anyone in this house. I was there when Stas brought the rumour that Warsaw had been taken by the Bolsheviks. A tense silence fell upon everybody, only the murmur of prayers muttered by the grandmother could be heard, and the ticking of the old clock.

"I can't believe it is true," said the young man, suddenly rising from the window-sill, "it must be a rumour – they won't give up Warsaw!"

"May God grant that you are right, Stas!" answered the mother.

I sat on the steps of the garden door, looking out over the fields glowing in the late afternoon sun, listening to these people so full of deep faith and so courageous.

It was getting late; I had a long way to go before reaching the centre of the town, but I was loath to leave these people so patient, so unflinching in their faith, so friendly to me. I wonder now whether their great faith was strong enough to carry them through the years that followed, when all hopes were thwarted, when the Polish Army never reached this town to bring them freedom. Where are Stas and his family now? I have forgotten their name, but I think I could still find my way to the little white house on the edge of Mogilev, where I learned so much about faith and true patriotism.

At the time Stas was right – the rumour had been a false one and Warsaw had not fallen. In fact, there was soon some firm news coming through about a Polish advance in our direction. This should have been good news for me, but there was an unexpected complication. With the Polish Army advancing in an easterly direction, the headquarters at Mogilev was to be evacuated and we, the entertainment artistes, had to shorten our programme and prepare to move. To be taken back east was an unbearable thought for me once I had managed to get so far towards the border. Officially I had bound myself for four months, and I would have to go with the actors wherever they should be sent. To remain in Mogilev with no job and consequently no valid papers would have been too risky, and to wander off on foot towards the frontier would be unrealistic at that distance. There seemed no other way but to find some new job which would take me in a westerly direction.

I would have preferred to join one of the refugee organisations either as a refugee or as some sort of employee – but such chances came seldom and were quickly taken up. There remained the Red Army, and the kind doctor's letter of recommendation. Could I really see myself joining the Red Army? Could I dare put myself forward, under the noses of the Cheka? It was a hard decision to make. Stasia thought I was crazy to attempt it, but her moans and complaints at being "left" in this way were unbearable to listen to and strengthened my resolve to do something now, at once.

The Red Cross detachment of the Red Army was moving from Mogilev in a few days' time. Yes, they were moving westwards, via Minsk. Yes, they were short of women helpers, and what could I do? I produced my letter from the doctor. No test of my medical knowledge, thank goodness, but an order to report for embarkation on the Red Cross train the following evening. If things had been calmer in Mogilev, no doubt there would have been more questions. But the whole town was in a state of upheaval because of the headquarters having to move, and the authorities had other things to do than look into the backgrounds of the latest batch of Red Cross volunteer recruits.

I returned to the school and spent the evening dropping remarks about the old aunt that I was going to visit the following day. This was the story I had prepared, and every-thing worked well. The next morning no one was surprised to see me pack my bags and set off from the building with apparent unconcern. Stasia played her part and left me well alone. I was grateful to her for her help, and for her promise to stick to the story of the aunt in the suburbs – whose address, "unfortunately", she did not know. She made no complaints this morning and seemed content to stay on with the artists' troupe. I think she knew she could have become a Red Cross volunteer like me if she had wanted to, but somehow the idea did not appeal to her.

There was one thing that I had not thought of until now. What should I do with my violin? It was a good instrument, and I felt responsible for it. I could not leave it in the room at the school, for things had a habit of disappearing from there; besides, if I had really gone to an aunt for a few days I would surely take my violin with me in order to practise before the next orchestral rehearsal. If I left it behind, suspicions would arise about the nature of my disappearance.

The director of our troupe was a quiet, elderly man who kept rather away from the others in the company of his wife and his little son. He had a kind face, and although I did not know him well I had a good impression of him as someone of integrity. I went now with my bags to his room at the other end of the building; it would look as though I were asking leave of absence for the visit to my aunt. He greeted me in a friendly way, asking me the reason for my call. To my surprise, I found myself telling him the truth. Somehow looking at him there with his wife sewing near the window and the little boy looking at a picture book and sitting on his father's knee – I felt that that man would understand me. I told him that I was not the lonely girl I pretended to be and, without giving my real name, I plainly said that all I wanted in life now was to find my three little boys again. And that meant getting out of the country. He nodded his head in understanding, but remained silent and for a moment I feared I had made a mistake. Then his wife looked

MOGILEV

up and asked questions about my boys, how old they were, where and when I had seen them last. I told them as much as I could, and explained that I had come to them for two reasons: first, to make sure that the violin was left in safety; and second, that Stasia would not be questioned or punished for her knowledge of my departure. Giving him then the story I had been spreading I begged him, if possible, not to look for me for the next two or three days, which would give me time to get further away from Mogilev.

"Don't worry," he said, "as the director of the company it is for me to see about its members, and as I know now what you have told your room-mates I can support the story. And later? Who knows where we shall all be later?" he added with a whimsical smile.

As I thanked him and took leave of the family, they both shook hands with me very warmly and the director said with a kind smile: "Good luck, and may God bless you and help you to find your children." Tears came to my eyes when I heard these words, this blessing from my supposedly "Bolshevik" boss.

Everything worked smoothly. I left the school, walked in a very round about way to the station, slipped into the Red Cross end of a long military train, and settled in the dark corner of the freight van on a large case which was to be my bed for the next four weeks.

18

THE MILITARY TRAIN

A slowly puffing engine, a monotonous row of closed red cattle-trucks, voices raised in discussion or dispute or song accompanied by the dull throb of the train's wheels; this was our military train winding its way steadily westwards; its pace was slow enough to teach us patience, and yet never so slow as to make me lose hope.

It was a quaint train – a little world of its own crawling along towards the Front, the war – and looking so extremely unwarlike. It was strange to watch, at stations or stopping-places of any kind, how the endless row of red, blind-looking vans suddenly became alive and poured out on the embankment an assortment of people who at first sight seemed to have little to do with the Red Army. There were some soldiers of course, and some Red Cross volunteers like me in a make-shift sort of uniform, but there were also women and children in light-coloured dresses, some of the women wearing society clothes they had picked up in the markets of Moscow while others were wearing the plain clothes and close-cropped hair which was the right style for a woman Communist. Children ran round playing hide-and-seek under the railway vans, while horses and other livestock were taken out to feed on the grass. There were horsedrawn vans and carts and even a motor car or two. The only thing that seemed to be missing was the usual "class carriage" or passenger coach for the commander of the train. I missed this carriage and always wondered who the commander of the train could be and why he kept his presence secret.

In my own van there were some twenty people, together with plenty of boxes, bales and even furniture. It was certainly quite crowded. Almost one half of the van, however, was occupied by just one family – the "Vanka" family as I called it privately. This family consisted of the father, Ivan, his wife and Vanka himself, a red-faced ever-howling ten-month old baby. Ivan's job was to look after the horses of the Red Cross detachment which formed part of the train. But he took life easily, drank hard when and where he could, performed his stable duties with the minimum of effort and slept the greater part of the time. Between him and the ever-howling Vanka, the mother had enough to keep her always busy and always in an atrocious temper. It was a noisy family altogether, but there was at least one thing I admired in them – namely, that they all knew what they wanted and always managed to get it. Vanka was greedy and howled until he was fed at any hour of the day or night by his ever-ready mother. Of course, a lot of slapping and scolding was administered first, but the meal would undoubtedly follow these punishments and Vanka had evidently found this out early in his life. The mother's one idea was to have a cup of tea, so she nagged her husband at every station until he fetched her some boiling water from the station kettle. If he seemed to be too obstinate and her nagging became too enervating, I volunteered to fetch the water – and soon she would sit sipping her tea with noise and gusto, a lump of sugar between her teeth. The father's aspiration was to get vodka and he somehow managed to get some, sufficient to keep him quiet for a time, and yet I never saw him drunk. He liked his sleep and certainly got plenty of it, and if he liked his comfort – well, he certainly had that too.

This was the reason why the Vanka family filled up half the cattle truck; if fate had been unkind enough to send Ivan to the Front, Ivan had managed to outdo fate by taking all his household goods with him – not to mention the family. In fact, the private apartment he had secured for himself in our van was crowded with furniture: two beds, a chest-of-drawers, two tables, chairs, boxes and baskets, and on the top of the van was fixed a flat peasant's sleigh – "For the winter in Poland" – Ivan had told me. This very individual way of preparing for war surprised and amused me at first, but by and by I noticed that many other warriors – or semi-warriors – had adopted the same policy and the most incongruous household apparatus could be seen emerging from the vans. Many other families – wives and children – were following the men to the Front, and I never really found out under what heading this part of the train's population was registered.

In a van quite near to ours there was a man who must have been some high official in the Red Army, for he and his family seemed to have the van all to themselves. His wife was a "real lady", dawdling along in gaily coloured dresses, a parasol on the shoulder and I think she even had gloves! The two little girls seemed to have a governess, and a soldier was clearly doing the work of an orderly, although the institution of orderlies had been abolished as incompatible with the self-respect of a proletarian. The father was the first to know whether the train would stop several hours at some particular spot, or whether it would proceed after a short rest only. Therefore, as soon as the "captain's family" (as I called them to myself) arranged their chairs and tables on the grass near the track, I knew I could safely walk off to a nearby village for food or to find some river for a swim. The family were so methodical and pedantic even in this unlikely setting: the governess gave lessons to the little girls who sat straight and demure on their chairs, their pigtails down their backs, their legs twisted around the legs of the chairs. The mother reclined in a deck chair, the parasol sheltering her face from the sun, and the orderly could be seen on all fours blowing hard at the samovar – in the good old style. Then cups and saucers would appear, even jam, for tea – and the tea-drinking ceremony would go on and on indefinitely. Two little dogs ran round the table or begged for sugar from the children.

Two carriages further on, there was a group of much less refined, but practical and comfort-loving people. They simply threw mattresses and blankets out of the van as soon as they thought it safe to get out for long. In this family the mother was the leader: I see her bare red arms gesticulating and I hear her shrill voice ordering about anyone and everyone, calling her three boys who seemed always to crawl too far away from her vigilant eye. They all crawled – the two eldest because they probably found it easier to get out of sight, and the youngest because he could not walk yet. I never made out who was the father of this family, for there were invariably four men all equally subdued by the woman's tongue – resting on the mattresses and seemingly content to let her run things her way. She was always bustling round the van and had plenty to do with the tying of their two piglets to the back wheels of the van, and their cock and three hens to the front wheels – all with individual long ropes. The piglets managed quite well and rarely squealed, but the hens were always so entangled round the wheels that it was a full-time job to unwind the strings and to pacify the frightened birds.

The van next to us was occupied by the staff of the Red Cross detachment, including the doctor who had accepted me in Mogilev. He was a kind and gentle man who always gave me a smile when he caught sight of me. One of the other doctors had with him his wife and a daughter of three or four. The child was very delicate, and whimpered and cried a good deal, much to the distress of her pale and worried-looking mother whose sad and careworn expression was pathetic to behold.

Further along the train – quite far away fortunately – was a van which seemed to contain the Communist "brains" of the train: all spectacles and pince-nez adorning big noses and lean faces. One or two spectacles sat on stumpy noses and pancake-like faces, but one feature seemed to be common to all inhabitants of this van, and this was to have hair that ran wild whether it was curly and crisp or yellow and streaky. The women were particularly repulsive with their hard expressions and the lack of all care about their appearance. They all smoked and talked and talked, and one was sure to hear the names of Lenin and Marx being mentioned in their discussions. I carefully avoided passing this van, as the peering and piercing eyes of some of its occupants made me feel very uneasy.

I felt uneasy, too, in the presence of a young man named Grigoriev who joined our van quietly and discreetly on the first day of our journey. He was a good-looking, tall and dark-haired fellow of about twenty-five. His grey eyes looked serious. He was attentive and silent, quiet in his movements and always looked clean – which could not be said of the other inmates of our van. Officially he was a corporal joining his unit somewhere at the Front, but I was sure that unofficially he was the "eye" of the Communist Party with the task of watching over the people in our particular group. I must say, he did his task in a very skilful and unobtrusive way, which made him all the more dangerous for anyone who needed to guard the secrets of a non-Communist conscience.

Grigoriev did not speak to me for several days, but showed attention by making some improvements in my sleeping arrangements: he pushed two boxes together so that I could rest more comfortably curled round if not stretched out on them, and he arranged a passage between bags and bales for me to approach my corner without having to walk over other people's belongings.

Very carefully and as if casually he found out where I came from, where I was going, what work I intended to do. Little by little, however, he became less "diplomatic", talked more freely, smiled naturally at some joke and discussed eagerly all topics except political ones. In fact, everybody seemed careful to avoid all discussion on political subjects. Sometimes, in a young and awkward manner, Grigoriev would start some long and rather dim argument about the aims of the Communist Party and the theory of its teaching, but such perorations sounded as a rule like a very poor lecture crowded with high-sounding words and flashy slogans. He had taken in too big a morsel of these teachings and had not yet been able to digest them.

We often sat together at the open door of the van as our train slowly wound its way through the endless forests of White Russia, and we talked about forests and fields and the way of life of the people here and in other parts of Russia. I had to be very careful not to display too much knowledge of different places, for Grigoriev easily jumped to conclusions and had a way of suddenly posing most awkward questions.

"You have seen lots of places, comrade. When did you have time? You are young still?" he asked me once.

"Well, my uncle the forester had to go to different provinces where he saw to the forestry works. He often took me with him as he did not like to leave me at home alone – after my mother died."

"I see, he was a schooled forester probably?"

"Yes, he went to a school of forestry and held a good post in the north." As I spoke thus of this mythical uncle I really saw him in my imagination, resembling rather the old Prince Regent of Bavaria with a pipe in his mouth, a long white beard and always a dog at his heels.

After a short silence Grigoriev put in: "Yes, an unusual childhood. I suppose this accounts for your different way of speaking – you have something of an accent."

"Oh, you too have noticed it." I laughed as cheerfully as I could, my heart sinking as I felt the shadow of a suspicion in the man's question. "I always thought my Russian was as good as that of any northerner – and here you notice the difference! I can't help it – it must come from my mother. You see, she was a French governess in Russia and she died from consumption when I was about ten."

"That must be it. She worked too hard teaching, I suppose, and could not stand the climate?" said Grigoriev, full of sympathy now, as a "teacher" was a worker and thus belonged to the right set of people in his eyes.

In fact, it must have been true that those of us who had been brought up by foreign governesses and who had spoken English, French or German from babyhood, had acquired in Russian a slightly foreign-sounding accent – or at least some foreign- sounding idioms had crept into our Russian. I had never thought much about it before, but when disguises became necessary I needed to develop a suitable story. Thus my supposed French mother and my imaginary uncle-forester pulled me through often enough and had to figure prominently in my conversations with people like Grigoriev.

After a week of travelling, which included several days of torrential rain, our train arrived in Minsk. By now I was becoming aware of the fact that, whether the Poles were far or near, I would have to get another pair of shoes. As long as the weather had been good my old tennis shoes were quite adequate, and I had too a pair of birch-bark sandals which had served me well. But neither of these pairs had stood the test of the recent rains, and I was now left practically barefoot with the birch-bark sandals falling off my feet. Shoes had to be got, and I could use for the purchase some money which I had got by selling two small brooches in Mogilev before I joined the military train.

I walked into the town of Minsk, taking my money and the names of some people who had been recommended to me by my Polish friends in Mogilev. I always liked to have a good look at a new place, and I made my way first to the main Catholic church which spoke of days of splendour and of devotion. I had a vague memory that some ancestor of Sasha's family had been buried in this church, and I tried to read the inscriptions on the dark tombstones. The place was absolutely empty, not even a beggar at the door, and no sign of clergy or altar boys. I had hoped to hear Mass, but no preparations had been made in either of the side chapels nor on the main altar. Finally, I walked into the vestry and found there a tiny, grey-haired old man who was shuffling about with a big bundle of keys. He turned round abruptly at the sound of my steps, a look of terror crossed his face, and the bundle of keys fell out of his hands. I realised that my attire as a Red Army member must have scared him, and to reassure him I addressed some words to him in Polish – in a whisper. The old man looked astonished but, still very scared, he came closer to me and whispered in reply: "No Mass can be said because all the priests are under arrest."

"All the priests? . . . And the bishop too?" I asked. This was a blow because I had a message for him from Father Bialoglowy in Mogilev.

"Yes, and the bishop too. All the priests in the town, except one young one still left at the new church near the station," whispered the old man, shaking his head repeatedly.

It was hard to believe, and so strange to think that this large church, in which Mass had been said regularly day by day, century after century, was now abandoned and silent. I began to feel scared, too, and as I turned to go the old man came closer and, touching my shoulder, said "You are not a Bolshevik if you care to hear Mass. You had better keep away from here – they are keeping watch over the people who come and go. You had better go out through this side door – it may not be watched . . ." and he opened noiselessly a small door from the vestry. I left, thanking the old man for his kindness and regretting that I would not be able to come back to this beautiful old church again.

On the following day I went in search of a cobbler's shop. There were many such shops in Minsk, but some were firmly closed and the few that I did find open were asking such high prices for all forms of footwear that I could not have paid for even one shoe – let alone a pair. This was depressing, but the sun shone warmly and I wandered on through the narrow side streets until, as I was passing a little white house with just one wide window and a door on to the street, the sound of a cobbler's hammer reached my ears. One or two pairs of boots stood in the window; the place looked modest and I decided to try my luck once more.

The cobbler, a man of about forty, was sitting on a low stool hammering away with regular quick strokes. He looked up as I entered, raised his eyebrows – but a quick glance at my disreputable shoes must have made it clear to him why I had come.

"Good morning, good morning, I see you want a pair of shoes?"

"Yes, I am looking for something strong and solid, something that can stand hard wear," I answered, quite cheered by his friendly greeting.

"There, I have only one pair of boots that could fit you and they cost 30,000 roubles. See them there in the window?"

"Impossible, I can't pay that price – I simply have not got the money – and I can't find anything cheaper anywhere . . ." I added, and my tone of distress must have sounded genuine, for the man looked again at my feet and said:

"You see, I cannot sell these boots for less – this is their real value. But certainly you can't go on in those sandals of yours. What about making a bargain after all? . . . You just marry me and you will have the boots!" and he looked up at me with a broad smile.

The joke was unexpected and harmless and taking it up I said, "That's all right, I see you are a very brave man if you are ready to marry a girl whom you see for the first time – I do admire you very much indeed."

"Oh no, I am not quite so simple. I know you already – there, you don't believe me? But I saw you buying apples in the square yesterday, and after that I saw you entering our big church and, what's more, never coming out of it again!" he added triumphantly, evidently enjoying the look of utter surprise on my face. I was certainly astonished and rather disturbed by the discovery that I was apparently so conspicuous. The man was looking at me and laughing.

"Yes, I was near the church and I saw you enter – and I rather liked you. So I waited for you to come out – but you never came and I gave up. You went to church, even though you are with the Red Army, and then you wear very bad shoes – it means that you do not know how to get things out of people – and this makes me like you more. So will you marry me?"

This time the offer sounded much more serious. Something had to be done, but I did not want to hurt the feelings of a man who had shown such very flattering perspicacity, and confidence in his choice.

As I hesitated, at a loss for an answer, he continued, "I am a bachelor, just forty-one. This house is my own, I am working all alone and I can provide for the two of us. You can ask the neighbours about me – they know I am no drunkard, just the right sort of man," he concluded.

"I thank you for your offer – but I am with the Army . . . and . . ." What was I to say?

"All this is nonsense. Why should a nice girl like you go with the Army. Why have you joined it anyhow? It is not the place for girls at all."

"Well, I was alone – I have no family – and I thought that I could be useful in the Army as I am not afraid of going to the Front. This is why I joined it, and besides, how could I marry you – I have no idea of household work, indeed I am most awkward at it and life would be very hard for you with a stupid wife." This argument seemed to be a good one and I was glad to have found it.

"I am an excellent housewife myself – look here, the place is clean, isn't it? It is not for nothing that I have been a bachelor for so many years. Life teaches one to do all sorts of jobs. Don't worry about all that – I can teach you how to clean the house and wash the linen, and how to cook too. Shall we make a start today? I have bought a joint of meat and will have to cook it later on, at three o'clock. Come in then and see how I do it – it is quite easy and I am an honest man – I will look after you."

"Yes, but the Army?" – this seemed to be my last plausible excuse. I laughed at myself inwardly for being so terribly helpless in finding the right way out.

"I already told you that a nice girl cannot stay with the Army. Go back and fetch your bag. Forget the Red Army – let it go – who wants it anyhow? Come back here this afternoon – be

Р. С. Ф. С. Р.

НАРОДНЫЙ КОМИССАРИАТ
ВНУТРЕННИХ ДЕЛ.

Петроградское Управление
по делам о пленных и беженцах.
(Петропленбеж).

" " января 1920 г.

№ 122

Петроград.
Вознесенский просп. 1.

УДОСТОВЕРЕНИЕ.

На основании соглашений Р. С. Ф. С. Р.
с Польским Правительством от 2 и 9-го
ноября удостоверяется, что пред'явитель сего *Мария Адам-
чевская*

является гражданским пленным подлежащим обмену и
направляется в Москву в распоряжение Комиссии по
проведению в жизнь вышеуказанных соглашений с
Польшей.

Пред'явитель сего *М. Адамчевская*
имеет право везти безплатно 15 пудов багажа.
Железнодорожным властям предлагается не чинить
препятствий к проезду *М. Адамчевской*
в г. Москву.

Комиссар Петропленбежа

Уполномоченный Комиссии

Управляющий делами

Permit issued on 12th January 1920 to "Maria Adamczewska" for
travel by train from Petrograd to Moscow. The intention was to join
the Krasinski family in Moscow and be "repatriated" with them to
Poland (see pp. 241–42).

False identity paper in the name of Evdokia Feodorovna Salogubova, dated 23 April 1920. The original blank identity form was genuine, but the handwritten details were filled in by friends who nearly spoiled the project by inattention to detail. Fortunately the inconsistencies remained unnoticed by the authorities (see p. 307).

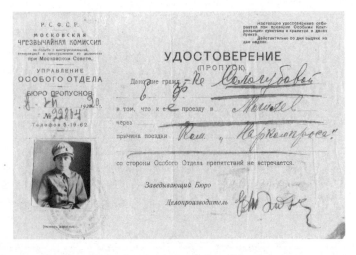

Permit issued on 8 June 1920 for "E. F. Salogubova" to join an actors' troupe travelling from Moscow to Mogilev. A general authorisation for the group was given by the Cheka, which meant that her name and photograph were not scrutinised too closely (see pp. 331–33).

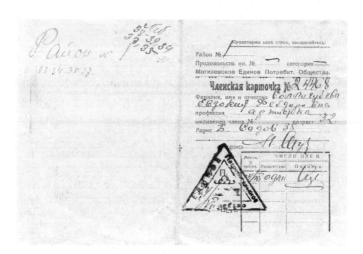

Personal union membership card carried by Edith as a musician member of the Mogilev troupe of "entertainment artistes". This card enabled her to move freely around the town, and meet friends who might help her escape (see pp. 346–48).

Handwritten permit to join the Red Cross detachment of the Red Army as a volunteer reserve recruit, issued on 31 July 1920. By the following evening Edith was at the railway station, boarding a military train bound for the Front (see p. 352).

Two official certificates from surgeon Dr Zurov of Field Hospital No. 8 of the 17th Division at Wolkowysk, recording Edith's arrival on September 5 and departure from the unit on 21 September 1920. The field hospital was about to join a general retreat (see pp. 404–17).

Handwritten appointment from the Wolkowysk station unit commander, dated September 22 and valid until 1 October 1920. A first-aid post had been set up to treat sick and injured soldiers. When the first-aid unit joined the retreat, Edith moved to the food distribution unit and worked there for a few more days before her final escape (see pp. 418–31).

In 1921, after four years of revolution and separation, mother and sons were reunited. The sailor suits, still worn by the two younger boys, remained as a link to earlier days.

here by three, for you must see how I cook the joint – it is quite easy, you'll learn it in no time – don't worry," and he patted my shoulder in an encouraging manner as he held the door open for me. I hurried away, rather distressed that once more I must let someone down, and at the same time amused at the unexpected episode. I felt ashamed of leaving him in the lurch, and I did not dare to leave the train again for fear of seeing him somewhere. Two days later we left Minsk and I lost my chance of owning there a nice little white house with a cobbler's workshop. I lost, too, the best chance of learning how to roast a joint – which was a skill that I never mastered during the rest of my life.

Back in the train, the daily life of my companions in the van imposed itself once more, and I had to play the part of the Red Cross nursing sister on the way to the Front.

Grigoriev was clever, watchful and observant, and I avoided whenever possible too much contact with him. I feared that I would have great difficulty in playing my part successfully before him, and indeed there were several times when he almost caught me out.

One day, I was having my early morning wash near the van, with my small rubber tub, a water jug and a plain silver mug all in a row on a pile of railway sleepers. Grigoriev, who was brushing his hair a few steps off, looking carefully into his pocket mirror as he made his parting, said to me:

"You have very nice arrangements for travelling, very useful and not like the others."

"I have been perhaps a little spoilt by my mother – she used to have things as they probably have them in France."

"Yes, I guess they have different things there – better things than we have here as a rule. But surely the bourgeois people all had such things bought from abroad, didn't they?"

"I suppose they did – if they were not too stupid," I laughed and continued to dry my face very energetically to conceal its expression. Was the fellow testing me again? It was quite a strain to remember to play a part, to say things not as I would naturally, but as such and such a person would have said them.

I wondered how I could manage to make my washing habits look rougher and less refined in future.

I remember, too, a rainy day when we were approaching Baranowiczi, advancing now more rapidly towards Warsaw. I was sitting in my corner considering as usual my chances of escape. Some of my companions were discussing a subject of morals, as far as I had noticed. A Communist Commissar in a black leather coat with two revolvers at his belt had entered our van asking for a lift as far as the next station. His presence was not reassuring, and I was glad to remain unnoticed in my corner. But Grigoriev was enjoying the discussion and the company of the Commissar. Suddenly, to my dismay, I heard him call out in my direction: "Comrade, sister – won't you help us to settle a question?"

"I don't know. What is it about?" I replied reluctantly.

"We were discussing various things just now, and we can't explain the difference between a principle and a prejudice. Can you help us?"

"I think I can – at least I'll try," was my reply. It was difficult to know what to do. If I gave a bad answer I would make Grigoriev look ridiculous in the eyes of the Commissar for having turned to me in the first place. Grigoriev had been helpful to me in many ways and I did not want to let him down. At the same time, I was unwilling to show that I might understand things which were not clear to the others. In a few words as plainly as possible I gave the desired explanation.

"Thanks, comrade," said the Commissar. "I understand what you mean – you put it quite clearly," and he went on talking until we reached the station. After that he was gone.

That evening, when I was cooking my supper on the track, Grigoriev strolled up to me and stood watching my preparations for some time. I was nervous lest my cookery should also brand me as "bourgeois", but on this subject he made no comment. He was still thinking about the earlier discussion.

"Strange, sister, there you are, a mere girl and not even a regular nurse, and you can understand and explain things which we Communists, members of the Party, cannot understand."

"It was a matter of chance that I knew – I had read about it somewhere," I put in casually.

"Maybe. But look at that fellow today. He was a Commissar, he had two revolvers, he has the power to decide over life and death, and yet he – like myself – could not make sense of these ideas which were so clear to you. Strange – and somehow it seems unjust," said Grigoriev, accompanying his last words with a vague shake of the head. He was perplexed, worried.

I pitied the man, for to acknowledge before me this lack of understanding must not have been easy for him, and his sense of justice and responsibility struck me deeply. I was thinking about him with a certain respect and, as I stirried the potatoes boiling in a small camp kettle over the fire, Grigoriev suddenly said to me:

"Look here, comrade, do you not belong after all to that family of Counts whose name is so much like yours?"

This was a shock. My spoon nearly dropped into the fire. What should I say? Must I deny? How could I?

"This is strange," I said, trying to sound indifferent. "What makes you think so all of a sudden?"

"Well, I don't know, something in your manners – in your hands – in the way they handle saucepans . . ."

"I am sorry if my hands are awkward, it is silly not to be able to use them better" . . . I was saying, and even now many years after I can remember the sound of my voice, the feeling of blood rushing to my face, the thoughts racing through my mind. What could I say? Only something blank and stupid – but not a denial, not a lie. Strange as it may sound, in all my months of danger I had always avoided telling such a direct lie – although the stories I had to tell and the parts I had to play were in themselves fantastic enough. Grigoriev muttered something insignificant, I can't remember what, and for once he did not persist. During the rest of our time on the train he never came back to this subject.

Weeks later, when our detachment was on the eve of being dissolved, when all my companions seemed to have been appointed to different posts, Grigoriev told me that he had been entrusted with a job in the special bureau of another division, and that he had asked to have me as his assistant. It was kind of him to have thought of me, but I had to refuse his offer which would have meant going to the rear, and I gave him as my reason an appointment that I had been offered in another division, at the Front. Grigoriev raised his eyebrows: "At the Front? Don't you really mind going to the Front? Are you not afraid?"

"Afraid? No – I suppose not," I said. "I am all alone in the world now and may just as well do the work there where risks run by others would grieve their relations."

"Pity for you, though," he replied with a smile. "Anyhow, remember, if you do not get your appointment I will always find work for you – just ask me." It was a touching end to our relationship. Grigoriev was out for the day when I finally left, and so I never said goodbye. I do not know what became of him afterwards, but I doubt if he ever made a brilliant career in the Party. He was too sensitive and fair-minded, and if he had not been a Communist I could have thought of him as a friend.

Meanwhile, we were still in our train and had reached the small, sleepy station of Stolpcy where we waited for news of the supply train that was supposed to be reaching us soon. It was high time for the distribution of food supplies, as ten days had elapsed since the last hand-out, and the rations we had received then were barely sufficient for six days. There was no regimental or communal kitchen on our train, and rations were distributed individually. The supply train had apparently been delayed somewhere up the line.

Thus the humour of my companions was not very brilliant. No complaints were uttered aloud but murmurs were heard here and there. Older men grumbled, the younger shrugged their shoulders, and all cast side glances at Grigoriev, waiting for news and feeling that it was all somehow his fault.

By now there was nothing left to eat. All individual larders were empty and nothing could be found in the little village but a few apples and, maybe, after much searching and coaxing, a couple of eggs in exchange for cigarettes or sewing cotton or other small trifles. The weather was mild and sunny and this was a consolation as I tramped hungrily off on an apple-and-egg hunt in the village. On my return to the train, I met to my surprise the majority of my travelling companions marching together, with cheerful faces and light steps, towards the fields.

"Come on, sister, we have just received permission to dig up potatoes in those fields. They once belonged to some runaway landlord. Fetch a bag and join us there – we'll have a regular feast tonight."

I nodded, mumbled something in reply and went on towards my van. I knew which fields they meant. They stretched from the railway line up a slope as far as a park, in the shade of which stood a long low country mansion surrounded by farm buildings. There was a large open lawn and a broad drive leading to the steps of a low veranda with four white columns. To the right, on the edge of the park, rose the high belfry of the village church and next to it was the priest's house. It was a picture so typical and so dear to me, and it had attracted my attention the moment we arrived in Stolpcy. The house was closed up, the place looked abandoned, and yet such order reigned everywhere that it looked simply asleep.

Now, as I sat on the steps of our van, I could see my companions and all the other groups, scattered over the fields, doubled up and looking like ants in the distance. Time passed slowly; my apples were good but did not do much to lessen my hunger. The sun was now low on the horizon, and I whistled a tune – to keep up my spirits.

"Not gone potato-digging?" said one of the doctors as he passed our van.

"No, sir, don't feel very inclined to," I answered lightly.

"Lucky you, that you don't feel hungry. All our people have gone," he went on. Oh dear! As if I didn't feel hungry! This was a nasty word to hear when it touched on the raw truth of the moment.

That night, a lovely smell of baked potatoes spread all over our train. All along the line, little camp fires were burning merrily and people bustled around them, joking, laughing, singing – and eating. I sat and looked at the moon and tried to whistle a little tune. How the delicious smell of the potatoes teased me – but could I go and steal potatoes in the fields of a fellow-landowner? No, I could not do it, even though he was no longer there, and I went hungry into my corner and curled round on my box and pretended to sleep.

The next day passed very slowly and in the same way. I bought three apples and they helped me through the morning. In the evening the same delicious smell of potatoes brought tears to my eyes. I pretended to have a headache and went early to bed, to avoid the many questions about why I had not joined the potato- digging party.

On the third day the supply train had still not appeared. Putting all my pride and my class sympathy deep in my pocket – or in a corner of my heart – I walked off with an empty bag on my shoulder towards the fields where my companions were already busy. It was hard to get there, my feet felt like lead, and when I started digging I felt miserable and guilty. It was hard on my pride, hard to give in just because of my hunger. If there had been nothing to eat I could probably have borne it, but it was impossible to stand the sight of the others cooking and eating each evening.

I never found potatoes as tasteless as those I baked that night in the embers of my small camp fire some way off the railway track, and in my heart I asked the unknown landowner to forgive me my weakness.

Our train was not the only one waiting for supplies. At last the news came through, the call being repeated from van to van all along the waiting trains: "The supply train is here!" Crowds rushed immediately to the main line on which presumably the long- expected train must have stopped. People jumped like frogs out of the luggage vans, swinging bags and baskets and looking eager and happy. The morning was bright and sunny, too hot perhaps as threatening dark clouds were gathering in the west. In a few minutes our train was almost deserted; here and there a figure sat in the shade of the van or fussed about with some household work, preparing the camp fire in view of the food to be fetched by other members of their family.

"Not gone to the food distribution, sister?" asked the good-natured doctor, the head of our Red Cross detachment, the one who had enlisted me at Mogilev.

"No, sir, not yet. The crowd will be too great at present and besides, I am not so hungry," I replied.

"Yes, I remember, you do not seem to have a very good appetite. You would not go for potatoes in the fields over there."

"My appetite is good enough, but my ideas about potatoes in other people's fields are not suited for times of war."

"That is what I had suspected – you see, I am a psychologist as well as a doctor, and I know that such ideas do not change very easily."

"No, my ideas are very stubborn, I fear. Besides, why change them?" I put in quite courageously. The doctor seemed in a talkative mood. I felt he could not be a militant Communist – if indeed he were a Communist at all.

"Life changes and ideas about life have to change, too – at least when too great struggles have to be avoided. You will learn this by and by, sister. Good appetite for the coming feast," and with a smile the doctor walked off to his van. I saw him climbing in slowly and patting the blonde head of the other doctor's little girl who was sitting on the doorstep.

A good man, this doctor, I thought. If I needed help or advice I felt I could turn to him. He would not betray me if he knew the truth – no – but he might not want me in his detachment if he knew about my plans for escape. He might try to shift me to some other organisation where I would be less of a liability. Better wait and say nothing, I thought, and be satisfied with the fact that our train was advancing towards the west, even though this advance was terribly slow.

By now people were passing me, carrying bags, parcels and baskets full of provisions, little camp fires began to send up columns of smoke all along the lines and I decided to make my way to the distribution centre where the main rush had to have subsided by now.

The controlling corporal did not even look at my papers and I soon found myself laden with sugar and salt in two shoe bags, semolina in my leather cap, tea, matches and cigarettes in my pockets and – at arm's length – a dangling bundle of salt cod which smelt appallingly.

As I turned back, the first drops of the approaching storm began to fall and a minute later the downpour came with such strength that I scrambled for shelter under the railway carriage nearest to me. Crouching there on all fours I tried to protect my stores from the rain which came now in rivulets all round me, splashing off the roof, running down the sides of the carriage into big overflowing pools. Dropped in my haste – and now at a good distance from me – lay the bundle of smelly cod which could only be improved by such a thorough rinsing.

"Hello, comrade," shouted a man's voice suddenly. I looked round and saw a man, on all fours like me and sheltering his goods, who had taken refuge under the next train. "Mind you keep low down," he shouted across to me. "You are on the main track and your train may start at any minute."

Should I really move? I would get soaked. And, after all, there was always a lot of whistling and engine puffing before a train started. I might just as well take a chance and hope for the best. But I did flatten myself as much as I could, and I thanked my neighbour for his kind warning.

A quarter of an hour later I was crawling out into the bright sunshine and splashing cheerfully through steaming pools as I made for "home". The engine of my shelter train was sending up clouds of black smoke, evidently preparing to move. Probably the engine driver had been waiting for the rain to stop. There was no timetable to keep to, and no one ever seemed to be in a hurry.

As I climbed up the board leading into our van, I noticed to my horror and disgust that my bundle of cod, refreshed by the rain, seemed fit to follow me into the van without my help. It looked terribly alive. With a swing of my arm I flung it out on to the embankment, much to the amusement of my companions.

"Ah, sister, that is not like you! If you don't want your fish give it to us. If we cook it it will be eatable," said Vanka's father. He reached across for the bundle – but I did not dare look at it any more.

Soon there prevailed for once a general tone of satisfaction and brotherly feeling along the length of our train. How much a good meal does mean in the making of good or bad humour, I thought. The arrival of supplies had brought together all the vans of the train, all the little red worlds strung together along the line. With no commander, our leaderless train seemed to drift along vaguely towards the Front. Each van had its life and its character, its habits and ways. Only the supply train brought us all together. After the evening meal, songs from the camp fires rose in the quiet evening air. Songs started by one group would be picked up by the next, and would thus link the string of little worlds. Tonight no one seemed to care much about time or destination. "The authorities know" was a sufficient answer to any question on these subjects – sufficient and conclusive. Before the revolution the Russian peasants used to say "The authorities know", which meant for them "Why bother to think for ourselves?" Things were not so different now on board our revolutionary military train.

19

BARANOWICZI

A hot August day with brilliant sunshine from the early morning. Not a breath of wind, laziness in the air, over the town, over our train. We had taken root in this place – the railway junction at Baranowiczi. Having arrived with the advancing troops we stopped and waited. Our train, stationary on a side track, looked more than ever like a travelling circus and less and less like a military train. The horses of our detachment had been taken out of their van and were grazing peacefully in the meadow at the foot of the railway embankment; pigs lay asleep in the shade of the vans, their hind legs tethered to the wheels; here and there some washing lay spread out on the grass to dry. The doctor's pale and wan little girl was sitting on the edge of the embankment trying to make sand cakes with her weak transparent little hands. My companions were asleep inside the van, except for Vanka who was evidently trying again one of his usual howls, accompanied by frequent energetic slaps from his sturdy mother. There was a lull in the movement of trains on the main lines – even the station looked drowsy and empty. What a dismal place, this little town of Baranowiczi! Rows and rows of low, unpainted weather-beaten houses, all grey, all equally ugly and tumbledown; no gardens, no flowers, no curtains on the windows, no shutters – and swarms of dark curly-haired and black-eyed children playing in the deep dust of the unpaved street. Hundreds of such urchins always intent on their games, always hurrying, never looking up dreamily at the passer-by, but glancing round furtively like hunted game, or gazing with a scrutinising look, old and speculative, on their small pinched faces. These children were Jewish and had learned to be cautious, to be ready to look for shelter quickly in their dingy, dirty, crowded homes. The people of Baranowiczi had seen many armies come and go and the mistrustful looks they gave us were scarcely to be wondered at.

Further, beyond the streets of the town, stretched endless fields, flat and monotonous, badly tilled and poorly sown. As I sat on the slope of the embankment looking west, as usual, and wondering if our train would ever move again, I noticed a small cloud approaching along the narrow road winding through the fields. A cloud of dust – I watched as it grew little by little until I discerned a group of men trudging along in the dust. There were some ten or twelve men: at the head the black leather jacket of a Communist of higher rank, behind him men or soldiers with rifles – and between them, trudging heavily along, three old village priests in their long black cassocks, their heads uncovered and bent low. My heart stood still: the blazing sunshine seemed to have lost its brilliance as I watched the dust, grey dust all round and those three miserable figures moving slowly on. At that moment a voice behind me said: "Well, they go away from their village church for the last time now – the villains. Their song is sung." I turned my head away and shrugged my shoulders, unable to look round into the face of the man who uttered such heartless words, but I knew it was Grigoriev, our Communist. I had the feeling that he said these words on purpose to see what effect they would have on me. I said nothing, and continued pushing pebbles down the embankment with my stick. The day had suddenly grown dark for me, and I could only hear the step of the three old priests going to their doom.

A week later the sleepy station – sleepy even in these times of war – was suddenly all movement and noise. It made me think of a Saturday cleaning in a small German town. Great

excitement reigned; the arrival of Trotsky, the great war lord of
the Soviets, had been announced. Spare engines ran backwards
and forwards dragging old vans, cattle trucks, carriages and
tenders. Trains with no special destination – such as ours, for
instance – were moved on to remote side lines. Women with
buckets of water splashed about right and left washing carriages, while others raked up the innumerable tins and papers
scattered on the lines. Even the reserve soldiers camping in
the endless military trains seemed to have been influenced by
this cleaning fever, and clusters of bearded men sat almost
naked round the well in the station yard washing their clothes,
scrubbing their bodies and hunting busily for insects – much
like apes in the zoo.

I was sitting on one of my favourite places along the
embankment, not far from some points and a signal box, and
was watching the efforts of an old engine with a queer funnel
opening wide at the top. It had just pushed our long train on to
another track, and now the engine driver was leaning out of his
cab, smoking a pipe and blinking at the sun.

"A lovely day, comrade," he said to me. "It's good to sit in
the sun. We are always warm enough in these engines but the
air is not so good up here."

"I agree, it's better to get warm in the sun than at the engine,"
I replied. "You have been running up and down the station all
the morning, and it's near dinner time now. Aren't you going
to stop soon?"

"Stop? You don't know our work here today! I have now to
shift this damned propaganda train and that'll take time to get
it to the right place. You just wait and see how they will make
me push it backwards and forwards – all for Trotsky to see it
the moment he arrives."

"He probably will be glad to see it at the best place."

"As if he had not seen it already hundreds of times at all
the big stations before this one! He must be sick of these
posters – nothing new in them, and what is their use anyhow
– eh?"

"I suppose he knows their use and likes them," I suggested, seeking to avoid any more definite statements about such high persons as Trotsky.

"You will have to join in the review too, comrade. Are you not on that train there?" put in the engine driver after a short silence.

"No orders have been given yet, so I don't really know," I answered, glad to have been warned thus indirectly of a possible ordeal in store for me. I certainly did not want to parade before Trotsky, and I would be careful now not to come near our train until the evening.

After a few more words with the engine driver, I strolled away making plans for the day. The few roubles in my pocket should be sufficient to get some apples and maybe, if I was lucky, a bun or a piece of black bread for my luncheon – and tea. What interested me more was the review, which I did not want to miss provided that I could be there as an onlooker only. I would creep away from my colleagues and especially from the vigilant eye of Grigoriev, and I would leave the station via the embankment and some back streets and then make my way through the outskirts of the town.

In due course the sound of military music drew me back to the centre – the review was apparently to take place in the market place. Troops were marching now towards this large open square where cattle markets were usually held once or twice a week. All the washing and cleaning had not done much to improve the appearance of these haggard, bearded soldiers in soiled and tattered uniforms. The majority were without rifles – at that time the rule was to arm the men only when they reached the very front lines. The only troops with any degree of smartness were some cavalry – the pride of the XVIth Army, I was told – who were now entering the square. It was true, the men looked cleaner and the horses were well fed and well groomed.

I squeezed into a corner near some tumble-down houses, hiding behind the backs of some local men who stood gaping at the troops. Our Red Cross detachment and the soldiers from our train were approaching to take up a position somewhere to the right.

After a good hour's waiting the "staff" appeared, but the rumour went round the crowd that Trotsky was not there. Never mind, the sight of this staff was a revelation in itself and really made the review worth seeing. What an agglomeration of quaint and entirely "unmilitary" looking men: and how they tried to adopt the airs of true army men, clicking their heels and getting entangled in spurs too long and boots with buttons! Some were on horseback, mounted on knock-kneed horses with melancholy drooping heads. These men clearly felt ill at ease in the saddle, swaying to and fro and grasping the knob of the saddle with one hand, if not exactly with both. The leader, a youngish fellow with a cap well tilted back, round shouldered and with ridiculously short stirrups, was evidently trying to show off as an experienced rider. He kicked the sides of his horse with his legs, keeping the spurs carefully out of the game, and his left arm rested on his hip while his right hand tightly grasped the reins – an arrangement which was so wrong that it really amused me a lot.

As I was thus enjoying this sight, a tall fellow in a ragged soldier's coat spat on the ground with a gesture of contempt, muttering half to himself, half to me: "That dirty chemist's assistant wants to play the general! Looks like a dog sitting on a fence with his knees under his chin." Stopping suddenly the man cast a side glance at me, evidently wondering how I would take this frank remark he had allowed himself. One of those looks we all knew so well – questioning, doubting and mistrustful looks which were our self-protection.

"He seems to have forgotten about the sword, with the reins in the right hand," I replied. We smiled now understandingly at each other and when I asked him "You surely served in the cavalry?", he answered at once, straightening his back: "In the Warsaw Uhlans" – and there was pride in his voice.

Whether the great Trotsky came to Baranowiczi that day I do not know. He may have come and gone again, but for the rest of us there was no coming or going – just endless days of waiting. It soon became clear that the Front was not advancing, was probably not even holding. The troop trains stopped going forward, and the lines became full of trains coming back. Wave after wave of retreating units, of fleeing soldiers passed us now day and night. Trains were packed: on roofs and on engines, on buffers and on steps, soldiers hung, sat and clung – looking so little like soldiers in their haphazard uniforms mixed with civilian clothes, with their long beards and hair hanging down to the collar. At the station they fell off their precarious seats and, stiff and tired, made their way to the steaming kettles to ask for some tea. They looked round anxiously and asked everyone whether the Poles were near, whether they had approached the town, whether the train would stop long enough to let them have a cup of tea. Poor fellows, I thought, how strained they looked, how hungry – and how quiet! They were subdued, frightened, lost – and so little conscious of the "great achievements of the revolution" for which they were summoned to fight. At the same time, how happy this fleeing crowd made me! I saw the moment approaching when I would be able to reach the Polish lines – to get out of this terror-stricken country into the free world once more.

As the hot August days went by I wished that I could find some lake, some river or pond where I could have a swim. But the land round Baranowiczi was dusty, dried out, flat and grey, with no water anywhere for a swim or a bath. None of the other people in the railway truck seemed to have any understanding of this desire, looking upon it as a bourgeois fancy – and it was wiser for me not to speak about it. They seemed perfectly content with their bit of face-and-hands washing every morning at the side of the track. This face-washing was an extraordinary operation which I watched, being quite fascinated by the skill of some of the men. The two women in our van were quite good at it, but one of the men – the stupid looking soldier with his hat always on the back of his head – was an ace in this art. He had, it is true, a very large mouth which must also have been extremely spacious on the inside, for when he drew in the water – he did it like a horse, lengthily and noisily – it seemed never-ending. Then, setting his legs well apart and stretching out his arms in front of him with the palms rounded and close together, he blew a strong jet of water into them and swiftly drew them over his face. All peasants washed like that, but this man had such a powerful jet and such a water storage capacity in his mouth that he washed, soaped and rinsed his face all from one jet. He would have provided much joy as a side-show at a fair, I thought.

Anyhow, I was looking for a bath and it occurred to me that railway guards might be a possible source of water. They lived independently beside the railway line, they had to have some water supply (for the trains) and their dwelling was usually a little more civilised than others of a similar social standing. On the outskirts of the main railway station I had noticed a clean looking little guard's house with masses of flowers in the tiny front garden, clean white curtains in the windows and a large tiger cat sitting on the bench under the window, eyes half-closed in the brilliant sunshine and with the tip of the tail twitching slightly as the eyes followed the movement of a spar-row hopping about on the ground. There was a pleasant look about the place. I entered the garden, found the guard's wife and, opening the conversation as usual on the topic of food, soon decided that it would not be too difficult to approach this woman on the subject of a bath. An hour later this great question was most satisfactorily settled: my turn for hot water would come after tomorrow's bread baking, provided it did not rain.

I arrived the next morning duly armed with a birch-twig broom to sweep the corner between the house and the wood-shed which was to be my open air bathroom, and an armful of ferns to use as a bathmat. A knotty pine branch supplied the pegs for hanging up my clothes, and a blanket served as a door. The bathroom was delightful, with the blue sky and the hot sunshine overhead and the fresh, strongly scented ferns at my feet. It was a most enjoyable bath and, to thank my hosts for their kindness, I took them two days' supply of wood from the nearby forest.

After this, I was treated as a friend of the family, and I spent many pleasant hours talking with them about harvests, gardens, flowers and vegetables. I loved listening to the guard's slow speech in the drawly half-Russian, half-Polish dialect which sounded to me so very picturesque. He liked talking about his railway, the difficulties he had in carrying out his job now, when orders and counter-orders were given and then either forgotten or misunderstood by those who forwarded them. At first he was very reserved towards me, but soon he realised that I was not a Soviet agent or propagandist and he then spoke frankly and freely, apparently happy to be able to talk with someone new and willing to listen to him. I learned from him many details about the local lines, the junctions, the functioning of trains, the nearest stations and stopping places, the position of bridges and shunting lines. All this was most valuable information, since I was now working on a plan to walk in the direction of Brest Litovsk – or, possibly, to Bialystock, where the Poles seemed to be firmly entrenched. I tried to learn by heart all the names of places and local expressions, not daring to write them down in case of being searched or arrested – who knew what?

Sometimes their nephew joined us in the evening, a tall lanky fellow from the post office. He had a dreadful squint, and as he sat on the bench next to me I had the impression that the unruly eye tried in vain to look over the flat nose and invariably got stuck squinting into the corner. It was painful to watch him, especially as he tried hard to appear at his best. I had a suspicion that my presence spurred him on to make a show of his knowledge and when, one day, he appeared with heavily oiled hair and a most enticing curl over the left eyebrow I had no doubt that such efforts were not intended for the uncle and aunt. I was only a simple Red Army girl, but he had found out that I could read Latin letters (as he could too because of

379

his work at the telegraph), and – even more important – I had long hair.

"Yes," the aunt had said the other day, "What are these new Communist girls doing? It is a real shame to look at them with their hair cut like a man's and a cigarette in their mouth!"

"Ah, yes, it's disgusting," the nephew had added. "In my view, a woman must have long hair if she is the right sort of woman ..." and the unruly eye stuck in the corner as he attempted to see what impression this wise statement made upon me. I agreed with conviction and smilingly nodded my head which carried the often tiring weight of two heavy tresses.

These were quiet evenings, with the scent of stock and tobacco plants mixing with the smoke of slowly passing trains. I knew it would be sad to say good-bye to these kind people, to that little spot of peaceful life in the midst of revolution and war.

After the ideally warm summer, the autumn rains set in about the middle of August with unpleasant ferocity. We were still stationed on our side track. There were still soldiers returning from the Front, and I would chat to them in the hope of gleaning some information about troop movements. An important shifting of forces seemed to be taking place, military trains crowded the junctions and Baranowiczi station now had heavy traffic from both directions as fresh troops arrived from the rear in increasing numbers. One day Grigoriev pointed out to me a group of high officials alighting from a military train, and among those that he named was Commissar K, the man mentioned to me by Father Bialoglowy in Mogilev. From a distance, all I could see was a man with small features and reddish hair. The officials splashed hurriedly away. The railway tracks were sodden, the passages between them were muddy paths in which innumerable empty tins, broken baskets, papers and other items of rubbish were stuck.

This wet weather was particularly unpleasant since the last pair of birch-woven sandals I had bought from a peasant in Mogilev were entirely worn out and I had been obliged to throw them away. The last week or two I had been walking barefoot and had actually stood this test quite well as long as the weather was dry. But now, with the rains, the mud had become ankle deep not only at the station but also all over the unpaved streets of the little town, and I found walking quite a difficult task as it meant avoiding odds and ends sticking out of the half-liquid chocolate-coloured mass. With the first cold morning I decided that the joke had gone too far and that I simply had to get boots. Thus, having fished a few Soviet 100-rouble notes out of their hiding place – the kneeband of my boy scout style breeches was my savings bank – I went into town in search of shoes of some kind.

All the shops had been closed since the arrival of the Soviet armies, but usually one managed to find some goods by looking closer through the windows into the low houses where signs still bore descriptions of former trading. But today, the same thing invariably happened at every place I enquired: first, vehement assurances that there were no goods to be found in the house; then, after some coaxing and persuading, the reply came that something might be found, perhaps, provided it would be paid for with Polish or even old Imperial Russian money – anything other than Soviet money. Soviet money was all that I had, and I wandered about greatly discouraged after these unsuccessful attempts.

Finally I stopped at a low doorway on the steps of which a man was hammering away at a boot while a Red Army soldier waited patiently for his boot to be ready. Of course my question received the same well-known answer – no goods left anywhere. But as the old cobbler looked less unfriendly and seemed to have been chatting quite readily with the soldier, I went on explaining to him my need, pointing out that the weather was really beginning to be too unpleasant for anyone to walk barefoot, and so on. The cobbler only shook his head, shrugging his shoulders, but the soldier took pity upon me and said:

"Well, sister, you'd better come across to where we are quartered. My mother bought a pair of shoes the other day

– very good shoes, too – but she can't wear them, they seem to be too small. You may be able to get into them. Just come and have a look."

I accepted this offer thankfully and duly appeared at his address an hour later. On my way I had been thinking with amusement about this typical Red Army arrangement: here was a soldier, in the Army, and quartered apparently with his mother – this was not unlike our train and the "Vanka family" arrangements.

The soldier let me in and introduced me to his mother as "the little sister who wants to buy your new boots". The fat and bulky old woman bustled away and reappeared with a marvellous pair of half-length boots with a row of black buttons on the side. I slipped them on to my bare feet and was made to walk up and down the rooms to make sure that they really fitted me.

"They seem to be all right – not too small," the soldier was saying, nodding his head as if he was an expert on fitting shoes, whereas in fact I could only just manage to shuffle along, the boots being miles too large. But I was glad to have something on my feet, and concluded the business after a little bargaining in which I attempted to get the boots for 1,000 roubles. Finally, I had to pay 1,100 roubles for the boots which, according to the fat mother, were "as fine a pair as one could find in the district". Off I walked, shuffling along pleasantly and thinking what a sight I must be.

Day by day more troop trains were arriving, including a train full of military supplies for the XVIth Army. Imagine my surprise when I discovered that the official in charge of this train was none other than the husband of Madame P, the provincial belle who had made friends with me in Mogilev. She had come with him and, together with two unmarried sisters and several servants (quite a "bourgeois" household), had taken up residence in a country place close by, in which they began to entertain the higher Communist officials and Red Army officers, of whom there suddenly seemed to be an increasing number in our little town.

Madame P had always had ambitions of being a successful social hostess, and her elegant tea-gowns alone must have impressed many of her guests as just the thing a lady would wear. Some of the guests, unused to such surroundings, would silently entrench themselves in their dignity – and if there were good things to eat would confine themselves to eating steadily and saying nothing. Others would become loquacious and loud, telling stories and spilling tea on the table cloth, determined to show that they were not overawed by such a social occasion. Madame P always managed to have plenty of good things to eat, so her guests of all types could busy themselves and feel satisfied – in all senses of the word.

When I first met Madame P in Mogilev I found that I could tell her more or less my true story and the object of my journey. She was a loyal friend and did not betray my trust, and when I called to see her again now she welcomed me into her house, in spite of my very modest post in the Red Army, giving as grounds for our friendship the fact that she had known a cousin of mine in former days. I frequently dropped in, appreciating the change and glad of an opportunity to glean some information on the progress of the war and the movements of the Army.

Perhaps I might even meet the Commissar K if he had not moved on. I was only too willing to grasp any opportunities which came my way. During the conversations around Madame P's supper table, most of the guests scarcely noticed me in my low position, and as a Red Army nurse I could be expected to be on their side in any case. My presence aroused no suspicions.

With the headquarters having been removed to the rear, it was clear that the war was going badly for the Red Army. There was no longer any question of our division advancing. Now we were merely waiting for orders to remove to the rear ourselves. This thought haunted me as I felt that it would mean the complete destruction of all my endeavours and would put before me the prospect of another winter in Russia, another year away from my children, and in conditions that were likely to be much harder than anything I had experienced until now.

For me, the mere thought of going back east, when all my striving was to go west, towards liberation, seemed to hurt me physically and make me feel sick and weak. I felt that at all costs I must go west geographically as well as ideologically – and the feeling grew stronger and stronger as I thought about my three boys who must be over there, somewhere. There was no time for any more hesitation; something had to be done, and I decided to trust my luck and start walking to reach the Polish lines on my own.

My plan was to go on foot from Baranowiczi to Brest Litovsk, a distance of some 125 miles. The distance was not so great as to frighten me, but the difficulty would be to cover this distance avoiding roads and villages, and passing instead through the forest of Bialowieca. Moreover, I did not know for certain where the Polish positions began, how far outside Brest Litovsk they would be by the time I approached. The questions of the rivers to be crossed worried me too, since I could not use the bridges on the main roads. A detailed map of the district was essential, but where could I get one?

There were no shops open in Baranowiczi, and even if there had been I could not have got such a map without arousing the suspicions of someone who might inform the Cheka. There was a soldier's library established at the station, but this contained only propaganda pamphlets, works of Marx and Lenin, and huge posters displaying anti-capitalistic propaganda. The map I wanted could only be found in some military office – but how could I get there?

Chance helped me. One day, Madame P, not feeling well, asked me to get her some medicines at the Red Cross dispensary and to call on her husband in his town offices to give him news about her. I did the errand and went to the office where I was told to wait as the Commissars were in conference. There, in the waiting room, hung a large and very detailed map of the very district I was interested in.

This was really a godsend; no map ever looked as beautiful to me as this military staff map. How eagerly I studied it, trying to learn by heart the names of the villages between Baranowiczi and Brest Litovsk, to estimate the distances separating them and to make myself a picture of their position. I jotted down on a slip of paper the main lines which would serve me as landmarks: the railway, two high-roads, the main curves of the larger rivers and the bridges across them. The greater part of the country I proposed to cross was covered with forest, and this was favourable to me. But the rivers seemed to be wide, and whether I would be able to cross them independently from the bridges was a question. Besides, Brest Litovsk itself had been an important Russian fortress and the Poles were said to have fortified it further. It would therefore be difficult for me to approach the lines. All these considerations turned about in my head as I stood in front of the map, trying hard to memorise every detail. I felt like a child learning a lesson by heart at the last minute before having to recite it.

As I was thus in the midst of my task, a door opened behind me and several military men came out. Among them was Madame P's husband. He was evidently astonished to see me here, and displeased, I thought.

"Have you taken the papers to be copied?" he asked me in a peremptory and loud voice. Standing to attention, I answered at once: "Yes, comrade. They are being copied and will be ready soon."

"All right. Wait here, as I have some more to give you," he said with a nod and walked out with the others. I was glad to have taken the hint and felt relieved when he returned alone, smiling.

"It's all right, now – thank you. What is the news from home?"

I gave him the message and left the premises after a last glance at the map, hanging there so temptingly, with pencil markings here and there, and traces of dirty fingers around the important centres. How I cherished the tiny slip of paper in my pocket, and went on repeating to myself the names of villages and rivers to be quite sure of them in the future.

My preparations did not take long. I told Madame P about my plan. She neither encouraged nor criticised it but kindly gave me some tins of food and a large piece of black bread for the journey. I hoped thus to be able to avoid all human dwellings and to live on my supplies and perhaps some wild berries for quite a few days.

It was not easy to take my belongings away without arousing the suspicions of my train companions. I therefore decided to abandon my coat, a small bag and my blanket which would remain on my couch to indicate my continued presence. I feared most the vigilant eye of Grigoriev. Fortunately he was out a lot these days, arranging apparently his own future, and I thus could carry away little by little all the things I wanted to take. The last preparations were made at the house of the railway guard whose wife had more than once given me hot water for a bath and hairwash.

At noon, when everything was ready, I decided to have a last look round Baranowiczi, so as to see which way I could get out of the town without being noticed by patrols. Leaving my things at the guard's house, I set out into the rain walking along the lines, between two walls of red luggage vans. With collar turned up, and hands deep in the pockets of my jacket, I trudged along, waiting for the end of this long uniform alley when, suddenly, a voice hailed me from the other side of the line to my left.

"Hallo, comrade, where are you going?"

"Out there, end of the line," was my reply.

"Stop and wait," came the unpleasant command and two men crawled out from underneath the van. They were two Cheka men – and my heart sank.

"Your papers, comrade." I handed them my documents. They looked at them closely. "Why are you not on the train?"

"I am free now as we are waiting for further orders and I have not yet been appointed anywhere."

"Where were you going in this direction?"

"I was going to the village yonder to the right of the line, some three versts further, to try to get some eggs." I hoped the food problem would be once more a good excuse.

"It is forbidden to go in this direction and to walk along the line anyhow," came the reply. "You had better follow me now and we'll look closer into the matter."

They marched off, with me between them. We crawled under several trains, came down the embankment and walked back towards the town, one man in front of me, one behind me. So here I was, once more in the hands of the Cheka. Fortunately I did not have my knapsack with me, or my excuse would have been very lame. And suddenly, I thought of my slip of paper with the outline of the map – the names, the distances . . . I would certainly be searched at the Cheka, and here was this slip in the side pocket of my shooting jacket. I could feel it – it seemed to burn my fingers. How could I get rid of it? The man behind me would notice my movement if I threw it out. I crushed and crumpled the poor slip of paper, trying to tear it between my fingers without moving my arm, with my hand thrust deep into my pocket. It was raining hard now: I got my hand wet, returned it to the pocket and worked feverishly at the map in the endeavour to make it unreadable. We were passing between crossroads, along a narrow path with bushes of blackberries and hedges of nettles on both sides. The man in front called out something to his comrade who, pushing me aside, passed on in front. I took the opportunity of this moment to throw the remains of my map into the bushes. What a relief it was. A second later the man turned back: we were on the road. I walked between the two and in a short while we reached the local section of the Cheka.

About twenty people were already in the large room into which I was pushed. Nobody seemed to pay much attention to a newcomer. All sat about the place on benches and on the floor; a few seemed to have made friends and were talking in hushed tones, but the majority kept silent. From time to time a soldier came in and called out a name; someone walked out and did not return, and involuntarily one made a conjecture as to his fate. Was he being set free? Was he being sent to prison? ... And the thoughts fluttered about in my head as if they, too, had been put in a prison and could not fly up higher than the ceiling of this low room.

Hours passed. It got dark. A lamp was brought in and hung from the ceiling, and for a long time it quivered gently, the circles of light and shade moving on the floor.

Finally, at about midnight, my name was called and I was brought before the Cheka authorities. My documents were in perfect order and my story was so old that it seemed to me to be absolutely true. I felt a bit of self-confidence returning. These Cheka men were very different from those I had had to deal with in Moscow. In Moscow they had been leading political men, mostly men with education. Here they were much rougher, coarser men who could more easily be diverted by a joke. There was a lot of laughing and joking which I did not really understand, and it was only afterwards when I thought about some of the questions that I realised many had a double meaning, and that this cross-examination was designed for women of a very dubious type.

In questioning me they insisted especially on my reasons for joining the Red Army, they wanted to know all the details about the troupe of artistes I had been with in Mogilev and, finally, insisted upon knowing what I had been doing in Moscow. My lies grew to mountains but everything held together until the final question: why in the first place had I wanted to leave Moscow? To join the Mogilev orchestra, to be near my aunts. Aha! Then why had I left Mogilev?

To join the Red Army. But why did I not stay with my orchestra? Because they were being withdrawn eastwards and I wanted to stay in Mogilev. Why, then, did I volunteer for the Red Cross when I must have known this would take me away from Mogilev also?

The men looked at me, amused and with evident satisfaction at having caught me. "So that's what it is! You did not want to go east. But you did want to go west. Why? You were running away from something. No use hiding things."

This was getting uncomfortably close to the truth, but I must try to get out of it somehow.

"One does not run away from anything," I answered stoutly. "But sometimes one has to remove oneself from certain situations. I was not wanted as a musician any more, but pressed to stay on with the troupe – there was one individual who wanted me to stay – and this did not suit me at all." The Cheka men exchanged knowing glances.

"Aha! What pride, quite unnecessary pride," said one of them with a leer. "And you really preferred running away?"

"Yes – to cut a long story short, I preferred to run away. And it did no harm to anyone. So why should I not run?" I left them to work their own meaning into these words.

"I suppose you may be right – why not run away? Mind only, don't try these tricks with the Red Army – there is no joking there, you know that."

"Oh, certainly I do – and I don't even want to try it. Besides, why should I, when I get my food rations – that's all I want."

The men exchanged a few words, then the one who had been talking to me said something about being careful to stay with my unit in the future and, handing me back my papers, told me I could go.

Out I walked, benumbed, tired, too terrified to be relieved. It had been a close shave. The Cheka along the front was quick in suspecting spies. All my lies, all those stories growing into monstrous buildings – how easily could they have crumbled down, and then there would not have been much chance left for me, I fear.

The days that followed were full of despair. My last hope had gone. I did not dare attempt my walk to freedom now. I did not dare visit Madame P either, for fear that the Cheka were watching me and I did not want to get her into trouble. And now the orders for our retreat were coming through. What could I do to stay in Baranowiczi and avoid this move to the rear?

There was a Refugee Committee working in Baranowiczi, helping the Lithuanian and Polish refugees. Perhaps I could get work there? Any post would do, as long as it meant staying here, and provided it gave me papers that would be valid in the eyes of the Cheka. For days I had roamed around this committee, trying first to make friends with the refugees – a difficult task as I had no grasp of Lithuanian and although I knew Polish I could not understand the thick local dialects. Finally I succeeded in finding out that one of the refugees happened to have a brother working in the committee office. This brother was to recommend me for a post if the office was allowed to expand, but against all expectations he was told that the committee was to cut down its activity and reduce its staff – and so of course he could not help me.

Thus I found myself finally without a string left to my bow. My identity papers would have no value the moment our detachment left, and orders to pack up had been given on the previous night. Besides, Grigoriev, the Communist, was still waiting for my reply regarding a post in his office somewhere at the rear – and I could not refuse his offer as long as I had no plausible excuse for doing so. He had to be managed with care and diplomacy and was too clever to be fooled by any kind of vague story. He was leaving tomorrow so I had to have an excuse today. Queer, how this one word "tomorrow" could look so black and blank and threatening.

All these considerations were turning in my mind as I walked away from the low building of the committee with its waiting crowds of refugees lingering outside. I tried in vain to think of some new way out. I felt utterly helpless. Apparently there was nothing, absolutely nothing for me to do now but to go with the general movement of retreat. And I could not bear this thought.

Wandering aimlessly about I came to the other end of the town where a few lime trees formed a poor semblance of a park. Barracks, a military hospital and military supply sheds clustered round these few spare trees. I was tired, my head felt blank and heavy as I sat down on the edge of the ditch separating the road from a meadow. Not a soul, not a breath of wind – and a heart as heavy as lead. I stared at the road, unable to stir up any new idea, any new plan for my future; I felt a lump in my throat and could not stop the tears.

It was a moment of true despair – the first on my flight – for here I was, alone, under disguise, facing a future without hope, and not a soul to trust or to ask for advice. The blankness in my brain, where before I had always found my imagination to help me, made me shiver and bury my face in my hands. I was sitting thus, head in hands and elbows resting on my knees, trying to gather my thoughts, when quick steps approached me down the road. I looked up and saw a man in military clothes, a thick leather case under his arm, hurrying past me towards the barracks. Absent-mindedly I looked at his face as he was passing me – and there, all of a sudden, I knew that I had seen that face before. It was the Commissar K, the same officer whom Father Bialoglowy had spoken to me about, saying that if ever I wanted help or serious advice in the XVIth Army, I should ask for Commissar K and say that I came from Father Bialoglowy. Yes, I was positive it was the same man. I jumped to my feet and ran after him.

"Excuse me, are you Commissar K?"

"Yes. What do you want?" He looked sharply at me with his greenish eyes. I fear he saw the traces of tears on my face.

"I come to you upon the advice of Father Bialoglowy. May I speak to you?"

The man raised his eyebrows, then said abruptly, "Where did you see him, and when?" And then, after I had explained that I was in Mogilev a month ago, a further question: "But you are not from Mogilev yourself. Did you know him somewhere else before?"

"You are right. I am not from Mogilev, and I met Father Bialoglowy several years ago in Petersburg." And I tried to tell my story in as few words as possible.

"You come at the last moment – it will be a matter of luck if I can still be of use to you. I am on my way now to hand over these documents that I am carrying to the Army Corps authorities today, before one o'clock. At two o'clock I am leaving to take up a new post in Vilna. But if you come along with me now I will see what I can do."

He strode away rapidly and I followed at a small trot, my hopes alive once more, not daring to believe my good luck and working out feverishly the details of what I would request. I had heard that the only division of the XVIth Army Corps which was to go forward rather than retreat was the 17th Division, leaving shortly for the Front in the direction of Bialystock. Once we were in the barracks I explained, as I answered more questions, that I had a close friend who was a nurse in the Red Cross detachment of the 17th Division and that I would like to be transferred to that division. The story would have been too thin without the support of the Commissar who, true to Father Bialoglowy's promise, was prepared to help me. Before long he had obtained from the military authorities a duly signed appointment which had also to be approved and signed by the Communist Commissar who acted as overseer of the military unit. The idea of having to appear before the eyes of this most powerful personage blurred all my joy in having obtained the appointment.

Commissar K took me now across the yard to the office of the Communist Commissar. After some knocking at the door, a sleepy voice finally called out something and we entered the office, a small room with a table, a chair and an iron bed on which reclined in an unbuttoned leather jacket a rather fat man with a brutal, sleepy face. On seeing my companion he rose and made an effort to look awake whilst the latter was telling him about my request.

"And now, Krestin, see what you can do for this comrade whom I recommend to you specially. Here are her papers for you to sign. I am leaving for Vilna in an hour's time, but you know that I will keep in close touch with you and the Party.

Goodbye, and thank you for your help in this matter. And goodbye to you, comrade, and good luck," he said turning to me. Before I could thank him, he had left the room and I heard his hurried steps on the pavement in the yard.

The Communist Krestin threw himself back on his bed and, with one leg dangling over the edge of the iron bedstead, he started cross-examining me. I was terrified but answered as coolly as possible, trying to look unconcerned and naive. The man's Russian was bad and his accent, as well as the hard cut features of his broad face, betrayed him as a Lett. This was not encouraging. Funny, however, how much he reminded me of a Lettish porter we had once in Petersburg.

"Why do you want to go near the Front? It is not a place for women. Remember – we are strict in these matters," he was saying now. I pretended not to understand what he meant, and answered him quite innocently:

"I want to go there as I have nothing to lose – I am alone in the world – and I can work willingly there where others may not want to work."

"I see, I see. Well, you want to join the detachment of Doctor Zurov. Do you know anybody there?"

"Yes, I know a girl who is a nurse there."

"So you want to be a nurse? You said, though, that you have no nurse's certificate – and work at the Front is not easy . . ."

What was the man driving at? I believe he was too sleepy to gather his thoughts and was trying to carry on the examination for the sake of appearances, so as not to make his agreement too cheap. He was repulsive in his fat, sprawling laziness, and the hard expression on his face jarred with the slow reaction of his thoughts and movements. I thought he might be going off to sleep when suddenly, turning round to rest on his elbow on the bed and facing me now, he asked:

"You want to go to the Front? But are you a member of the Party? You know that only members of the Party are allowed to occupy posts within an area of 25 versts from the enemy?"

My heart sank. "Yes," I boldly answered, "I know that. And I must admit that I am not yet a member of the Party."

"Why are you not *yet* a member?" came his question with an accentuation on the "yet".

"I have not had opportunity enough to learn the duties of a true Communist. It is too serious a step to join the Party, to do it rashly. To be a Communist gives rights, but it also implies great responsibilities and to be a true Communist means carrying out duties in a way which should serve as an example to others. I see it and fear that I am not yet sufficiently aware of the importance of these duties to be worthy of becoming a member of the Party."

This long speech was a brilliant improvisation. I delivered it so smoothly and so coolly that it seemed to me that I was listening to another person speaking. Queer things do happen at moments of emergency. The words and phrases must have come to me from Grigoriev, but the inspiration to use them just then was surely sent me from above.

The man lay there, nodding his head in silent approval, smoking his cigarette, spitting on the floor. I felt I had won my case.

"I am glad, comrade, to see that you are fully aware of the importance of a Communist's activity. You are on the right road and moved by a spirit I would be happy to find more often in young people. Yes, a Communist has great responsibilities – a hard life; he can't just lie on the stove and spit at the ceiling . . ."

My Communist here in front of me did not look overworked, and if he did not spit at the ceiling he was certainly spitting copiously onto the floor. Taking now my paper, he read it over again carefully and rising reluctantly from the bed, approached the table and put his signature to my appointment.

Could it be true? Could I now keep calm, and not let my joy betray me? He handed me the paper and I took it with hands that tried not to tremble, as he delivered his final blessing:

"Goodbye, comrade; abide in the spirit that moves you now and you'll soon be a deserving Communist."

20

WOLKOWYSK

I knew that my appointment to the 17th Division of the XVIth
Army would not please Grigoriev. Fortunately for me, he was
absent when I reached our van, and I knew that my chance
had come at last and that there was no time to be lost. I packed
as quickly as I could – others were packing now too and so
my activities passed without comment. It was late afternoon,
and the rain had started again, when I stepped down from the
van and wandered off with my bag and a knapsack along the
railway line towards the main station. There was still no sign
of Grigoriev, but the thought of a possible encounter cast a
shadow on my spirits. It was a muddy, dreary walk and my last
dismal impression of Baranowiczi.

Earlier, I had spotted a dilapidated woodshed near the station which could serve me as a temporary hiding place; and
now, in the gathering dusk, I crept into it to await the night.
The rain came down in torrents, the scanty lights on the platforms lit only small circles around them, trains came in slowly
as if searching for their way in the darkness. These were trains
coming from the Front, bringing the wounded and parts of
the retreating army. One train only was due to leave for the
Front and was expected at the station at about midnight. When
I saw it come in I emerged from my hiding place and walked
along the platform trying to find an open door to climb in. It
was an endless train and all doors of the trucks were carefully

closed because of the pouring rain; sentry after sentry posted on the platform asked me for my papers, checked my identity and my appointment and ordered me to climb in. And every time I began to open the heavy double doors, a wave of hot, stuffy and smelly air nearly knocked me down, while the muttered curses of the sleeping soldiers made me close the doors in a hurry. The train was full, the soldiers had obviously been herded close together into this last train, and I simply had not got the courage to find myself in their midst, in this total darkness and in that atmosphere – not to speak of the all too friendly invitations from those nearest the doors who caught sight of me in the faint light of the station lamps. "Come in, little comrade, come in . . ." I heard, in a tone of voice that made me shudder.

I was in despair as I knew this was my last chance of getting towards the Front. There were so few trains going in that direction, and my appointment to the 17th Division would be invalidated if I arrived later than September 5th – and it was already September 2nd today. I had been given a bare three days' "travelling leave". Four times I tried to hide myself in one of the small platforms placed at the rear of some of the trucks, and four times I was pulled down again by the sentries who said it was forbidden to stop there. Then the bell sounded – followed by a whistle which was the signal for departure, and with a jerk the train started to move. I stood near one of these small platforms, clutching my bag and my knapsack and waiting for my chance. The sentry on duty had his back to me and was hurriedly climbing into the truck. I swung my bags and jumped up – I was on the train at last, and even had a little roof over my head to shield me from the rain. I sat down on the top step and surveyed with joy my little kingdom. But my joy was short-lived. One of the last sentries to climb aboard had seen me and apparently decided to keep me company. I fear I did not enjoy the prospect of sharing with him this tiny place until the morning when we were due to reach our destination. I huddled down, making myself as small as possible.

The man stood silhouetted above me, remaining silent as the train slowly gathered speed and the station lights grew dim in the distance.

Presently the man stirred and, shuffling about in the dark with his rifle, pushed my bag saying, "Well, comrade, not asleep? Are you all right?" I muttered something about being quite all right, thank you. An uneasy cough on his part and a loud yawn suggested that he was at a loss for a topic of conversation. He stirred again, then seated himself next to my bag, grumbling something about the rain. I tried in vain to see through the darkness – but it was hopeless. Soon the man began to question me. I answered as well as I could – that is, in an evasive and vague manner avoiding all political topics. From questions about the object of my journey, my appointment, etc., the man came to more personal questions about the reason I had had for joining the Red Army, my name, my age, and so on. Well, my story was ready and had served me often enough but I hated to have to repeat it again on this dismal night, sitting there in clothes that were soaked, on the wet floor and in the company of a man whose face I could not see.

Suddenly, shots fell quick and fast to our left – the man jumped to his feet and gave two or three shots, while some more shots came from further along the train. The engine pulled on more strongly, we rolled faster, and soon only the occasional sound of a shot could be heard somewhere in the distance. What was it? Who was shooting? Had the Poles cut through the line? Had they cut off Wolkowysk? My heart beat faster and my hopes grew high.

"Poor little comrade, got a good fright, I am sure," and a big hand fell on my shoulder.

I shuddered, realising that I had to be right there with all my thoughts now. The conversation was resumed on a warmer tone on the part of the sentry; I wondered how to keep back his rapidly growing sentimental mood. As if deliberately to make things more difficult, a pale crescent moon appeared dimly between the heavy clouds, and a thick mist hovered above the forest.

In spite of the unpleasant situation, I could not help laughing inwardly at the funny picture we must have made. This moment of amusement helped me to gather my wits, and I remembered my favourite tactics in situations of this kind: instead of replying to his questions, I showered the man with questions about himself, about his country, his home, his family. He replied readily and took pleasure in describing his father's farm somewhere in Western Siberia, the cattle breeding they were going in for, the forests and field work there. This subject could not have suited me better. I could carry on the conversation with understanding and really grew interested in his father's work, about the game and shooting around their home, about the forests and the lumbering. The man forgot the moon, the sentimental moment, and was lost in recollections, in stories about his childhood, in plans for his future. My tactics had not failed; his thoughts were following a channel familiar to him and of interest to me, and the faint light of dawn found us talking like old friends.

The train progressed very slowly now, stopping frequently for unknown reasons. My friend, being on duty, got down when the train stopped and paced up and down beside the vans, climbing back on to our platform when the engine pulled on. I began to shiver piteously and was only too glad to throw over my shoulders the sheepskin coat which the sentry had in reserve. I could discern now the face of the soldier, a lean, clean-shaven face, small features, dark eyes, something of the Mongolian type with its serious and determined look. After a long silence, he suddenly turned to me and looking me straight in the face, said:

"Look here, you are the girl I want to marry. You know and understand our northern country and forests, you know our life and work. I will take you to my parents, they will like you, they will leave me the house in the forest and you will help me build a new farm there. Will you come?" – and shyly he put his hand on my arm.

All my tactics! Was this the outcome? What could I say? I was at a loss for words, for I did not want to hurt this boy who spoke so gently and respectfully and persuasively. We were approaching our destination now; would he wait for a reply in Wolkowysk? No, he said, he was not staying there but had to go some distance to the north. He would come back for me in two months' time, when his term of service would be over, and we would go then straight to Siberia, to his parents. Finally, I agreed – I was simply incapable of finding any plausible reason for a refusal. We wrote down each other's names and address, or rather the exact name of the division we each belonged to, and he took special pleasure in writing down in my notebook his name and troop number in a big round handwriting.

Our train slowed down; we had reached Wolkowysk. He helped me buckle my knapsack; we shook hands warmly, and he planted a respectful kiss on my cheek. A few minutes later I saw him marching off with his battalion – my supposed fiancé, Konstantin Konstantinov. I hope he got back to his Siberian farm, but to my relief I never saw him again.

Here I was at Wolkowysk – the last station before the front lines, and the point where I was to join my new unit in the 17th Division. After a sleepless, tiring night the idea of looking for this new unit was far from pleasant, and as I had two days in hand I resolved not to report straight away, but to see if I could find a temporary lodging somewhere in the town. The station buildings being apparently somewhat on the outskirts, I started to walk towards the centre. My knapsack seemed to weigh tons, my clothes were creased and uncomfortable, the strap of my bag cut painfully into my shoulders, and my hands and face were covered with a film of dirt. I was fully conscious of the hideous figure I must be at the moment, and this consciousness alone took away a lot of my self-assurance. With weary steps, mixing reluctantly with the crowds of the street, I began my search for a room.

Long rows of low brick houses with red tiled roofs ran either side of the narrow street. A small stream over which a low wooden bridge had recently been built was the only feature to break the monotony. Over to the left there was a view of low marshy meadows with the promise of wider marshlands beyond; and to the right, clusters of large trees overhanging the water made me think there might be gardens there with private houses hiding in them. But first I had to go into the centre where lodgings were more likely to be found.

I soon reached the market place, with a few old houses and a number of new brick buildings, uglier than ever with their corrugated iron roofs and clumsy attempts at decoration. Wherever I asked timidly for a room, suspicious eyes would look me up and down and a refusal followed immediately. It was evident that my looks were most unprepossessing. Discouraged, I decided to have one more try and, using a bolder approach, I turned towards one of the larger houses and walked right into the entrance hall, since the door stood open for the convenience of all the inhabitants of the place. A Jewish woman – all the people in this neighbourhood seemed to be Jewish – met me here and muttered in reply to my question that there might be room for me in the kitchen, if I were ready to share it with her two daughters. She opened the door into her apartment and beckoned me in. The dense, thick air of the place made me stagger. The apartment consisted only of the kitchen and a general living room; there was a strong smell of cooking, of garlic, and of humanity, and I could see children of all ages filling every possible empty space in the room which was crowded with the most incongruous bits of furniture. From a box to the left came the piercing wails of a tiny, black-haired baby towards which the woman rushed with motherly concern.

"Yes, these are all my children and two more are out in town," she said with evident pride.

"Oh yes," I muttered, looking in vain for some appropriate word of admiration. "I see you are already pretty crowded, I fear our arrangement won't work."

The mother turned briskly towards me "Ah now, you don't want to stay? The corner in the kitchen will do very well for you. Sarah can sleep on the bench with Ruthy and you can have the corner – if you can pay, of course."

Apparently the "corner" was regarded as an extremely luxurious place. However, I refused the pleasure of sharing it with Sarah and Ruthy and left the place to the loud giggles of the children accompanied by more remarks from the mother, who could not understand my reluctance to join them.

It really was discouraging, for as I looked in cautiously through the low windows of other houses, a more or less similar picture met my eyes and I came to the conclusion that Wolkowysk must be the most densely populated town on earth – and most of the people living in great poverty, besides. Tired and hungry, I retraced my steps towards the station, wondering where to spend the night. It was late afternoon already, a fine drizzly rain had set in again and I shivered. Before turning into the small square which separated the station from the street, I looked in once more into a low white house to my left. To my intense joy and relief I saw on the opposite wall a large picture of the Madonna of Czestochowa. At last a Christian house – here was a possible refuge. Without hesitation I knocked at the door which was opened by a worthy looking elderly woman, her grey hair parted in the middle, and straight eyebrows giving a somewhat severe look to her blue eyes.

"Please excuse me, I knocked at your door for I see you have the picture of the Madonna in your house. You are Christians – and I am a Christian, too. Could you find a room for me in your house? I have been wandering all through the town looking for one and have found only Jewish houses and . . ."

"I see," said the woman hesitatingly "I fear there is no room in my house. We do not take in strangers. Besides, you are a trooper, the military authorities must find a place for you."

Taking a step nearer, I whispered to her in Polish: "Have pity upon me. I am not a Bolshevik – I am a Catholic. Let me find shelter in some barn or garden shed of yours – anything will do."

I saw a look of understanding on her face and heard her say loudly in Russian as people were passing us in the street "Come back in an hour's time; I'll ask my husband who is still at his work on the railway."

I went away cheerful at heart, knowing that my request would be granted. The lonely drink of tea I made myself that evening in the station square over a camp fire made from a few dry twigs I had found under a heap of soaking boards tasted quite good.

I was right – the old woman let me in without a word and, having closed the door behind me, said in Polish that she could not arrange for me to stay in her house as they already had a lodger or two, but that she had found a room for me across the road, in the house of Polish people also working on the railway. It would be a passage room without furniture, leading to a room with some other lodgers – a Russian engine driver and his wife – but she hoped I would not be too uncomfortable and the owners who lived on the ground floor were kind-hearted people. Naturally I was delighted to have a place to sleep in, and having thanked her I walked across to the other house. The family met me there – evidently waiting for me – and I was shown the passage room and confidentially warned that the man in the next room did drink quite a bit and came home rather late and made quite a bit of noise but was not really bad. Everything seemed to be working out well at last. I said that I was sure the arrangement would be quite satisfactory and, having spread my coat on the floor as a mattress and using my knapsack for a pillow, I lay down and was so tired that I fell asleep at once, and for the first part of the night I slept like a stone.

However, the first night in my abode was not entirely peaceful. My neighbour, the engine driver, returned late from work or from some drinking session and for a long time I could hear him groaning and scolding his wife behind the thin partition. Also, the old burberry coat on which I lay did not give me the illusion of a mattress, and my knapsack was not a good pillow either. I even looked back with affection to the boxes with straw on top that I used to have in the military train, and which seemed by comparison to have been a fairly comfortable bed. Still, even if I could not sleep it was restful to be able to lie there and to know that downstairs there were friendly people with a ready smile, clean rooms and the picture of the Madonna on the wall; all this made me feel safer and happier.

As I passed the kitchen window in the morning, on my way to the station square where I planned to cook my breakfast, my hostess beckoned me in and made me sit down to a real breakfast with bread and butter and milk and even an egg. This was a treat after weeks of tea and dry black bread. She was a friendly, motherly woman who showed concern for my sleeping arrangements and promised to get a straw mattress for me as soon as she could, but such things were hard to come by in these difficult times.

Besides the father and mother, there was a daughter, a tall fair girl of seventeen, and a son – a cheerful boy of fourteen. We soon made friends on the subject of mushrooms and decided to go on a great mushroom hunt in the forest the same afternoon, as I was still free. It seemed incredible to me to be there talking about mushrooms – how many one could find of this or that kind, how one should cook them and eat them – and to discuss it all so naturally as if I had been with this family for years.

Our mushroom hunt was a great success – we brought back large, full baskets and had them for supper roasted in sour cream and butter. I was pleased to have an idea already of the local forests, of the roads leading out of them towards the west. I also found out about the measures taken by the Bolsheviks for the control of local traffic in these border regions, and was shown where it would not be advisable to go without a proper permit. The boy gave me a good idea of the footpaths leading through the swampy lowlands where duck and other waterfowl seemed to be plentiful. All this was precious information, as I still thought of continuing my way to the Polish lines independently from anyone – on foot and on my own.

The next morning I had to report to the Red Army unit to which I had been appointed. My little holiday had come to an end, but it had done me good and renewed my courage. I was thankful for this one long day out in the country, and I was happy to have found such kind and sympathetic people.

After some wandering about I found the unit I was looking for: the field hospital No. 8 of the 17th Division. As I asked the sentry at the gate of a long low building (probably it had been a school) for the chief doctor, surgeon Zurov, two men came out of the building. The sentry pointed out to me the taller one as Dr Zurov and told me to hurry as he was going away for a day. I went up and, handing him my paper, reported as I had heard soldiers do. The doctor, a tall fair-haired man in his thirties, with a rather sleepy look and slow movements, raised his eyebrows, looked at me and then at the paper, smiled and said:

"So you are appointed to this unit? But I never asked for more help, the staff here is complete. I am sorry, but I shall have to send you back . . ."

My heart sank. Would he really send me away? I must find an answer quickly.

"But the head of the personnel department on the staff interviewed me and gave this order. I am sorry if there has been some mistake. But I really can't go back, as they were all packing up and leaving for the rear. It will be so difficult to catch up with them now," I pleaded.

"Yes, yes, that is true. Perhaps you can be of some use after all. Your paper says that you are an assistant nurse, but I doubt if you are fit for this work which is hard and demands strength: you must carry buckets of water, wash the floors, lift the patients, carry the wood for the stoves, and so on. Can you really do work like that?"

I knew he was right and that I would not be strong enough to carry out such work. I was distressed but tried not to show it and suggested that the doctor might like to give me some other work if he thought I was not fit for the one mentioned on my paper. Turning to his assistant he said "What do you suggest, Derkin? Can't you find some job for this comrade?" Derkin scrutinised a paper he held in his hand and looked at me doubtfully. He muttered something in a low voice to Dr Zurov.

"Never mind – I know," said the doctor, and turning to me with an amused smile he said: "How would you like to take the post of Commander of the First Company of Stretcher-bearers?" It sounded impressive and terribly important – if only by the length of the title and grasping the humorous side of this suggestion, I straightened myself out "to attention", clicked my heels and saluting answered, "Ready, Sir".

Both men laughed heartily and, half-saluting, half-waving his hand at me, the doctor said that the matter was settled and I should report to him on Monday at nine o'clock. This gave me two more days of freedom, and with a light heart I set out to discover the beauties of Wolkowysk, and found that it really was quite a pretty place with delightful old houses – the town residences of local landowners, apparently. Of course, these houses were now requisitioned or nationalised, taken by the Government or the Party for use by local Soviets or for official Party organisations.

The gardens were uncared for: hedges and trees grew wild and lawns were trodden down; in some places nettles had already hidden all traces of former flower-beds; paths were overgrown with weeds; Virginia creeper fell in cascades over broken windows and entrance porches with knocked-in doors; ponds were covered with green water weed; and here and there roses still blossomed from among the wilderness of weeds and wild flowers. The place had charm: I loved the quiet little streets of the residential quarter with its rows of spacious one-storied private houses with white-columned porches and deep-set low windows. It looked like another town when compared with the centre where I had first come in my search for a room.

Finally, my walk took me to the outskirts of the town, past the station to a little hill which had already attracted my attention. I soon reached its summit and it turned out to be a former bastion; I concluded that it belonged to the series of Swedish bastions so frequently seen throughout the Baltic countries. The view from this bastion was delightful: one could see the range of sweeping hills on both sides of the marshy lowlands, the ploughed fields beyond the town on the northern side, and the vast forests to the north-east of it. It became my favourite walk in the weeks I stayed at Wolkowysk and I often lay there after the day's work, waiting for the sunset, looking at the line of dark forests on the horizon and listening to the distant rumbling of the guns – hoping for Polish success and speedy advance. It was a lovely warm September after the two rainy weeks at the end of August. The days were clear, the air soft and warm, the foliage still green but showing here and there some golden tints.

On that first Monday, at 9 a.m., I was at the field hospital and was duly introduced by Dr Zurov to the head of the office in which I was to work. Apparently, the high-flown title I had been given did not bear any relation to my actual duties, which were more those of a junior clerk in a room full of dull and sour-faced office workers. The head of the office was more sour-faced than the rest, and he soon took a strong dislike to me because I had no idea of office routine and made constant blunders in everything I tried to do. The poor man had to explain things which, in his opinion, "any idiot should know". My duty was to note down in some books the quantities of shirts and boots distributed by the organisation at certain times, and the demands made for them by other organisations. This was not really a complicated task, but having never looked into accounting work I was soon lost in the details of the right-hand and left-hand pages, the red and blue inks, and felt quite blank and stupid when my chief told me how I was to note things down. Finally, after a few days of assiduous work and many, many mistakes, I seemed to master to a certain extent the art of list-taking and gave my chief a little less trouble. I dreaded possible complaints from him about my inefficiency. I did not want to be moved elsewhere and lose the protection of Dr Zurov, who seemed to like me in spite of my failings.

Apparently all my colleagues were efficient clerks – at least I thought so, seeing them all working away on their books and tables with steady zeal. There was no chattering, no joking – all sat gloomily there, silent, busy, dull, only an occasional cough or loud sniff (to economise on handkerchiefs) breaking the silence. How I hated to see the sneering looks that accompanied me when I got up to ask the chief for some explanation, which he gave grudgingly and accompanied by a sour remark. Had these people always been so dull, so sour, I wondered, or was it the events of recent years that had made them so?

What a relief it was to leave the office at five o'clock, to go out of town for mushrooms for supper, and then back home via the station to glean information about the progress of the Poles. Would the Poles continue their advance? Would they come this way or take the direction of Vilna? Would they come before the cold winter set in? Were any parts of our 17th Division likely to be sent to the rear? All these were questions of vital importance to me, for I had to decide whether it would be better to try to escape right now, on foot, or by rail if I could be smuggled through, or whether it would be wiser to wait until the Polish Army came nearer.

Finally, I decided to try to get as near as possible to the Polish lines and to walk across those lines under cover of night. Twice I spoke to Dr Zurov, asking him to appoint me to the next field column to be sent out to the very front. He had nodded his head, answered in monosyllables and had looked sleepy – as he generally did. It became clear to me that – for one reason or another – the doctor had no intention of letting me live up to the name of my official title and lead a party of stretcher-bearers to the Front. After the inefficiencies I had already shown in the office, I suppose I could hardly blame him for thinking me somewhat incompetent. Having made no headway with Dr Zurov, I tried next to find some way to set out on a train bound for the Front, not in an official capacity but by asking some engine driver to smuggle me through. It was not difficult to get into conversation with the engine drivers manoeuvring on the shunting lines. I picked out a kindly looking, middle-aged driver and asked him to let me have a ride in the engine when he next went forward to the Front; I gave him the name of a village in that direction, saying that I had an aunt there whom I was anxious to see. He seemed to believe my story and promised to arrange such a visit – but he warned me that it would not be easy as the control on the line was very strict. He promised me an answer in a day or two.

On the appointed day he mysteriously told me that he had a plan but it was a great secret, that he could not tell me here, on the line, as his wife was very jealous and was sure to follow all his movements from her window yonder – but that at six o'clock she would go to the "Bania" in the town and we could meet then at the foot of the Swedish bastion. Very amused at this story of the jealous wife, and eager to hear about the great plan, I was well on time at the rendezvous. My engine driver arrived limping a little, but smiling as he told me:

"My wife has just left for the Bania in town – I even accompanied her as far as the bridge to make sure, so she is safe and we can have a talk," and he rubbed his hands together which produced a strange sound like the rubbing of glass-paper on leather.

"Splendid, but I am sorry if your wife is worried. Let us talk over the plan quickly and you can go home and get the samovar ready for her return."

"Bother take her," was his polite answer. "I don't want to think of her – nor of the samovar. Yes, my plan . . . well, it is a little complicated . . . I don't quite know how . . . in daytime you can be found so easily . . . in the night the control is very strict too and our Communist often boards the engine to keep warm, so you could not hide there . . ."

I saw at once that the man had no plan whatever but only a huge amount of objections. I must try to build a plan myself and adapt it as necessary – it was stupid of me to have counted upon any ingenious idea on the part of this mild-natured coward. In the meantime he had taken my arm and was suggesting a walk round the bastion. I could not refuse an arm-in-arm walk if I still hoped for a ride in his engine. And, besides, I could not anger him for he could easily report me to the Communist authorities, who would be interested to look closer into the case – and this had to be avoided.

Thus, arm-in-arm with the limping engine driver I strolled in the falling dusk around the foot of the bastion. All we needed now was the rising moon to complete the background for a romantic stroll. However, the sentimental element had to be banished – I felt that this was the first thing to tackle – and I plunged headlong into the enthusiastic praise of my dear aunt, describing her kindness, her exemplary life, her devotion to her husband. I felt quite thrilled at having such a relative – a real treasure – but my engine driver soon began to show signs of boredom and the pressure of his arm was lighter than it had been at the beginning of our walk. I think, too, that my good aunt was such a contrast to his own wife that it made him fear the latter the more. He suggested that we sit down for a while and although I much preferred to walk, I felt sorry for him with his limping leg and agreed to stop and sit down. Without giving him time to start a conversation of his own, I suggested various ways of carrying out my plan to board the train at the next station, or when he slowed down at some junction, or at the bridge some seven versts beyond the station. But somehow none of my suggestions found his definite approval; he said "yes" to them all and then invariably added "We will see". By this time it was getting very dark, no arrangement had been arrived at and I suggested that his wife might have finished her bath and that she certainly would be very thirsty after it.

"She will call out for the samovar, sure enough – I know her, and she'll ask me where I was and will ask all the neighbours when I came home and will ask the other men what my hours of work were today – oh, I know her, such a . . . woman!" He shook me by the hand, said he hoped we could repeat the pleasant walk, and limped away into the darkness. There was nothing to be done: I saw the plan would not work as the poor man was terrified of taking me on board and of being betrayed to his wife. So it was good-bye to another plan – and I went home a roundabout way as the engine driver had asked me to do, home to cook my supper of flour-water-salt on my camp fire before going to bed.

Every time an escape plan broke down, I felt a blankness in front of me, hopeless walls growing higher and higher around me, and then I would scold myself for this momentary depression and would start immediately working out something new. In the end one of my ideas would succeed and I would see my sons again – I was sure and certain of it.

The next day I decided to talk seriously to Dr Zurov once more. It would be better to try to see him alone, avoiding the presence of his assistant, my office chief, and so I decided to go after office hours to his private address. He was billeted in a small villa with a garden full of flowers. Fortunately he was at home, and let me in to the sparsely furnished room.

"Good evening, Comrade Salogubova. What is up? Something gone wrong?" and he sat down on his bed, balalaika in hand, humming a well-known gypsy song and looking at me inquiringly from under his sleepy eyelids.

"No, everything is in order – only I wanted your advice and you are always busy in the office. I did not dare interrupt you – and please forgive me for disturbing you here – I'll be brief."

"That's all right, go ahead, go ahead – and sit down there, on the box – it's my chair."

I started right away with my request to be sent to the front lines. I told him I was ready and willing to go there where others perhaps preferred not to go; I did not care about my own safety and would be very happy if I could live up to the ambitious title I had. The doctor laughed a big loud laugh and gave the same evasive answer as before, humming another well-known tune. As I listened to his answer, trying to prepare some further arguments in my mind, I saw through the window against the glorious red and golden sky of sunset, the long triangular stream of wild ducks flying south. Unable to keep my admiration to myself, I exclaimed in delight at the lovely sight. The doctor looked up at once – even walked towards the window and returning to his seat said: "Yes, it is a lovely sight. I wonder where they will settle for the night."

"Oh, I know where," I said, "they fly low already, they will surely settle round the bend of the river, beyond that hillock, where the swamps form a sort of lake all overgrown with reeds – that's where they always rest."

The doctor looked at me with astonishment. "You told me you are not from here – so how do you know all that?"

"Well, I love the country and I love shooting, and although I can't do any shooting now I always trace and follow all game I can – just a matter of habit, you know – one can't help it, I suppose."

"Yes, that's true, one can't help it. I love duck shooting and as soon as I can get a shotgun I will go out there. Will you come with me – since you know where the duck are to be found?" Of course I agreed with delight and we talked shooting, game, forests and country life until it got dark – both of us forgetting the original purpose of my visit. I had not noticed how time had flown and, realising that it was getting late, rose and said goodbye in a hurry.

"You can't walk home alone; have you far to go?" said the doctor, rising too.

"Not very far, through the town and towards the station. It is all right, I'll find my way," I answered, wondering how the thought had come to the doctor that I, a Red Army woman, could not go home alone.

"No, no, this won't do, a girl should not walk alone through the town in the dark – I'll come with you," and in spite of my assurances that I really did not mind going alone, the doctor took his cap and walked with me nearly to my door. I simply could not get over this courteous gesture and towards a supposedly Communist girl too! Anyhow, I felt sure that we were friends now and that I need not fear the doctor, even if my chief became too sour.

A day or two later, as I sat at my desk in the empty office, all the other clerks having gone out for lunch, I heard the door open behind me and Dr Zurov came out of his office.

"Hullo, what are you doing here alone? Don't you eat any lunch?"

"No, thank you. I had to finish some lists; it is too late for me to cook my lunch but I have eaten a piece of black bread. I was just trying . . ." and I was thinking desperately what to say about my travelling chessboard which lay on the table in front of me, half-covered by my hand.

"Is that a chessboard you have there?" exclaimed the doctor. "Do you play? Were you solving a problem? Would you like to have a game, by any chance?" and sitting down opposite me the doctor began to arrange the chessmen for the start of a game. We became deeply involved in this game and when after luncheon the clerks came back, they were quite astonished and probably shocked to find the head of the unit playing chess with the most junior – and most inefficient – clerk. The doctor rose quickly, as if ashamed of having been found out, and walked into his office giving some orders about papers for his signature. I packed my chessboard and bent over my accounts, not without noticing the sour smile of my chief and the knowing look of a younger clerk at the other window. Silence reigned – except for the scratching of pens and the scraping of my penknife correcting mistakes.

In spite of the doctor's friendly attitude, nothing seemed to advance with regard to my appointment to the field column. I did not like to insist too much in case this should arouse suspicion. It seemed clear that the doctor did not want me to go, though at the time in my naive way I had no inkling of the reason why. And anyhow, for the time being the retreat of the Red Army continued so that there was little chance of any more field columns being sent out. It became more likely day by day that the next move of the 17th Division would be towards the rear.

In the meantime I had been trying to get any information I could on the progress of the Poles, and had become acquainted with the family of another Polish engine driver, who being friends of my landlady, showed sympathy to me. More than once they offered to grill for me the mushrooms I gathered for my supper after office hours, and these meals were really luxurious. Their sons, two little boys of ten and twelve, became my friends; we made bows and arrows together and I often dropped in at their house on rainy afternoons. I did not imagine then of what great help these people would be to me at the end of my stay in the town.

However, I soon found out that it was not advisable for me to go to this house too often by the front entrance; across the street from it there was a house with Soviet officials, soldiers and especially sailors coming and going all day long, jesting and joking with two dark-haired young girls who seemed to be the daughters of the house. Their mother was always at the window and these sharp black eyes peering through the curtains made me feel uncomfortable. Was this house merely what it seemed, some sort of privately-run brothel, or was it something more? Once or twice I heard quite clearly the irregular nasal calls of a field telephone, then the typical ticking of Morse signals, coming from somewhere in or behind the house. Was this house some kind of observation post for the Cheka, reporting on the movements of the military and probably on the local people as well? Whatever was going on in there, I did not want the black-eyed woman to get to know me too well by sight. I discovered that one could get to my friends' house through a back lane and their vegetable garden, and this became my usual route.

I had heard no more from my limping engine driver, and before I had had time to develop any more plans, the Poles had made such rapid progress that one day the message was received at our office to pack up and prepare to leave the next morning in an easterly direction. It was a blow. I tried not to show any anxiety on hearing this news, but when allowed to go home to pack I rushed to my Polish friends to ask for news and perhaps for advice.

They, too, were in a state of alarm. The orders had been given at the station for the railway staff to prepare for evacuation. Many of the Russian railway people had already left, but the Polish group was reluctant, for their only desire was – like mine – to fall into the hands of the Poles. Fortunately, Nowicki, the father of my little friends, had been ordered to stay at the depot until further orders and the husband of my landlady, having been ill for some time, had not received any instructions. But both families dreaded the "last-minute" orders of forced evacuation which might be given at any time by the remaining representatives of the Cheka, and such orders could not easily be disobeyed. Some packing and arranging was therefore going on in advance, tears and sniffs and groans accompanying these preparations. Naturally, I could not expect any advice from these people and, not being able to help them either, I went out wondering what to do and where to go.

If the field hospital was to be sent to the rear, then somehow I must find some excuse for not going with it; this was the most urgent question and there was not much time to be lost. I walked to the station in the hope of picking up some news. I soon heard that all units were preparing to go and that the retreat was general. I pushed my way into the station which was crowded, packed already with civilian fugitives from the town – presumably those who had thrown in their lot with the Communists and who preferred not to stay and be denounced in front of the incoming Poles. There were soldiers, too, pushing through the crowd and asking for information about trains. "Ask the unit at the station office," shouted someone. "They'll be staying on here for a few days. They know more about the trains than the rest of us."

I pricked up my ears: a unit staying on. It was an outside chance – but might I be able to join it? With great difficulty I pushed my way through and into an office which was occupied by a mere three or four people who were busy writing, giving and receiving orders, distributing slips of paper, telephoning – all in great haste and obvious anxiety. The head, a small and very brisk uniformed man, was rushing round and complaining loudly about the lack of people to carry out the orders he was giving. This was my chance. I approached him, said that my unit was leaving but that I preferred to stay here because of my family, and that I would be ready to work at the station. He gave me a quick glance, asked whether I could write properly and if I knew the Latin alphabet which I would need to copy the Latin names of medical prescriptions, and when I assured him I was quite capable of doing this work, he agreed to take me then and there. But of course I must get the proper paper transferring me from my old unit to this one.

Not daring to believe my luck I rushed off, running, to the field hospital. Dr Zurov was not there, he had gone home. I ran to his private address and running up the steps of the porch I heard the strains of the balalaika coming from his room. "Come in!" he called in response to my urgent knocking, and I opened the door. There was Dr Zurov, half-lying, half-sitting on his narrow iron bed, a cigarette in his mouth, his hair tousled and his right hand lightly stroking the strings of the balalaika. It was scarcely the portrait of a militant Communist. I felt completely disarmed and all my false statements, my carefully prepared speech, seemed so inappropriate that I felt sure the time had come to tell him openly the whole truth. I thought that, Communist or not, the doctor was simply too lazy to bother about denouncing me, as this would involve too many reports and explanations and give him just the sort of extra work he always managed to avoid.

"Here you are again, little Sister Commander," he said with a smile at his own joke. "Not packing yet? Or packed already?"

"No, I have not packed and I don't intend to pack at all . . . May I ask you to let me stay here?"

"Stay here? Why? What for? No, I really can't allow it. But what is it that keeps you here?" He looked at me closely, and even stopped touching the strings of the balalaika.

"May I tell you the truth? I simply cannot go. I must remain here and wait to fall into the hands of the Poles. You see, I am not what you think I am, what I pretended to be . . . I am not a simple Russian girl, nor a simple Polish girl either, although I have pretended to be both these things in recent months. I am the wife of Count Alexander Sollohub, from St Petersburg. The revolution has separated us and I do not know where he is. We have three little sons whom I have not seen for two years either. They are over there, abroad, and my only aim and object in life is to get over, too, to join them."

It all came quickly, in one breath. Was it too much? Would this man betray me? The doctor's eyes were fixed on me; my speech seemed to have made a deep impression. Then he shook his head, puzzled and regretful. "This is strange, terribly strange – and it is a great pity. I liked you for yourself, you know, for what you are and never mind where you came from . . ." and he stopped short.

"I am sorry to have told you stories all the time even though you were kind to me. But I had to, for the sake of my sons. For two years now I have not known whom I could trust. And now I have hurt you – I am so sorry, really I am so sorry . . ." and we looked at each other quite stupidly in the awkwardness of the moment.

"So you want to go – I mean, you want to stay when the rest of us go. It is a pity, but it is quite natural and of course I do understand. But you are on active service – in the Red Army lists – I have not got the power to dismiss you," he said pushing back his fair hair and giving me a rueful smile. "It's a strange life, isn't it? I suppose now I must do my best to help you to leave me. You have a plan already? Come then, what have you planned in that enterprising head of yours?"

I told him of my provisional arrangement with the supply unit at the station. He agreed that a transfer to that unit would be possible. "I have not got the right to transfer you from one unit to another without the sanction of the Communist controller, but we are in an emergency – I can act on my own, and find an explanation for him when he notices your absence, which with any luck will not be for a day or two."

416

I felt very awkward, the man really was kind and was prepared to take this risk for my sake. He sat down now at his little desk and was writing out the paper which would transfer me to the new unit. He lifted his head and asked rather hesitatingly: "And do you think you'll like the unit there?"

"To tell you the truth, I did not like the looks of the men who were giving orders around the place. But – what can I do? I can't choose much!"

"Of course, nothing much to be done. But you must not trust them as you did me. Here is the paper, little Sister Commander. Must you take it to the place tonight?"

I said I had to go back there straight away. He offered to accompany me but I insisted that it would not look right for the unit commander to be taking such care of me, and that I must go alone. Dr Zurov gave a short laugh, and as I thanked him and bade him goodbye he added: "I had thought of taking care of you for quite a long time, you know. Run along then – and good luck in life. Be careful though, you are playing a difficult game. You did not quite deceive me with the peasant girl story, you know."

We shook hands. I could find no words to tell him how much I appreciated his kindness. The little wooden villa, the uncared-for garden, the gypsy songs – and the half-closed blue eyes with drooping lids, quite appealing in their laziness – all this remains in my memory very vividly as a friendly moment, a moment of true kindness. It was one of those images that I would never forget. I wished him goodbye and good luck in life, too. Then I turned and hurried away.

The field hospital left the following day. It was a noisy day in Wolkowysk with the evacuation of offices, hospitals and military organisations, and in the background the constant rumbling of artillery fire. From time to time this rumbling grew in intensity and we expected the Poles to break through at any moment, or so the rumour went. Feeling certain that my work with the new unit would not last more than a few days, I started it with an easy heart; however unpleasant it might be, it wouldn't last long – this was my consolation.

The little wooden building of the station was teeming with people. Train after train arrived and left. The traffic was in both directions: soldiers, rifles, orders, more soldiers – or rather peasants in ragged soldiers' coats – poured out of the smelly, dingy, overcrowded goods vans. Having duly reported to my new chief, I found myself appointed as assistant at the first-aid post just opening in the general waiting room. This was a bad beginning, I thought, for I had always dreaded anything connected with medicine and doctors. But there was no chance of getting out of it now. A doctor, with two medical students to assist him, was fussing round some boxes with medicines, scales, jars and bottles. Looking at me over the top of his spectacles, he told me to find paper and pencil and to keep a register of patients passing through the first-aid post.

A new train from the Front was just coming in, with much puffing and hissing of steam. The students rushed out to receive patients in need of immediate attention: doors banged right and left, people hurried past us, the doctor shouted in vain, "This is a first-aid post, get out of here unless you are a patient" – but with no effect. No one stopped, the doors went on banging and everybody seemed to rush through the room quite unconcerned. A few limping, stooping soldiers came in led by the two students; their wounds were hastily dressed, the commanding officer standing at the door and urging the doctor to hurry. "Anything will do – be quick, we must get off right away, never mind the bandages, plaster something on the top of them . . ." The men, too, were in a hurry to get back to the train – they were terrified of being left behind and patiently withstood painful dressings without a murmur, in order to be through quickly and to limp back into the waiting train. "Quick, sister, throw the coat over my shoulders – we must be off, the Poles don't wait" and they would limp and hobble away.

Through the wide open door of the vans I could see the grey mass of miserable humanity, the pale faces, the shaggy beards, the hollow eyes of those that lay inside. Every corner was filled with hunched figures of men crouching or lying – here and there a moan, a curse, and everywhere the words of hurry and anxiety: "Why don't we go on? What are we waiting for? They want us to be butchered like cattle . . ." As I helped one of the men to straighten out his tightly bandaged leg, his companion smiled at me and said, "You had better come with us, sister, the Poles will be here in no time – and it's no fun when they start bombarding from the air!" Strange life – their one idea was to go back east while my only thought was to go forward towards the west.

My task in the first-aid post was to note down the names of the men brought in and the nature of their wounds. As neither the doctor nor the students ever answered my questions, I had to use my own judgement and my own rather simplified definitions. The list was full of wounds to legs, arms, heads, backs – but no "middles" as those with serious wounds had to stay in the train and wait for proper assistance further in the rear. In spite of all the hurry and haste there seemed to be relatively good order in the first-aid post and I even succeeded in securing three mugs in which to give the men some water as they all seemed to be suffering from thirst. By the end of the day the doctor and the students looked grey and worn out, the supplies of bandages and dressings had dwindled considerably and my list had become quite long and important-looking.

The sun was low on the horizon, a red glowing sunset with narrow streaks of purple clouds; a train bound for the Front had come in and there was suddenly much to do again. Why were these men who had not yet been in the fighting line climbing out for medical attention? They were ill – they had been ill for some time before being allowed to see a doctor. They dreaded his decision and, alas, the truth was all too clear. My list was still more simplified now – it bore more or less exclusively the word "typhoid" attached to each name. Those shaking figures, those grey, drawn faces and sunken eyes haunted me for years afterwards. Misery, suffering, hopelessness – the sort of mute suffering of animals and something of the animal's absence of hope too. And the grey coats, bundles of grey, covering as if with one great blanket all the tormented humans herded together here in the little wooden station of Wolkowysk. There were no individuals any more – just one mass of grey and the red glow of the sunset through the windows.

Then suddenly, above the din of voices, the buzz of a plane's engine overhead, then a hiss, another hiss, explosions, and an incredibly rapid scampering of these grey figures. All ran with heads well down between the shoulders; they seemed to vanish as if by magic. In an instant our post was empty – except for one soldier with a broken leg and myself. Run? Where should I run to and why? It was a Polish plane overhead, and the mere thought of friends so near seemed to sweep away all thoughts of immediate danger. Another hiss, a bang – then the sound of a machine gun firing somewhere on the railway line, and the distant sound of a receding plane.

I went to the door and, looking out to see what damage had been done, I caught sight of the doctor, his pince-nez glittering in the red light, a bundle of cotton-wool firmly clasped in his hand, peering cautiously round the corner from under a pile of railway sleepers in the station yard, while one of the students hurriedly crept out from behind some trucks, brushing off the sand from his white overall. Figures began now to appear from all directions, and the station master was calling together some railway officials to inspect the tracks for any damage caused by the bombs.

"Here they come, the Poles," grunted the broken-legged soldier behind me, "no way of escaping them – even before we reach the Front. And your doctors – what good are they, scampering away like hares: they don't mind leaving a Christian soul to its fate!" and with a groan he tried to stand up. I helped him as well as I could and as we approached the train one of the students came up hurriedly, offering to help the man into the van. "Shake the earth from your clothes – we can manage without you," muttered the soldier with a sour smile, climbing

420

with difficulty into the van. "God bless you, sister, and thank you . . ." he added, his face paler than ever after the effort of the walk.

Someone called me: the order had been given to pack up without delay and prepare to board a train before nightfall. The first-aid post was joining the retreat. Frantic packing, hammering of boxes, orders and counter orders, and after an hour or two the waiting room had returned to its normal function and the doctor with his students were safely settled on their boxes in a goods truck, waiting for the train to start. My career as a first-aid assistant was quickly over, and I was to move now to the "courageous" section of the detachment who were not pulling out quite yet – the food supplies distribution post. I was to report there tomorrow morning for work beginning at eight.

I was dead tired now and the impressions of the day hung heavily on my mind. The faces of the wounded and of the sick, the regret at not having been able to help them more efficiently, haunted me. There were so many who needed help, so many that they lost their individuality; those hollow pale eyes, those hollow cavernous voices, all alike in texture as if the grey cloth of the uniform had spread also over the faces, the voices, the expressions of the men. One endless mass, moved by one common thought, one common striving – to get home, get back, get away from here. Only the recollection of the comic figure of the doctor emerging from his hiding place made me smile.

These impressions renewed in me the fear of falling ill, of getting an illness such as typhoid which would rob me of my independence. I dreaded being engulfed in the stream of "patients" evacuated to the rear, bundled together for some unknown destination, losing perhaps for ever my chances of escape. This thought made me shiver and when, exhausted after the long day's work, I reached my room, I shook properly as if with fever. It was late, and a fine autumn drizzle had set in; it would be hard to light my camp fire tonight, I thought, but I did need a cup of tea to warm me up.

As I came down with my kettle and a newspaper, ready to go outside, my landlady hailed me from the kitchen. She was a kind woman and offered me a cup of tea and a good slice of home-made brown bread with cheese – a luxury supper.

Half an hour later I was still sitting there, enjoying the cleanliness and the warmth and finishing my third cup of tea. The family were assembled there round the low paraffin lamp. The doors were closed, the Russian engine driver and his wife were no longer in the house, having been sent to the rear – we were alone. Still haunted by the fear of falling ill, I decided to confide in these kind people, to secure their help if necessary, to make sure that through them my boys should be able to trace my whereabouts and to hear at least of my attempts to reach them. Big, astonished eyes looked at me as I told my story; tears in the eyes of the mother, wonder and admiration in the eyes of the boy and the girl. I told them my life story, my name, my plans of escape. The boy carefully wrote down on two slips of paper the name and address of my boys in Estonia as well as my friends' address in Warsaw. One slip of paper was to be hidden in their house, carefully pushed down between the canvas and the rough wooden frame of an oil painting which decorated the wall of their small sitting room; the other slip would be carried the next day to the Nowicki family, the other Polish family who had befriended me, so that there would be two separate chances of the news of me getting through. This was a good idea put forward by the boy – it was a great adventure for him and he revelled in the excitement and mystery of my story. He and his sister promised to keep my secret faithfully and to watch over these slips of paper. Then, should anything happen to me, and should the Poles at last come and deliver them from the grip of the Soviets, they would send a letter to both the addresses I had given. I can still remember their awed faces, their kind smiles and the red excited face of the boy who did his best click-of-the-heels when he opened the door for me to go upstairs to my room.

Providence had given me these few hours of relaxation, this opportunity of finding sympathy and of confiding in people at a time when the nervous strain was just about unbearable. Of course, I realised afterwards that my imagination had carried me away in this dread of falling ill and of losing all chances of escape. But at the time it was a great relief to tell the truth, to gain a certain peace of mind and to benefit from the good night's sleep that followed. I had friends now, friends to whom I was my own self. As things turned out, the truth made my friends all the more willing to help me – and in a few days' time when I was badly in need of help they did not let me down.

It was with a light heart that I went to my new task the next day. When I reported at the food supplies distribution point, I found them on the point of moving away from the station. Evidently the bombardment of the previous evening had scared the authorities. A small house further down the street had been selected, and the entire day was spent in carrying across the office equipment – tables, chairs, papers and books, and in arranging the new premises. This gave me the opportunity of observing my new colleagues, and a first impression was very depressing. The few people employed there seemed to be all militant Communists – aggressive, talkative, intolerant. The head was a small, wiry and quick-moving man with a high-pitched voice, small black eyes, bristly hair and a spotless uniform of the latest military cut. The revolver and the long spurs were meant to enhance his militaristic appearance. His speech was accentuated by strong barrack-room expressions and it was evident that the man tried as hard as he could to pose as a true "soldier" and strict disciplinarian. His assistant was a tall and sinister looking individual with deep set eyes and tightly closed lips, who looked to me even more unpleasant and shrewd than the head. The three women seemed to be all local people, as they spoke of the local council as if it were a family affair including their husbands, brothers, cousins. There was also a fair-haired young man who seemed to be the most enthusiastic Communist of the whole lot, and who kept

423

up a constant stream of comment on the importance of our tasks, on the need for the true Communist attitude and fervent Communist zeal. He was constantly quoting the writings of Lenin or Marx in support of his loudly proclaimed statements. I was amused at the display of slogans and committed some of them to memory in case I should need them myself.

The next day our real work started. The task was to distribute food – limited now to bread and salt – to soldiers separated from their units, and then to share out what remained amongst the refugees who were flooding into Wolkowysk in increasing numbers. These were the refugees returning to their villages in Lithuania and Poland, having fled before the Germans during the war. I had seen such refugee families in all the towns I had been through in recent weeks – Orsha, Minsk, Stolpcy, Baranowiczi . . . stranded now at these railway stations near the Front, they could go no further and were left without food or shelter. Camping as best they could along the railway, in farms by the roadsides, or on the outskirts of the towns, they carried on a most precarious existence in utter poverty and in the knowledge that winter would soon be coming. These people were to receive a part of the food that remained after the soldiers had been supplied. They crowded the place, waiting patiently, dully, crouching on the steps, on the roadside, in rain or sunshine.

I had often watched these wretched families waiting at Wolkowysk, and wished that I could help them in some way. Thus I was glad to have a chance now of helping some of the refugees – but it was a dismal, depressing atmosphere to work in all day. The narrow room with two rows of desks along the walls was crowded throughout the office hours. We sat bent over our papers, people pushing us, pressing from all sides, bending over us to see whether we had written their names properly, whether we had counted correctly the number in the family. These families! There were haggard-looking mothers, crying babies, wan infants, pale children and pinched-looking adolescents. The one thought, the one desire that could be

424

read on their faces was how to get food, how to kill the hunger. The room was filled with a begging and entreating that never stopped – in Russian, Lithuanian, White Russian, Ukrainian, German, Yiddish – all were mixed with their various dialects and sounded like an inhuman babble. The air was thick, heavy, the smell at times unbearable – what a paradise for germs of all sorts and kinds, I thought. And certainly the germs were thriving, for soon I had to start a special column in my register for noting a variety of diseases, typhoid being predominant among these. Frequently relatives or friends endeavoured to get rations for those who were too ill to fetch them for themselves, and I was obliged to note their names and addresses as well as those who were present. The difficulty was to spell the long and very unfamiliar Lithuanian names properly, and to understand the mispronounced local addresses. The strain was both mental and physical, for there was no one else to take over my job and I had to continue all day with only a short break for lunch.

The only people who seemed to be quite pleased with life were some young people who were appearing at the food distribution post in ever-increasing numbers. All gave local addresses, and I wondered how far they could be considered refugees and whether they were really entitled to any rations. However, it was not for me to raise this question as I tried to remain as unnoticed as possible by my Communist colleagues. As the days went by, I noticed that the assistant head of our office, the tall, sinister-looking man, frequently singled out some of these young people and beckoned them, one at a time, into his office. Why, I wondered. One afternoon, I discovered the answer.

"Comrade Salogubova, have you a moment to spare? Will you type this list for me, and will you also make a note of the names and addresses of the people I interview privately in my office?" I had stood "to attention", my constant private joke, for it amused me to see how it flattered the Communist chief to be thus treated like an officer. I did not like the idea of having to work for the assistant head, and even less for the head who was also now involved in these private interviews. The lists I had been given to copy were lists of names and addresses of people beyond the lines – in Poland. As I stood on the doorstep of the private office ready to hand the head one of these lists, I saw him pick up a bundle of Polish banknotes which were swiftly slipped into the hand of the young man being interviewed, and I caught the last words of the conversation: "Here is the pass for our lines. You have nothing to fear on this side; they have been warned. Now be off immediately!"

The head saw me standing there, frowned slightly and took my list. I moved quickly back to my seat, terrified that my face might have betrayed me, for I now understood what they were doing under the guise of a food distribution post – and the idea horrified and disgusted me. I shuddered at the thought that I had to help in the Communist spying and propaganda work being carried on among the Poles on the other side of the lines, and my first thought was to run away from my work, which had suddenly lost any virtue that it once had. But where could I go? I would have no papers and would be a "deserter" with fewer chances still of ever getting across. No, I had to stay and carry on with the work, and I consoled my conscience with the thought that, once across, I could warn the Poles of the evil way in which the propaganda was being spread. I tried to memorise the names and addresses of the individuals sent, and of the proposed receivers across the lines. It would have been too dangerous to write down these names, as personal searches were frequent. But I did manage to memorise quite a few of the names, and after my escape I was able to repeat them to someone on the Polish side, who apparently found the information most useful.

21

ESCAPE

I have always been reluctant to approach the subject of my final escape, partly because I could not reconstruct accurately the military movements of these few days, and partly because the moment was so important to me personally that a written description seemed unable to do it justice – mere words on paper would be insufficient to convey what I did and how I felt. At Wolkowysk things were obviously working up to some sort of climax. Polish planes were coming over quite regularly now, some just circling above the town and disappearing again, some making straight for the railway line and the station and dropping their bombs with accuracy on the tracks. A train armed with two or three anti-aircraft guns had arrived, and when a plane appeared at its usual hour a wild cannonade rang through the quiet evening air. Meanwhile, the Polish ground forces must have been advancing, for the echo of distant gunfire could be heard now all the time, and in my imagination the sound grew louder and my hopes rose high.

I no longer felt as though my life was real, but rather I felt as if I was an actor in a play, the drama around me growing more and more intense, and myself trying to find the right lines to speak, lines that would fit the part that I was playing. No one had taught me these lines, I had to make them up as I went along. My whole personal world, my success or failure depended on the words I chose, the gestures I made, the decisions I had to take, from which there could be no return. The final curtain would mean for me either reunion with my boys, somewhere in the free west, or the black hopeless solitude of the prison world of Bolshevism.

How clearly some things stand out now, and yet how difficult it is to make a continuous story out of all the events that crowded these decisive days. Even the smallest things – the setting, the light, the weather – remain crystal clear in my memory and help me now to reconstruct the picture.

Thus I see myself, one late September morning, leaving the house where I stayed and approaching my place of work. It is as clear in my memory today as if it were a painting hanging on my wall. Every detail is clear: the light blue sky, the leaves still green on an old chestnut tree to my right, a mongrel busily scratching himself in the middle of the dusty street. The little peasant houses seemed to be taking a last airing before the autumn rains and cold – all windows were open; outside each hung bunches of tobacco leaves drying in the sun, and garlands of mushrooms threaded on thin string already looking shrivelled and crisp. I walked up the empty street towards the building that housed my unit. And just as clear in my memory are the violent thuds of my heart, the whirl of thoughts in my head, the tenseness of my nerves. For there, in front of our building, stands a rickety army lorry and several horsedrawn carts. The staff and a few odd soldiers are busily carrying boxes, crates, typewriters and loading them on to the transport. So once more I am faced with an immediate and momentous decision. Once more I have to say my lines with ease, calm and assurance. But the lines I have to say are in no book, no author wrote them for me, no older actor taught me how to move on this stage where everything is irrevocable, where there is no second chance, where every word and every move are so deadly dangerous.

One thing is clear: my unit is leaving, and I have only two or three minutes to think what to say, only the time it will take me to walk from the corner where I am now, into the busy scene before me. I cannot even stop and wait here where I am

428

until inspiration comes – because that will look suspicious and might arouse the attentions of some unfriendly eye behind a half-drawn curtain. As I put one foot in front of the other to walk on as casually as possible, the icy fingers that have gripped my heart begin to relax their hold, and a wave of warmth and courage rushes through me. How stupid of me! Of course I will find the right way! Have I not prayed and prepared for this moment for many months? Keep my head clear and keep calm, no impetuous action; this is just like game shooting – a matter of planning, of patience and a firm pressure on the trigger at just the right moment. Things become very clear.

It was really not surprising that the unit was packing for departure. This was to be expected. We were the last, except for the ubiquitous and ominous Cheka, who always used the final hours in a town to settle old scores, to hunt down potential escapees like myself, and to shoot any unfortunate hostages still held in the local prison. The Cheka will carry out their shooting. Well, in a way I shall carry out mine. I shall time my words and actions as carefully as I would a difficult shot. If I move too early, I will arouse suspicion and lose my chance. If I move too late, there will be no more chance left.

"Quick, comrade, hurry," said a voice when I joined the busy beehive of scrambling humanity, "Where are your personal files? Take a box and pack them."

"Yes, sir," said I, clicking my heels, for it was the head himself who had spoken to me.

"We are moving at eleven sharp, by road. No more trains left," he added.

Eleven. They would no doubt leave at eleven sharp. Punctuality was one of his main features, one of his ways of showing us and others that he was a real military man. Eleven was a firm time I could count upon and build my plan around.

More transport came up to the house. It had probably been "requisitioned" from whoever had a horse and cart in town. Even the two cabs that Wolkowysk could boast about in former days were drawn up to join the convoy.

Never have I packed things away with more zest and more pleasure. Goodbye to files and statements, farewell to badly printed forms. Let them leave with the fleeing Soviets, with these hard-faced, frightened men and women, smelling of fear – the smell of frightened humanity that makes horses bolt and makes dogs snarl and bite.

"I want everything ready for 10.30," said our head. "We will have thirty minutes left for checking up, and briefing. Each section to report as soon as ready."

"Files", I wrote on my boxes with a piece of chalk. They were neatly lined up and waiting for loading.

"Good idea," said a neighbour. "Can you write 'thermometers' on my box?"

"Of course, I will be glad to," and soon I was passing from crate to box and box to bag labelling the contents, much to the delight of all concerned, though our reasons were different. Whereas they were thinking of the trim and neat appearance of the unit, I was fondly visualising a Polish cavalry patrol overtaking the convoy and quickly sorting out the useful things such as thermometers, aspirins, salt and sugar from the other boxes containing files, statistics and Communist literature.

Ten fifteen on the station clock, just visible down the street. Ten twenty. Keep very cool. Fumble a bit more with the last items. Open and close drawers with a loud bang. Ten twenty-three. The checking and briefing will start in seven minutes. We will all have to stand at our places and show how we did our work. This was a regular drill, and our head is so systematic that the review and the briefing will last the full thirty minutes until eleven. In seven minutes it will be too late. Ten twenty-five. Five minutes margin. Now I must press the trigger. I am stone cold.

"Please sir," say I, clicking my heels once more and standing to attention. "All my boxes are packed. May I *now* rush and get my personal belongings? They are just round the corner."

The emphasis on the word "now" was heavy, and the head did not miss it. Here was an exemplary comrade, does all her work before thinking of herself, and is respectful too.

A careful glance at my things, a look at the clock, a trace of a satisfied smile on his important-looking face. "All right, run along but be sure to be back no later than five to eleven."

"Very good, sir, back at five to eleven." Another click of the heels, the last. A stony, matter-of-fact face. Now to walk away quickly but calmly. Not run. Especially not run. When all my soul is running, my every muscle straining to run. To put distance between these people and myself, to break their hold on me, to escape the leash. They have to let me go – but they don't know it. They will not know it for another thirty-five minutes. Don't run. Just walk briskly. Where will I be at five to eleven?

I cannot go to my abode and remain there. Some of the people in my unit must know where I lodge, and a few minutes past eleven the head would surely put someone on my trail. Losing one of his complement at this stage would not do him any good. In fact, it would be one of the things his orderly mind would resent most. So the least he could do would be to balance my disappearance in his files with the record of a report to the Cheka. And the Cheka are still here. They are always the last to leave.

I turn the corner and am hidden at last from the eyes that may still be following me; at last I can step more quickly, but still not run, not hurry too obviously for fear of other eyes, the cruel ever-present eyes of Cheka stooges.

So I head for the house of my other Polish friends, which I can reach by the back way and through the little garden. Only the wife is present. We quickly exchange our news. Her husband has gone away last night, having heard at the station that he might be called on to drive one of the trains heading east. So the safest thing for him was to go to the house of friends who had no connection with the railway, and where the authorities would not think of looking for him.

I explain to her that I, too, need somewhere to hide.

"I know of only one place where you *should* be really safe," says the dear kind woman, leading me out of the house into the backyard and garden. Seemingly built against the side wall of the house was a shed used for keeping gardening tools, various odds and ends and some of the wood stored for the daily fire in the kitchen and for winter heating. This shed was not a "lean-to" as one would have expected, but had its own walls on all sides, one running less than a metre from that of the house. This narrow space was boarded over with planks of wood on the street side, and painted the same colour as the house and the shed so that no space could be detected. But from the garden end the entrance was free, at least when there was no wood. At present the supply for the winter had been brought in and blocked any possible entrance almost completely.

It took us little time to move aside some of the wood, to get some hay into the passage, followed by a blanket, a large jug of water, half a loaf of bread, and myself. Two dozen short logs of firewood were quickly re-arranged from the outside and I was left alone in semi-darkness. Alone to listen and to think.

This time the die had been cast. I had no trace of any justification if things went wrong. Up to eleven this morning I had an assumed identity, some sort of papers to identify myself and a reason for my presence at a given spot at a certain time. That game was up. There was little chance of being able to talk myself out of my new situation if I were to be found. Either the Poles would arrive and save me – and how many others, I wondered? – or things would be really bad.

Fortunately there seemed to be no indication that the Red Army intended making a major stand at Wolkowysk. Firing even now was desultory and sporadic. It seemed to come from several directions and seemed to denote isolated contacts rather than the clear and persistent stand of a fighting line. I could hear no planes, no bombing, and no anti-aircraft fire, but there was some artillery active somewhere because three or four times shells whined over the town. I could hear both the sound of the guns and the distant impact of the shells as they fell.

Did time go on or did it stand still? I seemed to have no way of registering it although my watch still worked. Dead silence in the streets. An ominous suspense. Day gradually turned into night with the same kind of sounds, though they became less frequent. Apparently even soldiers on the move need some sleep. No more artillery either. We were already in a no-man's land.

I must have dozed. Or did I sleep, exhausted from the experience of the morning and the suspense of the day? Light and sound brought me back to consciousness. A ray of sun found a crack in the boards of the wall and hit my eye. The hum of a low-flying plane came at the same time. But it was not followed by any explosions, so no bombs had been dropped. More significant still, there was no anti-aircraft fire and none of those single rifle shots, pot-shots which soldiers could never resist taking at a plane.

"*Pani, Pani*, my friend, they are here . . ." came suddenly from behind the pile of wood, as some logs were pulled aside to provide an exit for me. Tears of joy were streaming down the cheek of my kind protector. Were they streaming down mine too?

Never was the sun so brilliant, never was the sky so blue, never was the morning air so clean and fresh, as we watched through our tears the Polish soldiers moving down our street. There seemed to be very few of them. Was it only a patrol? Would more be coming to back them up? Without waiting to think farther, the Polish inhabitants were streaming out of their houses, waving and shouting greetings.

But here words fail me. I sat down limply on the steps of the house and watched the scene in front of me. The thoughts, the emotions were too much, as it is too much today so many years afterwards, to try to express the inexpressible. It was the end, a fitting end, to my long and painful journey.

Desultory firing of small arms continued here and there for several hours. Occasionally a troop would gallop down the street, or a small unit pass on foot in a hurry. All did not seem to be yet in order, there was still a tenseness in the movements of our liberators, and a quick nod or a quick gesture was all they had time for in response to our joyful greetings. There was no relaxation yet, no feeling that the operation was successfully over, that the enemy had well and truly gone.

Suddenly, short angry bursts from a machine gun came from behind me – apparently coming out of my friends' kitchen. Something must be happening on the other side of the house. Half-crouching, half-crawling, I staggered through the house into the back garden, just a few steps from my hiding place. And there, facing the gentle slope down to the river was a young Pole firing his machine gun across the valley at a grey line of little figures moving in single file on the opposite slope. It was no more than 500 yards away, and I could see quite clearly when the young Pole hit his target and the group of grey figures began to fall over like bowling pins. Poor devils, I thought, most of them just mobilised muzhiks – peasants – and no more Communist than I was.

I stood fascinated by this almost theatrical demonstration of warfare. But this was not the time for standing still. The young Pole was all alone, his bursts of fire were short, too short, and there was nobody to feed the band into the machine gun. He had it over his right knee, coming up out of a box, but he had to correct his position constantly, taking great care so that his weapon should not jam. The gun itself, a water-cooled Maxim or Lewis, was steaming most unhealthily. He gave a worried look around him and, catching sight of me, cried "Water, *Pani*, please, – water!" So there I was for I don't know how many minutes dashing from the well to the machine gunner carrying water in the first thing I could get hold of and which I later realised was an old leather hat.

Then two more Poles were suddenly with us, the firing stopped, the machine gun was turned around and all three dashed out into the street where a horsedrawn cart was waiting. They were off in a hurry. Where to? War is full of mystery, even on the scale of individual movements. Now there were more carts and horses moving rapidly along our street. Were they leaving? Were they retreating? It seemed impossible to believe it. And yet they were in a hurry, they did not look happy, and firing grew more intense all around us. Had they been too small a unit, thrust too far forward with no support? I could not tell.

What I did know was that the ground was giving way under me. No, it was impossible to fall back into the hands of the Bolsheviks after having been free only a few hours. It could not be true, fate could not be so cruel, this could not be the final outcome of all my efforts. If the Poles were leaving, I had to go with them, even if it meant running after them on foot.

It was impossible to get on to any of their carts or army transports thundering down the road. It was impossible, after a few hundred yards, to keep pace with these healthy boys at the peak of their form. Impossible to follow . . .

Impossible to survive this final blow, I said to myself, once more back between the two walls of my hiding place, with the logs again obstructing the entrance. Impossible to come out of this black well of despair. How long did it last? I do not know. Perhaps a day and a night of utter quiet, the quietness of death I said to myself. Firing had subsided. No artillery was heard anywhere, no movement of any transport, no troops riding through. The Poles had gone – but the Bolsheviks had not returned. From time to time, my protector came to whisper through the logs and give me what news she could. The absence of anything to report was, in fact, news in itself. There was not a soul in the streets, neither military nor civilian. One thing was certain: there was no Cheka, either.

And then a date which I shall never forget – October 1st, 1920. It was a clear bright day. Once more there was the boom of artillery fire in the distance, and in Wolkowysk itself the heavy rattle of guns and army vehicles driving along the cobbled streets. At midday there were crowds in the streets, talking excitedly and waving their kerchiefs, while the last tall sunflowers waved too above the garden fences and the ripe chestnuts fell with a thud on the ground. I was in the street, happy, light-headed with happiness, my face all smiles now the tears were over. The Polish Army had entered the town in force, after pushing the Bolshevik rearguard well beyond the neighbouring hills. I felt so exuberantly free and independent. I had this one overriding sensation of being a free human being who had the right to exist, who was not a criminal merely because of the family and the society into which I had been born, a society which had been ostracised and doomed to annihilation.

That same evening, though, I was forced to realise that my feelings were a little premature and that a free life was not quite yet mine. Some woman in the street denounced me, saying that I was a stranger in the town and that I had worked at the station with a Bolshevik unit. Of course she was right in her way, and the Polish officers looked at me rather suspiciously as I stood there, in my clothing which was a sort of cross between the Red Army uniform and a home-made sports outfit. I asked to be taken at once to their headquarters where I would explain the situation. I told them the outline of my story and showed them my "leave-ticket" from the Moscow Lubyanka prison where I had been taken as Panna Maria Adamczewska, the Polish hostage, and their attitude changed at once to one of deference and kindness. Yes, for the time being I was obliged once more to be Panna Maria Adamczewska and felt ill at ease having to deceive these people who were kind to me and trusted my words. But I knew it would take more time to unravel the threads of my various false identities.

Only after I had found some of my own personal friends in Warsaw could I establish through them who I really was. I was given a permit of passage to Warsaw on the first available military train. I knew that when I arrived there I would need some sort of rest, for the strain of the past two years was having its effect upon me now. I must be well again before the last stage of my journey – back to the Baltics to look for my boys. I must be strong enough, now that I was free, to make my own way and live my own life. I was free – a free human being again, able now to make plans for the future, and to make them without the haunting fear of arrest. And my plan now was a very simple one: to see my sons again after more than two years of separation. As I boarded the Polish military train, I felt as if I were walking on air. I could hope to hear from my boys soon, very soon, for I was sure that my friends in Warsaw would help me find them. What did it matter if we had no money, no possessions and an unknown future? If we could be together, and if I could see them grow up honest and strong and freedom-loving, this would be my reward.

22

REUNION

The first few months after my escape passed in a haze of illness and gradual convalescence, watched over by kind friends, first in Warsaw and then in Paris. In Paris I had the first definite news of my husband since the day we had parted in Petrograd in November 1918. I learned that he had been killed fighting the Bolsheviks in southern Russia only a few weeks later. My feeling of being alone in the world was thus confirmed, and the burden of responsibility for my boys grew heavy once more. What would they be like now, after nearly three years of separation? News came that my sister Katya, having traced them through the international Red Cross, had gone to find them – still in Estonia but now at a different address. It was arranged that I would follow as soon as my health and strength returned.

My excitement was mixed with apprehension as I travelled to Estonia and made my way one June evening about sunset to the address in Reval, Baltischport Strasse, the home of the Manteuffel family from whom my sister Katya had rented a room for herself, the three boys and the devoted Elsa.

As soon as I entered, all apprehension vanished. My sister was just ladling out some soup for Alec and Nic, who were sitting at a table near the window at the far end of the room – a room which seemed to be largely taken up with beds. The reddish golden glow of the sunset threw a cheerful light on the little group, framed for me like a painting by the doorway as I came through the adjoining room.

It was a strange feeling to see them there, to feel them near me, so strange that I could not believe it was true. And yet – yes, Katya was real enough, there was nothing changed in her, Katya who knew what she was doing and why she had to do it. It was Alec who caught sight of me first and called out "Mama!" Little Nic looked delicate, sparrow-like, pale, and of course he did not remember me so well. But where was Vladimir? There were heavy steps behind me and, turning round, I saw Vladimir on the threshold, a much changed Vladimir, so tall and with a short haircut, wearing an American-style scout's uniform and an enormous pair of military lace-up boots. He was less good-looking now than when I left him, I found myself thinking. Was it really possible that all three of them were there with me again after these long months and years? Yes, they had changed of course, but not changed for the worse either in their character or in their manners and behaviour. It certainly was a relief, and my heart filled with gratitude to all the people who had helped them through this time.

The boys were a little shy of me at first, Nic especially, for he admitted shamefacedly that he did not recognise me and added in his piping voice, by way of explanation: "I always thought you would come on horseback." Apparently this was the last picture he had of me at home in Kamenka. But in the next few days he and I were able to get to know each other again, for the bigger boys were busy with school exams and little Nic was entrusted with the duty of showing me round the town of Reval, which I scarcely knew. The next few days we spent mostly in each other's company and I was very much amused at Nic's conscientious explanations and his comments on the historic monuments and the beauty spots of Reval. After having shown me round all the morning and part of the after-noon, he took me to the local public gardens and brought me to the foot of a monument, a large granite block with a bronze mermaid sitting on it. Apparently this was the highlight of the tour in Nic's eyes for when we were in front of it he said in a solemn voice: "And this is a monument to Saint Linda" – quite undisturbed by the fact that this particular saint had a fish's tail. Of course I was full of admiration and he then explained to me that it was the most beautiful statue in the town and the most respected one. Unfortunately I have forgotten the history of this statue but it certainly looked very nice on that glorious late afternoon in June, especially as reflected in the eyes of its young admirer.

During our days together I noticed to my great joy that Nic, who had been very wavering in his English on my arrival, seemed to feel much more at home with it now, and his English was becoming quite fluent again. Using German at school and Russian with his brothers, it was not surprising that his English had been almost forgotten. With the older boys there was no such problem for I had always spoken to them in English, quite apart from their solid nursery training from Miss Baker and Miss Taylor. How far away those days seemed now!

As soon as the big boys' exams were over, and when I had completed a round of calls to thank all the people who had shown interest in the boys and who had helped by having them regularly for meals and so on, we packed our trunks to go to Waldensee. The journey was complicated by the new frontier between Estonia and Latvia and so there were passport and visa formalities to undergo. It amused me and at the same time saddened me a little to see the "free" world no longer quite so free; I wondered what my father would have said. My father was very much in my thoughts as we set out by train for Wolmar. Waldensee belonged now to my two sisters, but to me it was still my father's house and to return there was the nearest thing to a homecoming that any of us could have in these changed times.

At Wolmar station Ivan was waiting for us – Ivan, our Waldensee coachman. He had not changed, perhaps a few more wrinkles round his small blue eyes and grey hair in his square reddish beard. He gave us such a warm welcome, lifting

Nic and the luggage into his cart to go home along the road, while the rest of us took the shorter way on foot through fields and pine forest. How often as children we had been along this railway embankment, picking and eating the exquisite wild strawberries which grew here in profusion. It was a lovely morning, the sun was bright, and we all enjoyed the walk after the long and tedious train journey. The boys rushed on in advance to meet the cart and Ivan with Nic, while Katya and I lingered behind as it was restful and quiet and a joy to live over again the series of recollections linked with these familiar views. I felt as if I were reading a book of stories of the past, or looking at an album of old photographs; everything reminded me of my father and of our childhood – my walks with my brother, my games with Katya and, alas, all too often the memory of some of our more indigestible governesses.

At last we were near home, near the garden which had no fence any more, which looked wilder now with trees and bushes growing in disorder, untrimmed, free and obeying only the law of the survival of the fittest. The house looked as cosy as ever, with its grey roof pressed deep onto the walls which now looked mildly brown and grey, a pleasant colour acquired by time and unspoilt by any fresh paint. Liza, Ivan's wife, met us on the terrace steps, looking as kind and as bulky as ever; and my sister Mary was there too, much changed and saddened by the war years, and clinging as before to her pet animals for comfort.

We soon settled down again in our part of the house, which had been patched up by Ivan as best he could. Window panes had been put in order, floors mended with bits of boards, and wallpapers had been re-pasted wherever possible. The traces of the passage of Russian, German, Lettish and Bolshevik troops were still visible but we soon got used to them. After all, good Ivan had managed to save a great deal during the war: he had settled down in the servants' quarters of the house and had taken into his rooms the best of the furniture, declaring to all passing army authorities that these were his own things and that, according to good democratic principles, he had a right as a family man to the possession of any furniture he needed. He thus managed to save the piano, several carpets, a lot of bed linen and blankets and a very appreciable quantity of furniture and crockery. As soon as sister Mary returned to the place, he had all these things brought back into the main part of the house – which now looked furnished and quite habitable.

Ivan farmed the land around the house and paid his rent to my sisters partly in cash but mostly in kind – that is, in flour, milk, potatoes, oatmeal, eggs, etc., which meant that we had the essential foodstuffs on the spot. The old orchard still existed and produced a lot of apples, pears, cherries, plums and quantities of berries such as currants and raspberries. The kitchen garden had been well stocked with vegetables for our use, and we certainly felt very grateful to have all these resources at hand and without having to ask anyone's permission.

In Waldensee a true sense of freedom returned to me, and with it the courage to face the future. So many problems lay ahead, and for the sake of my boys there were decisions to be made. We were happy here in Waldensee, but for how long? Where did their future really lie? Here in little Latvia, with the Soviet Russian border not very far away? Surely not. In Germany, where many Baltic families were settling now? No, that would not do either, especially for Alec who had already shown a towering anger against some elderly Baltic ladies whose enthusiasm for all things German made his Russian blood boil. In France, where I had been offered free places in Catholic schools for the two older boys? This was obviously a very attractive offer, but the difficulty was that the boys did not know any French. They knew Russian, German and English, but no French! It was really quite a problem.

At last Katya and I worked out a plan. I should remain in Waldensee for one winter, teaching the boys French; she would go to Riga to give lessons there so as to earn money to enable me to get a tutor for the boys in Latin and Maths. And Elsa, the devoted little Elsa, would remain with us to do the washing and cooking, on condition that she would have several free afternoons to go to Wolmar to the prayer meetings of her Adventists.

It was a cooperative effort on the part of everyone. I had to see to getting the books we needed, and with the help of an American friend procured a whole boxful of all sorts of French schoolbooks. Teaching French was a straightforward task for me, because my own first lessons had been in that language, and it was always to French that I referred subconsciously over any questions of grammar or construction. French was the language I had always spoken with my parents and sisters and brother, and so it felt quite natural to use it with my children too. The boys understood the importance of our task and worked willingly and with comprehension. Altogether the plan worked well, and at the end of 15 months Vladimir and Alec had learned enough French to be able to enter the French college and join the classes alongside French boys of their own age. This had been our aim and we were all delighted at the achievement.

In fact, looking back over my long life I find that this year in Latvia was one of the most full and interesting periods, and such an unexpected joy after the months of uncertainty and separation. It was wonderful to have the boys with me all the time, to get to know them again, to learn to understand them. We had some marvellous fun, with picnics by the river and swimming and mushroom-hunting, and in winter with music and charades and games with toy soldiers. There were visits from old friends, and walks in the forest where so many years before I used to take my dog Kars to hunt squirrels with my first little rifle. Now, in 1922, my old friend Konrad Knieriem had found a gun for me again, a 16-bore shotgun, which I stood in the corner of my room and looked at with a loving eye. But I could not afford the luxury of buying cartridges, as they were very expensive and all the money we had to spare was being put towards the cost of going to Paris. I went out once or twice with Vladimir, using the few cartridges we had and reminding ourselves of the old way of life that we both knew was over for us now.

The boys were growing fast, walking barefoot and healthy in the sunny weather. But the summer was coming to an end, and there were clothes and shoes to be bought or borrowed or made before we left. It had been a happy time, but we knew that it could not go on.

In October, 1922, I said goodbye to Waldensee and took my sons to Paris.

POSTSCRIPT

Some people have asked to know what happened to Edith and her sons in later life. She herself preferred not to chronicle her life in Paris, nor to write down details of her sons' progress. The following notes are, therefore, what remains from anecdote and hearsay, rather than documented fact.

Edith found modest lodgings in the 16th arrondissement, and a job as typist and translator at the American Embassy. She had very little money, not much furniture, and no cooking facilities. They seem to have survived on soup, bread and hard-boiled eggs. The two older boys were given free places in a French boarding school, but were not happy there. Vladimir was a gifted pupil, but he left early after being punished unfairly (in his view) for something which he had not done. He trained as a banker and financier, working for various international banking enterprises whose interests he looked after in Paris during the 1930s and under the Occupation. Later, in the post-war years, he became a successful businessman exporting French agricultural machinery. He married Elena Undurraga, a society beauty of Chilean extraction to whom he remained devoted until they both died in 1988. They had no children. Alec also left school early, in order to take up chicken-farming (the closest he could get to his land-owning background). His marriage to Franco-Italian countess Claudine Gnoli enabled him to continue farming, first in France, then in England, and finally in Italy. There were four children; one son died young, and Alec himself died in 1974. Some of his descendants live in England, and some in Italy. Edith's youngest son Nicolas attended French schools until he was given a free place at a small boarding school located outside Paris in the Château de Bures, run by a rich American philanthropist. From there he won a scholarship to Cambridge University, and began his academic career in England in 1931. Edith continued to live and work in Paris until the gathering war-clouds caused her to cross the Channel in 1939 together with Alec and his wife. A chicken-farm was rented in East Sussex, and this was the family home until after the war. Nicolas meanwhile had joined the academic staff at Dartmouth Naval College, where he taught French, German and Russian to naval officer cadets. In 1954 he moved to Winchester College, and taught there until his death in 1990. Edith had gone to live with him for the last ten years of her life. She died in 1965 and is buried in Winchester. In 1966 Nicolas married Valerie Drew; their four daughters have retained the Sollohub family name, and have passed it on to their children.

The fate of family and friends who were left behind in Soviet Russia is largely unknown. Communication with them was impossible from the West. Likewise, former servants could not be contacted for fear of reprisals against them. Word was received that the "Kursk" grandmother had died in the early 1930s. Friends such as the Riesenkampfs who settled in Poland were not heard of again after the outbreak of the Second World War. The boys' tutor, Vladimir Favre, worked in Germany as a musician and choirmaster, but he and his wife Anna seem to have disappeared in the 1940s. Family members who settled in Germany survived the war, though Edith's brother was bombed out of Berlin in 1945 and died a few months later. The two sisters lived on into the 1970s. They had left Waldensee in 1925, living unhappily together for some years in a small cottage in Fürstenfeldbruck near Munich. In 1938 Katya left Mary and went to Italy, where she worked as a freelance artist, while Mary stayed at home alone and became increasingly unkempt and eccentric. Each year in the 1950s and 1960s Nicolas went to visit Mary and thank the neighbours who helped to look after her. Finally, Katya came to Winchester for her last few years to help with the new generation of Sollohub children. Thus the family loyalties continued to the end.

Countess Edith Sollohub came to England in 1939 to live with her
son. She was accorded British citizenship in 1948, at the age of 62.
This was her passport photograph.

INDEX

INDEX

INDEX